Indigenous Peoples of the British Dominions and the First World War

This pioneering comparative history of the participation of indigenous peoples of the British empire in the First World War is based upon archival research in four continents. It provides the first comprehensive examination, and comparison, of how indigenous peoples of Canada, Australia, Newfoundland, New Zealand and South Africa experienced the Great War. The participation of indigenes was an extension of their ongoing effort to shape and alter their social and political realities, their resistance to cultural assimilation or segregation, and their desire to attain equality through service and sacrifice. While the dominions discouraged indigenous participation at the outbreak of war, by late 1915 the imperial government demanded their inclusion to meet the pragmatic need for military manpower. Indigenous peoples responded with patriotism and enthusiasm both on the battlefield and the home front and shared equally in the horrors and burdens of the First World War.

TIMOTHY C. WINEGARD is a Lecturer in the Department of First Nations Studies at the University of Western Ontario and a Postdoctoral Fellow in the Department of History at the University of Waterloo, Ontario. His books include *Oka: A Convergence of Cultures and the Canadian Forces* (2008) and *For King and Kanata: Canadian Indians and the First World War* (2011).

Cambridge Military Histories

Edited by

Hew Strachan
Chichele Professor of the History of War, University of Oxford and Fellow of All Souls College, Oxford

Geoffrey Wawro
Professor of History and Director of the Military History Center, University of North Texas

The aim of this series is to publish outstanding works of research on warfare throughout the ages and throughout the world. Books in the series take a broad approach to military history, examining war in all its military, strategic, political and economic aspects. The series complements Studies in the Social and Cultural History of Modern Warfare by focusing on the 'hard' military history of armies, tactics, strategy and warfare. Books in the series consist mainly of single-author works – academically vigorous and groundbreaking – which are accessible to both academics and the interested general reader.

A full list of titles in the series can be found at:

www.cambridge.org/militaryhistories

Indigenous Peoples of the British Dominions and the First World War

Timothy C. Winegard

CAMBRIDGE
UNIVERSITY PRESS

CAMBRIDGE UNIVERSITY PRESS
Cambridge, New York, Melbourne, Madrid, Cape Town,
Singapore, São Paulo, Delhi, Tokyo, Mexico City

Cambridge University Press
The Edinburgh Building, Cambridge CB2 8RU, UK

Published in the United States of America by Cambridge University Press,
New York

www.cambridge.org
Information on this title: www.cambridge.org/9781107014930

First published 2012

Printed in the United Kingdom at the University Press, Cambridge

A catalogue record for this publication is available from the British Library

ISBN 978-1-107-01493-0 Hardback

To my Longhouse

Contents

Figures

Maps

x

Tables

Acknowledgements

First and foremost, I would like to thank Hew Strachan, my doctoral supervisor at the University of Oxford, for his guidance and assistance. I have been extremely privileged to be the beneficiary of his knowledge and mentorship. I would also like to thank Adrian Gregory, Robert Johnson and John Darwin for their enthusiasm in this project. While conducting research, numerous people gave generously of their time, insight and help and deserve my utmost thanks. In Australia: Margaret Beadman, Garth O'Connell, Robert Hall, Peter Stanley and Christopher Clark. In New Zealand: Ian McGibbon, Christopher Pugsley and Dolores Ho. In South Africa: Cliff Bhekizizwe and Sophie. I would also like to extend a special thank you to P. Whitney Lackenbauer in Canada for his indefatigable enthusiasm and his unwavering friendship. A debt of gratitude must also be expressed to my caring editors, Michael Watson and Gillian Dadd, and the staff at Cambridge University Press.

To my family for the velvet allowance afforded me to follow the many crossroads I have chosen. To my sisters, Casey and Kelly (and Tom and Whitter), you are both such strong people, as evidenced by your amazing kids. Mom and Dad, although the 'Daytona Beach Accord' seems so distant, the resolutions have now, finally, been met. While mere words will never suffice, thank you both so very much for everything you have sacrificed for me. Your love, patience and wisdom of experience exist in such infinite vicinities for all of your children to unconditionally draw upon – for that we have no offerings of recompense; but alas, that question drowns in its own futility. Lastly, while I have enjoyed the generosity of colleagues, friends and family in writing and preparing this work, any errors remain mine alone. Nine years as an officer in the Canadian Forces taught me to seek and accept responsibility.

Camlachie, Ontario

Note on the text

This comparison will detail the participation of the indigenous populations of the five British Dominions – Canada, Australia, Newfoundland, New Zealand and South Africa – during the First World War. Any author investigating aspects of indigenous history must, if by peer scrutiny alone, delineate approaches to descriptive nouns and chronological representations. Given the multiplicity of indigenous nations within the respective Dominions, they did not represent monolithic, homogenous entities. Many indigenous peoples felt a stronger affiliation to clans than to either their nations or their indigenous collective (unknown prior to European contact). Moreover, enduring animosities still existed between traditional enemies. Therefore, grouping them as Aboriginal Australians, for example, is seemingly specious. Fundamentally, however, based on the dominant policies of Dominion and imperial governments, this generalization is not only unavoidable, but is also representative of trans-national themes, and is indicative of the social and political environments in all Dominions and the United Kingdom during the years of, and surrounding, the First World War.

Indigenous nations or groupings will be explored when they are important to the arguments or are imperative to understanding regional policies and decisions. Given the multitude of indigenous dialects within five diverse Dominions, the use of indigenous languages will be kept to a minimum unless central to explanation. For example, the Maori word for non-Maori peoples is *Pakeha*. This word will be used to describe non-Maori New Zealanders, as it was adopted into New Zealand society. In general, however, European terminology will be used, not out of ignorance or thoughtlessness; rather, to enhance readability and, more importantly, to adhere to contemporary convention.

As a rule, this work adopts the language present in the contemporary documents and bureaucratic discourses, although many of the terms used, such as kaffir or half-caste, are now deemed derogatory and politically incorrect. The term indigenous represents those peoples present in the Dominions prior to contact. Indian will be used to describe those indigenes of North America. The term Eskimo will embody the peoples of Arctic Canada and Newfoundland-Labrador. Métis will be used to describe a distinct people of European and Indian lineage. Indigenous Australians will be referred to as Aborigines, and at times as full-blood or half-caste, as this differentiation was paramount in Australian policy and practice. Indigenous South Africans will be referred to as black (or native) and coloured, as the Union of South Africa afforded different freedoms and management to these groupings. Lastly, the New Zealand Maori will be identified as such.[1]

The use of these labels, which many associate with subjugation, dishonour and Eurocentric ideology, is not a concession to their negative connections; rather, it is an attempt to relate accurately the contemporary attitudes, opinions and legal arrangements represented in these words by the societies, peoples and decrees which used them. To employ more current words or phrasings, or to surround in quotation marks to affirm the flawed construction of a label, is to impart a consciousness to policy makers and populations that did not exist at the time in which this history takes place.

Defining settlers from the British Isles is also challenging. Many considered themselves Scottish, Irish, Welsh or English. Conversely, settlers in the Dominions from the British Isles felt strong connections to the metropole and shared many of the same cultural and societal values and increasingly identified themselves with being British. Hence, in most instances, the term British will describe settlers from the British Isles.

Lastly, the term contact represents the first encounters between indigenous peoples and Europeans. This is not to impart that indigenous nations do not have, based on archaeological evidence, oral traditions and scientific theory, lengthy records of terrestrial occupation and socio-cultural evolution prior to the arrival of Europeans. Contact infers that indigenous peoples underwent an unavoidable cataclysmic crisis, unparalleled in their known previous histories, due to the introduction of disease and the adoption of killing potential through the use of European weapon systems. By the dawn of the twentieth century, indigenous populations, save for those of South Africa, were moribund, due to deadly disease, warfare, and contact with peoples of differing genetic dispositions and viral immunities.

---

[1] Although the Maori Contingent of the First World War was officially designated the 'Native Contingent', it is more commonly known as the 'Maori Contingent', and will be referred to as such. The term native was not officially, and legally, replaced with Maori until 1947.

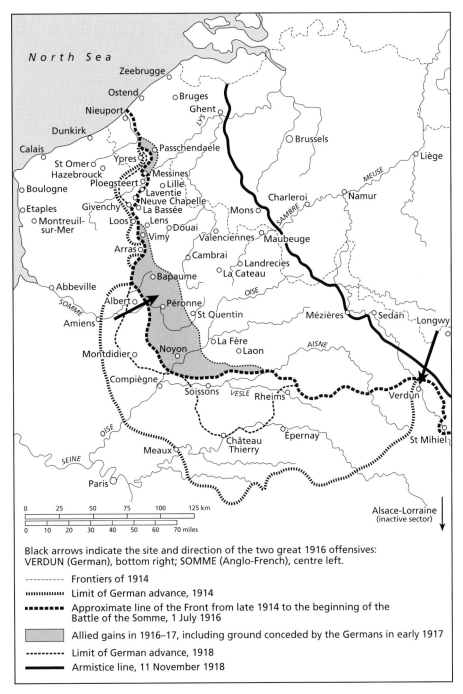

Black arrows indicate the site and direction of the two great 1916 offensives:
VERDUN (German), bottom right; SOMME (Anglo-French), centre left.

---------- Frontiers of 1914

▪▪▪▪▪▪▪▪▪▪▪ Limit of German advance, 1914

▪▪▪▪▪▪▪▪ Approximate line of the Front from late 1914 to the beginning of the
Battle of the Somme, 1 July 1916

▨ Allied gains in 1916–17, including ground conceded by the Germans in early 1917

- - - - - - - Limit of German advance, 1918

━━━━━ Armistice line, 11 November 1918

Map 1 The Western Front, 1914–18.

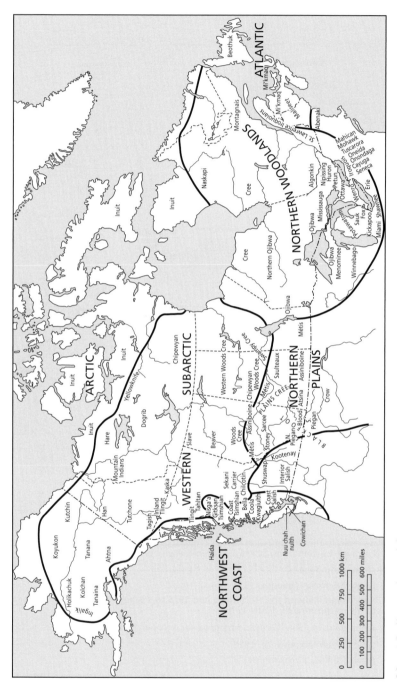

Map 2 Indian nations of Canada and Newfoundland.

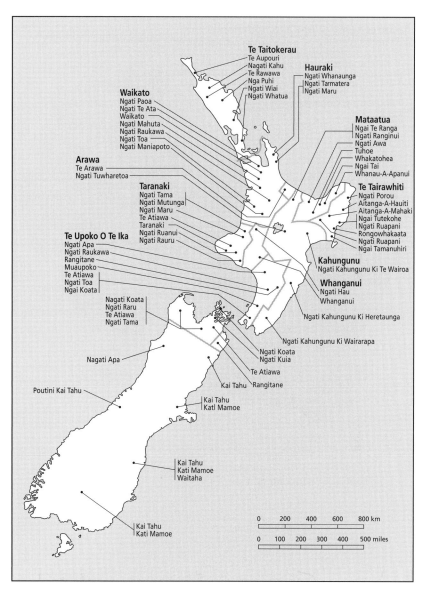

Te Taitokerau
Te Aupouri
Nagati Kahu
Te Rawawa
Nga Puhi
Ngati Wiai
Ngati Whatua

Hauraki
Ngati Whanaunga
Ngati Tarmatera
Ngati Maru

Waikato
Ngati Paoa
Ngati Te Ata
Waikato
Ngati Mahuta
Ngati Raukawa
Ngati Toa
Ngati Maniapoto

Mataatua
Ngai Te Ranga
Ngati Ranginui
Ngati Awa
Tuhoe
Whakatohea
Ngai Tai
Whanau-A-Apanui

Arawa
Te Arawa
Ngati Tuwharetoa

Taranaki
Ngati Tama
Ngati Mutunga
Ngati Maru
Te Atiawa
Taranaki
Ngati Ruanui
Ngati Rauru

Te Tairawhiti
Ngati Porou
Aitanga-A-Hauiti
Aitanga-A-Mahaki
Ngai Tutekohe
Ngati Ruapani
Rongowhakaata
Ngati Ruapani
Ngai Tamanuhiri

Te Upoko O Te Ika
Ngati Apa
Ngati Raukawa
Rangitane
Muaupoko
Te Atiawa
Ngati Toa
Ngai Koata

Kahungunu
Ngati Kahungunu Ki Te Wairoa

Whanganui
Ngati Hau
Whanganui

Nagati Koata
Ngati Raru
Te Atiawa
Ngati Tama

Ngati Kahungunu Ki Heretaunga

Nagati Apa

Ngati Koata
Ngati Kuia

Ngati Kahungunu Ki Wairarapa

Te Atiawa

Poutini Kai Tahu

Kai Tahu   Rangitane

Kai Tahu
Katl Mamoe

Kai Tahu
Kati Mamoe
Waitaha

0   200   400   600   800 km

0   100   200   300   400   500 miles

Kai Tahu
Kati Mamoe

Map 3 Maori *Iwi* (tribes) of New Zealand.

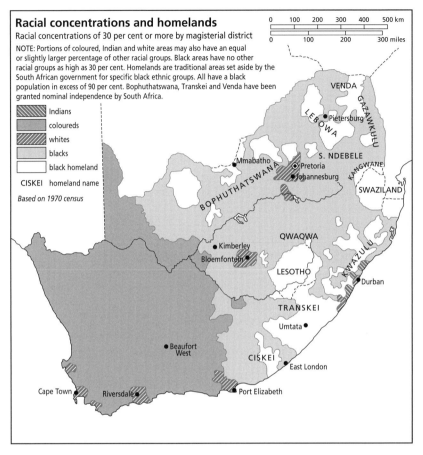

Racial concentrations and homelands

Racial concentrations of 30 per cent or more by magisterial district

NOTE: Portions of coloured, Indian and white areas may also have an equal or slightly larger percentage of other racial groups. Black areas have no other racial groups as high as 30 per cent. Homelands are traditional areas set aside by the South African government for specific black ethnic groups. All have a black population in excess of 90 per cent. Bophuthatswana, Transkei and Venda have been granted nominal independence by South Africa.

- Indians
- coloureds
- whites
- blacks
- black homeland

CISKEI   homeland name

Based on 1970 census

0   100   200   300   400   500 km

0   100   200   300 miles

VENDA

GAZAWKULU

LEBOWA   ●Pietersburg

S. NDEBELE

Mmabatho   ◉Pretoria   KANGWANE

BOPHUTHATSWANA   ●Johannesburg

SWAZILAND

QWAQWA

●Kimberley

Bloemfontein●

LESOTHO   KWAZULU

●Durban

TRANSKEI

Umtata ●

●Beaufort West

CISKEI   East London

Cape Town●   Riversdale●   ●Port Elizabeth

Map 4 The 1913 South African Natives Land Act: distribution of lands and ethnicity.

Introduction

The outbreak of the First World War shattered almost a hundred years of relative peace in Europe. Its nations had circumvented large-scale conflict since the defeat of Napoleon in 1815 through treaties, alliances and an aspiration to maintain a balance of power in Europe and empire. In place of war, European armies were deployed to the fringes of empire to gain territorial acquisitions within the imperial scramble, or to quell indigenous rebellions in existing colonies.[1] By 1914, the pan-European empire covered 84% of the globe, compared with 35% in 1800. The British empire encompassed one-fourth of the world and 445 million people lived under some form of British rule.[2] Within the social norms of this Victorian era, and the prevailing ethnocentric ideologies of Social Darwinism, indigenous peoples were seen as an unfortunate component of the 'white man's burden'.

At the onset of war, no imperialist European state, save for France, regarded its colonial indigenous populations as a source of military manpower for a European war.[3] Contemporary science, social biases and public opinion accepted that certain identifiable ethnic groups lacked the intelligence and integrity to fight modern war. It was also believed that since these groups were the subjects of vast European empires, prudence warned against allowing them to fight in a European war, thus forfeiting white racial supremacy. However, by late 1915, with mounting casualties and an increasing demand for manpower, Britain specifically requested the military inclusion of indigenous populations from the five Dominions.

---

[1] See: C. E. Callwell, *Small Wars: Their Principles and Practice* (Reprint. Lincoln: University of Nebraska Press, 1996).

[2] Tim Cook, *At the Sharp End: Canadians Fighting the Great War 1914–1916* (Toronto: Penguin Group Canada, 2007), vol. I, p. 10. Relative in the sense the Crimean War (1853–6), the Franco-Prussian War (1870–1) and the Balkan Wars (1912–13) never became general European wars.

[3] Hew Strachan, *The First World War, Volume I: To Arms* (Oxford University Press, 2001), p. 497.

1

The term Dominion was first used during the 1660s, to identify specific regions of Virginia and New England. British North America was officially designated the Dominion of Canada, with confederation in 1867. The first collective use occurred at the Colonial Conference (April to May 1907) when the title was conferred upon Canada and Australia. New Zealand and Newfoundland were afforded the designation in September of that same year, followed by South Africa in 1910. These were the only British possessions recognized as Dominions at the outbreak of war. In 1922, the Irish Free State was given Dominion status, followed by the short-lived inclusion of India and Pakistan in 1947 (although India was officially recognized as the Union of India). The Union of India became the Republic of India in 1950, while the Dominion of Pakistan became the Islamic Republic of Pakistan in 1956.

While India certainly has a place in other comparative investigations, these associations are beyond the compass of this analysis. Colonization in India, and its corresponding legislative and administrative structures, differed from that in the Dominions. They viewed India as an unequal and inferior imperial possession and actively restricted Indian immigration, creating a rift in British hegemony and British–Dominion relations.[4] In the five Dominions concerned, settlers, primarily British, sought to claim and secure enduring control of the land. Although regional exploitation of resources, such as fish, furs and flax (and the prospect of mineral riches), occurred, export development, after initial expeditionary commercial ventures, was a windfall to protracted settlement. In contrast, India was a colony based on the utilization of vast resources with indigenous and imported labour employed to extract the value of exportable trade commodities. The British demographic profile of exploitative or sojourner colonies was primarily adult males, who, after a period of administrative, military or economic service, returned home. Settler colonies, such as the Dominions, included women and children in a population intending to make a new home and country for future generations, under British sponsorship. More notably, the Indian Army of the British Raj, which mobilized 1.27 million *sepoys*, including 827,000 combatants, during the First World War, was vastly different in both construct and application from the national forces of the Dominions prior to, and during, the war.[5]

---

[4] For a detailed account see: Avner Offer, *The First World War: An Agrarian Interpretation* (Oxford: Clarendon Press, 1989).

[5] David Omissi, *Indian Voices of the Great War: Soldiers' Letters, 1914–1918* (London: Macmillan, 1999), p. 4. The pinnacle strength of the (combatant) Indian Army was 573,000. At the armistice, 943,344 Indian troops, both combatant and non-combatant,

Conversely, the United States of America shares extensive colonial commonalities with the Dominions. After the American Revolution (1775–83), however, Native Indian policy became inherently American. The United States, therefore, will generally be excluded from this investigation. Yet, the policies of the United States in relation to the military service of its Indian populations paralleled many of those of Canada, and will be used to highlight certain elements of the First World War experience common to all North American Indians. The traditional lands and contemporary reserves of many Indian nations straddled the US–Canadian border, a factor not germane to the island nations of Australia, New Zealand and, to some extent, Newfoundland. Most Indians did not recognize what, to them, seemed to be an arbitrary demarcation, nor were they obliged to do so under Articles II and III of the 1794 Treaty of Amity, Commerce and Navigation (Jay Treaty) negotiated between Britain and the United States in the aftermath of the Revolution.[6] Although the focal point of this study is founded on the five British Dominions, when pertinent, comparisons will be made with the indigenous peoples of India, the United States and with other British and European imperial possessions.

In the years approaching the First World War, national Dominion identities began to emerge and were solidified by the war itself, ushering in a more ambivalent stance towards imperial associations and British collectivism. Increased Dominion participation in the war effort was accompanied by demands for greater inclusion in the arenas of strategic council. As a result, Dominion prime ministers were included in David Lloyd-George's Imperial War Cabinet, convened in the spring of 1917. Its ratification of Resolution IX ensured full recognition of the Dominions as 'autonomous nations of an Imperial Commonwealth [with a] right … to an adequate voice in foreign policy and foreign relations'. This assertion was evidenced by individual Dominion representation at the 1919 Paris Peace Conference and in the League of Nations.

The First World War spawned national consciousness within the Dominions. Historians, especially those from the former Dominions, often use clichés to ally war participation with the creation of national identities. Although often overstated, they rest on truth, and are

---

were active in six theatres of war, although only 14.1 per cent of these were on the Western Front. The Indian Army suffered 64,000 dead and 69,000 wounded.

[6] Specifically, Articles II and III recognized the right of free movement over the border and the nullification of import duties. Article III states that, 'the Indians dwelling on either side of the said Boundary Line [should be able] freely to pass and repass by Land, or Inland Navigation, into the respective Territories and Countries of the Two Parties, on the Continent of America … and to navigate all the Lakes, Rivers, and waters thereof, and freely to carry on trade and commerce with each other'.

represented in the contemporary societies of all former Dominions. Canada has its imposing memorial at the 250-acre Canadian National Park at Vimy and boasts of the definitive war poem, *In Flanders Fields*, penned by its own (Lieutenant-Colonel) Dr John McCrae. Australia and New Zealand have their Anzac Day on 25 April; their young nationals take to the Gallipoli Peninsula in annual pilgrimage. Newfoundland-Labrador has its yearly, 1 July, Beaumont-Hamel provincial holiday and its towering bronze caribou rising above that battlefield at the Newfoundland Memorial Park. South Africa finds its war identity through the battle and memorial at Delville Wood, France. The individual war memorials throughout the former Dominions are evidence to the impact of the Great War on all communities of these young nations. Memorials are also scattered across indigenous territories, illustrating the shared responsibility taken by indigenes in all facets of 'The Great War for Civilization'.

The indigenous peoples of the Dominions willingly participated in all aspects of the First World War. Their calculated inclusion in Dominion forces was not a departure from, rather a continuation of, the pragmatic tradition of imperial and Dominion governments, which used them in a military capacity only when it suited British–Dominion interests and helped fulfil specific desiderata. This premise is exemplified by a catalogue of occurrences throughout the colonial warfare of all Dominions. During the First World War, the abilities of indigenes as soldiers, and the perception of their martial prowess, were measured against colonial experiences, including frontier warfare, and contemporary racial theories. Racial estimations were manifested in the differing policies of the Dominions and in the function, role and theatres of deployment of indigenes within their military forces. According to R. Scott Sheffield, 'This was clearly differentiation in practice, meaning that Aboriginal individuals were specifically recruited for, and their service was defined by, culturally and/or racially defined skills and characteristics.'[7] The evolution of indigenous participation during the First World War was an extension of this practice.

With Britain's declaration of war on 4 August 1914, indigenous communities and political leaders openly declared their loyalty and sought avenues to exemplify their allegiance and worth to both their Dominions and the Crown. Previous treaties and military alliances were fostered

[7] R. Scott Sheffield, 'Indifference, Difference and Assimilation: Aboriginal People in Canadian Military Practice, 1900–1945' in P. Whitney Lackenbauer and Craig Leslie Mantle (eds.), *Aboriginal Peoples and the Canadian Military: Historical Perspectives* (Kingston: Canadian Defence Academy Press, 2007), p. 58.

with Britain, not the Dominions. Many offered support of men and money directly to the King or 'the Great White Father'. Indigenous leaders acted as 'bridge people' between their cultures and Dominion political and social systems. Linda Tuhiwai Smith asserts that: 'Their elite status came about through the alignment of their cultural and economic interests with the colonizing group rather than with those of their own society.'[8] This interpretation, however, removes the dynamic and conscious participation of indigenous peoples within the colonial experience and the First World War.

Many believed that excelling, and showing themselves as capable as Europeans, in so-called European civilized pursuits, was a means to prove their worth as indigenous peoples both individually and collectively – in other words, selective assimilation for the aims of equality and autonomy. This is not to say, however, that these indigenes viewed themselves as assimilated, nor did it mean that they had rejected their indigenous culture. While certain commentators have criticized these people for abandoning, or becoming estranged from, their traditional roots, given contemporary racial attitudes, and socio-economic and political realities, this is unwarranted. The majority believed that by entering and engaging in Dominion society as indigenes, they could participate on equal terms and win the respect of the dominant European society in order to gain rights for their own peoples. Accordingly, many viewed the First World War as an extension of this approach. As such, what follows is, by necessity, as much a socio-political and cultural investigation as it is a documentation of strictly military history.

In effect, just as the war stimulated, and was used to promote, nationalist attitudes and demands in the Dominions in relation to the imperial government, the same can be said for indigenous nations in relation to their Dominions. As a microcosm, indigenous peoples sought the same recognition from their respective Dominion (and to a certain extent the Crown) as the Dominions sought from the mother country – equality and autonomy. For both parties, significant participation in the war represented one avenue to achieve these ambitions. In this sense, the patriotic reactions of many indigenous leaders in 1914, and their subsequent actions throughout the war, were no different from those of Dominion prime ministers and politicians. In an often overlooked premise, the Dominions did not cease to be evolving settler societies because of the Great War.

---

[8] Linda Tuhiwai Smith, 'Colonizing Knowledges' in Roger C. A. Maaka and Chris Andersen (eds.), *The Indigenous Experience: Global Perspectives* (Toronto: Canadian Scholars' Press, 2006), p. 97.

The First World War experiences of Dominion indigenes were analogous in most facets, despite their varied socio-economic condition and association with the dominant British-based settler societies. As A. G. Hopkins accurately explains:

Historians of India know little of Africa and vice versa; historians of Australia and New Zealand rarely make cross-references; historians of Canada have ceased, typically, to look beyond North America. In a world that is visibly shrinking, this is paradoxical to say the least ... Consequently, Maoris, Aborigines, Indians and others remain subordinated to a historical tradition that purports to emancipate them. An understanding of the imperial context would remove this false sense of isolation, open new possibilities for comparative studies of both settler communities and Indigenous peoples, and underline the widespread and growing significance of non-national affiliations.[9]

Similarly, Ken Coates argues that, 'historians are not well versed in the comparative dimensions of what has emerged as a major issue in national histories: the treatment of, and relationships with, Indigenous peoples'.[10] Indigenous participation during the First World War has been relegated to the peripheries of national histories, which in turn, generally represent Dominion and indigenous contributions as if detached from the governing political and military structures of the imperial government.

This thematic comparison of the participation of indigenous peoples of the Dominions during the war will place their involvement in a trans-national context, coupled to the British centre of influence, while identifying patterns of action and reaction by Dominion governments and indigenous peoples. As expounded by George Fredrickson: 'Cross-national history, by acquainting one with what goes on elsewhere, may inspire a critical awareness of what is taken for granted in one's own country.'[11] The historiography is void of any comparison between the Dominions and their indigenous peoples during the First World War. Most of the literature dedicated to the wartime experiences of indigenes falls within a dominant thematic tradition which P. Whitney Lackenbauer and R. Scott Sheffield label the 'forgotten warrior' genre.[12]

---

[9] A. G. Hopkins, 'Back to the Future: From National History to Imperial History', *Past and Present* 164 (1999), 216–17.

[10] Ken Coates, 'Learning from Others: Comparative History and the Study of Indigenous–Newcomer Relations', *Native Studies Review* 16/1 (2005), 5.

[11] George M. Fredrickson, 'From Exceptionalism to Variability: Recent Developments in Cross-National Comparative History', *Journal of American History* 82/2 (1995), 587–604.

[12] See: P. Whitney Lackenbauer and R. Scott Sheffield, 'Moving Beyond "Forgotten": The Historiography on Canadian Native Peoples and the World Wars' in P. Whitney

Within this construct, Dominion historians have recently resurrected the exploits of indigenous servicemen and women, to promote an agenda of recognition and commemoration akin to that bestowed on their white comrades.

Before the 1980s, the participation of indigenes in the First World War was virtually ignored by scholars, except for those from New Zealand, where narrative unit histories celebrated the racially homogenous Maori battalions of both world wars. This stagnation has seen considerable reversal over the last twenty years; however, most works are driven by narrative. The goal of these studies, which succumb to an interpretive orthodoxy based on recycled generalizations and anecdotal corroboration, is to ensure that indigenous veterans receive public recognition in the increasingly reconciliatory and apologetic western democracies.

In Canada, the literary tradition of the 'forgotten warrior' has its origins in the 1919 report of the Deputy Superintendent General of Indian Affairs from 1913 to 1932, Duncan Campbell Scott. Believing in the widely accepted vanishing race theory and promulgating an assimilationist policy, Scott had political motives for promoting the battlefield prowess and high enlistment rates of his Indian subjects:

In daring and intrepidity they were second to none and their performance is a ringing rebuttal to the familiar assertion that the red man has deteriorated ... These men who have been broadened by contact with the outside world and its affairs, who have mingled with the men of other races, and who have witnessed the many wonders and advantages of civilization, will not be content to return to their old Indian mode of life ... thus the war will have hastened that day, the millennium of those en-gaged [sic] in Indian work, when all the quaint old customs, the weird and picaresque ceremonies, the sun dance and the potlatch and even the musical and poetic native languages shall be as obsolete as the buffalo and the tomahawk, and the last tepee of the Northern wilds give place to a model farmhouse. In other words, the Indian shall become one with his neighbour in his speech, life and habits, thus conforming to that worldwide tendency towards universal standardization which would appear to be the essential underlying purport of all modern social evolution.[13]

Lackenbauer and Craig Leslie Mantle (eds.), *Aboriginal Peoples and the Canadian Military: Historical Perspectives* (Kingston: CDA Press, 2007), pp. 209–32.

[13] Duncan Campbell Scott, 'The Canadian Indians and the Great War', in *Canada in the Great War, Vol. III: Guarding the Channel Ports* (Toronto: United Publishers, 1919), pp. 327–8. Scott joined Indian Affairs in 1879 and worked as a clerk of various ranks and positions until 1896. He then served as the Chief Secretary until 1905, after which time he was posted as the Chief Clerk and Accountant until 1909. From 1909 until his promotion to Deputy Superintendent General in 1913, he was Superintendent of Indian Education. Scott was also an accomplished poet and wrote extensively on the Indian condition. His poetry is wrought with his belief of the fatal impact theory and

Two recycled narratives, Fred Gaffen's *Forgotten Soldiers* (1985) and Janice Summerby's *Native Soldiers, Foreign Battlefields* (2005), lend credence to the 'forgotten warrior' convention that has plagued accounts of Indian participation during the Great War.[14] In recent years, however, academics have begun to deviate from this motif by engaging in more scholarly appraisals of the overall Indian contribution as represented by L. James Dempsey's *Warriors of the King: Prairie Indians in World War I* (1999).[15] Detailed explorations of regional contributions and community-specific anomalies have also recently appeared. Nevertheless, the majority of accounts remain lodged in a national framework permeated by the 'forgotten warrior' approach.

In Australia, the service of Aborigines in the Australian Imperial Force (AIF) was wholly neglected until the late 1970s, aside from four brief articles on 'Aborigine Diggers' in the Returned Sailors and Soldiers Imperial League of Australia's 1931 and 1932 newsletters.[16] Aboriginal contributions were summarily, if not conveniently, ignored until Christopher Clark published two brief articles in 1973 and 1977 respectively.[17] Following Robert Hall's seminal work, *The Black Diggers: Aborigines and Torres Strait Islanders in the Second World War* (1989), a little more attention was given to Aboriginal involvement in the First World War.[18] David Huggonson produced a succession of anecdotal articles for obscure publications in support of his exhibition, 'Too Dark for the Light Horse', which toured Australia in 2000.[19] In 1990,

---

the assimilation of the remaining Indian population. For example, his 'The Half-Breed Girl' and 'The Onondaga Madonna' deconstruct the process of colonialism and the concept of Indians living in the cultural conflict of the convergence of two distinct societies.

[14] Fred Gaffen, *Forgotten Soldiers* (Penticton: Theytus Books, 1985); Janice Summerby, *Native Soldiers, Foreign Battlefields* (Ottawa: Department of Veterans Affairs, 2005).

[15] L. James Dempsey, *Warriors of the King: Prairie Indians in World War I* (Regina: Canadian Plains Research Center, 1999).

[16] Returned Sailors and Soldiers Imperial League of Australia (RSSILA), 'Aborigine Diggers: List Grows', *Reveille* (31 October 1931), 15; 'Many Served: A.I.F. Aborigines', *Reveille* (30 November 1931), 22; 'Lever on Britain: Prisoners Suffer', *Reveille* (31 December 1931), 10; 'A.I.F. Aborigines: N.S.W.', *Reveille* (31 January 1932), 20.

[17] C. D. Clark, 'Aborigines in the First AIF', *Australian Army Journal* 286 (1973), 21–6; C. D. Coulthard-Clark, 'Aborigine Medal Winners', *Sabretache* 18/4 (1977), 244–8.

[18] Robert A. Hall, *The Black Diggers: Aborigines and Torres Strait Islanders in the Second World War* (Sydney: Allen & Unwin, 1989).

[19] David Huggonson, 'Aborigines and the Aftermath of the Great War', *Australian Aboriginal Studies* 1 (1993), 2–9; 'Aboriginal Roughriders of World War 1', *Rodeo: Hoofs and Horns* (1990), 70; 'A Dark Past', *Army Magazine* 13 (1992), 26–7; 'Aboriginal Diggers of the 9th Brigade, First AIF', *Journal of the Royal Australian Historical Society* 79/3–4 (1993), 214–23; 'Aboriginal POW's of World War One', *Newsletter: The Historical Society of Southern Australia* 105 (1993), 9–12; 106 (1993),

Rod Pratt published four articles in *Sabretache*, entitled 'Queensland's Aborigines in the First AIF'. These articles remain the benchmark on Aboriginal participation during the First World War, highlighting the existing dearth of analysis in the Australian literary record.[20] Similarly, the contribution of Newfoundland-Labrador's indigenous soldiers has received no attention, aside from short biographies of Eskimo sniper John Shiwak.

Given that Maori were the only indigenous collective to have a homogenous combat unit during the war, a Maori Battalion history quickly followed. In 1926, the Department of Internal Affairs published James Cowan's *The Maoris in the Great War*. Cowan's assertion that, 'Not merely were the native New Zealanders superior to all the coloured troops ... but they proved superior to many of the white troops in directions which suited the genius of the race' is indicative of this panegyric narrative.[21] In 1995, Christopher Pugsley published the epigrammatic narrative, *Te Hokowhitu A Tu: The Maori Pioneer Battalion in the First World War*, which is heavily reliant upon the reproduction of nominal rolls and casualty and award registers.[22] P. S. O'Connor's enduring 1967 article, 'The Recruitment of Maori Soldiers, 1914–1918', remains the most analytical work.[23]

The involvement of the South African Native Labour Contingent (SANLC) on the Western Front, and of South African blacks in Africa campaigns, has garnered more academic interest in the past three decades than any other Dominion indigenous collective. This was the necessary by-product of the intense scrutiny afforded to the campaigns in East and West Africa, previously thought to be the forgotten fronts of the First World War.[24] Melvin Page, David Killingray, Hew Strachan, Geoffrey Hodges and Edward Paice have formed the vanguard for

---

8–11; 'Aboriginal Trackers and the Boer War', *Bourke Historical Society: The History of Bourke* 12 (1992), 20; 'The Dark Diggers of the AIF', *The Australian Quarterly* 61/3 (1989), 352–7; 'Too Dark for the Light Horse: An Australian in Germany', *Education* (1987), 24; 'Villers-Bretonneux: A Strange Name for an Aboriginal Burial Ground', *Journal of the Royal Historical Society of Queensland* 14/7 (1991), 285–8.

[20] These articles were reprinted, complete, in the 2007 edited volume by P. Whitney Lackenbauer et al., *Aboriginal Peoples and Military Participation: Canadian and International Perspectives* (Kingston: Canadian Defence Academy Press, 2007).

[21] James Cowan, *The Maoris in the Great War* (Auckland: Whitcombe & Tombs, 1926), p. 2.

[22] Christopher Pugsley, *Te Hokowhitu A Tu: The Maori Pioneer Battalion in the First World War* (Auckland: Reed Publishing, 2006).

[23] P. S. O'Connor, 'The Recruitment of Maori Soldiers, 1914–1918', *Political Science* 19/2 (1967), 48–83.

[24] Hew Strachan, *The First World War in Africa* (Oxford University Press, 2004), p. 185.

more acute research into Africa and the First World War.[25] As a result, the position of indigenous Africans has undergone a much needed reinterpretation.

The first publication detailing the SANLC was written while it was still active in France. Herbert C. Sloley, former Resident Commissioner of Basutoland and active member of the British Aborigines' Protection Society, ran a piece, 'The African Native Labour Contingent and the Welfare Committee', in April 1918, outlining the success of the 'experiment' of using natives as war labour outside of Africa. In a narrative enriched with praise for the efforts of his organization, Sloley concludes that, 'there is no reason to doubt that they [SANLC] will return with an increased idea of respect for the governing race'.[26] Scholarship, not to mention actual events, proved Sloley wrong and the wartime experiences of the SANLC in fostering black nationalism were seriously reassessed in the late 1970s. Albert Grundlingh took a leading role in re-evaluating the repercussions of the exposure of the SANLC to the more racially tolerant societies of France and Britain, and their interaction with soldiers from the vast conglomeration of Allied armies. In his own words, Grundlingh's systematic work, *Fighting Their Own War: South African Blacks and the First World War* (1987), 'analyzes their responses to and participation in the war, and also evaluates the wider ramifications of the war as these affected black people in South Africa'.[27]

Aside from secondary source material, the larger Dominion historiography shares a commonality in that the limited primary accounts were written by elite, literate indigenes, distorting the consensus of opinions on motivations, war service and soldiering by active participants. According to Smith, 'What is problematic is that this group of men have been named by the dominant non-indigenous population as individuals who represent the "real" leadership … idealized as the "saviours of the people."'[28] Indigenous leaders, or those in their counsel, often had veiled motivations for espousing indigenous contributions to the war effort. Only a select catalogue of works written by average (albeit

[25] See: Melvin E. Page (ed.), *Africa and the First World War* (London: Macmillan, 1987); Geoffrey Hodges, *The Carrier Corps: Military Labour in the East African Campaign 1914–1918* (Westport: Greenwood Press, 1986); Edward Paice, *Tip & Run: The Untold Tragedy of the Great War in Africa* (London: Weidenfeld & Nicolson, 2007).

[26] Herbert C. Sloley, 'The African Native Labour Contingent and the Welfare Committee', *Journal of the Royal African Society* 17/67 (1918), 210.

[27] Albert Grundlingh, *Fighting Their Own War: South African Blacks and the First World War* (Johannesburg: Ravan Press, 1987), p. ix.

[28] Smith, 'Colonizing Knowledges', 102.

literate) indigenous soldiers are available for consultation. Selections of interviews and primary accounts concerning indigenes and the First World War are spotted throughout a variety of secondary sources on a wide range of topics. The most valuable source of information is the archival records from various institutions of all Dominions and of the United Kingdom, although many indigenous-specific collections have been lost or destroyed.[29]

The First World War was, more so than its 1939–45 counterpart, the decisive chapter of the twentieth century for the Dominions. It forever altered the configuration of the empire and, through momentous Dominion participation, hastened the realization of full nationhood, both legally and culturally. The vast expeditionary forces of the Dominions, driven by the magnitude of the war and the incessant need for manpower, correspondingly led to a greater inclusion of indigenes than had been previously required or witnessed. Britain and its Dominions called upon their subject peoples, in varying degrees, to defend the institutions of their subjugation.[30] Although the Second Anglo-Boer War (1899–1902) marked the first occasion of noteworthy Dominion contributions to an external British war, white manpower was sufficient to exclude the enlistment of indigenes. Therefore, the elevated participation of Dominion indigenes during the First World War was the potential pivotal catalyst to accelerate their attainment of equal rights. For the first time in history, they had been summoned, in unprecedented numbers, to fight and labour on foreign fields alongside men from across the empire, and other Allied nations, for the common purpose of defending liberty and civilization.

The indigenous peoples of the Dominions shared equally in the burdens of war, both on the battlefields and the home fronts, and performed on par with their white comrades. They voluntarily aided the empire in its time of need and sought equality (akin to that created by soldiers in the trenches of France, Belgium, Gallipoli, Africa and the Middle East) as recompense. Arthur Marwick asserts that, 'in modern war there is a greater participation on the part of larger underprivileged groups in society, who tend correspondingly to benefit, or at least develop a new self-consciousness ... a strengthened market position and hence higher material standards for such groups; it also engenders

[29] For example, only 10–20 per cent of the First World War Maori collection was salvaged in the 1930s during relocation.
[30] George Robb, *British Culture and the First World War* (London: Palgrave, 2004), 'Nation, Race and Empire', pp. 11–12.

a new sense of status, usually leading to a dropping of former sectional or class barriers'.[31] The First World War was viewed by both indigenous political leaders and most soldiers as a medium to attain precisely these benefits, and the majority willingly supported the war effort.

---

[31] See: Arthur Marwick, *War and Social Change in the Twentieth Century: A Comparative Study of Britain, France, Germany, Russia and the United States* (London: Palgrave Macmillan, 1974).

1 Colonization and the settler state

European colonization of the Dominions occurred between 1530 and 1790. The colonial experience, including frontier warfare and cultural incompatibility, influenced the perceptions and policies of Europeans and their successive governments towards indigenous peoples. In all cases, indigenes were viewed as a deterrent to European expansionism and systems were implemented to control and subjugate indigenes and to expropriate their lands. All indigenous peoples actively resisted the European threat to their cultures and populations through violence and strategies to promote self-interest. None, however, could sustain opposition in the face of European technology, increasing settler populations and the drastic reduction of their own populations through disease and war.

All Dominions generally progressed through lengthy colonial experiences under British sponsorship. The Dominions were pioneer rather than sojourner colonies and were viewed as vacant for permanent European settlement. Land soon became the common currency, rapidly bringing settlers into conflict with indigenous peoples after the inevitable shift from beachhead frontiers to pastoral expansion into the hinterlands, culminating in protracted frontier warfare.[1] In 1516, at the onset of British imperialism, Sir Thomas More's *Utopia* foreshadowed the pervasive themes of land, warfare and assimilation that dominated settler–indigenous relations in all Dominions:

If the natives wish to live with Utopians, they are taken in. Since they join the colony willingly, they quickly adopt the same institutions and customs. This is advantageous for both peoples. For by their policies and practices the Utopians make the land yield an abundance for all, which before seemed too small and barren for the natives alone. If the natives will not conform to their laws, they drive them out of the area they claim for themselves, waging war if they meet resistance. Indeed they account it a very just cause of war if a people possess

---

[1] John Connor, *The Australian Frontier Wars, 1788–1838* (Sydney: University of New South Wales Press, 2002), pp. 25–7.

land that they leave idle and uncultivated and refuse the use and occupancy of it to others who according to the law of nature ought to be supported from it.[2]

The colonial process in all Dominions relegated indigenes to unwanted peoples – an unfortunate accessory to the 'white man's burden'. With the advent of Social Darwinism and racial theories in the mid-nineteenth century, Europeans created a 'scientific' framework to promote assimilationist and paternalistic agendas and to support the negative attributes ascribed to indigenous peoples. The exclusion of indigenes from most aspects of Dominion society, and their pragmatic use in military functions to satisfy white needs, was a reflection of their low status in the hierarchy of races and their inferior position in Dominion legal and social constructs. Colonial warfare, however, also created the contrasting but complementary concepts of martial races and of the savage, uncivilized indigene. The perceptions formed, and policies enacted, by settlers and their administrations during the settler state experience influenced most aspects of the lives of indigenous peoples, including their military value and function.

Prior to European contact, indigenous cultures were less technologically developed than some Asian and European cultures; nevertheless, multifarious trade and communication routes networking entire continents and oceanic islands had existed for millennia. Great indigenous civilizations, with complex political and social organizations, flourished. Warfare played an important role in political, social, cultural and genetic frameworks. Before contact, given the small populations of indigenous groupings, no standing warrior class could be maintained as in European nations or princely states. Any substantial loss of men was detrimental to the overall welfare of these small groupings of people. Additionally, the duration of any conflict was limited since participants, members of non-surplus producing economies, were forced to cease hostilities to resume food gathering and hunting.[3] During colonial warfare, these disadvantages accrued and left indigenous populations incapable of fighting the more robust standing European forces.

Canadian Indian warfare originated as a masculine sport. Battles were isolated and casualties low. Under proven war chiefs, raiding parties, usually numbering less than two hundred warriors, were sent to settle scores, to acquire provisions, or to avenge the deaths of, or replace, deceased clan members. The practice of incorporating prisoners into the tribe ensured the exchange of cultural information, the configuration of alliances, enhanced trading opportunities and the

[2] Thomas More, *Utopia* (Reprint. Illinois: Harlan Davidson, 1949), p. 38.
[3] Connor, *The Australian Frontier Wars*, pp. 1–6.

dissemination of broader genetic traits. Arranged marriages provided similar benefits. While these practices perpetuated a chronic state of war, the bloodshed remained minimal. Indian and Eskimo warfare of Newfoundland-Labrador was minor. Populations were smaller, had more access to resources and were more isolated from neighbouring groups. The Beothuk were homogenous and relatively few encroachments were made onto Newfoundland by the Mi'kmaq of Atlantic Canada or the Eskimos of Labrador prior to European contact.[4]

Maori warfare focused on *utu* (vengeance) and *mana* (prestige/influence). War was usually provoked by disagreements over land and resources (including women), the desire to avenge a death, to right a wrong, or to gain personal or tribal *mana*. Genealogy was instrumental in the formation of alliances for shared war aims. Although warfare was endemic, the season for war generally followed the harvest. Maori war parties were small, ranging from 30 to 140 warriors, under the inspiration of war chiefs. War could be averted through feasts, trade, diplomatic missions or arranged marriages.[5]

Aboriginal warfare was intermittent and localized. Given the non-hierarchical tradition in Aboriginal society and the isolation of tribal groups, coalitions were relatively unknown, making war parties autonomous units of five to thirty men. Engagements, to assert dominance over a neighbouring people, to acquire women or to avenge an insult or death of a tribal member, were sporadic and brief, with limited casualties.[6]

In southern Africa, membership of military organizations was the obligation of all able-bodied, free males and was a key component to social status. Armies tended to be larger than those of other Dominion indigenes. Leadership was bestowed upon men who had proven themselves in combat and had attained a prominent social and martial position. Women and children often accompanied their husbands on military forays, carrying provisions and cooking meals. Access to resources and slaves were the most prevalent motives for conflict.[7]

For all indigenous inhabitants of the Dominions the arrival of Europeans was the most significant threat to their populations,

---

[4] J. R. Miller, *Skyscrapers Hide the Heavens: A History of Indian–White Relations in Canada* (University of Toronto Press, 2000), pp. 7–14.

[5] Bradford Haami, 'Maori Traditional Warfare' in Ian McGibbon (ed.), *The Oxford Companion to New Zealand Military History* (Oxford University Press, 2000), pp. 303–6.

[6] K. R. Howe, *Race Relations, Australia and New Zealand: A Comparative Survey 1770s–1970s* (Sydney: Methuen Publications, 1977), pp. 5–6.

[7] Bruce Vandervort, *Wars of Imperial Conquest in Africa, 1830–1914* (London: Routledge, 1998), pp. 3–11.

civilizations and futures. As Charles Darwin noted in 1836, 'Wherever the European has trod, death seems to pursue the aboriginal. We may look to the wide extent of the Americas, Polynesia, the Cape of Good Hope and Australia, and we find the same result.'[8] The clash of mores was intense and included the introduction into indigenous societies of modern weapons, deadly diseases, Christianity and alcohol. Continental European wars were imported to select Dominions, most markedly North America, and indigenes were enlisted to participate. These wars, in combination with trade, fractured long-standing indigenous relations. Indigenous nations often formed alliances with a European belligerent to safeguard self-interest or seek revenge against traditional enemies. J. R. Miller asserts that, 'notions that one [indigenous] nation, or another took up arms to advance a commercial or strategical [sic] aim of the French or British were erroneous'.[9] Indifferent to underlying motives, European settlers used indigenes to satisfy their own purpose and need.

European colonizers and governments used an assortment of non-sequential strategies to undermine, subjugate or annihilate indigenous populations. Many of these were ongoing at the outbreak of the First World War, as the Dominions were consolidating the framework of a cohesive settler state. These approaches included, but were not limited to: waging decisive military campaigns; destabilizing or banning political organizations and power structures; removing or inhibiting identifiable cultural traits and language; creating economic and trade dependency; drastically shifting demographics in Europeans' favour; and, most importantly and antagonistically, expropriating and limiting the land base of indigenous peoples.

In 1583, Sir Humphrey Gilbert officially took possession of Newfoundland, England's first overseas colony, under royal prerogative of Queen Elizabeth I. John Guy established the first permanent settlement at Conception Bay in 1610. St John's, a natural harbour, became the principal headquarters and a port for a variety of European nations.[10] The relationship between the Beothuk, numbering roughly 1,200 to 1,500 in 1500, and European newcomers can be separated into three phases. The first, from the arrival of John Cabot in 1497 (excluding the brief Norse settlement at L'Anse aux Meadows around the year 1002) to permanent European settlement in 1610, can be

---

[8] David Maybury-Lewis, 'Indigenous Peoples', in *The Indigenous Experience: Global Perspectives*, p. 17.

[9] Miller, *Skyscrapers Hide the Heavens*, p. 76.

[10] Provincial Archives of Newfoundland and Labrador (PANL), MG145, Regulations for Fishing off the Coast of Labrador, 1765.

summarized as a period of relative cooperation, casual trade and occasional conflict. In the second phase, the remaining 500 to 600 Beothuk withdrew to a habitat beyond the coastal haunts of European fishermen. The final period of confrontation began in around 1750, when Europeans moved into the interior along the Exploits River, where the remaining 300 Beothuk were living. Competition for resources, disease and the increasing migration of French-allied Mi'kmaq into southern Newfoundland after 1713 led to the extinction of the Beothuk.[11] By 1811, seventy-two Beothuk were left and only thirteen by 1823. The last died in 1829.[12] Previous theories that the Europeans themselves, or through the Mi'kmaq, methodically eradicated the Beothuk are now discredited. Although the Beothuk were victims of murderous raids by individuals or small groups, they were not a people purposefully exterminated. According to Miller, 'they were not systematically hunted down, nor were they the objects of a campaign of genocide ... The fate of the Beothuk was a tragedy, not proof of European malevolence.'[13]

Following the Seven Years' War (1756–63), France ceded all possessions of New France to Britain, save for the islands of Saint-Pierre and Miquelon. The colony of Newfoundland received a House of Assembly in 1832 and was afforded responsible government in 1854. Its tiny residual indigenous population totalled roughly 2,000 to 2,500, comprised of Innu (Naskapi and Montagnais) and migratory Eskimo communities in Labrador, smaller numbers of peripatetic Cree in southern Labrador and diminutive groups of Mi'kmaq in southern Newfoundland.[14] The Dominion did not join Canadian confederation until 1949.

During the sixteenth and seventeenth centuries, relations between Canadian Indians, totalling an estimated 300,000 to 350,000, and the French and British, were generally peaceful and mutually beneficial through trade (see Map 2). Europeans came to the Americas for fish, fur, exploration and, finally, to promote Christianity. Originally, Indians tolerated the fishing, eagerly embraced the fur trade, cooperated with exploration, if it did not interfere with their own interests,

---

[11] Ingeborg Marshall, 'An Unpublished Map Made by John Cartwright between 1768 and 1773 Showing Beothuck Indian Settlements and Artifacts and Allowing a New Population Estimate', *Ethnohistory* 24/3 (1977), 223–49. The Beothuk covered themselves in red ochre for the practical purposes of defence against the cold and insects as well as ceremonial customs, giving rise to the term 'Red Indian'.

[12] Peter Calamai, 'Beothuk Mystery', *McMaster University Science Writer* (2005), 4.

[13] Miller, *Skyscrapers Hide the Heavens*, p. 114.

[14] Marshall, 'An Unpublished Map Made by John Cartwright between 1768 and 1773 Showing Beothuck Indian Settlements and Artifacts and Allowing a New Population Estimate', 223–49.

and indulged evangelists.[15] Cross-cultural marriages and sexual relations were frequent, since Indians viewed these unions as representative of trade alliance. Most prevalent with the French fur traders in Ontario and Manitoba, these partnerships produced the distinct French–Indian (and to a lesser extent Scottish–Indian) Métis populations. Two early historians of the Métis, only half-jokingly, wrote that, 'the Métis nation was created nine months after the landing of the first European'.[16] Nevertheless, European populations remained small and were protected by their commodities' value.[17] However, the fur trade, in conjunction with the dissemination of European wars, weapons and disease, began to unhinge the balance among North American Indians.

Indian campaigns to secure access to hunting grounds, to obtain furs to trade for European wares and firearms, transformed the traditional Indian landscape of North America. Those nations that secured furs, and in turn weapons, launched greater offensives against traditional enemies, resulting in the displacement or absorption of conquered tribes. The Iroquois Confederacy or Six Nations (Mohawk, Oneida, Onondaga, Cayuga, Seneca and, as of 1722, the Tuscarora) was the most proficient Indian coalition in this cyclical pattern and quickly monopolized the fur-for-firearms exchange east of the Mississippi River. The Iroquois used a combination of military might and skilled diplomacy to attain an empire, albeit short-lived, which served the British as a protective buffer between British North America and the French and, later, the Americans. The confederacy was a powerful British ally throughout the colonial wars. For example, in 1784, in recognition of their service to the British during the American Revolution, Mohawk Captain Joseph Brant and two thousand Iroquois, and allied Indian, followers were given land in Ontario – the Six Nations Reserve.[18] In this atmosphere of cooperation with the British and as a result of treaties signed by the Crown, Indian nations regarded themselves (and still do) as autonomous nations within the confines of North America.

Following the War of 1812 (1812–15), the Rush–Bagot Treaty (1817) demilitarized the Great Lakes and nullified future American threats.

---

[15] Miller, *Skyscrapers Hide the Heavens*, p. 31.
[16] J. R. Miller, *Lethal Legacy: Current Native Controversies in Canada* (Toronto: McClelland & Stewart, 2004), p. 19.
[17] At contact the only metal known to the eastern Indians of Canada was copper from the vicinity of Lake Superior, which was dispersed throughout eastern Canada and used for limited utilitarian and decorative purposes, given its soft metallic properties.
[18] Robert S. Allen, *His Majesty's Indian Allies: British Indian Policy in the Defence of Canada, 1774–1815* (Toronto: Dundurn Press, 1992), pp. 15–16.

As a result, Indians, including the vaunted Iroquois, lost their importance as military allies. They had been used as required and no longer
featured in British strategy. The British began to initiate policies of subjugation and assimilation rather than cooperation.[19] Indian nations east
of Manitoba had decreased in population by way of war and disease,
were relocated to reserves, by force or necessity, and left economically
destitute after the expropriation of their hunting grounds and the
collapse of the fur trade.

Indian reserves, incorporated in Crown protocol during the 1830s,
served two strategic purposes: they opened up land for unhindered
settlement and industry and established a framework by which Indians
could be integrated or, alternatively, easily monitored. Reserves, however, were never intended to be a permanent solution to the 'Indian
Question'. It was believed that the majority of Indians would die off
and that the remnants would willingly enter Euro-Canadian society.[20]
Furthermore, neither the 1763 Royal Proclamation nor Ottawa Chief
Pontiac's short-lived rebellion (1763–6) deterred European settlement
west of the Mississippi watershed. The Royal Proclamation forbade
colonists from settling, selling or buying land west of the Appalachian
Mountains, endowing the Crown with sole jurisdiction in any transac-
tions involving Indian lands.[21] These tenets were never enforced and
the ensuing westward expansion, in conjunction with the disappearance of the buffalo, threatened the survival of the Plains Indians in
both Canada and the United States. As westward settlement increased,
construction of the Canadian Pacific Railway (1881–5) eased the
passage for further settlement west of Ontario.

Indian Affairs was inherited from the British and remained under federal jurisdiction after Canadian confederation (1867). However, previous Crown policy, including over eighty treaties signed (in the Canadian
land-base) by the British prior to 1867, had predetermined the continuation of paternalistic authority over Indians. In 1869, the Gradual

---

[19] Ibid, p. 148.
[20] John L. Tobias, 'Protection, Civilization, Assimilation' in J. R. Miller (ed.), *Sweet Promises: A Reader on Indian–White Relations in Canada* (University of Toronto Press, 1991), pp. 127–44.
[21] The Royal Proclamation is viewed by Canadian Indians as their Magna Carta and is used in modern-day land-claim submissions and is their recognition as sovereign nations. The High Court of Australia determined in a 1992 Aboriginal land claims case that under the Royal Proclamation of 1763, 'all the Lands and Territories lying to the Westward of the Sources of the Rivers (west of the Mississippi River)' included the whole of Australia, as it was not settled by the British until 1788. However, the British rescinded the Proclamation in November 1768. With fear of a revolution, which inevitably came, the British under Sir William Johnson negotiated a treaty with the Iroquois for Ohio, dubbed the Treaty of Fort Stanwix, in November 1768.

Enfranchisement Act was conceded, placing the traditional political practices of Indians under governmental scrutiny, further undermining Indian leaders. The Act also removed 'status' from any Indian female who married a non-Indian, a penalty inherited by their offspring.[22] The Department of Indian Affairs (DIA) was unofficially formed in conjunction with the 1876 Indian Act, which after several revisions remains in force today. The core features of this policy included the resettlement of Indians to federally controlled reserves owned by the Crown, federal supervision of Indian political organizations and the banning of certain rituals. The Act also established the 'residential' school system whereby Indian children were removed from their communities for religious and agricultural instruction. In 1880, the Department of Indian Affairs was formally established and gave the federal government powers to impose elected councils in place of traditional Indian forms of non-elected leadership, such as the Iroquois Longhouse. The Indian Advancement Act of 1884 added a clause whereby Ottawa had power to depose any chief who was considered unfit.[23] A core feature of the original Indian Act was the assignment of Indian agents to reserves appointed by, and answerable to, the Superintendent of Indian Affairs, with his powers, in reality, vested in his Deputy Superintendent General – the office held by Duncan Campbell Scott during the Great War.

Unlike the other Dominions and the United States, Canada did not experience prolonged or incessantly violent frontier warfare, although it was not void of confrontation. Not all Indians welcomed confederation or the edicts of the Indian Act and the government immediately encountered insurrection in the form of the Red River Rebellion between November 1869 and August 1870, led by Métis Louis Riel. Although the resistance ended peacefully, Prime Minister Sir John A. Macdonald had ordered the deployment of a 1,200-strong armed force to Manitoba, under the command of Colonel Garnet Wolseley.[24] The 1870 rebellion made the Canadian government attentive to the unrest in western Canada and the problems associated with the influx of settlers to the vast prairies. To defuse the tensions among governments, settlers and Indians, a series of 'numbered treaties' (Treaties 1–10) were negotiated between 1871 and 1908 with jurisdiction over the majority

---

[22] Miller, *Skyscrapers Hide the Heavens*, pp. 145–6.
[23] Ibid, pp. 254–5. The US government also passed numerous similar pieces of legislation: the 1830 Indian Removal Act, the 1887 Dawes Severalty Act and the 1934 Indian Reorganization Act.
[24] J. M. Bumsted, 'The West and Louis Riel' in J. M. Bumsted (ed.), *Interpreting Canada's Past: Vol. Two, Post-Confederation* (Toronto: Oxford University Press, 1993), pp. 67–9.

of western Ontario, Manitoba, Saskatchewan and Alberta. These treaties were negotiated in haste to secure Indian lands in order to make
way for the deluge of settlers and the railway. Many treaties were initiated by chiefs to safeguard what remained of their land and livelihood
after the vanishing of the buffalo and the unregulated encroachment of
settlers onto their territories.[25]

On reserves, the Indians were dissatisfied with their static existence,
increasing starvation and the government's insistence on agricultural
and religious education. Portions of the treaties were not honoured
and some Indians viewed confrontation as a means to secure treaty
rights and promote their waning interests. Restless young Cree men
were beyond the authority of traditional chiefs and elders. The Métis
shared this discontent and began to mobilize, summoning Riel, in exile
in the Montana Territory, back to Canada. Riel established a provi-
sional government at Batoche on 19 March 1885, with eight hundred
Métis and Cree warriors (who had in the past fought over buffalo
hunting grounds).[26] The Northwest Field Force was dispatched under
the command of New Zealand War veteran Major-General Frederick
Middleton, comprising roughly 6,500 British regulars and Canadian
militia and 1,500 irregulars and North-West Mounted Police. After
a series of battles, and the capture of Batoche, Riel was apprehended
on 15 May and was hanged for treason on 16 November 1885.[27] The
unsuccessful North-West Rebellion effectively ended Indian attempts
to violently resist settler expansion and governmental policy. In 1907,
politician and farmer, H. C. Thomson, remarked that the Indian policy
was so successful in securing land for whites that it should be exported
to South Africa and Australia to secure large tracts of indigenous land
for white farmers.[28]

In Australia the use of force against, and extermination of, Aboriginal
populations to secure land was reaching its zenith, under the auspices of
Terra Nullius, after only fifty years of contact. It is estimated that in 1788
the Aboriginal population numbered approximately 300,000 to 350,000,
divided into 554 distinct tribes of semi-nomadic hunter-gatherers.[29]

---

[25] Alexander Morris, *The Treaties of Canada with the Indians of Manitoba and North-West
Territories* (Toronto: Belfords, Clarke, 1880); Department of Indian Affairs, *Basic
Departmental Data, 2003* (Ottawa: Department of Indian Affairs, 2003), pp. 87–103.

[26] Miller, *Skyscrapers Hide the Heavens*, pp. 207–24.

[27] Bruce Vandervort, *Indian Wars of Mexico, Canada and the United States, 1812–1900*
(New York: Routledge, 2006), pp. 218–22.

[28] Ronald G. Haycock, *The Image of the Indian* (Waterloo: Lutheran University Press,
1971), p. 19.

[29] Richard Broome, *Aboriginal Australians: Black Responses to White Dominance, 1788–
2001* (Sydney: Allen & Unwin, 2001), p. 15. Given the relatively large number of

John Connor labelled relatively peaceful settler frontiers, like that at Port Jackson/Sydney, 'beachhead frontiers'. Such British settlements founded on Australia's coastline between 1788 and 1837 experienced little initial contact or conflict with Aborigines, who still held the balance of power. However, as these settlements began expanding onto larger tracts of Aboriginal land, and with the Hobart General Orders of 1819 promoting the 'extension of grazing Grounds, and progressive occupation of the Country', frontier warfare began.[30]

As a result, many British referred to the 'Black War' on the frontier. The Aborigines of Tasmania were systematically eradicated during the late 1820s. In 1830, every able-bodied male formed an armed chain, dubbed the Black Line, to sweep the island in order to corral and kill the Aboriginal inhabitants. Those Aborigines that eluded their pursuers were ultimately relocated to the remote and inhospitable Flinders Islands, where their numbers continued to decline due to starvation and disease. By 1869 only a handful remained, living amongst white sealers.[31]

In 1822, in the midst of increasing violence, the British government lowered the duty on Australian wool to one-sixth that of German wool, leading to the immigration of over 200,000 British to Australia between 1832 and 1850. This resulted in the need for more pastoral land and an inevitable increase in settler–Aborigine conflict. 'Massacres' became more common.[32] According to Geoffrey Blainey, Aboriginal 'casualties might not, at first sight, seem large; but the death of two men in a battle involving forty meant that the casualties were approaching the scale of the Battle of the Somme. An aboriginal fight could absorb a large proportion of the adults within a radius of fifty miles – indeed, could involve a far higher proportion of able-bodied adults than any war of the twentieth century could possibly involve.'[33] The Pinjarra Massacre (28 October 1834) highlights Blainey's argument. It is estimated that the Pinjarra camp held roughly seventy to eighty people. Contemporary British reports estimate Aboriginal casualties at between twenty and thirty-five, while later journalistic reports offer figures of between seventy and eighty. Aboriginal traditions recite casualties in the hundreds;

Aboriginal tribes, it is not possible to include a map delineating their geographic locations as I have done for Indians and Maori. The following website, however, offers an excellent interactive map: http://mappery.com/map-of/Australia-Aboriginal-Tribes-Map

[30] Connor, *The Australian Frontier Wars*, pp. 27–34.

[31] Broome, *Aboriginal Australians*, pp. 41, 52.

[32] Ibid, pp. 41, 52.

[33] Desmond Ball, 'Introduction', in Desmond Ball (ed.), *Aborigines in the Defence of Australia* (Sydney: Australian National University Press, 1991), p. 10.

however, these should be seen as symbolic of the disastrous effect that Pinjarra had on the population of the Aborigines of the Murray River.[34]

The Aboriginal population decreased through violence, disease and starvation. The total number of deaths during the Australian Frontier Wars (1788–1890) is not known. Most academics estimate that some 2,000 to 2,500 Europeans died at the hands of Aborigines, while the conservative estimate of Aboriginal deaths is 20,000 to 25,000. This figure does not include the larger number of Aborigines who succumbed to disease, malnutrition and alcohol. By 1891, the Aboriginal population stood at 111,000 from a contact population of roughly 320,000.[35]

The Victoria 1869 Aborigines Protection Act was the first formal statute issued concerning Aborigines. Western Australia pursued its own Aborigines Protection Act in 1886, followed by Queensland's endorsement of the Aboriginals Protection and Restriction of the Sale of Opium Act of 1897. Finally, New South Wales (NSW) passed its Aborigines Protection Act in 1909 and South Australia (inclusive of the Northern Territory) generated the Northern Territory Aborigines Act in 1910.[36] The federation of Australian colonies occurred on 1 January 1901 to yield the Commonwealth of Australia. Jurisdiction for Aboriginal affairs was not transferred to the federal government and remained the responsibility of individual states, as outlined in Chapter 1, Part V, Section XXVI of the Commonwealth of Australia Constitution Act (1900):

The Parliament shall, subject to this Constitution, have the power to make peace, order and good government with respect to:–

(XXVI) the people of any race, other than the Aboriginal race in each State, for whom it is deemed necessary to make special laws.[37]

This policy was immediately challenged in the House of Representatives in July 1901 by Hugh Mahon from Western Australia: 'In this particular matter the reputation of the whole people of Australia is at stake. It is not a pleasant thing that the newspapers around the world should repeatedly contain references of slavery under the British flag.' Sir Charles Lucas, a member of the Colonial Office, noted after a trip to the Antipodes in 1909 that, 'Australians and New Zealanders have very

---

[34] Connor, *The Australian Frontier Wars*, pp. 82–3.
[35] Broome, *Aboriginal Australians*, p. 55; Jeffrey Grey, *A Military History of Australia* (Cambridge University Press, 1999), p. 36.
[36] Andrew Armitage, *Comparing the Policy of Aboriginal Assimilation: Australia, Canada and New Zealand* (Vancouver: University of British Columbia Press, 1995), p. 18.
[37] National Archives of Australia (NAA). Commonwealth of Australia Constitution Act (1900).

little or no experience of or training in the administration of natives, and it is unnecessary to emphasise the point that the Australasian view of coloured men does not coincide with our own.'[38] In January 1911, a committee was appointed to determine whether Australia should place Aboriginal protection under federal jurisdiction, similar to all other Dominions. The response of the federal government was that, 'According to moderate estimates about 75,000 or 80,000 Aborigines still survive, mostly in the northern part of the Continent ... they are already well cared for by their respective [State] Governments.'[39]

The various protection acts passed by Australian colonies/states created settlements to provide a 'pillow for a dying race'. This was done without treaty or indigenous consultation. These Crown-owned settlements, or reserves, were managed by protectors, usually members of legislature or police forces. The chief protector administered all aspects of Aboriginal life: where they could reside; in what occupations they could work; the control and dissemination of funds; the enforcement of alcohol, religious, linguistic and cultural bans; and the restriction of settler–Aborigine contact. Inclusive in this control was the protector's ability to remove Aboriginal children, with an emphasis placed on half-castes, for religious and industrial schooling focused on farm labour and domestic service.[40] On the eve of the First World War, the Australian Royal Commission on Aborigines submitted its 1913 year-end report: 'With the gradual disappearance of the full-blood blacks ... and the great increase in the number of half-castes and quadroons, the problem is now one of assisting and training the native so that he may become a useful member of the community ... To achieve this object we believe it is necessary for more direct [State] Government control.'[41]

New Zealand was the last Dominion inhabited by indigenous peoples and also the last to be colonized by Europeans. Maori arrived between 1100 and 1200 and spread across New Zealand, settling predominantly on the warmer, less formidable north island. By the early sixteenth century, after the depletion of large game, permanent agricultural settlements were centred on fortified and elaborate *Pa* (fortified

[38] Harcourt Papers, 468. October 1909: Notes on a Visit to Australia, New Zealand and Fiji by Sir Charles Lucas.
[39] NAA, A11915/6691: Protection of Aborigines Correspondence, 1901–14; NAA, A61901/232: Aborigines Protection Society London, Conditions of Aborigines in the Australian Colonies.
[40] Armitage, *Comparing the Policy of Aboriginal Assimilation*, pp. 34–5.
[41] Sharman N. Stone (ed.), *Aborigines in White Australia: A Documentary History of the Attitudes Affecting Official Policy and the Australian Aborigine, 1696–1973* (Victoria: Heinemann, 1974), p. 148.

villages or field fortifications).[42] Although the Maori population at contact is not known exactly, Captain James Cook's 1769 estimation of 100,000 appears to be relatively correct. This population was divided into approximately fifty tribes (see Map 3).[43]

As with initial relations in Canada, the first stage of contact between Europeans and Maori was one of cooperation; the Maori wanted European wares and traders wanted a market for their goods, in addition to land, food, wives and protection. Maori viewed these practices as a way to secure a trading monopoly and to enhance tribal alliances with Europeans.[44] The few hundred European missionaries, whalers and traders who cohabited with the Maori were protected by their value, not their power or numbers. James Belich asserts that Europeans came to New Zealand for 'flax, timber and whales; seals, sex and souls'.[45]

During the first three decades of the nineteenth century, Maori acquired muskets and continued their long-standing practice of traditional warfare. The continuation of hostilities with the advent of modern weapons led to larger wars with increased casualties. The period of Maori warfare from 1814 to 1833 is collectively known as 'the Musket Wars'. The violent upheaval that raged across the entire country resulted in significant Maori population migrations and deaths.[46] The musket wars abated after 1834, once all tribes had muskets and a balance of power was restored. Displaced tribes from Taranaki commandeered a brig and crew and invaded the Chatham Islands in 1835, killing or enslaving the entire Moriori population of roughly 1,800. By 1862, only 101 Moriori remained. The last died in 1933.[47]

The precise death rate during the Musket Wars is not known. Crude estimates range from 20,000 to 40,000, including deaths from disease, while another 30,000 Maori were displaced. The ramifications of the Musket Wars were important for future conflict between Maori and

[42] James Belich, *Making Peoples: A History of the New Zealanders from Polynesian Settlement to the End of the Nineteenth Century* (Auckland: Penguin Press, 1996), p. 80.

[43] D. Ian Pool, *The Maori Population of New Zealand, 1769–1971* (Oxford University Press, 1977), pp. 234–5; W. David McIntyre and W. J. Gardner (eds.), *Speeches and Documents on New Zealand History* (Oxford: Clarendon Press, 1971), p. 459.

[44] James Belich, *The Victorian Interpretation of Racial Conflict: The Maori, the British, and the New Zealand Wars* (Montreal: McGill-Queen's University Press, 1989), pp. 17–20. The first Maori visit to England occurred in 1805. Six thousand guns were imported from Sydney in the year 1831 alone, with the number of firearms in New Zealand doubling from 1829 to 1831.

[45] Belich, *Making Peoples*, p. 129.

[46] Tom Gibson, *The Maori Wars: The British Army in New Zealand, 1840–1872* (London: Leo Cooper, 1974), pp. 19–21; Belich, *Making Peoples*, pp. 160–5.

[47] Philippa Mein Smith, *A Concise History of New Zealand* (Cambridge University Press, 2005), p. 37.

the British. Firstly, the inter-tribal warfare flooded Maori communities with high-quality small arms and provided the opportunity for men to become skilled in their use. Secondly, due to the mass migration, the incorporation of certain tribes into others and the acquisition of prisoners and wives, Maori kinship was extended across a more diverse set of tribes than had occurred previously. Lastly, the vacancy of land resulting from Maori migration encouraged European settlement into these unoccupied districts.[48]

In 1835, a 'Declaration of Independence' was collectively signed by fifty-two Maori chiefs as the United Tribes of New Zealand, recognizing New Zealand as an independent state under British protection. Northern Maori believed this document was recognition of their sovereignty. Following an isolated outbreak of tribal warfare in the Bay of Islands, Governor Richard Bourke of NSW issued a proclamation on 14 January 1840 that extended its borders to include New Zealand. Bourke then dispatched Captain William Hobson, who arrived in New Zealand on 29 January 1840, and declared himself Lieutenant-Governor. Pre-empting these events, Colonel William Wakefield, as envoy of the New Zealand Company (NZC), purchased large tracts of land around Wellington in 1839.[49] Hobson, under pressure from land-hungry settlers and the New Zealand Company, summoned local Maori chiefs to a meeting at Waitangi on 5 February 1840. The Treaty of Waitangi has been the focal point of *Pakeha*–Maori relations since its signing and has been widely researched, theorized and disputed.[50] To the Maori the treaty was an affirmation of the coexistence of two sets of sovereignties in a partnership.

Nine versions of the treaty exist – the original in English and Maori, seven copies in Maori and one English reprint. Over five hundred chiefs

---

[48] Belich, *The Victorian Interpretation of Racial Conflict*, pp. 20–4. Maori small arms were not the 'sham dam iron' guns made in the factories of Birmingham and Liege for trade in Africa. These weapons sold for 5 to 6 shillings each, while the 8,000 muskets exported to New Zealand via Sydney from 1830–1 valued 26 shillings each.

[49] Richard S. Hill, *The Story of Policing in New Zealand Volume I: Policing the Colonial Frontier: The Theory and Practice of Coercive Social and Racial Control in New Zealand, 1767–1867* (Wellington: V. R. Ward Printer, 1986), parts I, II, pp. 76, 90. See: Patricia Burns, *Fatal Success: A History of the New Zealand Company* (Auckland: Heinemann Reed, 1989); Peter Adams, *Fatal Necessity: British Intervention in New Zealand 1830–1847* (Auckland: University of Auckland Press, 1977).

[50] See: Richard S. Hill, *State Authority, Indigenous Autonomy: Crown–Maori Relations in New Zealand/Aotearoa 1900–1950* (Wellington: Victoria University Press, 2004); I. H. Kawharu (ed.), *Waitangi: Maori and Pakeha Perspectives of the Treaty of Waitangi* (Oxford University Press, 1989); Claudia Orange, *The Treaty of Waitangi* (Wellington: Allen & Unwin, 1987); Michael Belgrave, *Historical Frictions: Maori Claims & Reinvented History* (Auckland University Press, 2005).

signed the treaty and all but thirty-nine signed a Maori version. Many other chiefs refused to sign, while others were not given an opportunity. Analysis of the treaty revealed inconsistencies between the Maori and English translations.[51] The most controversial facet of the treaty is the use of the word 'pre-emption'. The English version states that the Maori yielded to the Queen, 'the exclusive right of Preemption over such lands' they wished to vacate or sell. The Maori version made no reference to pre-emption. It promised the Queen the right to buy and sell these lands, but not exclusively, nor as the highest priority.

In reality, the colony's existence was predicated on buying land cheaply from Maori and selling it to settlers to encourage immigration. In order to facilitate this expansion, the government failed to comply with the treaty regulations and was unwilling to confront the New Zealand Company or settlers in safeguarding Maori rights. Conflict with settlers, and in turn the British, soon followed in the form of the New Zealand Wars (1845–72). Within this broad definition there were roughly twenty 'wars', separated into three main groupings: limited and localized conflicts during the 1840s and 1850s; major engagements between 1860 and 1864 involving British forces and the Maori King Movement (formed in 1857) in Waikato and Taranaki; and the diverse and pervasive fighting of 1864 to 1872 between colonial troops, their Maori allies (*kupapa*) and the supporters of Maori prophetic leaders.[52] Governor George Grey, who advocated a 'quick and complete assimilation' of Maori, foreshadowed this confrontation, remarking in 1845 that, 'aboriginal inhabitants are so numerous, and generally, I regret to say, are much better armed than our own men, that no force which Great Britain could spare, could hold military possession of the country until after a long and expensive war'.[53] It was the New Zealand Wars, not the Treaty of Waitangi, which ended Maori self-determination and solidified British authority. At the signing of the Treaty of Waitangi, the estimated Maori population was 65,000, compared to 2,500 Europeans. By 1858, marking the mid-point of the New Zealand Wars, the populations were balanced at roughly 59,000 each.[54]

By the end of the New Zealand Wars, 20,000 British soldiers and over 5,000 'settler soldiers' had been engaged to defeat a Maori

---

[51] See: Paul McHugh, *The Maori Magna Carta: New Zealand Law and the Treaty of Waitangi* (Oxford University Press, 1991).

[52] James Belich, 'New Zealand Wars' in *The Oxford Companion to New Zealand Military History*, p. 371.

[53] Hill, *State Authority, Indigenous Autonomy*, p. 18.

[54] McIntyre and Gardner, *Speeches and Documents on New Zealand History*, p. 459; Pool, *The Maori Population of New Zealand*, p. 237.

mobilization, led by the Kingites, of roughly 5,000 warriors. Australian colonies supplied British forces with supplies and 2,450 Australian militiamen.[55] By the end of Te Kooti's war in 1872, the Maori population numbered approximately 47,000, while the European population was nearing 300,000.[56]

The New Zealand Wars, in combination with government policies, drastically reduced Maori territorial holdings. In 1863, the New Zealand government passed the New Zealand Settlement Acts, allowing for the confiscation of Maori land on the north island. Subsequently, the government expropriated 1.2 million acres of land, mainly in the areas of the recently defeated Waikato and Taranaki tribes. An amendment to the Acts in 1865 abolished pre-emption, giving settlers the freedom to buy land directly from Maori. The Native Land Court, also established in 1865, extinguished traditional land rights and forced Maori to have their lands registered before private selling or leasing. In reality, this policy was introduced as an effective measure against communal Maori resistance to land sales, and undermined the collective stance of the King Movement. By 1891, with a diminishing population and at a nadir of 44,177, Maori held only 11.01 million acres of land (roughly 16 per cent of New Zealand), predominantly in the more remote regions of the north island. Of this total, 2.4 million acres were leased to Europeans, who, boosted by the gold rush of the 1860s, now numbered 626,658.[57] In 1894, the Advances to Settlers Act provided loans for land purchase to Europeans only. Furthermore, the Native Township Act (1895) allowed Europeans to settle on vacant Maori land. Lastly, the Native Land Act of 1909 removed all restrictions on land sale or transfer. By 1911, only 7.14 million acres of land belonged to Maori.

As the demographics of New Zealand changed, so too did its system of government. In 1852, the New Zealand Constitution Act established a General Assembly, followed by responsible government in 1856. The federal Ministry of Native Affairs was created in 1858. With a view to defusing Maori anger over land confiscation and the New Zealand Wars, all Maori men of 21 years of age and older gained the right to vote in 1867. Four Maori seats in Parliament were also created. In 1893, the vote was extended to all women, including Maori. All cabinets had a Maori minister between 1892 and 1934 and a Maori, Sir James Carroll,

---

[55] Frank Glen, 'Australian Involvement in the New Zealand Wars' in *The Oxford Companion to New Zealand Military History*, pp. 384–5.

[56] McIntyre and Gardner, *Speeches and Documents on New Zealand History*, p. 460.

[57] Colonial Office, *The Colonial Office List, 1916* (London: Waterlow & Sons, 1917), pp. 273–7.

was acting prime minister in 1909 and again in 1911.[58] In contrast to Britain and other Dominions, these enfranchisement extensions and government appointments were extremely progressive and had an immeasurable influence on the enhanced Maori management of their own war effort during the First World War.

In addition, Maori-specific education policies were created. In 1867, separate 'native primary schools' were established in an attempt to assimilate young Maori through the teaching of Christian, British ideology. By 1916, government-run native primary schools numbered 118, while 10 denominational boarding schools existed for Maori of secondary school age, with a total enrolment of 5,709 students.[59] By the 1880s these institutions were producing Maori who understood both their traditional and European cultures and laws. In 1894, Apirana Ngata became the first Maori to graduate from university and became the most influential Maori leader of the twentieth century. With the emergence of educated Maori, there were several attempts to form a Maori parliament, including *Te Kauhanganui* of the King Movement. Although never recognized by the New Zealand government, the King Movement unsuccessfully petitioned Parliament and Queen Victoria for an official Maori parliament.

In 1899, New Zealand instituted the Immigration Restriction Act designed to admit only British immigrants. By 1916, the Asian population numbered a mere 2,147. Like Australia, New Zealand was demonstrating its preference for a 'white only' society. As Australian Prime Minister, Edmund Barton, told the New Zealand representative at the Australian federation conference in March 1901: 'I should think that our objections to alien races and New Zealand's objections are practically the same, and that we have the same desire to preserve the "European" and "white" character of the race.'[60]

Unlike New Zealand and the other Dominions, European South Africans never attained demographic superiority, resulting in a relatively anomalous colonial experience. In 1652, Dutchman Jan van Riebeeck founded a station at modern-day Cape Town on behalf of the Dutch East India Company (VOC). Dutch settlers, bolstered by Germans and French Huguenots, gradually moved inland over the next 150 years, seeking large tracts of fertile land for farming and cattle ranching. Away from the domination of the VOC, these isolated *Trekboers* (peripatetic

---

[58] James Belich, *Paradise Reforged: A History of the New Zealanders from the 1800s to the Year 2000* (Auckland: Allen Lane Penguin Press, 2001), p. 191.

[59] Colonial Office, *The Colonial Office List, 1918* (London: Waterlow & Sons, 1919), p. 273.

[60] Smith, *A Concise History of New Zealand*, pp. 114–16.

farmers) began to refer to themselves as Afrikaners and their language as Afrikaans.[61] Conflict between Europeans and the Khoisan peoples of the Cape was instantaneous. The natives were summarily defeated by mounted Dutch farmer commandos between 1659 and 1676. By 1800 the majority of survivors were working as servants and labourers on Dutch farms or mission stations. In addition, between 1652 and 1800, over 60,000 slaves from India, Madagascar and Indonesia were brought to South Africa by the VOC. Sexual relations between these slaves, Khoisan peoples and Europeans spawned what came to be known by the 1830s as Cape Coloureds.[62]

By the late eighteenth century, *Trekboers* encountered the south-westerly expanding, Bantu-speaking Xhosa, whose primary occupation was farming and cattle keeping. Cattle were pivotal in the social order of Bantu peoples and represented a source of itinerant wealth and prestige.[63] The Xhosa were a large group who could mobilize significant numbers of warriors. The resulting competition for resources between the Xhosa and *Trekboers* on the 'Eastern Frontier' led to a series of at least nine wars, between 1779 and 1879, collectively known as the Xhosa (Kaffir) Wars or the Cape Frontier Wars.[64] The Xhosa cattle killings of 1856 and 1857 left the Xhosa in a state of severe famine.[65] This event, and the decline of the Xhosa population through subsequent starvation, effectively ended the protracted Xhosa Wars.

While Britain solidified control of the Cape in 1806, in the northeast Shaka succeeded to the Zulu throne in 1816. He united or incorporated neighbouring tribes through merciless military forays and initiated comprehensive cultural, military and political reforms. By 1825, Shaka had consolidated his empire – roughly the whole of present-day KwaZulu-Natal. The expansion and military might of the Zulu empire generated conflict with Afrikaner *Voortrekkers*, who, during the 1830s and 1840s, migrated into the interior to escape British domination and anti-slavery policies.[66] Conflict between the colonial rivals of South

---

[61] Julie Evans et al. (eds.), *Equal Subjects, Unequal Rights: Indigenous Peoples in British Settler Colonies, 1830–1910* (Manchester University Press, 2003), p. 22.

[62] Ibid, p. 23.

[63] See: James L. Newman, *The Peopling of Africa: A Geographic Interpretation* (New Haven: Yale University Press, 1995).

[64] Vandervort, *Wars of Imperial Conquest in Africa*, pp. 1–4.

[65] Timothy J. Stapleton, '"They No Longer Care for Their Chiefs": Another Look at the Xhosa Cattle-Killing of 1856–1857', *International Journal of African Historical Studies* 24/2 (1991), 383–92.

[66] See: Jonathan Sutherland and Diane Canwell, *Zulu Kings and their Armies* (Barnsley: Pen & Sword Books, 2004).

Africa – the Afrikaners and the British – was not manifest until after the subjugation of the native Africans.

The rise of the Zulu empire, and the consequent scattering of tribes during the *Mfecane* between 1815 and 1835, left portions of traditionally African land vacant for Zulu or Afrikaner settlement, bringing the two peoples into direct conflict. After a series of battles, the Boers declared the fertile Natal a Boer Republic in 1839. The short-lived republic was militarily annexed by the British in 1843 and became the second British colony in South Africa.[67] The results of the British annexation were two-fold: the migration of Natal Boers to the independent Boer Orange Free State and the Transvaal and the geographic expansion of British interests into Zulu territory. The discovery of diamonds near Kimberley on the frontier between the Cape Province and the Orange Free State in 1867, followed by the discovery of gold near Johannesburg in 1886, rejuvenated British–Boer acrimony and led to further violence in the form of two Anglo-Boer Wars.

In 1875, while conflict between the British and the Zulus was still latent, the Governor of Natal, General Wolseley, who had just defeated the Ashanti in Ghana, wrote to the Secretary of State for the Colonies, Lord Carnarvon: '[I do] not believe it possible for the two races to live together on perfect terms; one or the other must be the predominant power in the State; and if the very small minority of white men is to be that power, the great native majority must be taught not only to confide in its justice, but to realize and acknowledge its superiority.'[68] On 11 January 1879, 18,000 British and Natal Native Contingent soldiers, augmented by three hundred Zulu rivals of Cetshwayo, marched on Zululand against the wishes of Whitehall and without its knowledge.[69]

On 23 January 1879, a detachment of 1,700 British and native soldiers was routed by a Zulu force of 22,000 at Isandlwana, while 139 British and 160 African soldiers successfully staved off 4,000 to 5,000 Zulus at legendary Rorke's Drift. The British regrouped and decisively defeated Cetshwayo's armies at the Battle of Ulundi on 4 July. The Zulu empire was portioned among eleven chiefs on Wolseley's recommendation. The 'divide and conquer' tactic instigated a bloody Zulu civil war during the 1880s, destroying what was left of the Zulu kingdom. Thus, the way was paved for the absorption of Zululand (and Tongaland) by British Natal in December 1897.[70]

---

[67] Evans et al., *Equal Subjects, Unequal Rights*, p. 90.
[68] Vandervort, *Wars of Imperial Conquest in Africa*, pp. 103–4.
[69] Ibid, pp. 6, 104–5.
[70] G. A. Chadwick, 'The Anglo-Zulu War of 1879 – Isandlwana and Rorke's Drift', *South African Military History Journal* 4/4 (1978).

Between 1903 and 1905 the South African Native Affairs Commission investigated possible approaches to the 'Black Question'. The Commission's segregationist recommendations were incorporated into policy after the creation of the Union of South Africa on 31 May 1910, based on the 'necessary conclusion that you cannot give the Native his full rights as a citizen of a white State ... for whatever veneer of civilization he may have acquired will rapidly disappear, and unless he is controlled, he will rapidly relapse in barbarism, in which condition he will be a source of endless trouble and difficulty to his white neighbours'.[71] With the creation of the Union, the Ministry of Native Affairs was presided over by the federal government. Magistrates were appointed in the individual provinces. Regional magistrates were charged with liaising with chiefs, controlling native populations and enforcing policy. In 1910, natives outnumbered Europeans by a ratio of 4:1 and regulations matched the threat.[72] Segregation of blacks and protection of white interests were paramount in the formation of Union policies.

In 1911, both the Native Labour Regulation Act and the Mines and Works Act were passed, excluding blacks from skilled jobs, most notably in the mining industries. These Acts also promulgated a specific criminal code and labour offences for blacks, including strikes. The commission had also suggested that it was 'obviously far easier [to keep Africans] under some form of discipline when they lived as a native community'. In 1913 the Natives Land Act was passed, restricting black ownership to a mere 7.3 per cent of the total land mass of the Union. Included in the Act were regulations preventing purchase of land outside these geographic locations or reserves, and introducing anti-squatting and sharecropping measures and restrictions on employment within agriculture and mining (see Map 4).[73]

By 1914, all Dominions had successfully subjugated their indigenous peoples through direct military engagements, treaties and paternalistic policies. While Maori allegedly had equal rights, New Zealand introduced Maori-specific clauses and Acts to control Maori lands and culture. In all Dominions, white control over land, resources and government had been firmly established, with indigenes marginalized

[71] Saul Dubow, *Racial Segregation and the Origins of Apartheid in South Africa, 1919–36* (London: Macmillan, 1989), pp. 24–5.
[72] Colonial Office, *The Colonial Office List, 1916*, pp. 318–53.
[73] National Archives of South Africa (NASA), Cape Town Repository (KAB), Natives Land Act, 1913; Peter Walshe, *The Rise of African Nationalism in South Africa: The African National Congress 1912–1952* (London: C. Hurst & Company, 1970), pp. 44–5; Alon Peled, *A Question of Loyalty: Military Manpower Policy in Multiethnic States* (Ithaca: Cornell University Press, 1998), pp. 27–8.

to allocated parcels of land. Save for the Maori, indigenous peoples were denied civil rights and liberties and existed in varying states of deprivation. Children were forcefully removed to missions and schools to acquire religious and European education. Cultural attributes were outlawed and all aspects of life were controlled by agents, protectors or magistrates.

By 1900, the indigenous populations of Canada, New Zealand, Newfoundland and Australia were at their nadir, having been reduced through warfare, disease and socio-economic hardship. This proved to Dominion governments and populations that their indigenes were doomed to extinction, following the logic of Social Darwinism. Policy and the reserve systems, designed to be temporary, were intended to ease this demise, while providing assimilationist avenues to incorporate the civilized remnants into white society. For South Africa, policy was intended to subjugate and segregate the majority black population, so as to minimize the association of blacks with whites, while safeguarding white interests.

2   Racial constructs and martial theories

The paternalistic policies regulating indigenous peoples were dependent upon contemporary racial and class theories persistent in European dialogue and culture, imported by settler societies:

Colonial settlers, the offspring of European imperialism, refused to integrate with the indigenous population. Moreover, they kept Europe as their myth of origin and as a signifier of superiority even when formal political ties and/or dependency with European colonial powers had been abandoned. This sense of identification with the 'mother country' has not, however, mitigated the unevenness and fragility of settler identities, which were often forged in defence against metropolitan contempt.[1]

In the absence of large noble and gentry populations, the original convict and primarily lower-class British settlers of the 'white Dominions' instinctively filled the vacuum. While the colonies afforded both new opportunities and the ability to transcend the regimented tiers of European society, the hierarchies did not vanish. Settlers found in indigenous peoples, Asian labourers and inferior immigrants alternatives to fill the lower rungs of class and racial hierarchies.

The concept of martial races – the belief that certain identifiable peoples or societies had an innate and exceptional capacity for war – was a construct engineered in India and exported across the British and other European empires. Martial race theories were derived from a pragmatic approach to internal state security, as a consequence of the 1857 Indian Mutiny and the subsequent shifting of *sepoy* ratios in the Indian Army of the British Raj to favour men from the Punjab, Nepal and the Northwest Frontier (Afghanistan).[2]

[1] Daiva K. Stasiulis and Nira Yuval-Davis, *Unsettling Settler Societies: Articulations of Gender, Race, Ethnicity and Class* (London: Sage, 1995), p. 20.
[2] David Omissi, *The Sepoy and the Raj: The Indian Army, 1860–1940* (London: Macmillan, 1994), pp. 10–25; David Killingray and David Omissi (eds.), *Guardians of Empire: The Armed Forces of the Colonial Powers c. 1700–1964* (Manchester University Press, 1999), pp. 14–15.

34

Cynthia Enloe argues in *Ethnic Soldiers: State Security in Divided Societies* (1980) that the martial proclivities of minorities were judged by their 'political reliability', which included population ratios and proof of allegiance during colonial warfare. After a weighted assessment by governmental and military authorities, specific groups were assigned military occupations, or formed into minority units, consistent with maintaining state security. American Indian historian, Tom Holm, argues through a paradigm he labels the 'Gurkha Model' that, 'It was only after Indian assimilation policies had been put in place, the Native population had dwindled to less than one percent of that of the United States as a whole, and Natives soldiers and Marines had proven themselves in combat in World War I, that Indians were judged a politically "safe" minority group.'[3]

The categorization of indigenous peoples in the British empire was generated by an Anglo-Saxon assumption of superiority in the spreading of civilization, and of its religious and governmental appendages, to the vast expanses of the globe. Frontier warfare, and the increasingly vitriolic relationship between indigenes and colonials, magnified European and settler beliefs that the indigene was void of any appreciation of the benefits of European civilization. Mutual suspicion and profiling of the 'other' were the inevitable consequences of contact between incompatible cultures. These observations are corroborated by the reports and diaries of early explorers and settlers and through oral and historical remembrances of indigenous peoples.

Indigenous practices such as polygamy, human sacrifice, shamanism, communal land and a lack of any perceived political structures, misunderstood by Europeans, made the idea of the 'uncivilized heathen' credible. The more violent and cannibalistic rituals were perceived as intrinsic blood-lust. C. J. Jaenen comments that this was obtuse of Europeans, 'who believed in transubstantiation and literally eating their Lord in their communion service'. J. R. Miller elaborates that, 'Surely people of countries who guillotined, hanged, drew, and quartered those guilty of hundreds of offences, and who put heads on pikes as a warning to others, should have been able to understand the symbolic, cheerleading, and deterrent purposes of such native ... practices.'[4]

---

[3] Cynthia H. Enloe, *Ethnic Soldiers: State Security in Divided Societies* (Markham: Penguin Books, 1980); Tom Holm, 'Strong Hearts: Native Service in the US Armed Forces' in P. Whitney Lackenbauer et al. (eds.), *Aboriginal Peoples and Military Participation: Canadian and International Perspectives* (Kingston: Canadian Defence Academy Press, 2007), pp. 129–32.

[4] Miller, *Skyscrapers Hide the Heavens*, p. 75.

By the time Darwin published his *On the Origin of Species* in 1859, patriarchal administration and custodial practices regarding indigenes permeated Dominion policies and the concept of 'the savage' was engrained in settler perceptions. Social Darwinism and racial theories simply buttressed previously held beliefs and gave them a spacious framework in which to be modernized, employed and justified. Indigenes were, in a widely accepted belief, destined to extinction in their inevitable natural struggle against modernity and more advanced races. The residual populations would be assimilated, used as labour or absorbed through miscegenation (a term coined in England in 1863).[5] In 1910, Canadian journalist and poet, Ernest McGaffey, referred to the 'doomed races' of the empire: 'For it is so that the wilderness falls before the axe, that the old order passes as the new regime comes in; that you cannot stay the current development by a dogged refusal to go with the tide; and that the iron pen of history has written time and time again, the survival of the fittest is the law of nations.'[6]

Academic discourse during the nineteenth century created a relatively accepted belief that races varied in potential and in the progression of evolution. Darwin believed that civilized races had attained heights of progress through natural selection and racial struggle: 'Looking to the world at no very distant date, what an endless number of the lower races will have been eliminated by the higher civilized races throughout the world.'[7] Theorists generally agreed that the process of 'animality [sic] through savagery and barbarism to civilization was an uneven one, with many races confined to the earlier phases of evolution'.[8] This stagnation was viewed to be the condition of Dominion indigenes and manifested itself in the characteristics of lower intellect, an imitative childlike demeanour and a penchant for violent and erratic outbursts.

However, in a glaring contradiction of colonialism, indigenous women were the object of sexual attention. Kay Schaffer explains that the 'sexual exploitation of [indigenous] women was endemic to British imperialism – the romance between dusky, dark-haired maidens and pioneering heroes was at the core of the colonial adventure tale … so

[5] Victoria Freeman, 'Attitudes Toward "Miscegenation" in Canada, the United States, New Zealand, and Australia, 1860–1914', *Native Studies Review* 16/1 (2005), 42.

[6] Haycock, *The Image of the Indian*, p. 21.

[7] Paul Crook, *Darwinism, War and History: The Debate over the Biology of War from the 'Origin of Species' to the First World War* (Cambridge University Press, 1994), p. 25.

[8] Mike Hawkins, *Social Darwinism in European and American Thought, 1860–1945: Nature as Model and Nature as Threat* (Cambridge University Press, 1997), p. 244.

long as European women were absent, indigenous women could be used to satisfy what were perceived to be natural needs'. The chronicle of the Powhatan Indian, Pocahontas, who became a celebrity in London before her death in 1617, is illustrative of this observation. Conversely, the widespread conviction that Aboriginal and African men had an uncontrollable, sadistic sexual appetite for European women created the myth of the 'Black Peril' or 'Black Rapist' in both Australia and South Africa.[9]

Racial discourse existed within a pan-European deliberation about the differences of human populations and nations, allied to the extension of European empires. The word 'race' was used to describe variations of biology, nations and cultures. Most theories promoted the concept of an evolutionary stratum of racial tiers. The bottom was occupied by Aboriginal Australians, followed closely by Africans – the 'missing link between humans and apes'. North American Indians occupied the next tier, then Asians and Middle Eastern peoples, followed by Polynesians, including Maori. Eastern Europeans came next, followed by Mediterranean peoples. Western Europeans, who had formulated most theories, were the obvious apex of evolution, with Anglo-Saxons as the very summit in British opinion. This was the established categorization in the societies of most imperial European nations and of the Dominions.[10]

By 1860, the indigenous populations of Australia, New Zealand, Newfoundland and Canada, devastated by war and disease, were moribund (see Table 2.1). To the resident European populations, this was proof of Herbert Spencer's notion of 'survival of the fittest'.[11]

The elevated Maori position was the result of a blending of factors. Originally, it was believed that Maori 'will pass away and never be seen again'.[12] The declining Maori population, from contact through to 1900, supported this expectation of fatal impact; however, the relatively higher Maori resistance to European diseases, compared with other indigenes, slowed Maori population decline and they remained a sizeable percentage of the New Zealand population. This was evidence to *Pakeha* that Maori were a better breed of indigene. In addition, with a dearth of European women during the early decades of colonization, intermarriage was common and generally accepted in New Zealand. According to Belich, this was a deliberate Maori strategy to maintain

---

[9] Freeman, 'Attitudes Toward "Miscegenation"', 47, 52, 55.

[10] Hawkins, *Social Darwinism in European and American Thought*, pp. 191–240.

[11] Darwin did not use the term, borrowed from Spencer's 1864 *Principles of Biology*, until his fifth edition of *Origins* in 1869.

[12] Hill, *State Authority, Indigenous Autonomy*, p. 19.

Table 2.1: *Dominion non-indigenous and indigenous populations*[1]

Date	Canada	Australia	New Zealand	South Africa	Newfoundland & Labrador
Contact	*300,000–350,000*	*300,000–350,000*	*90,000–110,000*		*3,000*
1841	1,540,109	220,968	2,500		96,295
			65,000 (est.)		
1851	2,436,297	437,665	26,707		101,600
	158,960		*60,000 (est.)*		
1861	3,229,633	1,168,149	97,904		124,188
	115,000	*180,402*	*55,336*		
1871	3,689,257	1,700,888	254,928	1,084,200	152,517
	102,358	*155,285*	*47,330*	(total)	
1881	4,324,810	2,306,736	489,933	2,053,500	197,335 (1884)
	108,547	*131,666*	*46,141*	(total)	
1891	4,833,239	3,240,985	626,658	2,957,800	202,040
	107,638	*110,919*	*44,177*	(total)	
1901	5,371,315	3,824,913	772,719	1,116,806	220,984
	109,698	*94,564*	*45,330*	*4,059,018*	
1911	7,206,643	4,573,786	1,008,468	1,276,242	242,619
	103,661	*83,588*	*52,723*	*4,697,152*	
1914	7,879,000	4,917,949	1,099,449	1,383,510	251,726
	103,774	*80,000 (est.)*	*52,997*	*5,081,490*	*1,700 (est.)*
1921	8,787,949	5,510,944	1,214,677	1,482,464	263,033
	105,333	*75,604*	*56,987*	*5,444,936*	*1,200 (est.)*

[1] Indigenous populations are represented by the *italicized* bottom number. Numbers not italicized represent non-indigenous populations. The majority of statistics are taken from censuses conducted in the Dominions, with select early estimates taken from the most appropriate scholarly investigations and governmental demographic calculations. Those of Australia and New Zealand include both full and half-caste indigenes; South African statistics include both black and coloured; Canadian exclude Inuit (Eskimos). Estimates are based on the most reliable scholarly and governmental figures.

control of 'Our Pakeha'. One British settler surmised that, 'it is not safe to live in the country without a chief's daughter as protection'.[13]

Ernst Dieffenbach, a mid-nineteenth century New Zealand naturalist, described the Maori as 'people decidedly in a nearer relation to us, than any other; they are endowed with uncommonly good intellectual faculties; they are an agriculturalist nation, with fixed domicile, and have reached the farthest point of civilization which they possibly could, without the aid of other nations, and without the example of history'.[14] Maori cultural symbols, and the relative coexistence after the New Zealand Wars, thus became important elements of national identity. On a visit to New Zealand in 1909, Colonial Office representative,

[13] Belich, *Making Peoples*, p. 172.
[14] Evans et al., *Equal Subjects, Unequal Rights*, p. 72.

Sir Charles Lucas, reported that, 'most friendly relations seemed to exist between Maoris and whites'.[15]

During the late nineteenth and early twentieth centuries, models of an 'Aryan Maori' gained widespread acceptance. Initially, Maori were promoted as a 'lost tribe of Israel'. With the advent of Social Darwinism, the 'Semitic Maori' gave way to the 'Caucasian Maori'. Edward Treager's *The Aryan Maori* (1885) proposed that Europeans and Maori shared an Aryan origin. In *Hawaiki, the Original Home of the Maori* (1899), S. Percy Smith surmised that Maori descended from peoples of northern India or the Caucasus and placed Maori in the 'Caucasian family of the human race'. These ideas were promulgated in New Zealand well into the twentieth century.[16] In the words of William Herries, Minister of Native Affairs from 1912 to 1921: 'I look forward for the next hundred years or so, to a time when we shall have no Maoris at all, but a white race with a slight dash of the finest coloured race in the world.'[17] 'White Maori' gave *mana* to both Maori and *Pakeha*. While Australians shared geography with the lowest indigene, New Zealanders possessed the dignified Maori. During a visit to NSW in 1805, Maori Chief, Te Pahi, expressed a negative opinion of Aborigines and derided their lack of ingenuity in procuring food, their nakedness and their unmanly warfare.[18] According to Australian Chief Justice George Higinbotham, Maori were 'the noblest race of uncivilized men known in the world'.[19]

Belich argues that another motive for raising Maori onto a Caucasian platform was to alleviate anxiety over the poor performance of British and colonial forces during the New Zealand Wars; the British had fought a noble adversary of European descent, not a savage race of inferior warriors.[20] Sir John W. Fortescue, the historian of the British Army, recorded that British soldiers deemed Maori, 'on the whole, the grandest native enemy that [they] had ever encountered'.[21] Maori military

---

[15] Harcourt Papers, 468. Notes on a Visit to Australia, New Zealand and Fiji by Sir Charles Lucas, October 1909.

[16] Edward Treager, *The Aryan Maori* (Wellington: G. Didsbury Government Printer, 1885); S. Percy Smith, *Hawaiki, the Original Home of the Maori* (Auckland: Whitcombe & Tombs, 1921); Smith, *A Concise History of New Zealand*, pp. 12–13.

[17] Belich, *Paradise Reforged*, p. 190.

[18] Anne Salmond, *Between Worlds: Early Exchanges between Maori and Europeans 1773–1815* (Auckland: Penguin Books, 1997), pp. 350–4.

[19] K. S. Inglis, *Sacred Places: War Memorials in the Australian Landscape* (Melbourne: Miegunyah Press, 1998), p. 23.

[20] Belich, *The Victorian Interpretation of Racial Conflict*, p. 300.

[21] Robert A. Huttenback, *Racism and Empire: White Settlers and Colored Immigrants in the British Self-Governing Colonies, 1830–1910* (Ithaca: Cornell University Press, 1976), p. 19.

capabilities were thus recognized, and they were given a higher position on both the stratum of racial hierarchy and within the classification of martial races.

Although Maori as a collective were thought to possess a talent for, and love of, war, tribes from the north island, specifically those of King Country and the Bay of Islands, were thought to have greater martial capacities than those of the south island, who were perceived to be more 'Europeanized'. This was a reflection of both the dominance of the northern tribes during the Musket Wars and the sustained defence maintained by Kingite tribes during the New Zealand Wars. New Zealand Minister of Defence, James Allen, proudly declared in 1914 that Maori were, 'the chief of the dark races'.[22]

This belief, however, did not place Maori on equal footing with *Pakeha*. Maori were denied health care and the majority still lived in unsanitary camps or isolated communities. In 1900, infant mortality was three times higher in the Maori population compared with the remainder of New Zealand.[23] Nevertheless, Maori were, in principle, afforded legal equality within the Constitution and were eager to share in the responsibilities of citizenship and society, including politics and soldiering. The lofty status Maori were given in the hierarchy of races, and their pinnacle position among Dominion indigenes, significantly influenced their contributions and role as soldiers, and the administration of their own endeavours, during the First World War.

Canadian Indians did not share the same legal parity with Maori. They were not enfranchised until 1960 and the reserves and their inhabitants still remain wards of the Crown. Susceptibility to disease and alcohol, direct or circuitous involvement in colonial wars and socio-economic disparity drastically reduced Indian populations. To Canadians and Newfoundlanders, this was evidence for the fatal impact theory. Canada had instituted paternalistic policies controlling most aspects of Indian life with the aim of assimilating the surviving Indian population. In 1920, Duncan Campbell Scott wrote that: 'I want to get rid of the Indian problem ... Our objective is to continue until there is not a single Indian in Canada that has not been absorbed into the body politic and there is no Indian question, and no Indian Department.'[24] Miscegenation in Canada was not as widely accepted as in New Zealand; however, the Métis were evidence of its practice.

[22] Hill, *State Authority, Indigenous Autonomy*, p. 20.
[23] W. B. Sutch, *The Maori Contribution: Yesterday, Today and Tomorrow* (Wellington: Department of Industries and Commerce, 1964), table V.
[24] Library and Archives Canada (LAC), RG10, vol. 6810, file 470-2-3. Memorandum: Duncan Campbell Scott, Residential Schools and the Indian Question, 1920.

While inter-racial relationships were frowned upon in certain social circles, the Canadian government incorporated the frequent marriage of white men to Indian women into its assimilationist construct. The 1869 Indian Act removed 'status' from any Indian woman who married a non-Indian. This law also affected the woman's children and was not rescinded until 1985.[25]

According to Ronald Haycock, in his study of the perception and popular media coverage of Indians at the dawn of the twentieth century, there were three basic conceptions, singularly or in combination, about Indians. The first was that the Indian was doomed to extinction, like the Beothuk of Newfoundland, unable to survive the competitive evolutionary struggle. The responsibility of the white population and the government was to 'make the death struggle of the primitive as soft as possible'. The second analysis was that of the 'noble savage'. Indians had distinguished records of military allegiance to the British, which influenced their corresponding duality as both the noble and the savage. Canadians and Britons could not ignore the historical benefits of this alliance or the exemplary examples of Hendrick, Tecumseh, Crowfoot, John Deserontyon, John Norton and Joseph Brant, to name but a few.

The dichotomy of the Indian as a savage brute or as a noble warrior provided an exploitable and convenient framework whereby the Canadian population and government could justify the inconsistency of military and indigenous policies while maintaining a phlegmatic posture. The 'noble' Indian was extolled by government officials and citizens alike, but only when it suited their interests. The concept of this duality was also reinforced by common media, literature, such as J. M. Barrie's *Peter Pan* (1904), and 'Wild West Shows'. The Indian was either depicted as a treacherous, blood-lusting savage or as a righteous, astute warrior. James Fenimore Cooper's characters in *The Last of the Mohicans* (1826) illustrate this ubiquitous dichotomy; Chingachgook, the Mohican, represents the noble, while Magua, a Huron adopted by the Mohawk, represents the savage.[26]

The third conception was that the Indian had been unwillingly, or unknowingly, corrupted by the degenerate portion of the white population and that the honourable white segment was obligated by virtue to assimilate the Indian 'to hitherto unprecedented levels of civilization and salvation, fashioned on the white model'.[27] In 1910,

---

[25] Miller, *Skyscrapers Hide the Heavens*, pp. 145–6.

[26] James Fenimore Cooper, *The Last of the Mohicans* (New York: H. C. Carey & I. Lea, 1826).

[27] Haycock, *The Image of the Indian*, pp. 1–2.

journalist Elizabeth Walmsley summarized the position of the Indian in Canada:

The 'brave' no longer lives in a wigwam or 'tepee' as his forefathers did, more or less exposed to the inclemencies [sic] of all weather and consequently hardened to them, but in a 'shack' much like an immigrant settler's. But he cannot accustom himself to the white man's mode of life ... For the nature of the Indian is still Indian, and until he can be taught how to adapt himself to the higher standards of comfort which contact with civilization has brought him, the result must inevitably be extinction.[28]

In Canada, the Iroquois Confederacy, specifically the Mohawk, represented the pinnacle of martial attributes among Indians. The Iroquois had been the dominant military coalition in northeastern North America prior to contact, a position they maintained until the close of the War of 1812. The confederacy also established a long-standing alliance with the British Crown and rendered invaluable service during the colonial wars in North America. In western Canada, the Blackfoot Confederacy (Blackfoot, Blood, Piegan, and later the Sarcee) was also recognized for its military prowess, based on its long-standing animosities with the Crow, Sioux and Cree, and its penchant for attacking white settlers. At the outbreak of the First World War, the legal and social position of the Canadian Indian did not render him a suitable candidate to defend the empire, despite past allegiance to the British Crown.

Unlike Maori and Indians, Aboriginal Australians were thought to possess no redeeming qualities. In 1688, William Dampier, the first Englishman to visit Australia, described Aborigines as, 'the miserablest [sic] People in the world [who] differ but little from Brutes'.[29] The Reverend W. Yale reported to the British Parliament in 1835 that, 'I have heard again and again people say that they [Aborigines] were nothing better than dogs, and that it was no more harm to shoot them than it would be to shoot a dog.'[30] These attitudes had not been replaced by the First World War. Given that Aboriginal populations were in drastic decline, Social Darwinism confirmed for Australians and politicians the impossibility of Aborigines advancing through the evolutionary stages to civilization: 'The Australians [Aborigines] surely demonstrate, by their evident doom, that races below the level where self-prompted progress exists are unable to adapt themselves to the conditions forced upon them by civilization, and that, therefore, they must

---

[28] Dempsey, *Warriors of the King*, pp. 17–18.
[29] Broome, *Aboriginal Australians*, p. 29.
[30] Ibid, p. 34.

perish when brought into contact with it ... in fact, they represent the childhood of humanity itself.'[31]

Miscegenation was strictly controlled and permission from the Chief Protector of Aborigines was required for a white to marry an Aborigine. Furthermore, great emphasis was placed on the removal of half-caste children from Aboriginal communities to prevent further miscegenation. These children were offered redemption from Aboriginal licentiousness through education. According to John William Bleakley, Chief Protector of Aborigines for Queensland from 1914 to 1942:

> [T]he mating of an Aboriginal with any person other than an Aboriginal is prohibited. Every effort is being made to breed out the colour by elevating female half-castes to the white standard with a view to their absorption by mating into the white population ... The destiny of the native with Aboriginal origin, but not of full-bloods, lies in their ultimate absorption by the people of the Commonwealth, and it [Government of Queensland] therefore recommends that all efforts shall be directed to this end.[32]

Given their registered position as 'flora and fauna' until 1967 within the Constitution of Australia, Aborigines were denied inclusion into all elements of Australian society. No Aboriginal Australian nation was given preferential status. Aborigines were collectively viewed to be deficient of martial characteristics. The Colonial Secretary Andrew Bonar Law summarized this perception in a memorandum in December 1915: 'The Red Indian of Canada was more romantic and picaresque than the Australian Blackfellow.'[33]

South Africa represents a departure from the doomed race theory. The ratio of native to European was 4:1 at the creation of the Union. While war and starvation impacted upon native populations, they were not in decline like the indigenes of the other Dominions. Therefore, the ruling white populations adopted different perceptions and policies towards their indigenous wards, who were generally considered 'just like children ... intelligence of an average negro is about equal to that of a European child of ten years old ... Living among white men their imitative faculties enable them to attain a considerable amount of civilization. Left alone to their own devices they retrograde into a state little above their native savagery.'[34]

---

[31] Howe, *Race Relations, Australia and New Zealand*, p. 43.
[32] Colin Tatz, 'Confronting Genocide' in *The Indigenous Experience: Global Perspectives*, p. 127.
[33] House of Lords Records Office (HLRO), Andrew Bonar Law Papers, BL52/1. Memorandum on Canada and Australia Settler and Administrative Differences.
[34] Huttenback, *Racism and Empire*, p. 19.

Endowing blacks with a form of inferior intelligence justified exclusionist policies. It was widely held that the natural position of blacks, although prone to laziness, was one of labour, similar to that of American negroes. American racial theorist, Joseph Le Conte, argued in 1892 that: 'If, like the negro, the race was at an early stage of evolution and hence plastic, docile and imitative, then slavery was appropriate; if, like the redskin, the race had become more specialised and so more rigid, then extermination is unavoidable.'[35]

This perception suited the needs of the European population of South Africa. It rationally maintained their racial superiority, while fuelling the manpower requirements for agricultural and mining pursuits and, when required, labour in times of war.[36] There were, however, certain exceptions. Those nations that had engaged the British (and Boers) in hostilities were seen as having heightened martial abilities, specifically the Zulus, Xhosa, Matabele and Basutos, with the Zulu occupying the pinnacle position. According to a June 1914 Colonial Office Report on Zululand: 'In the case of the Zulus, civilization has one of its greatest opportunities, for certainly in them there is a spirit which can be led on to higher things.'[37]

---

[35] Hawkins, *Social Darwinism in European and American Thought*, p. 201.
[36] A. Adu Boahen, *African Perspectives on Colonialism* (Baltimore: The Johns Hopkins University Press, 1987), pp. 25–31.
[37] Andrew Bonar Law Papers, BL55/3. Colonial Office Report on Rhodesia and Zululand, 1 June 1914.

3   Precedents of military pragmatism

The inclusion of indigenous men in colonial and Dominion military structures varied and was conditional upon direct needs, managed at the discretion of imperial and Dominion administrations. In all Dominion experiences, indigenous peoples were utilized as scouts to fulfil British and colonial desiderata. The indigenous motivation for most participation was revenge on traditional enemies and to secure European favour to promote self-interest. In South Africa, where the native population greatly outnumbered that of Europeans, blacks were primarily 'recruited' by European powers as unarmed labourers during times of war. In addition, indigenous inclusion in Dominion expeditionary forces prior to the First World War was contemplated by all nations, but actual employment was dependent upon the assessment of needs. The official policy of indigenous exclusion, promulgated conjointly by the imperial and Dominion governments during the Second Anglo-Boer War, remained the precedent at the outbreak of the First World War.

The indigenous inhabitants of Newfoundland-Labrador did not participate in military campaigns during North American colonial wars because there were very few indigenous peoples left on the island and those present in Labrador were remote and reclusive. The Beothuk became extinct in 1829 and, although Mi'kmaq had settled on the southwest coast in 1720, they numbered no more than 175 by the end of the Seven Years' War. These Mi'kmaq did not militarily support their traditional French ally; rather, they were concerned with fishing and hunting to support the lucrative trade in furs.

Following the Seven Years' War, spending on British military garrisons in Newfoundland stimulated growth throughout the nineteenth century, with the population reaching 220,000 by 1900. The British garrison vacated Newfoundland in 1870 and the responsibility for defence passed to the government of Newfoundland. However, between 1870 and the outbreak of the First World War, no military organizations whatsoever were created.[1] During the 1880s, the Colonial Defence Committee in London repeatedly proposed the creation of small units of militia infantry and artillery and offered to cover all expenditures. The government of Newfoundland refused, believing that it would eventually be forced to financially contribute, and was not prepared to do so given the struggling economy of the colony within a global recession.[2] At the outbreak of war in 1914, Newfoundland was the least prepared of all five British Dominions to participate in a European war. Correspondingly, the remote and small Eskimo and Indian populations of Newfoundland-Labrador were accorded no attention as a source of military manpower, unlike those of neighbouring Canada.

Canada had a long history of British–Indian alliance throughout colonization. Indian nations, most conspicuously the Iroquois Confederacy, had been worthy British allies. Indians were given honorary British ranks, exemplified by a Mohawk, Captain Joseph Brant, and awarded British citations and medals.[3] Following the 1817 Rush–Bagot Treaty and the American Monroe Doctrine of 1823, which nullified future American and external European threats, Indians lost their importance as military allies. However, while Indians lost their military importance as a collective, individual Indians continued to support British military campaigns after the War of 1812, when mustered by Canadian authorities. Mohawks from the Six Nations Reserve accompanied Canadian militia units in defeating the Fenian Raids of the 1860s. Eighty-six Indians, predominantly Mohawk, were recruited as *Voyageurs* and paddled General Lord Wolseley's 1884–5 relief force up the Nile to the besieged city of Khartoum.[4] Wolseley had previously employed 140 Indian scouts on his expedition to restore order during the 1870 Red River Rebellion. Wolseley identified the need for Indian-specific skills during both operations and recruited accordingly.[5] Furthermore, Indian faithfulness to the British Crown was exemplified by the refusal of many Indian nations, including the powerful Blackfoot Confederacy, to join Métis-Cree forces during

[1] PANL, MG148, Catholic Cadet Corps (St John's) Fonds, 1905–20.
[2] Mike O'Brien, 'Out of a Clear Sky: The Mobilization of the Newfoundland Regiment, 1914–1915', *Newfoundland and Labrador Studies* 22/2 (2007), 402–4.
[3] Robert W. McLachlan, *Medals Awarded to Canadian Indians* (Montreal: Reprinted from *The Gazette* (1886), 1899); Melvill Allan Jamieson, *Medals Awarded to North American Indian Chiefs, 1714–1922 and to Loyal African and Other Chiefs in Various Territories within the British Empire* (London: Spink, 1936).
[4] Carl Benn, *Mohawks on the Nile: Natives Among the Canadian Voyageurs in Egypt 1884–1885* (Toronto: Dundurn Group, 2008). Also see: Carl Benn, *The Iroquois in the War of 1812* (University of Toronto Press, 1999).
[5] John Moses, *A Sketch Account of Aboriginal Peoples in the Canadian Military* (Ottawa: National Defence, 2004), pp. 48–54.

the North-West Rebellion and small numbers of Cree, Blackfoot and Ojibwa scouts were utilized by Middleton's forces. The long-standing military alliance between the Crown and Indians, although diminished, was not extinct by 1914. Given this pattern of allegiance to the British Crown, Indian enthusiasm towards the First World War was not historically unfounded.

Maori martial capacities had been known to the outside world since the arrival of European explorers and whalers. As early as 1817, Maori had been hired by traders as 'private police forces' to guard stations and stores. In 1845, the Governor of New Zealand, Sir George Grey, proposed to emulate the Native Police Corps of the Australian Colonies by raising a sixty-man all-Maori unit, officered by *Pakeha*, and structured similarly to the 'Cape and Ceylon Rifle Corps'. He believed this force could provide a cheap means of obtaining local military expertise. This force never materialized, due to *Pakeha* wariness about arming, and fighting alongside, Maori warriors. However, following Grey's suggestion, individual Maori were admitted as constables in police forces as early as 1846.[6]

The Musket and New Zealand Wars, during which *kupapa* Maori served with British forces, only reaffirmed the Maori warrior ethos in the minds of *Pakeha*. The first interest in harnessing Maori warriors for external service occurred in 1829, when it was unofficially suggested that Maori be used to track Aborigines in Tasmania shortly before the Black Line incident. In 1852, Grey suggested to the imperial authorities that, in the event of war with France, a force of four thousand Maori, officered by Europeans, be dispatched to seize Tahiti (a French protectorate since 1842). Five years later, during the Indian Mutiny, a similar suggestion was made by Colonel Robert H. Wynyard, commander of imperial forces in New Zealand. Neither offer was given consideration by the administrators of the Colonial and War Offices as they believed Maori to be 'changeable, capricious, and torn by tribal animosities'.[7]

After the New Zealand Wars, Maori corps were formed in the Volunteer Force as a result of the perceived 1878 and 1885 Russian threats to British interests in Afghanistan and India. Although most were quickly disbanded, the Wairarapa Mounted Rifles was praised and continued until 1907. Offers of warriors to aid Britain were also made by Maori themselves. During the 1884–5 Mahdi uprising in the Sudan, Ngati Haua Chief, Hote Tamehana, a British foe during the

[6] Hill, *The Story of Policing in New Zealand*, vol. I, pp. 53, 239–42.
[7] Cowan, *The Maoris in the Great War*, p. 5; Ian McGibbon, *The Path to Gallipoli: Defending New Zealand 1840–1915* (Wellington: GP Books, 1991), p. 4.

New Zealand Wars, offered two hundred of his warriors to the imperial government. Shortly thereafter, New Zealand contemplated sending a force of a thousand, including 250 Maori, to aid Britain in Afghanistan after Russian actions during the Pendjeh Crisis of March 1885, 'or any other part of the globe where Her Majesty's Government might require them'. Both offers were refused, as the War Office concluded that no New Zealand forces were required.[8]

As was customary during British colonial experiences, indigenous peoples were often contracted to scout and partake in expeditions against fellow indigenes, in aid of British units, colonial militia or police forces. In Australia, the use of police forces, which included Aborigines, rather than the British military, appears to have been a calculated policy of the British government after 1825. The 'Native Police Forces' of Australia, which helped end Aboriginal resistance, were established in Port Phillip in 1842, in NSW in 1848 and in Queensland in 1859. In certain instances, such as Moreton Bay, NSW, Aboriginal forces were raised by local farmers to protect their capital from raids. With the promise of uniforms, wages, horses, guns and the possibility of gaining women through their status as 'warriors' (a role traditionally monopolized by older men), young Aboriginal males joined these forces. The most important contribution of 'Native Police Forces' was that, unlike most British soldiers, they were able to track and pursue Aborigines into the bush. Although many killed fellow Aborigines, many others deserted, switched loyalties during raids, or killed their British superiors. However, Aborigines were never admitted into Australian military forces and were used predominantly for scouting when required by police forces, most notably in Queensland.[9] Following the relatively complete subjugation of Aborigines by 1890, 'Native Police Forces' were no longer of value and were disbanded throughout the 1890s. However, individual Aboriginal trackers remained a feature of local police forces until 1973.[10]

Like Canada, South Africa witnessed colonial warfare between European rivals. As early as the 1670s, Boer commandos were accompanied by 'Basters and Khoikhoi' on expeditions against the Xhosa and San. After 1774 a 'General Commando' was established in the Cape consisting of 150 coloureds and 100 whites.[11] The intermittent conflict

[8] Bradford Haami, 'Maori in the Armed Forces', in Ian McGibbon (ed.), *The Oxford Companion to New Zealand Military History* (Oxford University Press, 2000), pp. 301–3.
[9] Grey, *A Military History of Australia*, pp. 35–6.
[10] Huggonson, 'Aboriginal Trackers and the Boer War', 20.
[11] Kenneth W. Grundy, *Soldiers Without Politics: Blacks in the South African Armed Forces* (Berkeley: University of California Press, 1983), pp. 3, 34.

between Boer and Briton, beginning in 1795, provided an opportunity for African tribes to ally with, or be recruited by, a European power. The first instance of the organization of native soldiers in a distinct unit was the Afrikaner creation of the 'Corps Bastaard Hottentotten' or 'Corps Pandours' in 1781. The Cape Afrikaner administration deployed these coloured units against the British in 1795 and again in 1806.[12] Under British management, between 1817 and 1854, this unit became known as the Cape Corps or Cape Mounted Rifles (CMR). Although initially composed of coloured men officered by Europeans, the main body slowly enlisted Europeans. Nevertheless, this unit was active during the 4th to 7th Xhosa Wars and during the British occupation of Natal in 1842. From 1854 onward, with relative peace in the Cape Colony, recruitment of coloureds was discontinued and no coloured unit existed, although unaffiliated coloured men were frequently used in both combat and non-combat functions during frontier warfare, including the First Anglo-Boer War. Significant numbers of Swazi were mobilized by the Boers in their protracted struggles with the Pedi. Correspondingly, the British utilized over six thousand Swazi warriors during Wolseley's expedition against Pedi Chief Sekhukhune in 1879. The CMR was revived, and again recruited coloureds, in 1894 and was active during the Matabele campaign of 1896.[13]

However, no black units were officially authorized by either the Boers or the British during the period of colonial warfare in South Africa prior to the Second Anglo-Boer War. Nevertheless, many native tribes and warriors chose to fight alongside both European powers of their own accord. Blacks fought alongside European forces against traditional enemies or rival clans, as shown by British-allied Swazi and Zulu during the Anglo-Zulu War. Given the demographics of South Africa and the fear of black insurrection, the prevailing practice among the British and the Boers was to utilize blacks as wartime labour.[14] The reluctance to arm natives in South Africa represented a departure from the norm. David Killingray's assertion holds true for the remainder of Africa, and for the British in tropical Africa: 'European empires in Africa were gained principally by African mercenary armies, occasionally supported by white or other colonial troops. In what Rudyard Kipling described as "the savage wars of peace" the bulk of the fighting was done by black

[12] Ivor D. Difford, *The Story of the 1st Battalion Cape Corps* (Cape Town: Hortors, 1920), p. 2.
[13] Peter Warwick, *Black People and the South African War 1899–1902* (Cambridge University Press, 1983), pp. 11–13.
[14] Grundy, *Soldiers Without Politics*, pp. 35–8.

soldiers.'[15] However, blacks were recruited in large numbers by both Boer and British forces during the Second Anglo-Boer War.

The Second Anglo-Boer War serves as the most poignant example of indigenous military policy in the contemporary or future Dominions, including South Africa, prior to the First World War. The war initially met with varied responses from the governments of Canada, New Zealand and Australia. French-Canadian Prime Minister, Sir Wilfrid Laurier, hesitated to send forces to aid a British imperial campaign, as did the Australian colonies. New Zealand offered an expeditionary force shortly before the actual outbreak of war. All nations eventually committed considerable expeditionary forces to South Africa. The Governor of Newfoundland, Sir Henry McCallum, expressed his regret to the Colonial Office, simply stating that Newfoundland could not contribute men as the colony had no trained soldiers readily available. A small number of Newfoundlanders enlisted and served in Canadian contingents.[16] In Canada, New Zealand, Australia and within South Africa itself, the issue of including indigenous peoples in national forces penetrated governmental discourse and policy. The national precedents set during the Boer War ultimately survived as Dominion protocol for indigenous involvement at the outbreak of the First World War.

In Canada, Indians had been present in Non-Permanent Active Militia units (reserve units – the Permanent Active Militia represented Canada's small regular force) since the militia's official creation in 1868. The Militia Act did not bar them from service, and enlistment remained at the discretion of the commanding officer. Indian boys also received rudimentary military training through the residential school system, although this practice was by no means uniform throughout Canada. As early as 1896, William Hamilton Merritt, an honorary chief of the Six Nations Reserve, requested the formation of a regular unit composed of, and reinforced by, Indian boys from Canada's residential schools in

the form of a permanent Imperial Corps recruited from our Indians ... I would consider it very kind if you could ascertain from the Principals of the Industrial Schools how they would view the project of a certain picked proportion of their boys being drafted into a regiment on completing their education at the school, and how many it is likely could be supplied each year to recruit such a regiment if established. It has been held that the natural inborn instincts of the Indian lad suits him admirably for the profession of soldiering ... I suppose you would consider that there would be no difficulty in recruiting a regiment

[15] Vandervort, *Wars of Imperial Conquest in Africa*, p. 42.
[16] A. J. Stacey and Jean Edwards Stacey, *Memoirs of a Blue Puttee: The Newfoundland Regiment in World War One* (St John's: DRC Publishers, 2002), p. 15.

from the Indians of Canada who could speak English, and who are qualified to make excellent soldiers, and who have proved themselves to be true and Loyal Subjects of the British Crown.

Although Merritt even lobbied the War Office, the proposal was dismissed for two reasons. The first argument was the financial expenditure to educate the boys, only to deploy them on operations. Exporting educated, assimilated and 'worthwhile young Indians' would inherently deplete that same caste within Canada, diminishing the impact they could have on their communities. Secondly, it was deduced that the scheme would appear as a draft, without Indian approval, and could violate treaty agreements.[17] Nevertheless, certain residential schools did institute cadet training, predominantly in Manitoba and Alberta.[18]

There were also attempts to form complete Indian militia units in the decades prior to the First World War. Although the United States had formed all-Indian units as early as the Civil War (1861–5), and continued to do so through to General John Pershing's punitive expedition to capture the Mexican revolutionary, Pancho Villa, in 1916, Canada had no similar background.[19] The earliest attempts at forming an all-Indian militia unit in Canada coincided with the Second Anglo-Boer War.

In September 1866, the 37th Haldimand Battalion of Rifles was formed at Dunnville, Ontario, neighbouring the Six Nations Reserve. It was composed of six companies of which four (Dunnville, Caledonia, Oneida and Walpole) were predominantly Indian, save for a majority of white officers.[20] In addition, large numbers of Six Nations men were active in the 26th Middlesex Light Infantry. Given the high proportion of Indians in these militia units, in February 1896 Six Nations Chief Josiah Hill petitioned the Ministry of Indian Affairs, through his regional agent, Captain D. E. Cameron, to form a regiment on the reserve:

The Six Nations Indians feel on account of their loyalty to the Crown for over one hundred years, and having fought side by side with Soldiers of the Crown

---

[17] LAC, RG10, vol. 2837, reel C-11284, file 171/340. Letter from W. Hamilton Merritt to Deputy Minister Indian Affairs, 11 May 1898.
[18] Mike Mountain Horse, *My People, The Bloods* (Calgary: Glenbow-Alberta Institute and Blood Tribal Council, 1979), pp. 139–40; Dempsey, *Warriors of the King*, p. 18.
[19] Thomas A. Britten, *American Indians in World War I: At Home and at War* (Albuquerque: University of New Mexico Press, 1997), pp. 102–3; Bruce White, 'The American Army and the Indian' in N. F. Dreisziger (ed.), *Ethnic Armies: Polyethnic Armed Forces from the Time of the Hapsburgs to the Age of the Superpowers* (Waterloo: Wilfrid Laurier University Press, 1990), pp. 78–9.
[20] LAC, RG10, vol. 2837, reel C-11284, file 171/340. Composition 37th Haldimand Rifles.

in the War of Independence and the War of 1812–1814 that a Regiment bearing the name of the Royal Six Nations whose rank and file shall be composed of Indians with the head quarters at the Council House on the Grand River Reserve be established, over 1000 men can be raised if necessary ... To be commanded by Capt. Cameron our popular Indian Agent.[21]

Chief Hill's request was not endorsed by all council chiefs. Chief Isaac Hill protested to Indian Affairs that the council was unable to reach a consensus and 'they [did] not want to reject the ancient way of consulting on that affair'.[22] Nevertheless, Cameron proceeded to forward the request to Indian Affairs chief clerk, Duncan Campbell Scott, complete with drawings of a proposed regimental uniform (kilt with Indian headdress), colours and a *guidon* with battle honours, including the American Revolution and the War of 1812.[23] Enthusiastic, Scott approached the Deputy Minister of Militia, Colonel Charles E. Panet: 'I may say that this Department heartily endorses the proposed movement and is prepared, should the idea be favourably entertained by your Department, to encourage and assist the Indians in carrying out the proposal to a successful issue.' Although the idea was submitted to the Governor-General, John Hamilton-Gordon, in March, it was rejected on the grounds of funding and interdepartmental 'complications'.[24]

With the advent of hostilities in the Transvaal, and Canada's formal commitment of an expeditionary force on 13 October 1899, Josiah Hill sent a letter directly to Queen Victoria on behalf of the sovereign entity of the Iroquois Confederacy: 'I humbly beg herewith to transmit to Your Most Gracious Majesty a decision of the Chiefs of the Six Nations Council ... offering Your Majesty a contingent of Chiefs and Warriors, officered by Indians or those in connection with them to serve Your Majesty in the Transvaal, in conformity with the customs and usages of their forefathers and in accordance with existing Treaties with the British Crown.'[25] Also, during November, requests to send warriors were submitted through local agents by the individual Ontario

[21] LAC, RG10, vol. 2837, reel C-11284, file 171/340. Letter from Hill to Cameron, 14 February 1896.
[22] P. Whitney Lackenbauer and Katherine McGowan, 'Competing Loyalty in a Complex Community: Enlisting the Six Nations in the Canadian Expeditionary Force, 1914–1917', p. 97.
[23] Captain D. E. Cameron, 'Royal Six Nations Regiment', *The Indian Magazine Brantford* 3/4 (1896), 1–4.
[24] LAC, RG10, vol. 2837, reel C-11284, file 171/340. Letter from Scott to Panet, 26 February 1896.
[25] LAC, RG10, vol. 2991, reel C-11307, file 215/977. Letter from Six Nations Council Chiefs to Queen Victoria, 10 November 1899.

Chippewa (Ojibwa) reserves of Saugeen, Nawash and Sarnia, and by the Duck Lake Cree and Ojibwa of Saskatchewan.[26]

With offers of Indian warriors flooding in from across Canada, both the Colonial Office and the government of Canada finally dismissed the requests. The Colonial Secretary, Joseph Chamberlain, replied directly to Chief Hill on behalf of the Queen in February 1900: 'I have received Her Majesty's comment to desire you to convey to the Chiefs of the Six Nations our extension of Her sincere thanks for the loyalty and sympathetic assurances contained in the resolution and of Her regret at being unable to avail Herself of their patriotic offer.' In April, Indian Affairs followed the British exclusionist example and served notice to all agents that, 'no Treaty Indians can enlist for service'. There were reports and rumours circulating of Indians, mostly in western Canada in the wake of the North-West Rebellion, 'wishing to join the Boer force in the Transvaal' out of sympathy for the Boers' repression at the hands of the British. There was also a fear that the provision of military training and the organization of Indian regiments could be utilized against Canada itself.[27] The most palpable example of the British-Canadian policy barring Indians from service was that of John Brant-Sero, a Mohawk from the Six Nations Reserve: 'I have just returned from South Africa, disappointed in many respects, but I do not wish these lines to be understood as a grievance. I went to that country from Canada hoping that I might enlist in one of the mounted rifles; however, not being a man of European desent [sic], I was refused to do active service in Her Majesty's cause as did my forefathers in Canada ... I was too genuine a Canadian.'[28]

Although the government banned the enlistment of Indians for service in South Africa, a limited number did manage to evade this protocol. Since enlistment was on an individual basis and no account of 'race' was registered on any military records, the precise number of Indians who served is not known. However, a select number of Indian men were among the 7,368 Canadians to see service during the Boer War, including Private Walter White of the Anderdon Huron Reserve near Windsor, Ontario. White was killed on 18 February 1900 during the Battle of Paardeberg.[29] Private George McLean of the Okanagan nation of British Columbia served with the 2nd Canadian Mounted

[26] LAC, RG10, vol. 2991, reel C-11307, file 215/977. Correspondence: Indian Troop Contributions.

[27] LAC, RG10, vol. 2991, reel C-11307, file 215/977. Chamberlain to Lord Minto, Hill and Cameron, 13 February 1900; Circular: DIA to all Agents, 22 April 1900.

[28] Moses, *A Sketch Account of Aboriginal Peoples in the Canadian Military*, p. 61.

[29] LAC, RG38, A-1-a, vol. 111. Walter White Personal Records.

Rifles in South Africa. McLean enlisted during the First World War, being awarded the Distinguished Conduct Medal (DCM) during the Battle of Vimy Ridge (9–12 April 1917). His citation states that 'single-handed he captured 19 prisoners', whilst being wounded.[30]

Joseph Hanaven of the Six Nations Reserve served with the 6th Canadian Mounted Rifles. He was denied the allocation of a land grant for returning soldiers as he did not apply by the deadline. However, non-Indian soldiers who applied after the closing date of 31 December 1913 were 'grandfathered' and given parcels of land as outlined in the Service Act.[31] In addition to supplying men for active service, Canadian Indians actively contributed to the Canadian Patriotic Fund.[32] The patriotic response of Indians during the Boer War would be mirrored at the onset of hostilities in 1914.

In May 1899, shortly before the outbreak of the Second Anglo-Boer War, the idea of including Maori in an expeditionary force for service in Samoa was raised. With aspirations to sub-imperialism in the Pacific, New Zealand offered a contingent of men, including Maori, 'accustomed to bush life and with experience in the backwoods' to the imperial government.[33] This request was dismissed as the Treaty of Berlin (14 November 1899) partitioned Samoa. Germany gained the western portion and the United States the eastern, in exchange for Britain's gain of German New Guinea, an acquisition which appeased a burgeoning sub-imperialist stance in Australia. In compensation, New Zealand annexed the Cook Islands and Niue in June 1901, having previously acquired the Kermadec Islands in 1887.[34]

Maori assistance to the British in South Africa was offered prior to the official outbreak of the war. After the failed Jameson Raid between December 1895 and January 1896, and given mounting British–German rivalry, the Te Arawa tribe offered its warriors for service

---

[30] LAC, RG38, A-1-a, vol. 76. George McLean Personal Records; Summerby, *Native Soldiers, Foreign Battlefields*, pp. 14–15.

[31] LAC, RG10, vol. 2991, reel C-11307, file 215/977. Land Claim for Joseph Hanaven, 29 October 1930.

[32] LAC, RG10, vol. 2991, reel C-11307, file 215/977. Indian Donations to Canadian Patriotic Fund.

[33] Ian McGibbon, 'The Origins of New Zealand's South African War Contribution', in John Crawford and Ian McGibbon (eds.), *One Flag, One Queen, One Tongue: New Zealand, the British Empire and the South African War 1899–1902* (Auckland University Press, 2003), p. 8.

[34] Harcourt Papers, 508: Reports on Operations in British Dominions and Colonies and German Territories, 1914–1915; see: Wm. Roger Louis, *Great Britain and Germany's Lost Colonies 1914–1919* (Oxford: Clarendon Press, 1967); Angus Ross, *New Zealand Aspirations in the Pacific in the Nineteenth Century* (Oxford University Press, 1964).

in Africa.[35] Although no Maori were dispatched, twenty-two Maori Volunteer Force soldiers were included in the fifty-four-man New Zealand Contingent for Queen Victoria's 1897 Diamond Jubilee celebrations. This gesture was illustrative of a tacit recognition of an equal Maori position within New Zealand society. With the advent of war in South Africa, and the pledging of New Zealand units in September 1899, many Maori tribes offered warriors. These proposals were supported by all four Maori Members of Parliament, and Prime Minister Richard Seddon endorsed the idea of forming a Maori Contingent. However, both the Colonial and War Offices immediately forbade the use of Maori troops in a 'white man's war'. In addition, it was thought that Maori might not meet the conditions of service, predominantly acceptable English literacy.[36]

Nevertheless, Seddon, as well as Maori leaders and MPs, continued to endorse the idea of a Maori unit. In March 1900, Seddon relayed to the Governor-General that the Maori had offered a total of 2,000 troops for service, 'as good as any Boer who ever pulled a trigger'. The British authorities were also told of the Maori frustration, 'being not allowed to fight [to] prove their loyalty and patriotism having raised over £1,000 towards patriotic fund by means of carnivals'. In December 1900, General Kitchener petitioned the New Zealand government for further contingents. In response, Seddon suggested that 200 men be sent, including 100 Maori, and that the 6th Contingent contain 50 per cent Maori of acceptable literacy from the Volunteer Force. The Colonial Office rejected all proposals as the political situation in South Africa made the deployment of armed Maori 'impossible'. The Colonial Secretary, Joseph Chamberlain, sympathized with Maori frustration, observing that he 'would have been glad of affording opportunity of active service for the Queen to the Maoris who have so often proved their soldierly qualities and courage ... I am really sorry not to give these Maoris a chance. If they had sent them without asking and mixed them up with others no one would have known the difference. But [sic] as we promised that this should be a white man's war.'[37]

In February 1902, the government of New Zealand proposed an alternative use of Maori warriors, whereby a Maori force of 1,000 could

---

[35] Cowan, *The Maoris in the Great War*, pp. 6–7.
[36] Paice, *Tip & Run*, p. 286; Ashley Gould, '"Different Race, Same Queen": Maori and the War' in John Crawford and Ian McGibbon (eds.), *One Flag, One Queen, One Tongue: New Zealand, the British Empire and the South African War 1899–1902* (Auckland University Press, 2003), pp. 120–1.
[37] Gould, '"Different Race, Same Queen"', pp. 120–1.

be deployed elsewhere in the empire to release imperial soldiers for use in South Africa. The Colonial Office rejected this offer on the grounds that Maori were 'merely children' and would be 'a great trouble'. The Colonial Office tried to placate New Zealand by asking for Maori to be included in the New Zealand Contingent at the coronation of King Edward VII in August 1902. Thirty-two Maori performed a *haka*, as part of the 122-man Contingent. Prior to this representation, a Maori Contingent was sent to Melbourne for the opening of the Commonwealth Parliament of Australia.[38]

Although Maori support for the war effort was evident, it was by no means universal. Many tribes in King Country, still bitter over land confiscation and the New Zealand Wars, voiced their disapproval of Maori support for a British war. In addition, the Maori of Hokianga were found by Governor-General, Lord Ranfurly, to have 'a Pro-Boer element which has been fostered by some local Dutch and German Priests'. In reality, anti-government sentiment within the Hokianga tribes was fostered by the 1898 'Dog-Tax Rebellion', and the use of 180 troops to confront Maori protesters.[39]

Despite the restrictions placed on military service, Maori men fought in South Africa. It is known that at least twenty-one men of Maori descent, including four 'full-bloods', served with the New Zealand Contingents, which totalled 6,500 soldiers. John Callaway attained the rank of Lieutenant in the 9th Contingent.[40] All of these volunteers possessed anglicized names, many adopting them solely for the purpose of enlistment. The concept of 'half-castes' was not as pronounced in New Zealand as in Australia. In the 1901 census, only 5,540 half-castes were identified, 3,133 living as Maori and 2,407 living as Europeans, out of a total Maori population of 45,330.[41] The probability is that most Maori men who served were half or quarter-castes living as 'Europeans', who had access to education and prior Volunteer Force service.

At the outbreak of the South African war, Australia consisted of five self-governing British colonies. Each colony was responsible for its own defence, policing and Aboriginal policies. As individual colonies were formed, they created militia units, which supported British regulars until their departure in 1870. Colonial defence policies, such as the Queensland Defence Act of 1884, contained no mention of racial

---

[38] McGibbon, *The Path to Gallipoli*, pp. 121–2.
[39] Belich, *Making Peoples*, p. 268.
[40] Gould, '"Different Race, Same Queen"', p. 123.
[41] Colonial Office, *The Colonial Office List, 1916*, p. 277.

exclusion. This was not a gesture of racial tolerance, simply a tacit understanding that Aborigines were not people and required no specific mention of exclusion.[42] Nonetheless, some men of Aboriginal descent, albeit very few, did serve in Australian colonial militia units prior to the Boer War, such as Darug Aborigine, Gerome Locke, who served with the New South Wales Rifles throughout the 1880s. He and his three sons served in the AIF during the First World War.[43]

During the Second Anglo-Boer War, after some hesitation, Australian colonies offered expeditionary forces. In light of this commitment, Archibald Meston, co-administrator to the Queensland Aboriginal Protection and the Restriction of the Sale of Opium Act (1897), privately recruited fifty 'expert Aboriginal horsemen and marksmen', for service in South Africa. Correspondingly, the Victorian Protector of Aborigines appealed to his charges to 'fight for the homeland'. No record exists of any Aboriginal volunteers. Given the limited number of positions within the expeditionary forces and the high enlistment rates of white Australians, these Aboriginal offers were summarily rejected.[44]

However, individual Aborigines did see service alongside 16,175 Australians. These Aborigines were recruited for specific skills, solely to meet the needs of the expeditionary force. A tracker named 'Billy', attached to a Queensland contingent, caused British officers to lose a bet when he successfully tracked five men in a pre-arranged test.[45] Private Mulumphy and Trooper William Stubbings also saw service in South Africa with the 3rd (NSW) Mounted Rifles.[46] Following Australian federation, which occurred during the war, Lord Kitchener asked the Australian Prime Minister, Edmund Barton, to send Aboriginal trackers with future contingents. Correspondingly, the Commissioner of Queensland Police dispatched four Aboriginal trackers (including 'Billy') for service with the Bloemfontein Police in South Africa.[47]

---

[42] Rod Pratt, 'Queensland's Aborigines in the First AIF', *Sabretache* 31 (1990), 18. NOTE: This was a series of four articles that appeared consecutively in this journal in Volume 31: (1) January/March 1990; (2) April/June 1990; (3) July/September 1990; (4) October/December 1990.

[43] Suzanne Kenney, *Mount Tomah: Darug Aboriginal Connections* (Sydney: BestwayBerk Printing, 2000), p. 15.

[44] Lindsay Watson, 'Better Than a One-Eyed Man: An Incomplete History of Queensland's Indigenous Soldiers of the Boer War and World War One' (Unpublished paper, University of Queensland, 1999), 4; Pratt, 'Queensland's Aborigines in the First AIF' (January/February 1990), 19.

[45] Watson, 'Better Than a One-Eyed Man', 4.

[46] Mrs Margaret Beadman, Australian War Memorial (AWM), Private Collection; Kenney, *Mount Tomah*, p. 15.

[47] Huggonson, 'Aboriginal Trackers and the Boer War', 20.

Another Aboriginal who contributed his skills to Australia's Boer War effort was Jerry Jerome of Queensland, who broke over a thousand horses for service. Many Queensland Aborigines were expert horsemen due to a clause in the 1897 Aborigine Act requiring them to be employed in rural positions, mainly as farm hands and ranch aids.[48]

The native inhabitants of South Africa were directly implicated in the war, including military service. In 1900, the population of South Africa was made up of 1,116,806 whites, 4,059,018 blacks, 500,000 coloureds, and roughly 100,000 Indians and Asians, the latter primarily in Natal.[49] At the outbreak of war, no formal agreement forbidding the use of blacks as combatants existed between the Boer and British governments. However, the British government internally agreed that only white troops, including those of British colonies, would be employed in combat roles. The martial law regulations (*krijgswette*) of both Boer republics specified that all male inhabitants ages 16 to 60 were liable for service, including coloureds. The Hague Convention of July 1899, ratified months before the outbreak of war, made no specific reference to the employment of black troops (or any other race) in a combat, or any other, function of war. During the initial months of conflict both sides accused the other of using natives as combatants. While many instances were fabricated or exaggerated, both sides had used armed natives for defensive purposes and as scouts, in addition to large numbers of black labourers. Both sides had also taken black prisoners. Although the Boers relied on Africans for intelligence and used black scouts, they were not normally armed, unlike those employed by the British. As the war progressed, both sides began arming blacks for offensive operations. In addition, beginning in 1901, Zulu warriors independently supported the British effort, guided by British liaison officers, and frequently raided Boer positions and depots.[50]

While the initial historiography perpetuated the pretence of a 'white man's war', Peter Warwick's seminal work, *Black People and the South African War 1899–1902* (1983), dispelled these myths. Warwick concludes that over a hundred thousand blacks served in a wide range of non-combat occupations for both the British and the Boers, and, 'At least 10,000, and possibly as many as 30,000, blacks were fighting within the British army as armed combatants by the end of the war.' While the number of blacks armed by the Boers is unknown, both

[48] Pratt, 'Queensland's Aborigines in the First AIF', 19.
[49] Colonial Office, *The Colonial Office List, 1916*, pp. 318–54.
[50] Warwick, *Black People and the South African War*, pp. 17–27, 75–90.

Kitchener and the Boer general, Jan Smuts, later acknowledged that they had knowingly allowed the use of black combatants. In addition, 116,000 'Black Boers' were interned in concentration camps, with over 14,000 dying of starvation or disease.[51]

The Second Anglo-Boer War marked the first instance of the deployment of significant expeditionary forces from Canada, Australia and New Zealand in aid of a British imperial campaign. The First World War was a continuation of this commitment on an amplified scale.

[51] Ibid, pp. 4–27; Jan C. Smuts (eds. W. K. Hancock and Jean Van Der Poel), *Selections from the Smuts Papers, Vol. I: June 1886–May 1902* (Cambridge University Press, 1966), pp. 482–4.

4   Dominion defence acts

The Boer War exposed the deficiencies in British doctrine and the neglect and inadequacies of Dominion military capacities. After British forces withdrew from the Antipodes and Newfoundland in 1870 and Canada in 1871, military expenditure and reform were left in relative abeyance. Given the experience of the British Army during the New Zealand Wars, the North-West Rebellion, and the striking similarities between Maori, Métis/Cree and Boer tactics, New Zealand Prime Minister Richard Seddon made reference to the New Zealand campaigns of the 1860s. He believed that the British should have adopted modifications, based on Boer threats, similar to those applied against Te Kooti in New Zealand: 'What is wanted in South Africa at the present time, is some more Von Tempskies [sic].' Seddon also claimed that, had 5,000 well-trained Maori warriors been dispatched to South Africa under their own war chiefs, the Boers would have been defeated much earlier.[1] Similarly, Aborigine Matthew Kropinyeri remarked to his protector in 1914 that:

The war was in progress in South Africa a few years ago there was great excitement ... that was more a 'blackfellows' war ... I remember when the news came through of some of the mistakes made by the British troops in South Africa because they were not accustomed to the style of warfare adopted, the old men felt that they would be equal to the occasion ... They seemed to think they could do better, because they were more accustomed to sneaking on their game.[2]

---

[1] McGibbon, *The Path to Gallipoli*, pp. 119, 122; Belich, *The Victorian Interpretation of Racial Conflict*, pp. 294–5. Gustavus von Tempsky was a Prussian-born adventurer and journalist. He joined the irregular Forest Rangers and served as a Major in the Waikato and Taranaki Wars of the 1860s. The arrogant von Tempsky was an excellent tactician and adopted and used Maori tactics. He was greatly respected by his peers, including the Maori, who called him Manu-Rau. He was killed in action on 7 September 1868 and is alleged to have been eaten by the Maori (a sign of respect), as his body was never recovered nor its resting place disclosed. His Maori adversaries returned his sword and scabbard to his widow.

[2] Doreen Kartinyeri, *Ngarrindjeri Anzacs* (Adelaide: Aboriginal Family History Project, South Australian Museum and Raukkan Council, 1996), p. 15.

Between 1904 and 1912, as a consequence of the Boer War, all Dominions enacted new, or amended, national defence acts which drastically altered the structure of their military forces. Included in these new policies were directives pertaining to force strength, mandatory militia and cadet training, compulsory combatant service in times of war, and specific clauses referring to those segments of society not eligible for volunteer or mandatory service, including indigenous men. The clauses specifically mentioning or encompassing indigenes varied, depending on the circumstance and needs of the individual Dominions.

In New Zealand, the original 1845 Militia Ordinance required all able-bodied men aged 18 to 65 to attend twenty-eight days of annual training if mustered to do so. The 1858 revision, influenced by the ongoing New Zealand Wars, provided for the formation of Volunteer Force units, which were liable for duty anywhere in New Zealand. These units were primarily used for garrison duty, while those members who wanted battlefield service joined the 'armed constabulary' or 'special units', such as the Forest Rangers or the Taranaki Bush Rangers. These formations were created to meet local and immediate needs and, as the New Zealand Wars waned, they were gradually disbanded. By 1901 the Volunteer Force numbered 17,000, including the Maori Wairarapa Mounted Rifles. In April 1902, Seddon announced a government proposal to raise a 5,000-strong Maori corps, but it never materialized for economic reasons and because of the fear of arming such a large, domestic Maori entity. However, select corps had Maori sections under Maori officers, while individual Maori served throughout various formations of the Volunteer Force.[3]

The 1909 Defence Act introduced cadet training for boys aged 12 to 17 and compulsory military service in the Territorial Force for all men aged 18 to 25. After five years' service in the Reserve Force, men were obliged to join a rifle club until the age of 55. By 1913, 52,356 males were active under this arrangement, supervised by a cadre of 625 British officers and instructors.[4] Although the 1909 Act drew no distinctions between Maori and *Pakeha*, the government decided not to apply compulsory service to Maori. Only the ecclesiastical boarding schools, which were obliged to conduct cadet training, and which in 1914 had 577 Maori boys on their rolls, trained Maori compulsorily.[5] Nevertheless, many Maori men volunteered and entered units of the

---

[3] Rolfe, *The Armed Forces of New Zealand*, pp. 3–5; McGibbon, *The Path to Gallipoli*, p. 200.
[4] F. W. Perry, *The Commonwealth Armies: Manpower and Organization in Two World Wars* (Manchester University Press, 1988), pp. 175–6.
[5] Colonial Office, *Colonial Office Lists, 1916*, p. 273.

Territorial Force. In vicinities with large Maori populations, distinct Maori sections or platoons were created, many commanded by Maori officers and senior NCOs, a residual precedent from the Volunteer Force. Although the imperial officers of the general staff thought Maori soldiers were 'dirty in their habits and untrustworthy as regards care of arms, equipment, and clothing issued to them', they also recognized their merit as soldiers. Exclusion from the Territorial Force was never considered, nor was it technically permissible under the current law.[6]

Also in 1909, Australia amended its 1903 Defence Act, mandating that all males aged 12 to 25 receive military training, while men older than 25 years of age form the reserve. By 1914, 45,000 men aged 18 to 25 comprised the adult portion of the Australian Militia Force.[7] Within this 1909 alteration, Section 61(h) stipulated that:

The following shall be exempt from service in time of war, so long as the employment, condition, or status on which the exemption is based continues: –

(h) Persons who are not substantially of European origin or descent, of which the medical authorities appointed under the Regulations shall be the judges ...

Provided that, as regards the persons described in paragraphs (h) and (i) [Conscientious Objectors] of this section, the exemption shall not extend to duties of a non-combat nature.[8]

Given that Aborigines were not of European descent, they were exempt from military service under this clause; however, the ambiguity was whether, by being exempt, they were also unable to volunteer. The federal government under the 1901 Constitution had the power to 'make peace, order and good government with respect to ... the people of any race, other than the Aboriginal race in each State', yet the federal Defence Act seemed to contradict this clause.

Although these discrepancies could be used to argue in favour of the voluntary enlistment of Aborigines, they were neither of European descent nor citizens under the Australian Constitution; therefore, they were deemed irrelevant in the formation of defence or other federal policies, unless specifically mentioned. However, the sub-section referring to non-exemption from non-combat duties for 'Persons who are not substantially of European origin or descent' raises the question as to whether this clause was inserted with the realization that Aborigines

[6] Haami, 'Maori in the Armed Forces', 302.
[7] Jane Ross, *The Myth of the Digger: The Australian Soldier in Two World Wars* (Sydney: Hale & Iremonger, 1985), pp. 39–40.
[8] Government of Australia, *Defence Act 1903* (Canberra: Office of Legislative Drafting and Publishing, 2005).

and other non-whites could be used for labour both within and outside Australia during times of war.

Although there were governmental regulations prohibiting Aborigines from direct military and cadet service, in 1912 a group of north Queensland missionaries raised their own Aboriginal cadet unit of young Weipa males. It met for, 'military drill … every Friday afternoon, and I [the missionary in charge] was extremely interested in witnessing the many varied evolutions some two dozen of the boys had been taught to perform'. In reality, this was an exercise to instil the soldierly virtues of self-restraint and obedience rather than tactical military training.[9] In 1913, the Governor-General of Australia, Thomas Denman, summarized both the work of the missionaries in civilizing the Aborigine and, also, the common perception of most Australians towards their indigenous population at the outbreak of the First World War:

The fashion in these days … is to regard the aboriginal as something beneath our contempt. In fact one of our great scientists – [Ernst] Haeckel – has gone so far as to say that the Australian aboriginal is little better than the anthropoid ape. Those of us who know the aboriginal at all, believe this to be entirely false. They are, it may be said a child race, and they are often very troublesome children. Still they have the keen observation of children and can be taught and influenced; and it is on this fundamental basis that our missionaries are working amongst them to-day.[10]

Following the Treaty of Vereeniging, the Union of South Africa was formed in 1910 after much negotiation and deliberation. Former Boer general, Louis Botha, became the first prime minister, and Minister of Native Affairs as of 1912, and held these posts until his death in 1919. He was succeeded as prime minister by fellow Boer veteran, Jan Christian Smuts, who served as Botha's minister of defence from 1912 onward. Both men, former British adversaries, dominated the South African war effort during the First World War.

The Union Defence Act of 1912 made all European males aged 17 to 60 liable for military service in times of war, and obliged those aged 17 to 25 to undergo compulsory training. The Union Defence Force (UDF) was primarily composed of a small body of five permanent mounted rifle and artillery units totalling 2,500 men and an 'active citizen force' of 25,000 soldiers. A Cadet Training Corps for boys aged 13 to 17 was also instituted.[11] In provisions echoing those of the Australian 1909

---

[9] Pratt, 'Queensland's Aborigines in the First AIF', 21.

[10] The National Archives, UK (NA), HO-45/10667/216857. Albert Medal, 2nd Class to Australian Aboriginal Neighboni or Neighbour.

[11] Perry, *The Commonwealth Armies*, pp. 187–8; Strachan, *The First World War in Africa*, p. 65.

Act, the Union Defence Act of 1912 officially denied natives armed service in the UDF.

Chapter 1, Article 7, of the Act stated that the liability to render combatant service in wartime, or any obligation to train under prescribed military arrangements,

shall not be enforced against persons not of European descent, unless and until Parliament shall by resolution determine the extent to which any such liability shall be enforced against such persons: but nothing in this section contained shall be deemed to prevent the voluntary engagement at any time of such persons for service in any portion of the Defence Forces in such capacities and under such conditions as are prescribed.[12]

The clause excluded non-Europeans from wartime service in a combatant capacity and from peacetime training. However, the clause could be changed by a majority vote in Parliament and, more importantly, a qualifying condition safeguarded the opportunity for the clause to be repealed summarily in times of war. Given the black involvement on both sides during the Boer War, Article 7 was carefully crafted to deny blacks immediate combatant status, but enabled, if required, their services in any variety of non-combatant roles, and even as combatants if thought necessary by Parliament.

Smuts, who drafted the clause, stated that Article 7 'is simply that no compulsion shall be laid upon any coloured citizen to serve or train in any military capacity, unless Parliament has otherwise decided. But no provision was laid down by which coloured citizens may not volunteer and offer services to the country, and a proposition like this will always be considered by the Government.'[13] The arrangement satisfied Afrikaners wary of arming blacks by denying blacks and coloureds compulsory service. The clause also mollified the black and coloured communities by not outwardly denying them the ability either to volunteer or to serve when required by the Union to do so. It placated British South Africans and the imperial government, concerned that blacks and coloureds should not be wholly subjugated.

At the close of the Boer War in 1902, the Canadian permanent force numbered 1,000 men, whose daily pay was half that of an unskilled labourer, while the part-time militia consisted of 35,000 poorly trained civilians of limited military value. The 1904 Militia Act authorized the expansion of the Canadian permanent and militia forces.[14] In 1909, the

---

[12] NASA, Pretoria Repository (SAB), Union of South Africa, Statutes, 1912, Act No. 13, Clause 7.

[13] Grundy, *Soldiers Without Politics*, pp. 46–7.

[14] J. L. Granatstein, *Canada's Army: Waging War and Keeping the Peace* (University of Toronto Press, 2002), pp. 45–7.

Canadian Defence League was formed and called for universal military training and mandatory cadet instruction for schoolboys. Such a drastic programme was neither economically feasible nor sanctioned by the government, but by 1911 six provinces, including Quebec, offered cadet training. By 1913, 40,000 Canadian boys were active in this programme, including many of the 4,655 Indian boys aged 16 to 20 years old within the residential school system.[15] During that same year, the Permanent Force peaked at 3,100 and the militia at 43,000, both still well under the authorized strengths of 5,000 and 60,000 respectively.[16]

The 1904 Militia Act also identified those Canadians liable for military service. Section X stated that, 'All the male inhabitants of Canada of the age of eighteen years and upwards, and under sixty, not exempt or disqualified by law and being British subjects, shall be liable to service in the militia; provided that the Governor-General may require all the male inhabitants of Canada capable of bearing arms.'[17] Those 'exempt under law' were listed and included conscientious objectors, such as Doukobors, and 'unexpendable' professionals. However, the Act made no specific mention of Indians.[18] Given that Indians were 'British subjects', it is unknown whether this implied Indian service or was a conscious omission based on treaties. Significant numbers of Indians were active in the Canadian militia and training as cadets at one of forty-five residential schools across Canada.[19] Within the twelve military districts of Canada, commanding officers of militia units had the freedom to recruit directly from the local population. Commanders of units centred in regions with high Indian populations, such as the 37th Haldimand Battalion of Rifles headquartered astride the Six Nations Reserve, enlisted Indian volunteers who were fit for service.

Unlike its counterparts, the diminutive Dominion of Newfoundland had no governmental portfolio dedicated to, or encompassing, defence and no regulations pertaining to military service for any Newfoundlanders, let alone for its small, secluded indigenous populations. Its sole official

---

[15] Office of Census and Statistics, *The Canada Yearbook 1914* (Ottawa: King's Printer, 1915). Saskatchewan did not institute Cadet training, and given the high proportion of residential schools and Indians in that province, many Indian boys were excluded from Cadet training.

[16] G. W. L. Nicholson, *Canadian Expeditionary Force: 1914–1919* (Ottawa: Queen's Printer, 1962), pp. 6–10.

[17] LAC, RG24, C-1-a, vol. 6564, part I. Revision of the Militia Act, 1904.

[18] John Herd Thompson, *Ethnic Minorities during Two World Wars* (Ottawa: Canadian Historical Association, 1991), pp. 4–9.

[19] Suzanne Fournier and Ernie Crey, 'Killing the Indian in the Child: Four Centuries of Church-Run Schools' in Roger C. A. Maaka and Chris Andersen (eds.), *The Indigenous Experience: Global Perspectives* (Toronto: Canadian Scholars' Press, 2006), p. 147.

military organization was a single branch of the Royal Naval Reserve at St John's, formed in 1902. The detachment had an authorized strength of 600 sailors and one vessel. Newfoundland's main pseudo-military programme consisted of four church-sponsored cadet corps divided along sectarian divisions. In 1892, the Church Lad's Brigade (CLB) was formed by the Church of England, followed by the Catholic Cadet Corps in 1896, the Methodist Guards in 1900 and, finally, the Presbyterian Newfoundland Highlanders in 1907. Only the CLB had representation outside St John's. The only other organizations remotely related to soldiering were one registered rifle club in St John's and the non-denominational Legion of Frontiersmen operating out of St John's and St Antony's on the island and at Nain, Mud Lake and Hopedale in Labrador.[20] By 1914, the Legion consisted of 150 men who had either, 'seen active service in a war … had training at sea [or] knocked about in the wilds'.[21]

The defence acts enacted by the Dominions between 1904 and 1912, and the clauses relevant to indigenes, remained in place at the outbreak of the First World War. South Africa and Australia included clauses which specifically pertained to their indigenes. Both national acts excluded indigenous men from combatant service, while allowing their inclusion as labourers in times of war when deemed necessary by governmental institutions. Given that black South Africans had been employed as labourers and carriers by both Boer and Briton during frontier warfare and the Boer War, the clauses in the Union Defence Act remained consistent with past policy and practice. Australia had used Aborigine trackers when necessary, but the Defence Act remained on a par with overall exclusionist policies evident throughout colonization and recent Australian military contributions.

The Defence Acts of Canada and New Zealand made no specific reference to Indians or Maori, although both were active in militia formations, which raises some interesting questions. Specifically, Indians had a long history of allegiance and military service alongside British and Canadian soldiers. Given that both Indians and Maori were 'British subjects' by both Constitution and treaty, was it simply implied that they were included, most notably because they were active in the militia? Within the military districts of both Dominions, commanding officers of militia/volunteer units had the freedom to recruit directly from the local population. Commanders of units centred in regions

[20] Stanley I. Hiller and the NFLD RNR, 'For King and Country', *Newfoundland and Labrador Heritage Project* (2007). www.heritage.nf.ca/greatwar/home.html
[21] O'Brien, 'Out of a Clear Sky', 404–5.

with high Indian or Maori populations enlisted volunteers who were fit for service. Was this, perhaps, a conscious omission, on the part of both Canada and New Zealand, to avoid confirming official policy, whereby Indians and Maori could be denied service when suitable to authorities or, when required, utilized at the discretion of the government in the future?

Indeed, the failure to mention Indians and Maori is puzzling, and the only clear answer is that no official policy existed concerning service in the militia, home defence forces, expeditionary formations, or under conscription legislation. The absence of an official policy was manifest immediately at the outbreak of the First World War and led to confusion within government, among recruiters, Indian and Maori volunteers and their councils. However, the Maori were the only Dominion indigene afforded the rights of citizenship. Therefore, the New Zealand Defence Act, theoretically, required no specific legislation regarding military service. Strangely then, the British government refused to include Maori in the New Zealand force for the Boer War.

5   1914: Subjugated spectators

Following Britain's declaration of war on 4 August 1914, men and materials were immediately offered by all Dominion governments. The commitment of the Dominions was affirmed in the Canadian House of Commons by Prime Minister Sir Robert Borden: 'As to our duty, all are agreed; we stand shoulder to shoulder with Britain and the other British dominions in this quarrel ... not for love of battle, not for lust of conquest, not for greed of possessions, but for the cause of honour.'[1] Until the 1931 Statute of Westminster, Britain retained control of Dominion foreign policy, including the ability to declare war independently. Therefore, unlike at the outbreak of the Second World War, former Canadian Prime Minister Sir Wilfrid Laurier's 1910 maxim, 'When Britain is at war, Canada is at war. There is no distinction', was the legal arrangement for all Dominions in August 1914.[2]

The Dominions had the autonomy, however, to decide the scope of men and materials offered to the imperial war effort. New Zealand formally committed a contingent of 8,000 soldiers on 30 July, with Canada following suit with a pledge of 25,000 men on the 31st. On 5 August, Australia pledged a force of 20,000 men.[3] On 4 August, South Africa, alone among Dominions in that it was still garrisoned by British troops, immediately offered to replace British regiments with UDF units. The last British troops left South Africa on 10 August to supplement the British Expeditionary Force (BEF) bound for the Western Front.[4] On 8 August, Newfoundland pledged '500 troops for land service abroad' and doubled its Naval Reserve quota to 1,000 sailors.[5]

---

[1] Robert Borden, *Special Session of Parliament, August 1914* (Ottawa: King's Printer, 1914).
[2] Nicholson, *Canadian Expeditionary Force*, p. 5.
[3] Grey, *A Military History of Australia*, pp. 80–1.
[4] The first British units on the Western Front engaged German soldiers on the morning of 22 August during the Battle of the Frontiers north of Mons, Belgium.
[5] PANL, MG136, Sir Walter Davidson Papers, file 2.02.007. Diary Entry 9 August 1914; file 2.04.001. Diary Entry 7 August 1914.

Dominion competition was immediate, as heightened trade and export potential accompanied war. All Dominions sought to secure enhanced portfolios and new contracts for munitions, materials and agrarian products to boost economies in the midst of recession.[6] George H. Perley, Canadian High Commissioner to Britain, told Borden at the onset of hostilities that, 'This war sure [sic] to alter situation and relationship various parts Empire. What Canada does at this time immensely appreciated and will not be forgotten.'[7] The brood of the mother country was fighting for accolades and the position of the favourite child. Maurice Hankey, Secretary to the Committee of Imperial Defence, later remarked that, 'The dominions are as jealous of each other as cats.'[8]

The pledging of expeditionary forces was one avenue to gain favour in the contest for British and other Allied war contracts. On 7 September, Borden requested that Perley 'confidentially sound [Colonial Secretary] Harcourt [as to] our expeditionary force being increased to say forty thousand men [but] no more should come than we can manage to pay for'. In the same telegram, he instructed Perley to ascertain in confidence, 'How many Australia and New Zealand propose to send'.[9] Like Canada, Australia, Newfoundland and New Zealand also recognized the benefits of shouldering the financial responsibility for their own contingents and calculated their initial troop commitments accordingly.[10] In Newfoundland, the war, by way of participation, was viewed by politicians as a medium to earn, 'a distinguished place in whatever scheme is developed for closer Imperial Federation when the war is over'.[11]

Manpower was foremost in the Dominion rivalry for accolades and for financial recompense via war contracts. The Colonial Secretary, Lewis Vernon Harcourt, in the principal position between the contending Dominions, recognized the situation and tendered a memorandum on behalf of the King on 8 September:

The Dominion of Canada, the Commonwealth of Australia, and the Dominion of New Zealand have placed at my disposal their naval forces which have

---

[6] Offer, *The First World War*, Chapter 11.

[7] Department of External Affairs, *Documents on Canadian External Relations, Vol. I, 1909–1918* (Ottawa: Queen's Printer, 1967), p. 48. Perley to Borden, 10 September 1914.

[8] Margaret MacMillan, *Paris 1919* (New York: Random House, 2003), p. 45.

[9] Department of External Affairs, *Documents on Canadian External Relations*, pp. 47–50. Borden and Perley, 7, 29 September 1914.

[10] PANL, MG136, Sir Walter Davidson Papers, file 2.02.007. Diary Entries 7, 9 August 1914.

[11] O'Brien, 'Out of a Clear Sky', 402–3.

already rendered good service for the Empire. Strong expeditionary forces are being prepared in Canada, in Australia and in New Zealand for service at the front, and the Union of South Africa has released all British troops, and has undertaken important military responsibilities, the discharge of which will be of the utmost value to the Empire. Newfoundland has doubled the number of its branch of the Royal Naval Reserve and is sending a body of men to take part in the operations at the front ... All parts of my overseas Dominions have thus demonstrated in the most unmistakable manner the fundamental unity of the Empire amidst all its diversity of situation and circumstance.[12]

With the Anglo-Japanese Alliance of 1902 (and extensions of 1905 and 1911), both Australia and New Zealand were determined to prevent Asian immigration and to limit Japanese expansion. Both Dominions harboured sub-imperialist designs on adjacent archipelagos, islands and German Pacific colonial possessions, which could serve as a buffer against southern Japanese expansion. Likewise, South Africa viewed both neighbouring British protectorates, such as Bechuanaland and Basutoland, and German Southwest Africa (GSWA), with sub-imperialist interest. By extension, the war – by way of significant contributions of men and materials – could serve as a means to expropriate these territories during the war itself, or through a negotiated peace. Britain, by way of Dominion assistance, would be forced to settle outstanding Dominion concerns and grievances over past British policies.[13]

Recruiting stations in the Dominions, possessing little contingency planning for mass mobilization, were overwhelmed with volunteers during the first months of the war and attesting officers had the ability to be highly selective. This outpouring of support, although driven by patriotism, was also the result of high unemployment rates throughout the empire, in the midst of a global recession. Nevertheless, positions within initial Dominion formations were quickly filled by men of European, primarily British, stock. The majority of indigenous peoples greeted the war with enthusiasm and immediately offered their services to King and country. Indigenous elites and political organizations viewed war service as a tool to gain equality and respect within the broader spheres of Dominion politics and society. Dominion politicians and military officials viewed indigenous service as a pragmatic necessity to meet national war aims, while also using participation as an instrument of

---

[12] Department of External Affairs, *Documents on Canadian External Relations*, pp. 47–8. Harcourt to Dominion Governors General, 8 September 1914.

[13] Harcourt Papers, 508–9: Reports on Operations in British Dominions and Colonies and German Territories, 1914–1915; 479: Private Correspondence with Sir Ronald Munro Ferguson, Governor-General of Australia, 1914–17. See: Ronald Hyam, *Britain's Declining Empire: The Road to Decolonisation, 1918–1968* (Cambridge University Press, 2006).

assimilation or, in the case of South Africa, segregation. Although the majority of indigenous leaders and peoples offered their immediate support to the war effort, their active participation remained dependent on existing Dominion defence acts or, in the absence of any clear policy, on the whims of national governments. Throughout 1914, the general policy towards indigenous service adhered to contemporary racial assumptions, and past policy and practice, and remained one of exclusion or of limited involvement in non-combatant roles. Throughout 1914 and early 1915, in the absence of vast deployments to European theatres accompanied by inevitable casualties, white manpower was sufficient to meet the demands of Dominion commitments, still in relative infancy, within the context of a war which it was believed would be short-lived. No Dominion units were active on the Western Front until the independently raised Princess Patricia's Canadian Light Infantry (PPCLI) Battalion entered trenches near Ypres on 6 January 1915.[14]

In 1914, the population of Canada was 7.88 million, excluding 103,774 Indians and 3,447 Eskimos. Of the total population, 54% were of British ancestry, with 10.89% born in Britain itself. Of the 36,267 soldiers of the first Canadian Expeditionary Force (CEF) Contingent, 9,635 (27%) were English-speaking born Canadians, 1,245 (3.4%) French-speaking born Canadians and 23,211 (64%) were British by birth. By the end of 1914, Canada had enlisted 59,144 soldiers for service overseas. The percentage of French-Canadians would not increase over the course of the war. Although they accounted for 30% of the total Canadian population, French-Canadians made up only 4% of all Canadian volunteers and recruitment levels in Quebec were the lowest of any province.[15] Of the 4.92 million Australians in 1914 (excluding an estimated 80,000 Aborigines), 13.3% were British-born and roughly 84% were born in Australia. Men of British birth composed 27% of the first contingent of the AIF, totalling 20,626 men. By the close of 1914, Australian enlistment totalled 52,561 – a per capita ratio comparable with that of Canada.[16] New Zealand's 1914 population comprised

[14] LAC, RG9III-D-3, vol. 4911, reel T-10703. War Diaries: Princess Patricia's Canadian Light Infantry, 1914–1915. The PPCLI was independently raised, and funded, by Montreal millionaire Captain Andrew Hamilton Gault. The PPCLI was absorbed into the Canadian 3rd Division on 22 December 1915.

[15] Census and Statistics Office, *The Canada Yearbook 1914*, pp. 60–75; J. L. Granatstein and J. Mackay Hitsman, *Broken Promises: A History of Conscription in Canada* (Toronto: Oxford University Press, 1977), pp. 23–4; Nicholson, *Canadian Expeditionary Force*, Appendix C.

[16] E. M. Andrews, *The Anzac Illusion: Anglo-Australian Relations during World War I* (Cambridge University Press, 1993), pp. 43–4; J. G. Fuller, *Troop Morale and Popular Culture in the British and Dominion Armies 1914–1918* (Oxford: Clarendon Press,

1.1 million *Pakeha* and 52,997 Maori. The British-born percentage of *Pakeha* was 22.2%. Of the 8,417 men of the first contingent of the New Zealand Expeditionary Force (NZEF), 6,241 (74%) were born in New Zealand, with 2,157 (25.6%) born in the United Kingdom.[17] In 1914, the population of Newfoundland, roughly 252,000, was spread over more than 1,300 isolated villages and fishing settlements, with St John's boasting the largest population at a mere 32,000. By the end of October 1914, however, 1,076 men had been attested into the Newfoundland Regiment and the Naval Reserve had risen from 500 to nearly 800 sailors. Eighty per cent of these men were of British heritage from St John's.[18]

Although no Dominion directly recruited indigenes for combatant service in 1914, the precedent for the employment of indigenous men as combatants was set by both Britain and France during the opening battles of the war, as the Dominions hastened to form expeditionary forces. France quickly put into effect its plans to mobilize indigenous colonial soldiers for a European war, and dispatched them to the Western Front. Four battalions of Moroccans, dubbed *les Bataillons des Chasseurs Indigènes*, were incorporated into the Sixth French Army on 20 August 1914 and, on 1 October, two battalions of colonial Algerians arrived in France.[19] In October, a Senegalese brigade (*Tirailleurs Senegalais*) suffered a casualty rate of nearly 75 per cent when successfully holding its portion of the line on the Yser River.[20]

Britain, in need of manpower, as the Dominions were scrambling to train expeditionary forces, deployed a British Indian contingent, Indian Expeditionary Force A, consisting of the 3rd (Lahore) Division, the 7th (Meerut) Division, the 4th (Secunderbad) Cavalry Brigade and auxiliary units, which arrived at Marseilles on 26 September 1914. By

---

1990), p. 171; L. L. Robson, *The First A.I.F.: A Study of its Recruitment 1914–1918* (Melbourne University Press, 1970), pp. 49–54.

[17] NZEF (1914), *Europe War Diary* (Wellington: Government Printer, 1915); Fuller, *Troop Morale and Popular Culture in the British and Dominion Armies*, p. 171; McGibbon, *The Path to Gallipoli*, p. 250.

[18] PANL, MG136, Sir Walter Davidson Papers, file 2.02.008. Diary Entry 1 December 1914; PANL, MG632, Patriotic Association of Newfoundland, 1914–19, file 1. Minutes 23 October 1914.

[19] Driss Maghraoui, 'Moroccan Colonial Soldiers: Between Selective Memory and Collective Memory – Beyond Colonialism and Nationalism in North Africa', *Arab Studies Quarterly* 20/2 (1998), 21–5.

[20] Shelby Cullom Davis, *Reservoirs of Men: A History of the Black Troops of French West Africa* (Westport: Negro Universities Press, 1970), pp. 142–3; Charles Mangin, *La Force noire* (Paris: Hachette, 1910). In his 1910 book, *La Force noire*, General Charles Mangin predicted the French could raise 40,000 men from its West African colonies (4 per cent of the total population of 10.65 million). By the end of the war, France had enlisted 200,000 soldiers from these same colonies.

the close of 1914, over 2,000 *sepoys* had been killed on the Western Front. The Indian units, however, had a difficult time adjusting to new equipment, language barriers and the Continental climate, resulting in poor morale. Following actions at Neuve-Chapelle (March 1915) and Ypres (April 1915), the infantry divisions were withdrawn to Egypt in October 1915 before the onset of winter, although the cavalry units remained on the Western Front until their transfer to Egypt in March 1918.[21]

The inability of the *sepoys* to adjust to European weather made the War and Colonial Offices question the feasibility of using Dominion indigenes, in both combatant and labour roles, on the Western Front. Nevertheless, the early deployment of these French and British colonial troops did not go unnoticed by the indigenous peoples of the Dominions. In their initial efforts to promote equal military service opportunities for their peoples, indigenous leaders (and at times government officials) in all Dominions frequently referred to these combatants and questioned the validity of denying their own 'races' the same privileges.

On 7 August 1914, the same day that New Zealand agreed to assault German Samoa, South Africa was asked by the imperial government to invade German Southwest Africa. On 10 August, the Union Government agreed to the request, as both Botha and Smuts were convinced that by conquering GSWA with Union troops, the colony could be formally annexed by South Africa after the war. Botha's decision, however, was met with resistance from Afrikaner opposition leaders and senior officers in the UDF, who supported Barry Hertzog. An Afrikaner nationalist and former Boer general, Hertzog formed the Nationalist Party in January 1914, stealing much Afrikaner support from Botha on the eve of the war. One-sixth of the Afrikaner population was of German heritage and GSWA had been used as a sanctuary for diehard Boers following the Boer War.[22]

Despite these objections, during mid-September Union forces initiated the invasion of the German colony, igniting a Boer rebellion of 10,000 to 12,000 dissenters. Botha met the rebellion with a force of 30,000 Boer Unionist soldiers. He believed that using Boer soldiers to defeat the rebellion was a better option than using English-speaking South Africans, Britons, or Indian *sepoys*, or accepting Harcourt's

[21] Omissi, *Indian Voices of the Great War*, pp. 2–4. Of the 130,000 *sepoys* who served on the Western Front, almost 9,000 died.

[22] Harcourt Papers, 508–9: Reports on Operations in British Dominions and Colonies and German Territories, 1914–15.

offer of 30,000 Anzac soldiers, volunteered by the imperial government to be redirected to South Africa while en route to Egypt. Harcourt's offer of Australian and New Zealand soldiers illustrates the absence of Dominion control over the deployment of their own forces. The governments of both countries were never notified of this possibility before Botha's calculated rejection of the offer on 9 November. On 24 November, General Alexander Godley, the General Officer Commanding (GOC) New Zealand forces, wrote to the Minister of Defence, James Allen: 'I shall be very interested to know why we were under orders to go to the Cape while we were at Albany [Australia]. I have heard nothing yet, and I hope you will let me know. It was only at the eleventh hour that it was altered again, and that we went by the original route.'[23]

The Boer rebellion, which suffered from a lack of coordination, was all but over by December 1914 and officially ceased with the surrender of Major J. C. G. Kemp on 4 February 1915. It was the manifestation of the dissident political and cultural environment within the Union of South Africa between British and Afrikaner. Although the ethnic divisions between the French and the English in Canada could be racially comparable, they were by no means as volatile. Nevertheless, Smuts alluded to this comparison: 'They [Afrikaners] think that in that way they will be better able to preserve their language, their traditions, and their national type … They point to the precedent in Canada, where French-Canadians are also standing aside from the general current of Canadian life and national development for the same reasons.'[24]

Aware of the ethnic tensions in his country, and with war imminent, on 1 August 1914 Botha released an official statement regarding the hostilities in Europe and the natives of South Africa:

There is, however, little probability at present of any trouble which need seriously affect the natives … the opportunities for employment of natives, the Gold Mines will continue to offer work to those who desire it. The Government therefore trust that the Natives will display their customary loyalty to His Majesty and of the Union of South Africa by going quietly about their daily work and paying no heed to idle rumours; resting assured that the Government … will carefully watch over their interests.

In addition, magistrates and commandants of police forces were instructed 'of the importance of moving about among the people and

---

[23] Harcourt Papers, 471: Estimates of Rebel Forces, September–November 1914; 508–9: Reports on Operations in British Dominions and Colonies and German Territories, 1914–15; ANZ, Godley Papers. Cable from Godley to Allen, 24 November 1914.

[24] J. C. Smuts, *Jan Christian Smuts* (London: Cassell & Company, 1952), p. 193.

keeping more than ever in touch with the Chiefs and other persons of influence'.[25]

South Africa's direct participation in the war heightened the ever-present fear of black insurrection. Many members of Botha's Union Party (and the entire Nationalist Party) were certain that participation in the war, of any nature, would place a strain on the maintenance of the status quo and present the native population with an opportunity to challenge white domination. In addition, politicians and civilians were concerned that draining the country of able-bodied men for external service would create a vulnerable environment within South Africa. To justify these apprehensions, allusions were made to real or imagined attacks on whites by blacks during the Boer War, to the Herero rebellion in GSWA in 1904, to the 1906 Bambatha (Zulu) rebellion in Natal, and, most immediately, to the recent sporadic violence following the 1913 Natives Land Act.[26]

For the native inhabitants of South Africa, the war and the rebellion afforded them the opportunity to contrast their allegiance to both the Union of South Africa and the British Crown with Afrikaner disloy-alty. According to Solomon (Sol.) T. Plaatje, Secretary of the South African Native National Congress (SANNC): 'Nor could we conceive of any reason why the Boers, who have now more freedom than they ever dreamt of possessing under their own flag, including the right to partially enslave blacks, should suddenly rise up against the English, whose money and brains are ever at the beck and call of the Dutch!'[27] Stimela Jason Jingoes, who eventually joined the Western Front-bound SANLC in 1917, wrote of his emotions at the outbreak of war: 'The present war is a world war. Every nation must take part in it. Even we Bantu ought to play our part in this war ... Why should I hesitate? I must go and die for my country and my King!'[28]

Many natives, however, shared the view 'that this was only one more of those wars to which the Europeans, who ought to know better, were accustomed, and that in any vital sense it was not a [Native] concern'. Others commented on self-declared civilized peoples waging such

[25] NASA, KAB, 1BIZ, vol. 6/2. Botha to Natives, 1 August 1914; Memorandum: Botha to all Magistrates, 15 August 1914.
[26] The Bambatha rebellion was an armed Zulu uprising in Natal against British rule and taxation policies led by Chief Bambatha kaMancinza. In all some three thousand Zulus were killed, with another five to seven thousand imprisoned or flogged.
[27] Sol. T. Plaatje, *Native Life in South Africa* (London: P. S. King and Sons, 1916), p. 296.
[28] Stimela Jason Jingoes, *A Chief is a Chief by the People: The Autobiography of Stimela Jason Jingoes*. Recorded and compiled by John and Cassandra Perry. (Oxford University Press, 1975), pp. 72–3.

destructive war upon each other. More (ignorant of the cruel German treatment of their colonial native populations) remarked that joining the Germans could secure freedom from the repressive Union regime. There was no unanimous stance within the black and coloured populations concerning the war.[29] However, the reaction of black and coloured leaders to the war, and to the rebellion, was one of support and allegiance to the Union and the King.

The South African Native National Congress (SANNC), the forerunner to the African National Congress (ANC), was formed in January 1912 to lobby for native interests and grievances. A delegation arrived in London in June 1914 and fruitlessly petitioned the King and the Colonial Office over the terms of the 1913 Natives Land Act. When war was declared, the SANNC President, the Reverend John Dube, was briefing the congress at Bloemfontein on the activities of the delegation in England. On 6 August, a dispatch was sent to Botha outlining the loyal position of the SANNC:

The Executive of the South African Native National Congress desires to assure the Union government that this Congress is absolutely loyal to the Union of South Africa and to inform the government that during the present European crisis if any assistance or sacrifice is required by the government from us we shall be ready and willing to be in our places. We fully realise that our lot is one with that of white South Africans. Moreover, in order to prove our loyalty to the government, the Executive has unanimously decided to suspend all agitation against the Natives Land Act until the present unrest is over.[30]

The acting Minister of Native Affairs, F. S. Malan, replied to the SANNC, stating that it had made a 'very wise step which would be likely to impress Parliament to consider their cause sympathetically'.[31]

In addition to verbal allegiance, on 20 October the SANNC, through its Vice-President, the Reverend Walter Rubusana, offered 'a native levy of 5 000 able-bodied men' as combatants for GSWA, 'provided the Government is prepared to fully equip this force for the front'. An answer from the Ministry of Defence was relayed on 2 November:

With reference to your letter ... refer you to the provisions of Section 7 of the South Africa Defence Act, 1912, and to state that the Government does not desire to avail itself of the services, in a combatant capacity, of citizens not of

---

[29] NASA, KAB, 1BIZ, vol. 6/2. Memorandums: Botha to all Magistrates, 15 August, 2 September 1914. These differing reactions and opinions are well-documented in Grundlingh, *Fighting Their Own War*, ch. 1.

[30] Ian Gleeson, *The Unknown Force: Black, Indian and Coloured Soldiers Through Two World Wars* (Cape Town: Ashanti Publishing, 1994), p. 11.

[31] NASA, SAB, GNLB, vol. 187/14. Report: Meeting of SANNC with F. S. Malan, 31 October 1914.

European descent ... the present war is one which has its origin among the white people of Europe and the Government are anxious to avoid the employment of its native citizens in a warfare against whites.[32]

Plaatje immediately questioned the validity of this argument: 'For weeks before Dr. Rubusana sailed from Europe the Turcos and Algerian and Moroccan troops had been doing wondrous deeds on the Continent for the cause of the Allies ... while the Canadian troops on Salisbury Plain included Red Indians.'[33] The SANCC nevertheless agreed to set up a sub-committee to aid the government in recruiting African labour for GSWA.

Like the SANNC, the African Political Organization (APO), representing coloureds, also declared in August 1914 that it would cease political campaigning for the duration of the war, while providing loyal service to the empire. An offer to raise 5,000 men was forwarded directly to Smuts. This tender was repeated on 23 October, after the outbreak of the rebellion. Both offers were rejected. On 6 November the APO received a letter from the Ministry of Defence, mirroring the exact wording of that sent to the SANNC four days earlier.[34] In addition, individual chiefs from the Zulus, Tembus and Pondos offered the services of their warriors. Leaders from the British protectorates of Swaziland, Basutoland and Bechuanaland also offered volunteers. Indian leaders in Pretoria wrote to Smuts stating that they 'could get together a very serviceable lot of men – old Gurkas, Bengal Cavalry, Bombay Lancers, Pathars, Sikhs – all trained men, as keen as mustard'.[35]

While no official offers from native, coloured or Indian political organizations were accepted by the Union government, blacks and coloureds were active in both the GSWA campaign and the Boer rebellion. By November, the Union forces deployed to GSWA had grown from the initial 30,000 to almost 60,000. Smuts was 'concerned about the serious position created by the formidable shortage of transport natives which threatens virtual suspension [of] real progress [in the] campaign'. To meet this need, the recruitment of natives and the efforts of the SANNC sub-committee were placed under the jurisdiction of Colonel S. M. Pritchard, Director of the Government Native Labour Bureau, in November 1914. Pritchard, who realized the importance of SANNC and native support in securing recruits, worked in close

---

[32] South African National Defence Force Documentation Centre, Pretoria (SANDFDC), DC623/190/9199. Rubusana to Botha, 20 October 1914; Reply, 2 November 1914; Plaatje, *Native Life in South Africa*, pp. 303–4.
[33] Plaatje, *Native Life in South Africa*, p. 305.
[34] Grundy, *Soldiers Without Politics*, pp. 51, 55.
[35] Gleeson, *The Unknown Force*, p. 12.

cooperation with the SANNC, chiefs and headsmen, often inviting them to discussions and meetings. SANNC President Dube remarked, in January 1915, that Pritchard was, 'the one official of the Government who was administering Native Affairs in the right direction – namely, by consulting the Natives in matters in which they are interested and for not hesitating to take them into their confidence'.[36]

Recruits, however, did not volunteer in the numbers expected or required, even with the incentives of a limited four to six month contract, free uniforms, rations and a monthly pay of £3 (10 per cent higher than that in the mines). Despite the assurances of Pritchard that 'the system of obtaining labourers … would not be compulsory [and] no pressure or other influence would be exercised in order to induce Natives', the circumstances surrounding enlistment were hardly voluntary.[37] Various pressures, threats and bribes were used by magistrates and chiefs to secure labourers. The Ministry of Defence contemplated imposing martial law on the native populations, enforcing conscription. The fear of civil unrest meant that such drastic action was not taken as the Union had no substantial force remaining to counter a rebellion. In all, 33,546 coloureds and blacks (and a very small number of Indians) served in non-combatant roles as carriers, drivers and animal pack leaders with Union forces during the GSWA campaign, which ended on 9 July 1915. Of this total, aside from 1,326 from Bechuanaland and 58 from Basutoland, all were South African. Of the South African total (32,162), roughly 28,000 came from the Eastern Cape and the Transvaal.

In the Eastern Cape natives had historically been under more liberal British control and white domination was less pervasive than in other areas of the Union. The native population of the Transvaal was significantly smaller than in other regions of South Africa. However, severe drought and deteriorating conditions, in combination with more drastic recruitment, made enlistment a viable means to secure income in the face of disease and starvation. The Zulu, still smarting from the brutal suppression of the Bambatha rebellion and the 1913 Land Act, represented only a small token of the overall number. Given their legacy of war with Europeans, and in light of the rebellion, government representatives exercised little pressure to recruit them. This pattern would be repeated with the recruitment for the SANLC between 1916 and 1918.[38] Native casualties were incurred, but the figures are unknown.

[36] Grundlingh, *Fighting Their Own War*, pp. 57, 59.
[37] Ibid, p. 59.
[38] NASA, SAB, NTS 11/363/9107. South African Native Labour Recruiting Statistics, 15 January 1919.

A column of transport riders were captured by German forces in September 1914 and most showed signs of torture and mutilation at the hands of their captors after their liberation in July 1915.[39]

During the rebellion a special Native Intelligence Branch was formed, under Captain Allan King (Native Magistrate Pretoria District), to gain information on rebel strengths and movements. There is evidence to suggest that blacks were recruited, cajoled and forced into service by both parties, despite the Union government's assurance that, 'no armed Natives or Coloured persons were employed to assist in the suppression of the rebellion'.[40] It seems likely that many Union scouts were armed, as unarmed informants had little chance of returning with valuable information in the event of contact with rebels. There is also evidence that certain rebel leaders forced blacks into service as both combatants and labourers, using threats of violence and castration.[41] However, if armed blacks were present in the ranks of both forces, the number was minimal and most associated with either side were used as labourers.

The use of armed blacks by both sides during the rebellion was similar to that during the Boer War. Arming blacks was not outwardly endorsed and was not common practice. Given the short duration of the failed Boer insurrection, the employment of armed blacks received scant attention outside official circles, aside from the usual public rumours circulating about the ever-present fear of black revolt. In contrast, the use of blacks and coloureds in labour capacities was never questioned and was always, in the South African tradition, intended to be a vital element in the make-up of the overall Union forces. In January 1915, Colonel Pritchard made a public announcement stating that blacks were used 'not for fighting purposes, but for that class of employment [labour] that was exclusively and ordinarily suited to Natives'.[42]

On 6 August, a request to occupy German Samoa was extended to New Zealand by the War Office. On 7 August, New Zealand agreed and, after a brief delay, the 1,383-strong Samoan Expeditionary Force disembarked at Apia on 29 August. No resistance was offered and the German Governor surrendered on the 31st.[43] This campaign raised the question of Maori participation in the First World War. Since the

---

[39] Grundlingh, *Fighting Their Own War*, p. 87.
[40] H. J. and R. E. Simons, *Class and Colour in South Africa 1850–1950* (Harmondsworth: Penguin Books, 1969), p. 177.
[41] Grundlingh, *Fighting Their Own War*, pp. 23–4.
[42] B. P. Willan, 'The South African Native Labour Contingent, 1916–1918', *Journal of African History* 19/1, World War I and Africa (1978), 64.
[43] Harcourt Papers, 508: Reports on Operations in British Dominions and Colonies and German Territories, 1914–15.

outbreak of war, Maori chiefs and tribes had been lobbying the government and the five Maori MPs to create a distinct Maori unit for overseas service. Many Maori chiefs wrote directly to the King offering troops in the name of Queen Victoria, under whom the Treaty of Waitangi was signed.[44]

Unlike the indigenes of all other Dominions, Maori were equal to *Pakeha* under New Zealand law and in 1914 were represented in government by five Maori Members of Parliament. New Zealand was also witnessing a revival of the King Movement under King Te Rata and Princess Te Puea, in addition to more localized spiritual organizations on the north island, led by prophetic leaders such as Rua Kenana in Urewera. Between April and August 1914 (at the same time as members of the SANNC were in London remonstrating against the 1913 Natives Land Act), a delegation of the King Movement was in England protesting that the 1909 Native Land Act was an infringement of Maori rights as outlined in the Treaty of Waitangi. Maori leaders held an audience with King George V on 4 June 1914 and with representatives of the Colonial Office in early August, before leaving for New Zealand on 10 August, six days after the British declaration of war.[45]

The New Zealand government never intended to deny Maori the ability to serve: 'It is our earnest hope that, though the Maori Race is among the smallest of those within the British Empire, its name may not be omitted from the roll of the peoples who are rallying to maintain the "mana" of King George the Fifth.' The question, however, was in what capacity Maori could serve within the overall British imperial forces, as the War Office had barred them from the New Zealand force raised during the Boer War.[46] Although the Department of Defence stated on 11 August that, 'it is unlikely that a Native Contingent will be sent to the front', on 1 September, Prime Minister William Massey addressed the issue and alluded to indigenes active on the Western Front: 'There is an embargo that a Native force should not take part in wars between the White races. But as Native troops from India have arrived in Europe ... a way has been paved for the offer of the Maori people ... our equals in the sight of the law. Why then should they be deprived of the privilege of fighting and upholding the Empire when assailed by the enemy?' On

[44] Archives New Zealand (ANZ), AD1, box 734, record 9/32: Maoris: Offering Services in Expeditionary Force; AD1, box 734, record 9/32/1: Maori Contingents NZEF.
[45] Michael King, *Te Puea: A Biography* (Auckland: Hodder and Stoughton, 1977), pp. 73–5.
[46] ANZ, AD1, box 734, record 9/32/1. Department of Defence Notice to all Maori Tribes, 1 September 1914; AD1, box 734, record 9/32: Maoris: Offering Services in Expeditionary Force.

3 September, the Governor-General, Lord Liverpool, relayed the Maori requests to Lord Kitchener: 'The Maoris in New Zealand are most anxious to volunteer for War service and my Prime Minister hopes that His Majesty's Government will agree to their doing so. If so my Prime Minister will place the matter before Cabinet with a view to settling the numbers and the training necessary.'[47]

On 6 September, Harcourt advised Massey that, 'the Army Council would gladly accept contingent not exceeding 200 for service in Egypt'.[48] After receiving a letter from the Minister of Defence, James Allen, concerning the training and officering of an all-Maori unit, General Godley, the General Officer Commanding (GOC) New Zealand forces, immediately intervened in any further organization of a Maori unit which would be placed under his command:

The best way to arrange for the organization of the Maori Contingent, if offered, would be that it should be done by a committee of leading Maori gentlemen and of others particularly connected with the Maoris. I would recommend ... Hon. Dr. Pomare, Sir James Carroll, Dr. Buck, Hon. Mr. Ngata, Mr. Parata ... They should have full power to appoint officers in whatever way they think best, also non-commissioned officers ... We don't want to get mixed up in their tribal jealousies, degrees of rank etc.

Godley also stated that any Maori contingent should include adequate initial reinforcements of 5 per cent of the total force, must be dismounted and 'let it be understood by those who are offering that, if accepted, their term of service will be for the duration of the war'.[49]

Following this advice, a Maori War Management Committee was established, holding its first meeting on 18 September. Representing the Maori were all five Maori Members of Parliament: Hon. Sir James Carroll (MP Gisborne, non-Maori riding), Hon. Maui Pomare (MP Western Maori), Hon. Apirana Ngata (MP Eastern Maori), Dr Peter Buck (MP Northern Maori) and Taare Parata (MP Southern Maori). Collectively, with other prominent, educated Maori, they had been dubbed the Young Maori Movement. Pomare was given ministerial control over the Cook and other Islands in 1912 (and again in August 1915), while Buck resigned his seat to join the First Maori Contingent as a medical officer. He was replaced by Taurekareka Henare in the

---

[47] ANZ, AD1, box 734, record 9/32. Colonel E. W. C. Chaytor to The Reverend W. T. Fraser, 11 August 1914; Harcourt Papers, 468: General Correspondence 1910–15. Speech by Massey, 1 September 1914; Liverpool to Kitchener, 3 September 1914.

[48] Harcourt Papers, 468. Telegram from Harcourt to Liverpool, 6 September 1914.

[49] ANZ, AD1, box 734, record 9/32/1. Allen to Godley, 11 September 1914; Godley to Allen, 14 September 1914; Memorandum: Godley to Department of Defence, 19 September 1914.

10 December 1914 election. James Carroll was elected for the Eastern Maori seat in 1887. He became the first Maori to hold a cabinet position – Minister of Native Affairs from 1899 to 1912 – and served as acting prime minister in 1909 and 1911. In 1893, Carroll was elected to the non-Maori seat of Gisborne, a position he held until 1919. In 1912, he became the first Maori to be knighted.[50] Throughout the war, this association, chaired by Pomare, wielded tremendous influence in dictating Maori policy within the overall New Zealand war effort. The power given to these Maori leaders was far greater than afforded to any other Dominion indigenous leaders during the First World War. This was a direct reflection of the equal legal status which Maori enjoyed and of their pre-eminent martial position among Dominion indigenes.

Prior to the 18 September meeting, the committee had been informed that two Maori forces would be dispatched for garrison duty with 'preference to those who have seen service abroad or who have been volunteers in New Zealand'. The Department of Defence stated that 200 men for Egypt and 300 men for Samoa would be raised 'to relieve ... European men for other fronts'. The Maori committee formed quotas for each electoral district based on population: 180 western Maori, 180 eastern Maori, 102 northern Maori and 40 southern Maori (south island). Responsibility for direct recruitment rested with local sub-committees answerable to their regional Members of Parliament on the main Maori board. Although the Maori contingents were part of the NZEF, they were tasked with garrison duty, as the government of New Zealand was still unclear of the imperial policy with regard to indigenous combatants. Godley thus believed that one month's training would suffice. On 22 September, a notice was issued to military districts and Maori communities asking for volunteers aged 21 to 40. Prior to this announcement (and throughout the war) a small, but unknown, number of individual Maori, the majority active in the pre-war Territorial Force, enlisted and served in other NZEF units.[51]

On 22 September, the Department of Defence also approved the committee's request that it be allowed to choose all officers. The department, however, insisted that the commanding officer (CO) and the adjutant be *Pakeha*. These two positions were filled by the Department of Defence in consultation with the committee. The rationale was that, by allowing the committee to select the junior officers, the fact that

---

[50] ANZ, AD1, box 734, record 9/32/1. Quotas for Districts, 18 September 1914.
[51] ANZ, AD1, box 734, record 9/32/11. Defence Department Memorandum, 28 September 1914; AD1, box 734, record 9/32/1. Quotas for Districts, 18 September 1914; 'A Notice', 22 September 1914.

Maori were to be deployed as non-combatant garrison guards would be forgiven or publicly overlooked by Maori. It was also believed that Maori soldiers would respond better to junior officers, with whom they would have the most direct contact, if they were Maori. Lastly, by filling the two most senior positions with *Pakeha*, the Department of Defence maintained overall control of the unit, preventing a situation whereby the department could be deliberately, if not underhandedly, excluded from decisions made by the committee or by the actual CO of the Contingent itself.[52] After the initial choices for CO and adjutant failed their medical examination, with the consent of the committee, Brevet Major Henry Peacock was selected as CO and Captain William Ennis as adjutant.[53]

There were immediate problems and apprehensive responses from governmental departments concerning the formation of distinct Maori units. The first concern came from the Colonial Office. Harcourt questioned whether the Maori required any special considerations once deployed, given their Pacific origins. Second, the Minister of Public Health, as well as district health officials, warned the Ministry of Defence that, given Maori susceptibility to tuberculosis and other diseases, Maori units should be quartered 'separate in camps and troopships and away from European troops and towns. Have all of them vaccinated [against typhoid] and maintain proper sanitary conditions. From our experience ... it was impossible to train them to observe sanitary precautions ... Do all in your power to discourage Defence Department in any proposal to concentrate Maoris for military purposes.'[54] The New Zealand authorities were not alone in their concern about disease and the deployment of indigenes. All the Dominions harboured similar fears.

Colonel Robert Logan, commander of the Samoan Expeditionary Force, urged Allen, on 27 October, not to deploy any Maori to Samoa. He argued that native Samoans 'look down on the Maori as being of an inferior race ... and could not fail to bitterly resent the presence of armed Maori in their midst'. He also alluded to the perception that Maori were uncouth and drank intoxicating liquor (the Samoans did not drink), and was concerned that the example set by the Maori might be imitated

---

[52] ANZ, AD1, box 734, record 9/32/1. Godley to Allen, 22 September 1914; Allen to Pomare, 22 September 1914.

[53] ANZ, AD1, box 1108, record 43/210: Officers: Maori Contingent.

[54] ANZ, AD1, box 734, record 9/32/1. Harcourt to Liverpool, 11 October 1914; Minister of Public Health to Allen, 16 September 1914; Dr R. H. Makgill (District Health Officer Auckland) to Lieutenant-Colonel Parkes (Medical Officer Auckland Military District), 17 September 1914.

by the 'cleanly and courteous [Samoans] with disastrous results'. Logan shared the anxiety of health officials about the possibility of Maori soldiers infecting the local population with disease.[55] The Maori committee was privy to Logan's communication and quickly issued a statement outlining their desire to see all Maori proceed to Egypt in a single contingent. It can be reasonably assumed that this request was made in order to save face due to the racial undertones in Logan's reasoning. On 29 October, Allen reiterated this wish to Harcourt, who responded favourably. The offer of a single Maori contingent, 500-strong, for garrison duty in Egypt was officially accepted on 9 November.[56]

There was no shortage of volunteers to meet the quotas set by the Maori committee. It was noted that many of the first were 'Europeanized Maori' or students, current or graduates, of *Pakeha* and mission-run schools. Most tribes were represented by the original recruits, save for the Waikato. Upon his return from England in late September, King Te Rata, although not directly supporting the New Zealand war effort, stated on behalf of the Kingites, '*Waiho ma he hiahia*' (leave to the desire of the individual). Te Rata's view was that, if individual Maori wished to enlist, they could, but none should be forced to serve. In reality, Te Rata, Te Puea and other Kingite leaders actively discouraged enlistment and no recruits from King Country were among the first two deployments of the Maori Contingent.[57]

Health concerns were heeded as volunteers arrived at the segregated Maori Avondale Camp, near Auckland, between 17 and 22 October 1914. Initially, Maori recruits were split up into two companies on no logical basis; for example, the tallest men formed one company. The ramifications of this were that tribal affiliations were divided and recruits were separated from their elders, who were nominated and sent by local recruiting committees to uphold tribal *mana* and *kawa* (customs). While some of these elders held ranks and deployed with the contingent, others were only present during the training period at Avondale.

The committee was divided on whether to maintain mixed tribal companies, as supported by Pomare and Parata, or to form sections and companies based on tribal affiliations, as supported by the three other members. It was ultimately decided that all eight platoons would be structured on tribal (devolving to sub-tribal for sections) membership

---

[55] ANZ, AD1, box 734, record 9/32/11. Logan to Allen, 27 October 1914.
[56] ANZ, AD1, box 734, record 9/32/1. Allen to Harcourt, 29 October 1914; Reply, 7 November 1914.
[57] King, *Te Puea*, p. 77.

based on Maori custom, in the interest of creating efficiency through tribal competition. It was realized that recruiting and morale might be enhanced, and it was believed inadvisable to mix tribes with traditional animosities. The quota of forty south island Maori, who were considered 'much more Europeanised', were grouped together in a single platoon of individual sections of south island tribes.[58] With this decision, Allen issued instructions to the Avondale training authorities on 28 October 'not to offend Maori feeling or custom with respect to tribes and Hapus [sub-tribe] ... In organizing the Maori Corps do not split up the tribes or hapus more than is absolutely necessary.'[59]

Training commenced on 21 October. Although the Maori Contingent was intended to be a garrison unit, its training was identical to that received by NZEF units bound for active theatres of war. Free time was spent boxing, wrestling, playing football and rugby and in song and dance. A twenty-piece Maori band was formed in January 1915. A library was also established at the camp, the majority of books being military in nature, with military law and financial instructions translated into Maori. Many soldiers also took to the beach to supplement their diet with mussels, eel and *puha* (coastal thistle) and Maori families were invited to attend a traditional Maori *hangi* feast over Christmas 1914.[60]

General leave was granted every Sunday, with many soldiers spending this time in nearby Auckland. Maori private, Rikihana Carkeek, noted in his diary that, 'some of the marrymakers [sic] made friends with Mr Booze and occasionally one or two of the black sheep carried their intimacy too far'.[61] Carkeek enlisted at the outbreak of war at 24 years of age, following higher education at Te Aute College. He was wounded at the Battle of Sari Bair (Gallipoli) on 6 August 1915. While on the Western Front in 1917 he contracted influenza. Upon his recovery he was sent for officer training at Cambridge, and subsequently served as an aide to Captain Peter Buck. Carkeek survived the war and returned home to become a farmer and an interpreter for the Maori Land Court.[62]

---

[58] O'Connor, 'The Recruitment of Maori Soldiers', 51–2; Wira Gardiner, *Te Mura O Te Ahi: The Story of the Maori Battalion* (Auckland: Reed Books, 1992), pp. 14–16.

[59] ANZ, AD1, box 734, record 9/32/1. Allen to Colonel Hume (GOC Auckland), 28 October 1914.

[60] ANZ, AD1, box 1132, record 45/67. Memorandums NZMF, 15 January, 26 January 1915; AD1, box 758, record 51/276. Establishment of Library Maori Contingent, 30 January 1915. 'Hangi' refers to the Maori method of cooking in the ground with hot stones, or to the underground oven so created, and to the food cooked.

[61] Rikihana Carkeek, *Home Little Maori Home: A Memoir of the Maori Contingent 1914–1916* (Wellington: Totika Publications, 2003), pp. 10–11.

[62] Ibid, pp. ii–iii.

Following complaints from locals and Maori soldiers about alcohol, standing orders and canteen sales were amended, excluding alcohol from camp. This was not an uncommon procedure in *Pakeha* training facilities and there is no evidence to suggest that charges related to alcohol were any more frequent among Maori than *Pakeha*. However, given that the Maori Contingent was under the microscope of the Defence Department, stereotypes prevailed and Allen commented about 'venereal and drink ... and was not pleased with the Maoris'.[63]

As training progressed, other problems were immediately recognized. Although trivial, numerous Maori soldiers complained about foot problems caused by boots 'quite unsuitable for Native wear'. It was deemed that the issued boots were too narrow 'for the shape of Maori feet'. Secondly, the uniforms initially issued were surplus from the Volunteer Force, unlike those of other units of the NZEF. Alternative boots and proper uniforms were procured for Maori soldiers to avoid the 'risk of public discredit'.[64] The newly issued uniform was complemented with a Maori Contingent badge, consisting of a crown intersected by traditional Maori weapons, bearing the inscription 'Te Hokowhitu A Tu'. The latter, 'the seventy twice-told warriors of the war god', was chosen since 140 was the favoured size of a traditional Maori war party.[65]

Lastly, although Maori soldiers received pay and benefits equal to *Pakeha*, strict instructions were given to officers to have 'allotments to dependants operate *immediately after the men are paid* so that Allotment Warrants may be issued at once'. This directive was given as it was thought that Maori did not understand financial protocol or that they might neglect support payments to their families.[66] The Department of Defence insisted on the production of birth certificates before granting children's allowances to Maori soldiers, although prior to 1913 there was no legal obligation for Maori to register births. Parents of babies born after 1913 were given two months to register their births, after which no registration would be acknowledged by the government. In addition, enlistment of men with more than three children was initially forbidden. Problems arose, given the fact that many Maori children were unregistered and that some soldiers had more than one wife and three children. The policy regarding registration of births was rescinded, by

[63] ANZ, AD1, box 1021, record 32/23. Canteen Maori Contingent, Avondale 1914; AD1, box 1278, record 51/361. Standing Orders Maori Camp.
[64] ANZ, AD1, box 1135, record 46/104. C. J. Parr (Mayor of Auckland) to Allen, 12 October 1914; Auckland Patriotic Fund to Allen, 15 October 1914.
[65] ANZ, AD1, box 810, record 13/67. Memorandum Cap Badge, 29 October 1914.
[66] ANZ, AD1, box 992, record 31/419/20. Memorandums Maori Contingent, 21 November, 7 December 1914.

the Native Court and the Department of Defence, to allow for the registration of any previously unregistered dependants of Maori soldiers, regardless of when they had been born. Although some Maori soldiers had more than three children, it was deemed that they would not be released from service; instead, 'Maoris ... must be treated exactly the same as Europeans ... [no] pay for more than 3 children.'[67]

With uniforms and financial arrangements made, after just over two months of training, the Maori Contingent began to mobilize for deployment. Yet, racial anxiety regarding the Contingent still persisted. General Godley wrote to Allen on 10 January 1915 about his concerns for the welfare of the Maori once in Egypt:

I am very doubtful about the Maoris coming here, and am afraid it is a risky experiment ... as regards treatment they are likely to receive at the hands of other people here, who do not, and can not, realise that in New Zealand the coloured race is treated on exactly the same footing as the white ... I am afraid that the Maoris may be looked upon in the same light as the Egyptians and Soudanese [sic] here ... and may then resent it ... However, I have not heard that there has been any difficulty with the Indians [*sepoys*] on the [Suez] canal ... but I must say that it would be better if they could go straight to the [Western] Front and fight.

Godley obviously saw no reason why they could not be used in combat. Allen dismissed Godley's concern, believing that it would be obvious to all that Maori were superior to 'the ordinary coloured race',[68] and that the Maori were, 'chief of the dark races living under the sun and alongside white races'.[69]

Unlike New Zealand, which allowed the inclusion of Maori into the NZEF in 1914, albeit as non-combatants, Australia did not endorse the acceptance of Aborigines into the Australian Imperial Force. Given the overwhelming numbers of white volunteers throughout 1914 and 1915, no thought was given to allowing Aborigines to enlist and the Defence Act forbade them from entering military service. Exclusion of Aborigines, as in the past, was the policy of the Australian government in 1914. The majority of recruiting officers adhered to this principle, which had been outlined in their *Recruiting Regulations Booklet*: 'Aborigines and half-castes are not to be enlisted. This restriction is to be interpreted as applying to all coloured men.' However, officers had the ability to enlist men at their personal discretion and a small number

[67] ANZ, AD1, box 1007, record 31/1077. Allowances Maori Soldiers, 24 November 1916; Department of Defence Memorandum, 8 March 1918.
[68] O'Connor, 'The Recruitment of Maori Soldiers', 52.
[69] Pugsley, *Te Hokowhitu A Tu*, p. 29.

of 'half-castes' were enrolled by officers who viewed recruits without prejudice. All but two were dismissed in Australia during the medical evaluation for being 'too dark'.[70] The government of Australia and the policy disseminated to military recruiters whole-heartedly rejected Aboriginal applications for service. Only two 'half-castes' are known to have successfully enlisted in 1914.

Like Aborigines, Canadian Indians did not have the rights and responsibilities of citizenship; therefore, the government of Canada did not expect or need them to take up arms in a foreign war. Indians remained wards of the Crown, and the British government agreed, stating that, 'such an appeal to all the scattered remnants of tribes throughout the immense domain, and in varying degrees of civilization, would be practically impossible'.[71] The Ministry of Militia was concerned that, 'While British troops would be proud to be associated with their fellow subjects [Indians], yet Germans might refuse to extend to them the privileges of civilized warfare ... Therefore it is considered ... that they had better remain in Canada to share in the protection of the Dominion.'[72] This exact phrasing was widely disseminated as unofficial policy by the ministries of Militia, Indian Affairs and Justice from its first use by the Minister of Militia, Sir Sam Hughes, on 8 August 1914 until December 1915, when official sanction was given to enlist Indians. There was also apprehension that including Indians in an expeditionary force could violate treaties.

During the negotiations of Treaties 1–6 (1871–86) – which covered roughly the southern half of the provinces of Manitoba, Saskatchewan, Alberta and western Ontario – Indian chiefs specifically asked about military service. In October 1873, during the discussions of Treaty 3, governmental representative, Alexander Morris, was asked by an Ojibwa chief from Fort Frances, Ontario, 'If you should get into trouble with the nations, I do not wish to walk out and expose my young men to aid you in any of your wars.' To this Morris replied: 'The English never call Indians out of their country to fight their battles.'[73] Morris echoed this sentiment to Cree chiefs at Fort Carlton and Fort Pitt, Saskatchewan, in August 1876 during consultations over Treaty 6A: 'I assured them, you will never be asked to fight against your will; and I trust the time will never come of war between the Queen and the great country near us

---

[70] Watson, 'Better Than a One-Eyed Man', 3–5.
[71] 'Canadian Indians and World War One', *Saskatchewan Indian Federated College Journal* 1/1 (1984), 67.
[72] LAC, RG24-c-1-a, vol. 1221, part 1, file HQ-593-1-7. Hodgins to Hughes with Reply, 8 August 1914.
[73] Dempsey, *Warriors of the King*, pp. 38–9.

[USA] ... My words, where they are accepted are written down, and they last; as I have said to others, as long as the sun shines and river runs.'[74]

Collectively, treaties were signed, not by Canada, but in the name of Queen Victoria; thus, Indian nations saw treaties as an alliance with the Crown through Canada, but not with Canada itself. Like the Maori, Indians often related more to the British Crown than to their host Dominion, as treaties signed on behalf of Queen Victoria signified sovereignty in partnership with Britain. Many Indians referred to her as 'the Great White Mother' and in 1914 acknowledged that the 'Queen's grandson needed help'.[75] In August 1914, the Ojibwa of Sucker Creek, Ontario, offered $500 to defray, 'the enormous expenses in which our Great King is engaged at present. In the wars of 1812 our forefathers fought faithfully under the British flag. In 1870 four members of this Band went on the war expedition with Sir Garnet Wolseley to Red River.' Chief F. M. Jacobs, of the Sarnia, Ontario, Chippewa (Ojibwa) Reserve, wrote to Duncan Campbell Scott that his people were willing to offer, 'help towards the Mother Country in its present struggle in Europe. The Indian Race as a rule are [sic] loyal to England; this loyalty was created by the noblest Queen that ever lived, Queen Victoria.'[76] This belief was not only guided by treaties, but also by the 1763 Royal Proclamation. It stated that Indian affairs and any political activities between Indian nations and the state remained the responsibility of the Crown; thus, it was a historic recognition of the Indian nations' sovereign status.[77]

The most poignant example of this affiliation to the Crown and belief in Indian sovereignty was that of the Six Nations Reserve, the largest Indian community in Canada, which boasted a population of 4,716 in 1914. When war was declared, the band council offered troops and money directly to Britain. The chiefs told Scott that the Six Nations, 'do not belong to Canada and wish to make their contributions direct [through] their brother Chief Ka'rah'kon'tye the Duke of Connaught Governor-General of Canada ... as a token of the alliance existing between the Six Nations and the British Crown'.[78]

---

[74] Ibid, p. 39. The assumption in the language is that Indians would only be drafted to fight in the advent of war with the United States.
[75] James Dempsey, *Aboriginal Soldiers and the First World War* (Ottawa: Library and Archives Canada, 2006), p. 1.
[76] LAC, RG10, vol. 6762, reel C-8508, file 452-2-1. Chiefs of Sucker Creek to Indian Agent W. McLeod, 26 August 1914; Jacobs to Scott, August 1914.
[77] Allen, *His Majesty's Indian Allies*, p. 193.
[78] LAC, RG10, vol. 6762, reel C-8508, file 452-2-1. Minutes Band Council Meeting, 15 September 1914; Gordon J. Smith (Indian Agent) to Scott, 16 September 1914 with reply 21 September 1914.

The vast majority of Canadian Indians and band councils greeted war with enthusiasm and offered immediate support in men and in money. With no pan-Indian political organization comparable to the SANNC or the Maori committee, individual reserves and councils relayed their support through their Indian agents or directly to Scott. It was not only the traditionally warlike Indian nations, such as the Blackfoot and Iroquois Confederacies which offered warriors, so too did nations with little martial prowess, such as the Nkamaplix of British Columbia.[79] Scott recognized that the Indians of British Columbia were 'not so warlike in disposition as those of the central and eastern parts of the Dominion'.[80] As an alternative, on 1 September 1914, Thomas Deasy, agent at Massett, British Columbia, offered the Haida Indians for local home defence to relieve white soldiers for overseas duty. His offer was duly dismissed.[81]

In August 1914, Indian men rushed to recruiting depots for reasons other than loyalty to the British Crown. Although the warrior ethic had stagnated as a result of residential schooling, religious education and isolation on reserves, it had not been completely repressed. While many joined for money, adventure and employment, as did their white comrades, scores of others enlisted to revive the warrior tradition and gain social status within their communities.[82] War in Europe seemed a feasible means to circumvent governmental policies and the Indian Act, while offering freedom and escape from docile reserve life. According to Mike Mountain Horse, a Blood from Alberta, who joined the 191st Battalion in 1916:

From the outset of this colossal struggle the Red Man demonstrated his loyalty to the British Crown in a very convincing manner ... My uncle, Chief Bull Shield, had been a great warrior of the plains. But the war proved the fighting spirit of my tribe was not quelched [sic] through reservation life. When duty called, we were there and when we were called forth to fight for the cause of civilization, our people showed all the bravery of our warriors of old.[83]

In 1914, although the 1904 Militia Act made no specific reference to Indians, the government unofficially forbade their enlistment despite the fact that many were active in militia units. Although Scott bluntly stated on 12 August 1914 that, 'no unit composed solely of Indians

[79] P. Whitney Lackenbauer, *Battle Grounds: The Canadian Military and Aboriginal Lands* (Vancouver: University of British Columbia Press, 2007), p. 35.
[80] Scott, 'The Canadian Indians and the Great War', 223.
[81] LAC, RG10, vol. 6766, reel C-8511, file 452-13. Deasy to DIA, 1 September 1914.
[82] Cook, *At the Sharp End*, pp. 28–30.
[83] Mountain Horse, *My People, the Bloods*, pp. 139, 144.

will go to the front with the Canadian Contingent', neither he nor his department (or the Ministry of Militia) promulgated any official policy concerning individual enlistment.[84] Many Indians applied for overseas service. Most were immediately turned away. Many others were released after their Indian status was discovered. However, under the frenetic 'call to arms' of the Minister of Militia, Sir Sam Hughes, units recruited directly from their regions, without interference from the ministries of Militia or Indian Affairs. Local recruiting officers, therefore, had absolute discretion over whom they enrolled, provided recruits met the medical standards.[85] This policy was reiterated by the Chief of the General Staff (CGS), Lieutenant-General W. G. Gwatkin, in a 13 November 1914 memorandum concerning 'coloured enlistment', which included not only Indians, but also blacks and Asians.[86]

The success, or failure, to attest Indian volunteers, therefore, depended on two factors. The first was the need for battalion commanders to fill their unit quotas. Given the overwhelming response to recruitment, officers had little trouble meeting demands and, as the statistics show, filled initial positions with men predominantly of British origins. The second, and more likely, factor depended on the recruiters' racial perceptions of Indians within the dichotomy of the 'noble savage'. While many would have viewed Indians with disdain and rejected volunteers, others assumed Indians possessed martial talents and enrolled them accordingly.[87] Although 'race' was not recorded on enlistment documents, some recruiting officers listed 'Indian' under the section entitled 'Description of [Name] on Enlistment – Complexion' on the attestation form.[88] Many Indians circumvented the unofficial exclusionist policy, with or without the collusion of their commanding officers. The 1st Canadian Division, which disembarked in England on 14 October 1914, did contain a small number of Indian soldiers, as did the independent PPCLI Battalion, which included at least two Indians. Many of these Indian soldiers were snipers and scouts, including the famed Ojibwa sniper, Corporal Francis Pegahmagabow of the 1st Battalion. According to R. F. Haig of the Fort Garry Horse, some British civilians were disappointed to witness that the newly arrived colonial soldiers

---

[84] Dempsey, *Warriors of the King*, p. 21.
[85] LAC, RG24, vol. 1221, file 593-1-7. Correspondence: Ministry of Militia and Ministry of Indian Affairs, 1914–15.
[86] James W. St G. Walker, 'Race and Recruitment in World War I: Enlistment of Visible Minorities in the Canadian Expeditionary Force', *Canadian Historical Review* 70/1 (1989), 4–5.
[87] Sheffield, 'Indifference, Difference and Assimilation', 61–2.
[88] LAC, RG150, box 2648, 15–25. Personal Records First World War.

from Canada were not all red-skinned, decorated and dressed in feathers and pelts, wearing traditional headdress.[89]

Shortly after the declaration of war in August, there were numerous unsuccessful attempts to create all-Indian units throughout Canada, despite the fact that historically there was no such precedent. The first effort was made in October 1914 by Glen Campbell, Chief Inspector of Indian Agencies for western and northern Canada, and militia veteran of the 1885 North-West Rebellion. Campbell proposed the formation of a corps of scouts or irregular cavalry made up entirely of Indians, similar to the mounted infantry unit in which he confronted Métis/Cree forces during Louis Riel's second uprising.[90] Concurrently, in Alberta, the Reverend John McDougall, a Methodist missionary to the Alberta Indians, petitioned Indian Affairs, suggesting that: 'Indians at one time fought in battles amongst themselves, and some of them are the best scouts in the world ... I would suggest the taking of a certain number of Indians from each tribe and from each reserve, and making up a regiment of about 500.'[91]

On 1 November 1914, Colonel William Hamilton Merritt, honorary Chief of the Six Nations Iroquois, tried, as he had done during the Boer War, to arrange with the Ministry of Militia the formation of two Six Nations companies, which he personally offered to fund. He did not, however, consult the Six Nations Council. On 26 November, the council rejected the offer to mobilize a distinct regiment, asserting that they would only respond to a request from King George V. By allowing the Canadian government control of a Six Nations regiment, the council would tacitly acknowledge the government's jurisdiction, something they were not prepared to do. While the council supported the war effort, the decision was made to force the government to recognize the Six Nations Confederacy as a sovereign ally of Britain equal to the Dominion of Canada. According to Scott Trevithick, 'By making their acceptance conditional upon recognition of their independent political status the Chiefs hoped to force the government to make a concession. When the government did not, it provided a further affront to Six Nations nationalism.' The Militia Council in Ottawa had also decided that the offer was simply 'too inconvenient', and bluntly stated that

[89] Cook, *At the Sharp End*, p. 71.
[90] LAC, RG10, vol. 4063, reel C-10204, file 402890 – Correspondence Regarding the Appointment of Glen Campbell as Chief Inspector of Agencies, Reserves and Inspectorates in Manitoba, Saskatchewan, Alberta and the Northwest Territories; LAC, RG150, 1992–93/166, 1434. Service Records Glen Campbell.
[91] Dempsey, *Warriors of the King*, pp. 19–24.

'under no circumstances [would the government allow] the Canadian-Indians to furnish a contingent for war service in Europe'.[92]

All attempts to create all-Indian units or sub-units were rejected conjointly by the ministries of Indian Affairs and Militia throughout the early months of the war. Scores of requests, however, continued to be sent by band councils, Indian agents and private citizens to both ministries regarding the enlistment of individual Indians or the formation of Indian units. In response, Indian Affairs issued its first official statement concerning the individual enlistment of Indians, in a directive to all agents in late December 1914. It stated that men could enlist, but there was to be no direct recruiting on behalf of the agents themselves.[93] Despite this instruction, there remained confusion among Indian communities, their agents and district military commanders as to the regulations on Indian enlistment. This ambiguity was only rectified by the Ministry of Militia in December 1915, after the 1st Division had been drained of manpower in the 1915 battles at Ypres, Givenchy and Festubert. As the CEF expanded, and suffered greater losses, the need for manpower increased and governmental policy slowly shifted in favour of recruiting Indians to meet these mounting demands. Official policy, however, was only issued after the British requests for indigenous soldiers in October 1915.

Unlike the other Dominions, in August 1914, Newfoundland had no organizations, political or otherwise, devoted to defence. Although the government of Newfoundland, under Prime Minister Edward P. Morris, committed 500 men for imperial service on 8 August, there was no department or organization to oversee this, or any future, commitment. Furthermore, there was a dire lack of military experience or expertise in all parties of government and in the general populace of Newfoundland. More importantly, for Morris and his People's Party, any defence organization had to include Liberal and Union opposition party support, as the current government was a minority and its election in 1913 was based on regional and religious affiliations.

To appease the opposition, and safeguard power, Morris consulted the British Governor, Sir Walter Davidson, who agreed to shoulder the responsibility for leading Newfoundland's war effort. On 12 August, the Newfoundland Patriotic Association (NPA) was established, with Davidson at its head, to coordinate defence activities. This organization was a non-governmental, non-partisan body of fifty-five leading

---

[92] Lackenbauer and McGowan, 'Competing Loyalty in a Complex Community', 96–7.
[93] LAC, RG10, vol. 6762, reel C-8508, file 452-2-2. Memorandum: DIA to Indian Agents, December 1914.

men of St John's. Forty-five sub-committees, totalling 300 men, were established in outports under the control of local magistrates or influential citizens. While decisions rested with the NPA, no action could be taken until approval was given by both the prime minister and the leader of the opposition.[94] This arrangement lasted until the creation of an official Department of Militia in July 1917.

The NPA officially began recruitment on 22 August and by 28 September, 973 men had been enrolled in the Newfoundland Regiment, which was based on the standard size of a British battalion of roughly a thousand men.[95] Unlike the Newfoundland Regiment, the members of the Newfoundland branch of the Royal Naval Reserves were dispersed throughout the Royal Navy. On 2 August, the roughly five hundred active reservists were mobilized without difficulty. On 8 August, the imperial government authorized an increase in strength to a thousand sailors, and recruitment began in November. This goal was not met until April 1915. Davidson blamed the lack of recruits on the CO, Captain MacDermott, whom he believed to be 'just a waster ... he just loafed along'.[96]

On 4 October 1914, the first of twenty-seven Newfoundland contingents sailed for training in Britain. The 'first 500' (actually 540) arrived at Plymouth on 14 October, fearful that they would be amalgamated into a Canadian brigade. According to Captain J. E. J. Fox, 'there was the fear that our identity would be lost with some Canadian unit'.[97] Lieutenant Owen Steele further remarked that the members of the regiment were, 'very particular that [they] not be classified as Canadians ... much prouder of distinction as Newfoundlanders'.[98] This distinction was quickly made by their English hosts, as Private Frank Lind commented in a letter home: 'The English did not seem to know that Newfoundland is not Canada, but they thoroughly understand now that Newfoundland is NOT Canada and that we Newfoundlanders, NOT Canadians.'[99] Initially, imperial authorities suggested that the regiment join a battalion from Nova Scotia. The fear of amalgamation into the CEF, however, was allayed. Following the arrival of the second

[94] PANL, MG632, Patriotic Association of Newfoundland, 1914–19, file 1. Minutes 17 August 1914, 29 August 1914, 28 September 1914.
[95] Ibid.
[96] PANL, MG136, Sir Walter Davidson Papers, file 2.02.008. Diary Entry 1 December 1914.
[97] J. E. J. Fox, 'From Pleasantville to Englebeimer', *Veteran Magazine* 7/1 (1928), 69–70. Newfoundlanders were paid on par with Canadian rates.
[98] MF, 147: Diary of Owen Steele. Centre for Newfoundland Studies, Memorial University of Newfoundland. Letter of 2 December 1914.
[99] Frank Lind, *The Letters of Mayo Lind* (St John's: Robinson & Co., 1919), p. 23.

contingent, the Newfoundland Regiment, now at battalion strength, was shipped to Inverness, Scotland, for training in December 1914, safely isolated from the Canadians in southern England. The regiment remained distinct within the BEF for the duration of the war.[100]

The original members of the Newfoundland Regiment came primarily from St John's and the surrounding communities of the Avalon Peninsula. When recruiting was resumed after the sailing of the first contingent, only 68 of the 607 men enlisted between 30 November and 10 December 1914 came from outside St John's. Given the remoteness of many communities in Newfoundland and Labrador, including those of the majority of Eskimos, Mi'kmaq and Cree, recruiting efforts were confined to the more populated areas of the island.[101] From the onset of war, however, the NPA maintained that, 'Correspondence is being kept up with the Outport Recruiting Offices, with a view towards encouraging recruiting in the Outports.' Davidson believed that, 'when the Outports get going we shall have 1000 more'.[102] No indigenous men were part of the first contingent, and there was only one indigenous enlistment in 1914. Eskimo Joseph Michelin ('Complexion: Rather Dark, Eyes: Brown, Hair: Very Black') from Hamilton Inlet, Labrador, enlisted in St John's on 14 December 1914. The machine-gunner, a former 'fisherman and sailor', was wounded at Gallipoli on 29 November 1915. The circumstances of his anomalous enlistment are not known.[103]

War was generally met with a jingoistic outpouring in the British segments of the Dominions and support for the imperial government was given in the form of men, material and money. While outwardly supporting the empire, Australia, South Africa and New Zealand harboured sub-imperialist ambitions and, as the war progressed, nationalism became more pronounced in all Dominions. Although not engaged in the main theatres of war, by the end of 1914 Dominion soldiers had participated in 'sideshow' campaigns, and the training of substantial expeditionary forces had commenced.

The outward support for the war given by indigenous leaders in all Dominions did not in all cases reflect the opinions of those whom they

[100] PANL, MG632, Patriotic Association of Newfoundland, 1914–19, file 21b. Correspondence from Prime Minister's Office, 1915.
[101] PANL, MG632, Patriotic Association of Newfoundland, 1914–19, file 1. Minutes 11 December 1914, 30 March 1915.
[102] PANL, MG632, Patriotic Association of Newfoundland, 1914–19, file 1. Minutes 11 September 1914; MG136, Sir Walter Davidson Papers, file 2.02.008. Diary Entry 1 December 1914.
[103] PANL, GN19, B-2-3, reel 56. Service Records Joseph Michelin.

purportedly represented. Many indigenous peoples, in all Dominions, did not support the recruitment of indigenous soldiers for a European war. This was no different from the divisions within the European populations in the Dominions and should be viewed as such. In Canada, most French-Canadians did not support the war effort. In South Africa, opposition was voiced by segments of the Afrikaner population, some to the point of open rebellion. In Australia, many Irish immigrants voiced their disapproval – 23 per cent of the total population being of Irish-Catholic descent.[104]

Offers of indigenous troops were made (and recorded) by the literate and often politically motivated elite, within the indigenous communities. The Maori committee's near-fanatical attitude about Maori inclusion in the war effort must be viewed within this contemporary context. Pomare's assertion, about the 'rush of the Maori to offer his life in the nation's service', was far more evident in the actions of the committee than within actual Maoridom.[105] The South African elite, as SANNC President Dube expressed it in 1917, 'were not loyal because their treatment was good in South Africa, but because they wanted to show that they were loyal and that they were deserving of fair and just treatment'.[106]

For indigenous leaders, participation in the war by way of offering support directly to the Crown was viewed as a means to force or lobby the imperial government to pressure the Dominions to alter oppressive laws to allow full and equal inclusion. Members of both the SANNC and the Maori King Movement were in England advocating and petitioning the British government for precisely this when war was declared. The SANNC remarked that the African elite were, 'far too loyal to England to entertain for one moment the idea of active resistance to the laws of this [South Africa] country'. In Canada, the actions of the Six Nations Council surrounding the creation of a distinct Six Nations battalion offers no better example of the recognition of this demand and belief. Many other indigenous leaders also cited treaties, and offered support, in the name of Queen Victoria, to illustrate this principle, while seeking acknowledgement of sovereignty from both their respective Dominion governments and the Crown.

---

[104] Robb, *British Culture and the First World War*, p. 27.
[105] King, *Te Puea*, pp. 80–1.
[106] Grundlingh, *Fighting Their Own War*, p. 14.

6   1915–1916: King and country call

By the close of 1914, the 125,000 'old contemptibles' of the BEF had suffered 90,000 casualties. Although the Dominions mobilized expeditionary forces and conducted training both at home and abroad, no Dominion forces participated in major campaigns during 1914. During 1915 and 1916, Dominion forces expanded and became key components of the fighting strength of the BEF on the Western Front and at Gallipoli. High casualty rates accompanied this participation, and the swelling expeditionary forces required increasing reinforcements to sustain these national formations. The escalating overall strength of Allied armies was accompanied by the immediate need for service and support auxiliaries, such as labour battalions, forestry corps and pioneer battalions. Britain increasingly looked to her Dominions as a source of men and materials. Amplified Dominion participation, however, was accompanied by greater demands for inclusion in strategic and operational counsel by Dominion prime ministers to satisfy nascent domestic national consciousness.

Within this general atmosphere, in October 1915, the War Office issued the three most important imperial documents of the war pertaining to indigenes of all Dominions. Inclusion of indigenes in Dominion forces and the alteration of Dominion policies between 1915 and 1917 were directly allied to these requests of the imperial government. While scholars of individual nations have noted the drastic shift in specific Dominion policy towards greater inclusion after October 1915, not one has referenced these documents, or offered a comparative explanation for the collective shift towards the inclusion and recruitment of indigenes for expeditionary forces. The level of inclusion varied within the Dominions and was based on pragmatic requirements, domestic attitudes and contemporary racial philosophies and anxieties. These decrees also affected the formation and deployment of indigenous expeditionary forces from other British colonies and protectorates, and the inclusion of other minorities in Dominion formations. Moreover, these British decisions directly

influenced France to alter policy and practice concerning the recruitment and tenure of colonial soldiers.

On 8 October 1915, all governors-general and administrators of
British Dominions and colonies received a confidential memorandum
from the Canadian-born Colonial Secretary, Andrew Bonar Law:[1]

The [War] Cabinet have asked for a report as to the possibilities of raising
native troops in large numbers in our Colonies + Protectorates for Imperial
service. What is wanted is an estimate of the numbers that could be raised; the
length of time needed for training; an opinion as to their fighting value; and
any pertinent remarks on such points as climatic restrictions on their employment, the influence of religion … + the difficulty of officering.[2]

Ten days later, on the 18th, the Colonial Office issued a memorandum solely to the five Dominions, specifically addressing the question
of raising native troops from South Africa for imperial service:

The *Union of South Africa* is the only one of the self-governing Dominions
which need be considered in this connection. There are a number of warlike
natives – Zulus, Matabele, Basutos, &c. – south of the Zambezi [River], but it
would not be practicable to raise a force of natives without the consent of the
Union Government. No proposal for training natives upon a large scale is likely
to be acceptable to that Government or to the British or Dutch inhabitants of
the Union, as the return, after peace, of a large body of trained and disciplined
black men would create obvious difficulties, and might seriously menace the
supremacy of the white. With the possible exception of the Basutos, no South
African native could stand a European winter – even the Basuto is liable to
pneumonia. It is conceivable, assuming the Union Government would consent, that a corps of, at most, a few thousand natives might be trained and sent
to the Persian Gulf to relieve the Indian troops now serving there.[3]

A third request, encompassing the indigenes of all Dominions, was
forwarded on 25 October. War exigencies now required the military
inclusion of indigenous men.

On 9 October 1915, one day after the first British memorandum, the
French issued a decree extending war contracts of all French indigenous colonials for the duration of the war. On 19 October, one day after
the second British memorandum, the French issued another decree

---

[1] On 25 May 1915, Law replaced Harcourt as Colonial Secretary. He was born in New
Brunswick and moved to Glasgow at the age of 12. He remains the only British Prime
Minister to have been born outside of the United Kingdom.
[2] Andrew Bonar Law Papers, BL/55/16. Memorandum: Colonial Office to Governors-
General and Administrators of British Dominions, Colonies and Protectorates,
8 October 1915.
[3] Andrew Bonar Law Papers, BL/55/16. Cabinet Memorandum to the Dominions:
The Question of Raising Native Troops for Imperial Service, 18 October 1915. (Also
contained in Harcourt Papers, 445.) *Italics* are original.

placing all colonials under French military law and 'recruitment' of French Indo-Chinese labourers was accelerated. On 16 August 1916, all French colonial contracts were extended for the duration of the war plus six months. By the end of the war, 40,000 French Indo-Chinese labourers had served, predominantly on the Western Front, but also in Mesopotamia and Macedonia. In total, 845,000 French colonial 'natives' served in various roles in the First World War, 500,000 of these in Europe.[4] In 1920, African-American political activist, W. E. B. Du Bois, remarked that, 'the darker world is held in subjugation to Europe by its own darker soldiers'.[5]

In 1914, the New Zealand Department of Defence, in consultation with the War Office, and in partnership with the Maori committee, began the process of organizing, training and deploying to Egypt a Maori Contingent for garrison duty. The issue of using the Contingent in a combatant role had been raised by Godley on 10 January 1915, and was revisited during the final inspection of the Contingent on 6 February 1915 by Lieutenant-Colonel Hume, commander of the Auckland Military District: 'I am of the opinion, however, that two capable Company Commanders, who are not Maoris, are necessary, if the Contingent is to be employed in active operations in the field.'[6] The Contingent sailed from Wellington on 14 February, onboard the SS *Wairrimoo*, bound for Egypt. Carkeek wrote that for 'the first time in New Zealand history did all the tribes unite to fight one common enemy'.[7]

The *Wairrimoo* docked at Albany, Western Australia, on 25 February. Lending credence to Maori health concerns, Major Peacock, seriously ill with typhoid contracted from his soldiers, was returned to New Zealand. He was subsequently designated commander of the Maori training camp at Narrow Neck, Auckland.[8] Private Carkeek recorded, in his Albany diary entry, that upon going ashore, 'I spotted one or two Aborigines'. On another occasion, while moored at Colombo, Ceylon (Sri Lanka), Carkeek commented on the native population: 'They are a very scraggy looking people with poor physique … It's nothing but beg, beg, beg everywhere you go. "Sir, sir – meester – penny please!"' Upon arrival in 'Gypoland' (Egypt), he recounts the 'natives were

---

[4] See: Richard S. Fogarty, *Race and War in France: Colonial Subjects in the French Army, 1914–1918* (Baltimore: The Johns Hopkins University Press, 2008).

[5] Killingray, *Guardians of Empire*, p. 10; Vandervort, *Wars of Imperial Conquest in Africa*, p. 213.

[6] ANZ, AD1, box 1062, record 39/91. Inspection Report, 6 February 1915.

[7] Carkeek, *Home Little Maori Home*, pp. 9, 15–17.

[8] ANZ, AD1, box 1062, record 39/110. Progress Reports 3rd Reinforcements and Maori Contingent.

selling "Oringis"'.[9] For the Maori, other indigenous peoples, including Aborigines, provided a sense of curiosity and comparison. The official Australian war correspondent, Charles E. W. Bean, noted that, 'the New Zealand men are not used to dealing with "real niggers" and place them on the same level with Maoris'.[10] When docked at Cape Town, Percival McIntosh, RSM of the New Zealand Contingent, noted the higher qualities of the Maori, compared with the 'local kaffirs of South Africa'.[11]

The 508-man Maori Contingent arrived in Egypt on 26 March. On 18 March, Major A. H. Herbert had been given command in succession to Peacock. After training in Egypt, prior to the Contingent's deployment to Malta as garrison troops, the Maori made an impact on Godley, who had previously been suspicious of their abilities.[12] In a report to Allen on 2 April, Godley commented that the Maori had 'behaved extremely well and have earned golden opinions by their smartness and bearing and general efficiency. We all think very well of them, and I am sorry they are not coming with us [to Gallipoli] ... the Maoris would be a valuable reinforcement for my Division and I should be very glad to have them with me.' Godley also reported that General Sir Ian Hamilton, commander of the Mediterranean Expeditionary Force, had cabled Lord Kitchener expressing the Maori 'desire to serve and fight with the New Zealanders, and that he [Hamilton] recommends that they be allowed to do so'.[13]

On 3 April, it was arranged that the Maori Contingent perform war dances, *hakas* and songs for senior commanders and dignitaries. Many Maori soldiers resented the fact that they were seen as a travelling show and were not deemed 'good enough to fight' (see Figure 6.1). Captain Buck announced during a speech that, 'We would sooner die from the bullets of the enemy than from sickness and disease ... Though we are only a handful, the remnant of the remnant of the people ... we are the old New Zealanders. No division can be truly called a New Zealand Division unless it numbers Maoris in its ranks ... Give us an opportunity for active service with our white kinsmen.'[14] Nevertheless, on 4 April, while Anzac readied for Gallipoli, the Maori Contingent was sent to

---

[9] Carkeek, *Home Little Maori Home*, pp. 20, 25, 29.
[10] Belich, *Paradise Reforged*, p. 107.
[11] Queen Elizabeth II Military Museum (QEII MM), record 1999.3226. RSM Percival McIntosh, 12 August 1918.
[12] ANZ, AD1, box 734, record 9/32/1. Memorandum: Mediterranean Force HQ to Hamilton, 18 March 1915.
[13] ANZ, AD1, box 734, record 9/32/1. Godley and Allen, 2 April 1915, 5 April 1915.
[14] J. B. Condliffe, *Te Rangi Hiroa: The Life of Sir Peter Buck* (Christchurch: Whitcombe & Tombs, 1971), pp. 126–8.

Figure 6.1 The Maori Pioneer Battalion welcoming Prime Minister William F. Massey and Sir Joseph G. Ward with a *haka* at Bois-de-Warnimont, France, June 1918.

Malta. Anzac landed on the Gallipoli peninsula, on 25 April, alongside British and French units, and indigenous troops from India, the Orient and Senegal, and was followed by the Newfoundland Regiment.[15]

On 2 May 1915, with mounting casualties at Gallipoli, Harcourt informed Allen that the 'ARMY COUNCIL propose sending MAORIS on SERVICE ... and ask whether New Zealand Government can supply drafts of 250 men every THREE MONTHS'. On 8 May, senior officers of the Maori Contingent expressed the desire to form a complete battalion and requested reinforcements, 'if not enough Maori then Pakehas'. On 12 May, the Maori committee and Allen approved active service for the Maori Contingent, adding that a first reinforcement of 300 Maori would be raised. Allen added that it was 'difficult to guarantee further Maori Reinforcements but it seems probable that a third could be sent'.[16]

---

[15] The 29th British Indian Infantry Brigade, 26th Indian Mountain Battery and the French Oriental Expeditionary Corps (including four Senegalese Battalions) landed at Gallipoli.

[16] ANZ, AD1, box 734, record 9/32/1. Harcourt to Allen, 2 May 1915; Herbert to CGS Wellington, 8 May 1915; Allen to Liverpool, 12 May 1915.

The committee insisted that the Department of Defence be responsible for recruiting reinforcements. The committee avoided active recruiting in order not to upset elders and chiefs, many of whom were opposed to Maori military service, primarily in Waikato and Taranaki. Chiefs from the Bay of Islands wrote to Massey, 'the word of Queen Victoria ... was that her Maori people were to die in New Zealand, and were not to die in foreign lands'.[17] In June 1915, Allen made reference to this issue in relation to Maori reinforcements in a letter to Godley: '[W]hether we shall be able to keep the Maori reinforcements is difficult to say, as the Maoris seem to have a disposition not to serve led by some of their chiefs who are beginning to feel sore over the land question [1913 Native Land Amendment Act]'.[18]

The decision to deploy the Maori Contingent to Gallipoli was based on two themes relating to manpower. The first was the competition between Dominions. On 4 March 1915, Prime Minister Massey confidentially cabled his Canadian counterpart, Borden, without the collusion of the other Dominions or of the Colonial and War offices: 'Have you any objection to telegraphing me strictly confidential number men Canada has already sent to the front, secondly number men in train[ing] and thirdly what Canada intends to do for the future in this connection'.[19] New Zealand was determined to keep pace with Canada and Australia. Secondly, at Gallipoli, the New Zealand Brigade suffered 700 casualties during the initial landings. By 8 May, total casualties for the brigade exceeded 2,000. The NZEF needed reinforcements. Given its proximity to Gallipoli, the Maori Contingent was mobilized.

The Maori continued training at Malta as a pioneer battalion, where they were exposed to a variety of soldiers of other nationalities. Given that Malta was the choke-point for casualties evacuated from Gallipoli, the Maori interacted with soldiers from across the British and French empires (see Figure 6.2). According to Godley: 'I am glad to say that the Maoris are coming here [Gallipoli] ... It is still noticeable that there are a good many people who do not know the difference between Australians and New Zealanders, and who think the Maoris are savages.'[20] The Mediterranean Expeditionary Force Headquarters asked Godley if the Maori had any special dietary or other requirements: 'I replied that there were 500 of them but the question of their diet should offer no

[17] ANZ, AD1, box 734, record 9/32/1. Chiefs of the Bay of Islands to Massey, 30 September 1914.
[18] King, *Te Puea*, p. 82.
[19] Department of External Affairs, *Documents on Canadian External Relations*, p. 65. Massey to Borden, 5 March 1915.
[20] ANZ, AD1, box 734, record 9/32/1. Godley to Allen, 24 June 1915.

Figure 6.2 Maori diggers at Malta, May 1915.

difficulty as I trusted that, during their stay with the Division, enough Turks would be killed or taken prisoner to go round [eaten]. Sir Ian [Hamilton] was much amused.'[21]

The decision to employ the Maori as pioneers reflected the realization that at present strength (roughly five hundred), in conjunction with the uncertainty of further recruitment to replace casualties, the Contingent was not large enough to form an infantry battalion.[22] Pioneers were primarily infantry soldiers trained to perform basic combat engineering assignments in the front lines. However, they were not support troops, like those of entrenching battalions, railway companies or tunnelling companies, nor were they educated and skilled engineers, like those of the engineering field companies. Pioneers were armed, trained in infantry tactics and employed in combat roles when not performing minor engineering tasks, such as installing

[21] Alexander Turnbull Library, P920GOD1949. Godley to Arthur Lord Kilbracken, 3 July 1915.
[22] Pugsley, *Te Hokowhitu A Tu*, p. 34.

communication wire, building trenches and erecting defensive obstacles. There is no justification to support James Cowan's assertion that the pioneer role was selected because Maori were acknowledged by the government in the following way: 'Coming from a race of fort-builders, the Maori soldier was a natural military engineer ... the military genius of the race was recognized.'[23]

Given the need for more men, in June the maximum weight restriction for Maori was raised to 13.5 stone (189 pounds), 'provided that Medical Examiner is satisfied men are fit otherwise'.[24] Lieutenant-Colonel Malone, commander of the Wellington Battalion, described the Maori as 'mostly big hulking gone-in-the-knees walking men. I think the War Lords don't quite know what to do with them.' One Maori officer weighed 275 pounds.[25] Military standards were being circumvented to meet Maori enlistment needs before any casualties had been sustained. In addition, Maori, training with other units, were given the opportunity, if desired, to be transferred to the Maori training base at Long Neck.[26]

When the 477-strong Maori Contingent landed at Anzac Cove on 3 July 1915, many Maori soldiers had long since been involved in the fighting at Gallipoli. According to Christopher Pugsley, 'The nominal rolls and casualty lists of both the infantry and mounted rifles of New Zealand Expeditionary Force show they [Maori] were in every unit from the 6th Haurakis, the 11th Taranakis, and the Auckland and Wellington Mounted Rifles ... They had enlisted in the companies of the provincial battalions, not conscious or concerned about race.'[27]

The Maori Contingent was initiated into combat in the Battle of Sari Bair (6–21 August 1915). Maori losses between 6 and 9 August were: seventeen killed, eighty-nine wounded and two missing, excluding those who were in hospital with sickness and disease. Following the battle, commanders, including Generals Hamilton and Birdwood, praised the performance of the Maori.[28] Godley wrote to Allen reiterating that, 'All speak most highly of the individual bravery and courage of the men, and of their gallantry during the fight.' However, Godley concluded that excess Maori casualties were suffered because they were

[23] Cowan, *The Maoris in the Great War*, pp. 3–4.
[24] ANZ, AD1, box 757, record 9/276, parts 1–2. Maori Force Memorandum to all Districts, 10 June 1915.
[25] Gardiner, *Te Mura O Te Ahi*, p. 18.
[26] ANZ, AD1, box 757, record 9/276, parts 1–2. LCol. Hume to NZMF HQ, 23 June 1915.
[27] Pugsley, *Te Hokowhitu A Tu*, p. 36.
[28] Andrew Bonar Law Papers, BL/56/XI/4. Hamilton to Kitchener, 11 August 1915: 'The Mounted Rifles and the Maori Contingent were conspicuous by their gallantry.'

a small independent unit and that they 'would be better off in one of our New Zealand Brigades'. While he thought the performance of the majority of Maori junior officers and men 'upheld the warlike traditions of their race', Godley criticized both Maori company commanders and two other 'troublesome Maori officers'. He also revealed that he had broken up the Maori Contingent, attaching one-half of a company to each battalion of the infantry brigade, to provide reinforcements and also to allow the Maori to fight alongside 'fellow-countrymen of the Dominion' – a malleable explanation for legitimate practicality and clandestine assimilation.[29]

The break-up of an identifiable Maori unit and the public disgrace of these officers compounded problems that existed between Major Herbert and many of his Maori officers, and added to the political stalemate between the Maori committee and the government of New Zealand. Shortly before the Battle of Sari Bair, Herbert requested a Maori second-in-command: '[M]ilitary education will not be required so much as [to] have complete knowledge of language and customs to act as a go between, between CO and other officers. He must be of high standing, influence and mana.' Herbert's ability to communicate with his Maori soldiers was hampered, as not all spoke English. Certain officers misinterpreted, on occasions deliberately, his commands and instructions, despite the persistent efforts of Captain Buck and Maori chaplains, who acted as intermediaries. Privately, Godley believed Herbert and thought the handicap was that officers had been chosen by the Maori committee with little regard for military competence.[30] However, it was Godley himself who had originally proposed this arrangement at the outset of the creation of the Maori Contingent.

On 3 September, three Maori officers left Egypt for New Zealand. The fourth was medically discharged. The discrediting of these officers and the dissolving of a distinct Maori unit immediately aroused the ire of the Maori committee: 'We could not ourselves go before our people to ask for further men to reinforce a Maori Contingent that does not exist … you should understand that it was the existence of the force as a unit, however small, representing the Maori race alongside other races fighting for the one flag … that the recruiting Maori tribes had always before them.'[31]

---

[29] ANZ, AD10, box 20, record 42/4. Godley to Allen, 20 August 1915.

[30] ANZ, AD1, box 734, record 9/32/1. Godley to Allen, 24 July 1915; O'Connor, 'The Recruitment of Maori Soldiers', 55–8; Gardiner, *Te Mura O Te Ahi*, pp. 20–1.

[31] ANZ, AD1, box 734, record 9/32/1. Maori Committee to Department of Defence, 9 December 1915.

The October imperial memorandum, the unyielding objections of the committee and the enlargement of the NZEF all influenced the reconstitution of a distinct Maori Contingent. On 7 December 1915, the committee presented Allen with correspondence outlining several key demands: that the returned officers be reinstated; that the Maori Contingent be reconstituted into one body; that all Maori in *Pakeha* units and camps be transferred to the Contingent or to Narrow Neck camp; and that Lieutenant-Colonel Herbert be replaced by Captain Peacock.[32] Over the next several months, these demands were met by the Department of Defence. In actuality, by September 1915 there were only sixty Maori active at Gallipoli. By the time of the evacuation of Anzac on 14 December 1915, the Maori Contingent's marching state was 2 officers and 132 other ranks.[33]

As of December 1915, all Maori serving in other units were again invited to join or train as reinforcements for the Maori Contingent, 'although I [Allen] did not feel it was right to compel them'. Secondly, on 25 December, in what all evidence points to as a favour to the Maori committee, Godley relented and reinstated all three returned officers for overseas service, under the stipulation that they would not be placed in a position higher than platoon commanders, where their 'future conduct and efficiency will be judged'. In addition, in early January 1916, Herbert was assigned to General Base Depot, in Cairo, on the nominal role of NZEF HQ; however, Peacock was still too ill to command.[34] Godley maintained that the re-creation of a separate Maori unit was inadvisable, given that he would be forced to give them a non-combat role, which would be sure to anger the Maori population and committee: 'I have explained to the Contingent, (and I hope it is clearly understood in New Zealand), that the incorporation of the Contingent into the New Zealand Brigade is done purely in the interests of the contingent and of the Maori Race ... Their fighting efficiency will be made much greater.'[35]

The Maori committee's threat to halt recruiting was evident from the fact that only 120 Maori were training at Narrow Neck camp in January 1916. However, a New Zealand Division had been formed under Godley's command in January 1916, and became part of

---

[32] ANZ, AD10, box 20, record 42/4. Allen to Major-General Sir Alfred Robin, CGS, 7 December 1915.
[33] ANZ, WA97, box 3/1. Numerical Roll and Gallipoli.
[34] ANZ, AD10, box 20, record 42/4. Allen to CGS, 7 December 1915; AD1, box 734, record 9/32/1. Correspondence: Allen, Godley and Maori Committee, 24 January 1916.
[35] ANZ, AD10, box 20, record 42/4. Godley to Allen, 20 October 1915.

I Anzac Corps (II Anzac Corps as of July 1916). This re-organization provided the opportunity to end the political stand-off and reunite all Maori soldiers into a single unit.[36] On 20 February, the New Zealand Pioneer Battalion was formed piecemeal from the remnants of the original Maori Contingent and the newly arrived 2nd and 3rd contingents, which formed two companies, including officers. *Pakeha* soldiers from the depleted Otago Mounted Rifles and the New Zealand Mounted Rifles formed the other two companies. The Battalion's regimental badge consisted of a Maori warrior's tattooed face above a crossed pick and axe, and the inscription 'NZ Pioneers'. Maori platoons remained organized according to tribal affiliations.[37] Godley proposed to Allen that, 'All the Maori reinforcements will be posted to this battalion and eventually it will become practically entirely Maori ... I am very glad to be able to meet your wishes and those of the Maori so fully.'[38]

Immediately, there were complaints from members of the Maori community regarding the 'degradation of the Maori Military contingent from first-line soldiers to pioneers'. These complaints, however, came from private citizens. The Maori committee did not protest, as all of their original demands had been met. Although the battalion was not solely Maori, all Maori were now collected under one command, save for those refusing to be transferred from other units. Allen assured the committee, asking them to relay the message to Maori chiefs and communities that, 'Maoris need have no cause for disquiet regarding their transfer to a Pioneer Battalion. The Pioneer Battalion takes seniority of an Infantry of the Line.' The members of the Otago Mounted Rifles were also angry at losing their identity and becoming pioneers.[39]

The newly promoted New Zealand divisional commander, Major-General Sir Andrew Russell, recognized the difficulties surrounding the unit and placed a very competent major, George Augustus King, a regular officer of the Staff Corps, in command. Captain Buck was persuaded to fill the role of second-in-command. It was also arranged that all future Maori reinforcements would join the Battalion, with a view to creating a homogenous Maori unit. All company commanders were

---

[36] O'Connor, 'The Recruitment of Maori Soldiers', 60.

[37] ANZ, AD1, box 734, record 9/32/1. Department of Defence Press Release, 13 March 1916; Pugsley, *Te Hokowhitu A Tu*, 45.

[38] Joseph F. Cody, *Man of Two Worlds: Sir Maui Pomare* (Wellington: A. H. and A. W. Reed, 1953), p. 118.

[39] ANZ, AD1, box 734, record 9/32/1. Fred J. Foot to Hon. Dr R. McNab, 27 May 1916; Allen to Maori Committee, 12 June 1916.

Pakeha, while all company second-in-command positions were filled by Maori, except one.[40] According to Captain Buck:

> In the evacuation of Anzac ... there were no Maori Platoon Officers left ... All who have come through the Gallipoli Campaign ... where the Pakeha and Maori have shared ... recognize that the Maori is a better man than they gave him credit for and have admitted him to full fellowship and equality ... make this known to the Maori Race in order that recruiting may be kept up ... we will emerge from this war, with a higher respect for ourselves and receiving higher not only from New Zealanders but from the peoples of the British Empire.[41]

The 3rd Maori Contingent arrived at Suez to join the newly formed Pioneer Battalion on 16 March. In addition to 111 Maori, this reinforcement also consisted of 140 Niue Islanders and 47 Rarotongans. Soldiers who were classified as Rarotongans and Niue Islanders also came from: Samoa, Fiji, Norfolk Island, Tonga, Hawaii, Society Islands, Tahiti, Chatham Islands, Gilbert Islands (Kiribati), Ocean Island, Penrhyn Island and the French territory of the Tuamotus.[42]

At the outbreak of war, the Resident Commissioner of Niue, H. G. Cornwall, immediately offered a Niue Expeditionary Force to New Zealand, made up of European officers and indigenous soldiers. Only thirty islanders, out of a total population of roughly four thousand, were European. By November 1914, 200 to 250 soldiers were training as the 1st Niue Regiment, under the control of Cornwall and Sergeant Frederick Holmes, chief constable and a Boer War veteran.[43] On many of the individual Cook Islands, such as Rarotonga, Mauke and Atiu, military training was also being conducted, under the command of the resident agents and local constabularies. Both the Cook Islands and Niue also raised £117 and £165 respectively for the New Zealand Red Cross Fund.[44]

Recruitment for the 2nd and 3rd Maori contingents had been markedly lower than expected (especially in Pomare's Western Maori district, which included King Country), partially due to the fact that the Maori unit had been disbanded. In a transparent design of Maori

---

[40] ANZ, AD1, box 1108, record 43/175. Appointment Second in Command Maori Contingent; AD1, box 734, record 9/32/1. Godley to Allen, 7 March 1916.

[41] ANZ, WA1, box 1/4/2, record 11. Sir James Carroll to Maori Contingent, January 1916; Buck to Carroll and Maori Committee, 13 January 1916.

[42] ANZ, AD78, box 6, record 22/4. Memorandum: Secretary of NZEF Demobilization Sub-committee, 12 September 1918.

[43] Margaret Pointer with Kalaisi Folau, *Tagi Tote E Loto Haaku – My Heart is Crying a Little: Niue Island Involvement in the Great War, 1914–1918* (Niue: Oceania Printers, 2000), pp. 4–6.

[44] Dick Scott, *Years of the Pooh-Bah: A Cook Islands History* (Auckland: Hodder and Stoughton, 1991), pp. 131–3; Pointer, *Tagi Tote E Loto Haaku*, p. 4.

sub-imperialism, Pomare, realizing that the Maori Contingent could only be reconstituted if appropriate reinforcements were forthcoming, saw the islands under his ministerial control as a source of 'nominal Maori' manpower. In September 1915, the 'Cook Island Maori' Contingent arrived in Wellington and was led into Parliament by Pomare, ironically, to sing for the assembled politicians. At his own desire, Pomare sailed to Niue in October 1915 to raise a contingent.[45]

Although the minimum enlistment age for the NZEF was still 20, no official birth or marriage records were kept on Niue, and many under-age soldiers were part of the Niue contingent. Many enlistment papers record only '1895' as the date of birth as this was the year that 'officially' made recruits 20 years of age.[46] Similarly, in November 1915 Pomare instructed the Cook Islands Resident Commissioner, Henry William Northcroft, to lower height restrictions to 158 cm (5 foot, 2 inches) and to take 'anyone over 18'.[47] It appears that Pomare, given his ministerial position and the ignorance of the islanders (due to their isolation), was circumventing official policy in order to secure more soldiers, in the hope of pressing for a reconstituted Maori Contingent.

The 1st Niue Regiment arrived in New Zealand on 19 October 1915 and problems were immediately evident. Although Holmes, who accompanied them to Narrow Neck as sergeant-major, spoke some Niuean, only ten to twelve soldiers spoke fragmented English. Only one (a teacher) was competent and he acted as the interpreter. The remainder were given ranks, ranging from sergeant to lance-corporal, based simply on their ability to speak some English. Secondly, the Niueans were not accustomed to wearing any sort of footwear or heavy clothing, and the introduction of boots created numerous medical problems, as did the bulky military uniforms. In addition, the food issued at Narrow Neck was unlike their usual island diet and was, as they complained, heavy on meat and the 'animal flesh was not cooked'. Health and digestive tract problems ensued until their diet was altered to include less meat and more fresh fish and fruit. Lastly, they were very susceptible to climatic changes and suffered increased health problems, as they had less immunity to disease compared even with Maori. Allen advised Godley that, 'there are great difficulties encountered in fitting them for active service ... I do not quite see how you will get on with them when we send them to you.' Allen also alluded to

---

[45] ANZ, AD1, box 813, record 13/148. Cook Islanders Joining Maori Contingent; MA1, box 376, record 19/1/473. Maori Battalion Embarkation Rolls, 1914–18.

[46] Pointer, *Tagi Tote E Loto Haaku*, p. 11.

[47] Scott, *Years of the Pooh-Bah*, p. 133.

the possibility that they should remain in the warm climates of Egypt as garrison troops.[48]

By April 1916, 52 per cent of the Niue Contingent was hospitalized with illness. On 7 April, only sixty Niueans were part of the 976-strong Pioneer Battalion that struck camp in Egypt for the Western Front. After familiarization training near Hazebrouck, the Pioneer Battalion was sent forward on 15 May near Armentières. Niuean soldiers continued to be hospitalized with sickness and the majority had persistent troubles with the weather of northern France. In late May, all Niuean soldiers were returned to Niue, with only 18 per cent of the total completing the round-trip without having been hospitalized. The experiment was not repeated and no more Niueans were enlisted for service.[49]

There were two more reinforcements of Rarotongans in July 1916 and February 1918, totalling 268 men; however, due to climatic concerns, these soldiers were sent not to the Western Front but to the Middle East. At the armistice, a fourth contingent of ninety-three men was training at Narrow Neck, with a fifth contingent being recruited. Although the Niueans were rotated out of the Pioneer Battalion and discharged, the initial contingent of Rarotongans remained in France until January 1918, whereupon it joined the main body of Rarotongans deployed to Palestine.[50]

In late August 1916, the Pioneer Battalion was the first New Zealand unit to move to the Somme front. According to Pugsley, it was the British units, with which the Pioneer Battalion initially served, that created the nickname 'diggers', because the work of the battalion involved digging trenches. This nickname was then gradually applied to all soldiers of the two Anzac Corps.[51] The first New Zealand action on the Western Front came at the Battle of Flers-Courcelette (15–22 September 1916), in conjunction with the Canadian Corps. Maori casualties on the 15th alone were twelve killed and forty wounded. After the battle, Pomare wrote to Buck, celebrating that, 'Your boys have proved beyond a doubt what the race is capable of' (see Figure 6.3).[52]

In France, Maori soldiers found comfort in their collectiveness and continued certain traditional practices. The unit had one Maori chaplain

[48] Pointer, *Tagi Tote E Loto Haaku*, pp. 18–22.
[49] ANZ, AD1, box 869, record 24/146. Niue Islanders: Instructions Discharge; Pointer, *Tagi Tote E Loto Haaku*, pp. 38–45.
[50] ANZ, MA1, box 376, record 19/1/473. Maori Battalion Embarkation Rolls, 1914–18; Scott, *Years of the Pooh-Bah*, pp. 136, 140.
[51] Pugsley, *Te Hokowhitu A Tu*, p. 55.
[52] Christopher Pugsley, 'The Maori Battalion in France in the First World War' in John Dunmore (ed.), *The French and the Maori* (Waikanae, New Zealand: The Heritage Press, 1992), p. 146.

Figure 6.3 'The Spirit of his Fathers': from the *New Zealand Observer*, Christmas Issue December 1915.

for each company and Maori nurses were present in New Zealand field hospitals.[53] During Christmas 1916, Maori soldiers bought pigs and fowl and cooked traditional *hangi*. During leave or when billeted in rear rest areas, many Maori helped French farmers with their crops and gardens, and marvelled at some of the most recent technological equipment and techniques, and the fact that women also worked the fields.

[53] ANZ, AD1, box 1339, record 59/152. Chaplains Maori Contingent, Prisoners of War; AD1, box 758, record 9/296. Allen to Pomare, 3 September 1915.

Like all soldiers, they frequented the estaminets, and performed Maori dances and songs for French civilians and other soldiers: 'On one occasion … a hall was cleared of young women because of the ferocity of these New Zealand "dances".'[54]

Aside from the PPCLI, the 1st Canadian Division was the first Dominion unit to participate in a major theatre of war. The division arrived in France on 16 February 1915. On 3 March, battalions entered the lines at Fleurbaix and took part sparingly in the Battle of Neuve Chapelle (10–13 March 1915). The 1st Division suffered 320 casualties in March, in what was labelled a 'familiarization period'. During its tour in the Ypres salient, between 15 April and 3 May, the division suffered 6,104 casualties out of roughly 16,500 engaged (37 per cent) – the majority between 22 and 25 April. During these four days, although the number of Indians present in the division was small, eight became casualties, including five killed.

The day of 22 April is likely to have seen the death of the first Canadian Indian in the First World War. Private Angus Laforce, a Mohawk from Kahnawake, Quebec, went missing on the evening of 22 April. The following day, Lieutenant Cameron D. Brant of the Six Nations of the Grand River, great-great-grandson of Joseph Brant, was killed leading his men in a counter-attack. His body was never recovered. His commanding officer, Lieutenant-Colonel Arthur Birchall, a Briton on loan to the CEF, remarked that Brant was 'quiet and unobtrusive [but] The Boys will follow him everywhere'. Like his forefathers, Cameron was a worthy ally of the British Crown, prompting Six Nations elders to predict that, 'such nobility of purpose and sacrifice of life will go far to further cement the many units of our citizenship into one great unified front'.[55]

Private Albert Mountain Horse, a Blood from Alberta, described the fighting at Ypres in a letter to his brother Mike:

As I am writing this letter the shrapnel is bursting over our heads. I was in the thick of the fighting at Ypres and we had to get out of it. The Germans were using the poisonous gas on our men – oh it was awful – it is worse than anything I know of. I don't mind the rifle fire and the shells bursting around us, but this gas is the limit. I have a German helmet I want to give you … my it's a good one. I took it from a Prussian Guard. I gave him the steel through the mouth and then took his helmet.[56]

---

[54] Pugsley, *Te Hokowhitu A Tu*, pp. 59–60.
[55] Jonathan F. Vance, *Death So Noble: Memory, Meaning, and the First World War* (Vancouver: UBC Press, 1997), p. 247.
[56] Moses, *A Sketch Account of Aboriginal Peoples in the Canadian Military*, p. 65.

During his childhood, Albert Mountain Horse learned and practised the traditional customs and beliefs of the Blood, while being educated at the nearby Anglican St Paul's Mission Boarding School. Like many young Indians of the time, Albert was torn between his traditional mores and the government's insistence on residential edification and assimilation. Nevertheless, Albert was described as, 'one of the brightest and most enlightened boys on the Reserve', and thrived in St Paul's cadet programme. He volunteered for the militia summer training programme at Calgary and, after completion, was commissioned a lieutenant in the Canadian Militia. At the outbreak of war in 1914, Albert was serving as a cadet instructor with the 23rd Alberta Rangers. He volunteered and was accepted into the Canadian Expeditionary Force (CEF) on 23 September 1914, taking a demotion to the rank of private to minimize further officer training, in order to be deployed more quickly. Albert proudly exclaimed that he was 'going forth to fight for my King and Country'. He sailed with the 10th Battalion as part of the First Canadian Contingent in October 1914. Due to unofficial regulations excluding Indians from service, he was one of only a handful of Indians in the initial deployment of over 31,000 men: 'I do not think the Germans will stand any chance when we get over there ... I am very anxious to get to the war.'[57]

Albert survived the fighting at Ypres only to be gassed twice more and was never able to make the gift of the souvenir helmet to his brother. He was hospitalized because of gas poisoning and, with acute respiratory distress, subsequently contracted tuberculosis, a disease twenty times more prevalent among Indians than whites: 'I told him [the doctor] I would sooner die like a man in the trenches than have a grave dug for me.' On 19 November 1915, only one day after arriving in Canada, 21-year-old Albert Mountain Horse died at Quebec City. His body was shipped home to Macleod, Alberta, and Albert was given a military funeral, presided over by his St Paul's school master the Reverend Samuel Henry Middleton: 'One of the Empire's greatest sons who fought to uphold the prestige and traditions of the British race, and having gained all the honours and respect which can be shown to a soldier and a man, has cast a brilliant reflection on the Blood Indians of Alberta, proving to the world at large he was truly an Indian warrior.'[58]

---

[57] Dempsey, *Warriors of the King*, pp. 53–4.
[58] Ibid, pp. 54–5. According to a February 2010 report, the rates of tuberculosis among First Nations are 31 times higher, and those of Inuit 185 times higher, than Canadian-born, non-indigenous peoples. Bryn Weese, *Parliamentary Bureau*, 10 March 2010.

Shortly thereafter, Albert's older brothers Mike and Joe enlisted, as official sanction to enrol Indians had been granted in December 1915. According to Mike, 'Reared in the environment of my forefathers, the spirit of revenge for my brother's death manifested itself strongly in me as I gazed down on Albert lying in his coffin that cold winter day in November 1915.' Joe was wounded three times and survived the war. Mike was buried alive for four days at Cambrai in October 1917, leading to his hospitalization for shell-shock. Upon returning to action, he was twice wounded, attained the rank of sergeant and won the Distinguished Conduct Medal (DCM) for bravery. Following the war, Mike became a translator for the Royal Canadian Mounted Police (RCMP), a locomotive mechanic for the Canadian Pacific Railway, a journalist for local newspapers and a member of his band council.[59]

After its bloodletting at Ypres, the 1st Canadian Division suffered an additional 3,000 casualties during subsequent actions at Festubert (22–24 May) and Givenchy (15 June). Furthermore, while the division was not involved in any large-scale battles until St Eloi in March 1916, 'wastage' accounted for roughly 650 casualties per month from September 1915 to March 1916.[60]

Compounding the need for manpower, in the face of these casualties, was the drastic expansion of the CEF in 1915. The 2nd Division, authorized on 9 October 1914, joined the 1st Division in France in September 1915, facilitating the creation of the Canadian Corps. On 30 October, Borden increased the authorized strength of the CEF to 250,000, despite sober counsel from Gwatkin that, 'there is a limit to our production ... You cannot put every available man into the firing line at once. Casualties must be replaced. It takes 3,000 to place 1,000 infantrymen in the field and to maintain them there in numbers and efficiency for a year.'[61] Nevertheless, a 3rd Division was formed from surplus reserves in France, on 24 December 1915. On 31 December, Borden doubled the authorized strength of the CEF to 500,000, accompanied by this threat to the British government:

It can hardly be expected that we shall put 400,000 to 500,000 men in the field and willingly accept the position of having no more voice and receiving no more consideration than if we were toy automata. Any person cherishing such an expectation harbours an unfortunate and even dangerous delusion. Is this war being waged by the United Kingdom alone or is it a war waged by the

---

[59] Mountain Horse, *My People, the Bloods*, pp. vi–ix, 140–2.
[60] Bill Rawling, *Surviving Trench Warfare: Technology and the Canadian Corps 1914–1918* (University of Toronto Press, 1992), p. 218; Cook, *At the Sharp End*, pp. 159, 206, 214.
[61] Granatstein and Hitsman, *Broken Promises*, p. 36.

whole Empire? ... Procrastination, indecision, inertia, doubt, hesitation and many other undesirable qualities have made themselves entirely too conspicuous in this war ... Another very able Cabinet Minister spoke of the shortage of guns, rifles, munitions, etc., but declared that the chief shortage was of brains.[62]

Since the beginning of October, Borden had been relentless in demanding greater involvement in the direction of the war. Although the 'upright and handsome' Borden, as representative of the senior Dominion, took the lead in voicing these anxieties, his concerns were shared by the 'thick-headed and John Bullish' Massey of New Zealand and the 'hot-tempered, idiosyncratic' Australian Prime Minister William Hughes.[63] According to Borden, nationalist considerations could not be ignored if recruitment was to be sustained, as the 'Governments of Overseas Dominions have large responsibilities to their people for conduct of war and we deem ourselves entitled to fuller information and to consultation respecting general policy in war operations'.[64]

In late 1916, Borden craftily enhanced Canada's position within London political circles. In November, he forced the resignation of the Minister of Militia, Sam Hughes, explaining that, 'his conduct and speech were so eccentric as to justify the conclusion that his mind was unbalanced'.[65] Borden thought it 'essential to curtail the activities of Hughes and to place in the hands of a responsible Minister in London, the disposition of all such matters affecting the welfare of the Canadian Army ... and thus relieve the Government of the unfortunate results of Hughes' visits abroad'.[66] To circumvent the legalities of British control over Canadian foreign affairs, Borden used the 1914 War Measures Act, internal to Canada, to achieve his desires.[67] On 28 October 1916, the Ministry of Overseas Military Forces of Canada was established in London, to ensure that Canada was kept informed of developments and to express concerns 'in all matters connected with the government, command and disposition of the overseas forces of Canada'; it 'shall be responsible for the administration of the affairs of the military forces of Canada in the United Kingdom and on the Continent

---

[62] Department of External Affairs, *Documents on Canadian External Relations*, pp. 103–4. Borden to Perley, 31 December 1915; Borden to Perley, 4 January 1916.
[63] MacMillan, *Paris 1919*, pp. 48–9.
[64] Department of External Affairs, *Documents on Canadian External Relations*, pp. 93–4. Borden to Perley, 30 October 1915.
[65] Michael Bliss, *Right Honourable Men* (New York: HarperCollins, 1994), p. 81.
[66] Alan R. Capon, *His Faults Lie Gently: The Incredible Sam Hughes* (Ontario: Floyd W. Hall, 1969), p. 140.
[67] LAC, MG27IID23, vol. 1, file 8. Borden to the Governor-General in Council, 22 September 1916.

of Europe'.[68] No other Dominion initiated any matching organization, although in June 1917 Smuts became a permanent member of David Lloyd George's Imperial War Cabinet, which included sporadic attendance by Dominion prime ministers.

In reality, Borden's commitment of 500,000 men, in light of casualty rates, would require the immediate enlistment of 250,000, and an additional 25,000 men per month (300,000 annually) if its strength was to be sustained. Senator James Mason reported to his colleagues that these figures 'will not be obtained under the present system of enlistment'.[69] As of January 1916, the total strength of the CEF stood at only 218,260, and on 20 January, a 4th Division was authorized by Borden. The total enlistment for 1915 was 158,859 – an average monthly enlistment of 13,238.[70] To meet Borden's imperious and idealistic promises, Canada needed to significantly bolster recruitment.

To meet the demand for manpower in November 1915 the government authorized prominent individuals and communities to recruit and raise battalions for overseas service outside of official military circles, with the consent of the Ministry of Militia, which did not forego financial responsibility. Throughout 1915, confusion prevailed as to the legality of enlisting Indians and scores of requests were submitted to the ministries of Militia and Indian Affairs. For example, in October 1915, Cape Croker Chippewa Indian agent, A. J. Duncan, questioned Indian Affairs as to why three men from his reserve were denied enlistment at four different stations while other Indians had been accepted. In November, Scott simply replied to offers and complaints that, '[I] would not put any obstacle in your way [but] The Militia Department, however, does not seem to be very willing to enlist Indians for overseas service' (see Figure 6.4).[71]

In November, F. R. Lalor, MP for Dunnville, Ontario, and Lieutenant-Colonel Edwy Sutherland Baxter, CO of the 37th Haldimand Rifles, appealed to Sam Hughes for permission to raise a battalion in the Dunnville–Caledonia–Six Nations area. Although it was to include Indians, it was not initially intended to be solely an Indian unit. Baxter was known to the Six Nations and was 'one of the most popular men in the opinion of the Indians', according to a December 1915 article from the local *Brantford Expositor*. While the Ministry of Militia approved the battalion, no mention was made

[68] LAC, MG27IID23, vol. 1, file 8. Ordinance: Overseas Military Forces of Canada.
[69] Ronald G. Haycock, 'Recruiting, 1914–1916' in Marc Milner (ed.), *Canadian Military History: Selected Readings* (Toronto: Irwin Publishing, 1998), p. 67.
[70] Nicholson, *Canadian Expeditionary Force*, Appendix C.
[71] LAC, RG10, vol. 6766, reel C-8511, file 452-13. Correspondence Scott and Indian Agents, November–December 1915.

FILE HILLS INDIAN RECRUITS
OCT. 1915

Figure 6.4 Cree Indian recruits from File Hills, Saskatchewan, October 1915.

concerning Indians, as recruitment remained within the discretion of local commanders, in this case Baxter. He believed that he could muster 200 to 250 Indians from the Six Nations Reserve, many already active in his militia unit. On 3 December 1915, Baxter received formal authorization specifically to recruit Indians for his 114th Battalion. This policy was extended to all district commanders, battalions and Indian agents across Canada on 10 December.[72] According to a November 1917 report from the Ministry of Militia, the question was raised,

Whether there was any General Order of the Department by which Indians were not allowed to enlist. No such General order was issued. Towards the latter part of 1915, the number of Indians who volunteered to enlist was continuously increasing, and representations were made from the Crown ... that they should be allowed to do so, and the circular letter was issued on December 10, 1915. This regulation has never been altered since that time.[73]

---

[72] LAC, RG24-c-1-a, vol. 1221, file HQ-593-1-7. Hughes to Baxter, 6 December 1915; Ministry of Militia Circular, 10 December 1915.
[73] LAC, RG24-c-1-a, vol. 1221, file HQ-593-1-7. Ministry of Militia to A. G. Chisholm, 26 November 1917.

For the first time in the war, two months after the British requests, Canadian authorities relented and officially allowed Indians into the CEF. While Indians were given admittance, other minorities, such as blacks and Asians, were still barred from military service for the time being.

The response to the change in Indian policy was overwhelming. A clear example of this shift was the enlistment of American Oneida brothers Albert and Enos Kick of Wisconsin, who were attested as 'Indian' on 28 January 1916 into the 135th Middlesex Battalion (London, Ontario):[74]

My brother [Albert] and I enlisted almost at the same time, first month of 1916, because we have families and didn't want to see Germans kill the little ones. We tried to go over in 1914, but we couldn't on account of us being Indians, so we couldn't very well pass as a white man, so we waited until our chance came, so both of us went to the same Battalion and the same Company and everything the same ... But I miss my brother Albert, he is over there yet [killed by a sniper at Cambrai in October 1918].[75]

The 135th Battalion left for England in August 1916 containing 77 Indians, including the American Kick brothers. On 13 April 1916, Indian Affairs received a letter from Jennie Kick, wife of Enos, living at the Muncee Reserve, Ontario (original spelling and punctuation):

I cannot support my 4 Poor little Indian children ... I am not healthy I am sickly most of my life and cannot be with out my husband. We need him in the worst way. We have no place to go to. But when my husband is here we allways have a place to go too, he left us at his fathers and his mothers, and they turned us out on the road and every since that we are all over the reserve. We do not Belong here. Our home is near Green Bay Wisconsin place called Oneida Wis., Brown County. So I Beg and Beg you to have my husband Enos W. Kick Released ... anybody can tell you the way we are fixed should you want to know more about it ... I am begging every night and day for God sakes sent my husband to us. We are poor every since my husband is away. We want help so send my husband to me.

Indian Affairs simply replied that it could not force his release and that discretion remained with Enos himself. Enos survived the war and returned to his family in December 1918.[76]

It is not known how many American Indians served in the CEF prior to the US declaration of war on 6 April 1917. In total, 35,612

[74] LAC, RG150, box 5135-5-6. Service Records Albert and Enos Kick.
[75] Susan Applegate Krouse (original documentation by Joseph K. Dixon), *North American Indians in the Great War* (Lincoln: University of Nebraska Press, 2007), p. 21.
[76] LAC, RG10, vol. 3180, reel C-11335, file 452, 124-1a. Letter Jennie Kick to Indian Affairs, 13 April 1916, reply 21 April 1916; *Hordenville Weekly Review*, 'Oneida Killed at Front', 28 June 1917.

Americans served in Canadian units during the war.[77] The Indian population of the United States, in 1917, was roughly 330,000 (three times larger than that of Canada). Similar to Canada, the exact total figures for American Indian service are not known. An accurate estimate, based on the 1920 Annual Report of the Commissioner of Indian Affairs, Cato Sells, and secondary sources, reveals that between 10,000 and 12,000 American Indians served in the American Expeditionary Force (AEF) – 6,509 are known to have been drafted and another 5,000 to 6,000 are thought to have voluntarily enlisted. (By comparison: 3.9% of the total Indian population of Canada voluntarily served, compared to 3.3% of the US total who volunteered *and* were drafted.) This discrepancy can be attributed to the late entry of the US into the war, and to the fact that, unlike Canadian Indians, those in America did not possess a strong allegiance to the British Crown. Like his Canadian counterpart Duncan Campbell Scott, Sells also viewed the military service of Indians as an avenue of assimilation. By November 1918, 17,000 (including the 6,509) had been registered for the draft. Sells stated, in his 1918 report, that, 'many Indians from our northern reservations enrolled in Canadian military organizations before the declaration of war by the United States'. According to Thomas A. Britten, 'press reports indicated that hundreds of Native Americans from the United States enlisted in the Canadian army between 1915 and 1917'.[78]

In 1919, Joseph K. Dixon interviewed and surveyed 2,846 American Indian veterans. Of the 2,315 who listed a specific national formation, seven reported that they had served in the CEF. An extrapolation of this percentage, based on the total service of 12,000, would place the overall number of American Indians in the CEF at 36. Given that Dixon used American enlistment papers to locate his subjects, his sample group would have excluded most Indians with CEF service. While the number is certainly higher than the projected totals of Dixon's surveys, it is doubtful that it exceeded 300.[79] In August 1919, an inquiry was made by the US administration as to how many American Indians served in the CEF. The reply from the Ministry of Militia simply stated that, 'no

[77] Fred Gaffen, *Cross-Border Warriors: Canadians in American Forces, Americans in Canadian Forces from the Civil War to the Gulf* (Toronto: Dundurn Press, 1995), p. 14.
[78] See: Britten, *American Indians in World War I: At Home and at War*; Russel L. Barsh, 'American Indians in the Great War', *Ethnohistory* 38/3 (1991), 276–303; Michael L. Tate, 'From Scout to Doughboy: The National Debate Over Integrating American Indians into the Military, 1891–1918', *Western Historical Quarterly* 17/4 (1986), 417–37.
[79] Krouse, *North American Indians in the Great War*, p. 36.

differentiation between Indians and other Canadians was attempted in the Canadian Forces'.[80]

Although he initially formed the 114th Battalion, Baxter's tenure of command lasted just over two months. He died of disease on 15 February 1916 and was replaced by Lieutenant-Colonel Andrew T. Thompson, born in Cayuga, astride the Six Nations Reserve.[81] Pedigreed by an affluent, aristocratic family, Thompson had previously served in the Canadian Militia as private to colour sergeant with the Queen's Own Rifles of Canada. He then joined the 37th Haldimand Rifles as a captain in 1892 and proceeded to serve as the regiment's commanding officer for eight years. He went on to command the 5th Infantry Brigade for four years and served as commander for the Canadian Coronation Contingent at the crowning of King Edward VII in January 1902.[82] Thompson, a lawyer and editor (he was editor of the *Canadian Military Gazette* for many years) by trade, also served as Member of Parliament for the constituency of Haldimand and Monck from November 1900 to November 1904 in Prime Minister Wilfrid Laurier's Liberal government.[83] Given his prior service with the 37th Haldimand Rifles and his political experience, Thompson was a logical choice to command the 114th Battalion, given its Indian composition. In addition, his grandfather had fought alongside Six Nations warriors at the Battle of Queenston Heights (13 October 1812) with Major-General Sir Isaac Brock, and Thompson's two sons, Andrew and Walter, were serving lieutenants, having joined the 114th on 8 December 1915. Thompson himself was an Honorary Chief of the Six Nations; his Iroquoian name was *Ahsaregoah*, meaning 'the sword'.[84]

In March, Thompson was given special permission to enlist Indians, both within and outside the Battalion's military district. He was also afforded the opportunity to arrange for the transfer of Indians serving in other units to the 114th. The Ministry of Militia, however, refused to make transfers mandatory. This arrangement was supported by Brigadier-General W. A. Logie, Commander of No. 2 District Toronto, and also by Duncan Campbell Scott: 'I thought I should write

---

[80] LAC, RG24-c-1-a, vol. 1221-1, file HQ-593-1-7. Letter from Attorney Charles F. Fitzgerald to Ministry of Militia, 9 August 1919, with Reply, 12 October 1920.

[81] LAC, RG150, 1992–93/166, 9622. Service Records Andrew T. Thompson.

[82] LAC, RG150, 1992–93/166, 9622. Service Records Andrew T. Thompson. Five generations of Thompsons (of Scottish ancestry) lived at the Ruthven Park estate outside Cayuga from 1845 to 1993, including Andrew Thompson. The 1,500-acre Ruthven Park is now a Canadian National Historic Site.

[83] Parliament of Canada, Senators and Members – Andrew Thorburn Thompson, at: www.parl.gc.ca

[84] Scott, *Report of the Deputy Superintendent General*, p. 7.

you [Logie] and state how much I am interested in the welfare of the 114th Battalion; I hope to see a solid half of the battalion composed of Indians, and I trust that District No. 2 may be able to produce them. It is in the interest of the Indians, I think, that we should have at least two full Indian companies. Personally and officially I have been doing everything possible to bring this about.'[85]

During active recruiting and in the media, the 114th was advertising itself as 'the Indian Unit', and at least a dozen battalions transferred their Indian recruits to the 114th. In a gesture of solidarity, Indian Affairs lent the 'only male Indian employed at the Service in Ottawa', Ojibwa-Mohawk Charles Cooke, to the 114th Battalion as a recruiting officer. Bestowed with the honorary rank of lieutenant, Cooke toured Ontario and Quebec reserves throughout 1916 recruiting for the 114th. By the end of his first week, Cooke had recruited ninety Indians.[86] However, not all Indians wanted to serve in the 114th Battalion, as they preferred 'not to fight alongside Mohawks'. During the colonial wars, Iroquois warriors had earned a reputation as fierce combatants (specifically Mohawk) by conquering or assimilating other nations, some to the point of near extinction, as in the case of the Huron and the Mahican Confederacies.[87] This reluctance to transfer to, or join, the 114th lends credence to Gwatkin's concerns on 6 January 1916 about forming an all-Indian unit:

If 500,000 men are to be raised, we must take all we can get; but it is useless to enlist Indians, and train them, unless we intend to employ them at the front ... If they are employed as a battalion, or by companies, we must come to some understanding with the War Office ... after consultation with the War Office to earmark one or more companies as Indian companies, and keep them up to strength by drafts specially prepared. How Indians would stand trench warfare I do not know; nor do I know whether, coming from different tribes, they would fight among themselves.[88]

The practice of transferring Indians to the 114th was abolished in February, due to complaints from other battalion commanders who

---

[85] LAC, RG24, vol. 4380, file 34-7-89, vol. 1. Scott to Logie, 31 May 1916.

[86] LAC, RG10, vol. 6765, reel C-8510, file 452-7. Scott to Logie, 19 January 1916, Reply 21 January 1916; Baxter to Scott, 21 January 1916, Reply 25 January 1916; RG24, vol. 4383, file MD2-34-7-109. Scott to Logie, 19 January 1916, Reply 20 January 1916; Logie to Baxter, 22 January 1916; Scott to (No. 2 District Recruiting CO) Maj. George Williams, 31 January 1916, Reply 2 February 1916; Cooke to Scott, Report Ending 14 February 1916; *The Globe*, '96 Indians Join 114th Batt.' (Toronto, 8 February 1916).

[87] LAC, RG24, vol. 4383, file MD2-34-7-109. OC 227th Bn to Logie, 4 May 1916.

[88] LAC, RG24-c-1-a, vol. 1221, file HQ-593-1-7. Gwatkin Memorandum (6 January 1916).

were trying to fill their under-strengthened units. In July 1916, a report of the No. 2 Military District revealed that the 114th had 348 Indians (including 5 officers), while another 211 were represented in 15 other units.[89] Many Ojibwa from Ontario and certain chiefs from the Six Nations, however, actively resisted Cooke's attempts at recruitment and men were not as forthcoming as Cooke had expected or hoped. Given the lower than expected recruitment rates and the non-mandatory transfer policy, an all-Indian battalion was unsustainable. In all, 353 Indians (287 from the Six Nations Reserve) served in the 114th Battalion, of which two of the four companies, including most of the officers, were Indian. A thirty-five-man regimental band was also formed. The band toured the British Isles for recruiting and patriotic purposes and included traditional garments and war dances in their performances.[90]

Although only two companies were comprised of Indians, special concessions were asked for by Thompson in a letter to the Ministry of Militia on 25 March 1916:

This battalion is recruiting largely from the Six Nation Indians. Already more than two hundred of them have enlisted, and I confidently expect three hundred and fifty to four hundred more. The ancestors of these men fought for Great Britain in every battle on the Niagara frontier in the War of 1812, and were with General Brock in large numbers when he fell at Queenston Heights. To this day they venerate his memory, and the name for which I ask, 'Brock's Rangers' would greatly add to our prestige with them, and gratify them exceedingly. The 'white' half of the battalion comes from Haldimand County, one of the Niagara Peninsula group, and many of these men too had ancestors with Brock in 1812.

Permission was granted to use the name 'Brock's Rangers' two days later.[91] Like the Maori Contingent, the 114th had a cap badge reflecting its unique constituency. The regimental crest featured two crossed tomahawks below the regimental motto 'For King and Country'. The crest also bore the name, 'Brock's Rangers', and a crown, all superimposed on a maple leaf. The Six Nations Women's Patriotic League embroidered a 114th Battalion flag, which they adorned with Iroquoian symbols. Thompson proceeded to gain approval from the Ministry of Militia for his battalion to carry this flag alongside the King's Colour

---

[89] LAC, RG24, vol. 4383, file MD2-34-7-109. Report: Indians at Camp Borden, 13 September 1916; Correspondence Battalions June–July 1916.

[90] LAC, RG9-II-B-10, vols. 31, 38. Nominal Rolls, 114th Overseas Battalion; LAC, RG24-c-1-a, vol. 1562, file 1. Pay Sheets, 114th Overseas Battalion.

[91] LAC, RG24, vol. 1562, file HQ-683-173-2. Thompson to Adjutant-General, Ministry of Militia, 25 March 1916.

and their regular regimental colour.[92] The Battalion was mobilized to proceed overseas on 29 September 1916. The last inspection before sailing was conducted on 17 October 1916, at Camp Borden, by Major-General F. L. Lessard, who concluded that: 'This is a good Battalion in which there are 300 Indians ... 15 men trained in Scouting ... of Good Class and Physique'.[93]

The only other CEF unit to mirror the Indian composition of the 114th was the 107th Battalion, raised in Winnipeg, Manitoba, in December 1915, shortly after permission was granted to enlist Indians. Lieutenant-Colonel Glen Campbell, who had attempted to construct a similar unit in 1914, was responsible for recruitment as the command-ing officer. Campbell, as 'Chief Inspector of Agencies, Reserves and Inspectorates in Manitoba, Saskatchewan, Alberta and the Northwest Territories', was loaned to the Ministry of Militia by Indian Affairs.

If Canadians created legendary folk heroes, like those of the United States, Campbell would be equivalent to the celebrated American frontiersman, soldier and politician David 'Davy' Crockett. Glenlyon Archibald Campbell was born on 23 October 1863 at the Hudson's Bay Company Post, Fort Pelly, Saskatchewan. Glen's father, Robert Campbell, an immigrant from Glen Lyon, Scotland, was a fur trader for the Hudson's Bay Company (HBC) for interrupted periods between 1830 and 1871.[94] Through his trading expeditions, he helped map the final portions of northern Canada, giving name to many geograph-ical features in Yukon Territory. In fact, in 1840, he became the first known non-Indian or Eskimo to cross into the Yukon River watershed from the east. The present day 602 km-long Robert Campbell Highway (Highway 4) in the Yukon roughly conforms to his 1840s route.[95]

Robert Campbell's vocation had an early impact on his son Glen's life. In 1870, Glen and his two siblings accompanied their mother to Scotland, where shortly thereafter she died of typhoid.[96] The children were taken in by an aunt in Perthshire and spent their time between

---

[92] LAC, RG24, vol. 1562, file HQ-683-173-2. Thompson to Adjutant-General, Ministry of Militia, 25 March 1916.

[93] LAC, RG24, vol. 1562, file HQ-683-173-2. Inspection Report, 114th Overseas Battalion, 17 October 1916.

[94] Robert was a descendant of the Campbell Clan, members of which were the perpe-trators of the Glencoe Massacre (Scotland) on 13 February 1692 during the era of the Glorious Revolution and Jacobitism. Seventy-seven members of the MacDonald Clan, including women and children, were killed (or died as a result of the massacre) by Captain Robert Campbell and his followers.

[95] Grant MacEwan, *Fifty Mighty Men* (Saskatoon: Western Producer, 1958), pp. 116–19; Kenneth Stephen Coates, *Dictionary of Canadian Biography – Robert Campbell*. www.biographi.ca

[96] Glen also contracted typhoid at this time.

Scotland and Manitoba. In the process, Glen attended Glasgow Academy and Merchiston Castle School in Edinburgh. By 19 years of age, Glen found himself in the Montana Territory, due to his father's request for him to work on a cattle ranch and learn stock-raising. In 1884, Glen returned to Manitoba to live with his father on the family ranch near Riding Mountain in the Russell District of Manitoba.[97]

Unlike Andrew Thompson, prior to taking command of the 107th Battalion, Campbell's only military service had come during the 1885 North-West Rebellion. In early April 1885, Major Charles Arkoll Boulton was given permission from the Canadian government to recruit an irregular mounted infantry unit from the population of the Russell-Birtle District in Manitoba. The unit, known variously as 'Boulton's Mounted Infantry', 'Boulton's Horse', and more commonly as 'Boulton's Scouts', consisted of 5 officers and 123 men, including Glen Campbell. The unit joined General Frederick Middleton's column as the advance guard en route to Fish Creek and the Métis capital of Batoche. On 13 May, following the Battle of Batoche, Major Boulton promoted Campbell; the previous two troop leaders were casualties of action: 'I now appointed Captain Campbell, a son of an old Hudson's Bay officer ... He was installed amid cheers of the men.'[98]

In actuality, the Campbell/Riel connection dated back to the Red River Rebellion (1869–70). In fear of Métis pillaging and reprisal, Glen's father, by then a Chief Factor in the HBC, sent his year's quota of furs to London, England, via Sioux country, which was engulfed in the American–Sioux War (1862–90). Glen, his mother and his siblings accompanied the military escort from Manitoba and disembarked in London. This action led to Robert's dismissal from the HBC the following year.[99]

After his brief period of military service, Glen Campbell returned to ranching, hunting and trapping and in 1897–8, during the Klondike Gold Rush, he unsuccessfully attempted the arduous overland route from Edmonton to Dawson City. Like his counterpart, Thompson, Campbell, too, became a politician. After being defeated for the seat of Dauphin in the Legislative Assembly of Manitoba in 1892 and 1896,

[97] Desmond Morton, *Dictionary of Canadian Biography – Glenlyon Archibald Campbell*; MacEwan, *Fifty Mighty Men*, pp. 116–18.

[98] Charles Arkoll Boulton, *Reminiscences of the North-west Rebellions: With a Record of the Raising of Her Majesty's 100th Regiment in Canada, and a Chapter on Canadian Social and Political Life* (Toronto: Grip Printing and Publishing Co., 1886), ch. XIV – 'Batoche Captured'; LAC, RG150, 1992–93/166, 1434 – First World War Service Records Glen Campbell.

[99] Coates, *Dictionary of Canadian Biography – Robert Campbell*; Vandervort, *Indian Wars of Mexico, Canada and the United States*, pp. 161–91.

he won the reconstituted constituency of Gilbert Plains[100] in 1903 and again in 1907 as a Conservative. In 1908, aided by his brother-in-law, MP Clifford Sifton, he was elected to the House of Commons for the federal riding of Dauphin.[101] From all accounts, the 6'4" Campbell made an impression on his fellow Members of Parliament with his 'towering figure, bronzed swarthy face, large brown eyes, capped off with a cowboy hat'.[102] Although he spoke infrequently, on 17 March 1911, Campbell was involved in a bellicose dialogue with an Alberta MP, in a confrontation labelled 'one of the tensest situations and exciting scenes ever witnessed in Canadian Parliament' by *The New York Times*.[103] On another occasion, after listening to a speech by an eastern member who used eloquent yet confounding language, Campbell made his rebuttal in a combination of Cree and Latin.[104]

Campbell, although a Conservative, was defeated in the 1911 election which saw Robert Borden replace Wilfrid Laurier as prime minister. However, he was appointed Chief Inspector of Agencies, Reserves and Inspectorates in Manitoba, Saskatchewan, Alberta and the Northwest Territories within the Ministry of Indian Affairs by the new Conservative administration. Campbell had strong ties with the Indian communities of Manitoba through ranching and trapping. He had also married Harriet Burns, daughter of Saulteaux (Ojibwa) Chief Keeseekoowenin, in 1886. Campbell remained in this position with Indian Affairs, centred in Winnipeg, until July 1915.[105]

---

[100] According to the town of Gilbert Plains, Manitoba, in 1884, Campbell rode his horse over the Riding Mountains into what is now known as the Gilbert Plains, finding only one man, Métis Gilbert Ross, and his wife, living in a small cabin. Campbell traded his horse for the cabin and moved in. See: O. E. A. Brown, *Settlers of the Plains* (Gilbert Plains: The Maple Leaf Press, 1953).

[101] MacEwan, *Fifty Mighty Men*, pp. 120–1; Morton, *Dictionary of Canadian Biography – Glenlyon Archibald Campbell*; Parliament of Canada, Senators and Members – Glenlyon Archibald Campbell. Sifton was the MP for Brandon, Manitoba. He was Minister of the Interior and Superintendant General for Indian Affairs in Laurier's cabinet from 1896 to 1905. He was largely responsible for the influx of eastern Europeans (some three million) to western Canada at the turn of the century. He was knighted by King George V on 1 January 1915.

[102] Morton, *Dictionary of Canadian Biography – Glenlyon Archibald Campbell*.

[103] *New York Times*, 'Branded as Liar in Ottawa House', 18 March 1911.

[104] MacEwan, *Fifty Mighty Men*, p. 121. Another anecdote reportedly has Campbell re-enacting his account of riding a Bull Moose for members of the House of Commons.

[105] LAC, RG10, vol. 4063, reel C-10204, file 402890 – Correspondence Regarding the Appointment of Glen Campbell as Chief Inspector of Agencies, Reserves and Inspectorates in Manitoba, Saskatchewan, Alberta and the Northwest Territories. Also Subsequent Work while on Loan to Department of Militia & Defence and Death as Lieutenant-Colonel in France. Saulteaux are a branch of the Ojibwa Nation within the Algonquian language grouping. They are also referred to as Anishinaabe. Harriet Campbell (nee Burns) died on 17 May 1910, at the age of 44.

As mentioned, in October 1914, Campbell unsuccessfully petitioned Ottawa to raise an irregular unit of Indian scouts similar to that in which he had served under Major Boulton during the 1885 rebellion. On 9 July 1915, he was loaned to the Ministry of Militia by the Ministry of Indian Affairs, given the rank of major and tasked to assist in raising the 79th Battalion in Brandon, Manitoba. On 24 November, Campbell was transferred from the 79th and mandated to raise the 107th Battalion in Winnipeg and was appointed its commander as a lieutenant-colonel.[106]

On 3 February 1916, Campbell sought permission from Scott to recruit Indians from the Elkhorn and Brandon Industrial Schools in Manitoba. Campbell argued that these young Indians 'would be under closer and more kindly supervision than in any other Battalion in the west ... even if they were not quite eighteen years of age'.[107] Scott endorsed the proposal with trepidation, concerned that parents and band councils might complain if Indian Affairs used its influence to persuade under-age Indian pupils to enlist, but added, in paradoxical logic, that those who did so would be 'breaking their treaty obligations, as they promised to be loyal citizens and it is anything but loyal to prevent recruiting'. Scott went on to state that, 'there should be some good material at Elkhorn', as the students received drilling instruction within their curriculum. He also encouraged Campbell to visit western reserves for recruiting prospects.[108]

The recruiting drive by Campbell was a success. Unlike the 114th Battalion, which was linked to the one-half Indian militia unit of the 37th Haldimand Rifles, the 107th did not have the benefit of such a relationship. Complete with a pipe and drum band and the regimental march, 'The Campbells are Coming', Lieutenant-Colonel Campbell enticed 1,741 volunteers, both Indian and non-Indian, to join his battalion. He rejected over 600 of these men and achieved full strength

[106] LAC, RG150, 1992–3/166, 1434 – First World War Service Records LCol. Glen Campbell.

[107] L. James Dempsey asserts that perhaps Campbell's initial motivation to recruit underage Indians was simply to increase his battalion's strength. Campbell could also have been using his former position of power within the Ministry of Indian Affairs and the Ministry itself to undermine or intimidate parents, chiefs and band councils into agreeing to this policy.

[108] LAC, RG10, vol. 6766, reel C-8511, file 452-13. Campbell to Scott, 3 February 1916; Reply 7 February 1916; Office of Census and Statistics, *The Canada Yearbook, 1916*, p. 640; Duncan Campbell Scott, *The Administration of Indian Affairs in Canada* (Ottawa: Canadian Institute of International Affairs, 1931), p. 17. At this time in Manitoba, 795 Indian boys were attending various 'Indian Schools and Institutions'. In Canada, for the fiscal year of 1915–16, 12,799 Indians were enrolled in one of the 350 residential and day schools.

within three months of the Battalion's conception – 45 officers and 861 other ranks. Over 500 of these soldiers were Indian. However, unlike the 114th, all but one officer of the 107th were white, lending credence to the comments of the Inspector-General that the 'NCOs and men are very good, of good physique and above average intelligence, though very few hold certificates'.[109] For the most part, a non-battlefield commission in the CEF still required an education, a qualification which excluded most western Indians. In 1914, according to Indian Affairs, only 31% of Manitoba Indians spoke English, 22% in Saskatchewan and 15% in Alberta, compared with 67% in Ontario, home to the 114th Battalion.[110]

Many of the Indian soldiers of the 107th did not speak, or spoke very little, English and they came from a variety of nations, predominantly the Blackfoot Confederacy, Cree and Ojibwa. To remedy this, Campbell often instructed training, and conducted administrative and disciplinary matters, in Indian languages, as he was fluent in the dialects of Cree and Ojibwa. English language instruction was also given to Indian soldiers in the Battalion.[111] The 107th had a cap badge which embodied its Indian configuration. It was composed of a crown bearing the Battalion number, reinforced with a backdrop of a stalking wolf.

The 107th became unofficially known as the 'Timber Wolf Battalion'. The origin of the cap badge and nickname was explained by Steven A. Bell:

My Grandfather was a rancher in the Canadian West during the Great War. Four of the Native Canadians who worked for him joined the 107th. Only one returned. He gave my family a 107th cap badge. He claimed the Timber Wolf was selected because it was a common totem to many of the Native soldiers. He used the name 'Timber Wolf Battalion' to refer to the unit. No other explanation regarding the origin of the cap badge was discovered in the records at the National Archives.[112]

Another theory, according to Glenlyon Campbell (the great-grandson of Lieutenant-Colonel Campbell), was that Campbell's wife, Harriet,

[109] LAC, RG10, vol. 6766, reel C-8511, file 452-13. Campbell to Scott, 3 February 1916; Morton, *Dictionary of Canadian Biography – Glenlyon Campbell*.

[110] *The Canada Yearbook 1914*, p. 640. Statistics for the rest of Canada: PEI – 61%; Nova Scotia – 62%; New Brunswick – 50%; Quebec – 26% English, 48% French; BC – 33%.

[111] LAC, RG9III-D-3, vol. 5010, reel T10859, file 725. War Diaries 107th Canadian Pioneer Battalion; Dempsey, *Warriors of the King*, 25.

[112] Steven A. Bell, 'The 107th "Timber Wolf" Battalion at Hill 70', *Canadian Military History* 5/1 (1996), 78.

'was full-blooded Ojibwa, daughter of Chief Keeseekoowenin, and her family was Wolf Clan. I assume that is why the 107th had the timber wolf on their patch.'[113]

The 32 officers and 965 other ranks of the 107th arrived in Liverpool on 25 October 1916, followed by the 30 officers and 679 other ranks of the 114th on 11 November. Like many Canadian battalions raised after 1915, the 114th was broken up soon after its arrival in England, its members used to reinforce other units. Some Indian members, primarily officers, were transferred to the 107th but the majority were sent to bolster the 35th (Toronto) and 36th (Hamilton) Battalions. The 114th's regimental band toured until the end of 1917, when its members were sent to active formations.[114]

A number of other battalions raised after December 1915 also had a high percentage of Indians, although none rivalled the 114th and 107th. The 135th Middlesex, 149th Lambton, 160th Bruce and 52nd 'Bull Moose' New Ontario Battalions, all from Ontario, and also the 188th Saskatchewan were dispatched overseas containing a large segment of Indians (see Table 6.1).[115] In November 1916, one year after the official sanction, the distribution of known Indian enlistments was released by Indian Affairs.

The numbers are reflective of two factors. Firstly, initial recruitment efforts were directed at Indians in eastern Canada, who were less isolated, more assimilated and spoke more English. Secondly, by extension, higher enlistment rates occurred east of Manitoba within the more traditionally warrior-based nations with a history of allegiance, such as the Iroquois.[116] By late 1916, this trend was brought to the attention of Scott, who authorized a second major shift in policy. To enhance Indian recruitment in western Canada and on the more isolated reserves in eastern Canada, a military recruiter, often an Indian repatriated from the front, was paired with a member of Indian Affairs, as proposed by Lieutenant Maxwell Graham. He further recommended that, 'select Indians now overseas be brought back for recruiting purposes ... that photographs be shown the Indians of this Dominion, of their compatriots in uniform'. Charles Cooke again offered his service to recruit

[113] Interview by author with Glenlyon Campbell, 15 January 2008.

[114] LAC, RG9II-B-10, vols. 31, 38. Nominal Rolls – 114th Overseas Battalion; RG24-C-1-a, vol. 1562, file 1. Pay Sheets – 114th Overseas Battalion; RG150, 1992–3/166, 1434. Service Records Glen Campbell.

[115] LAC, RG24, vol. 4383, file MD2-34-7-109. Report: Indians at Camp Borden, 13 September 1916; LAC, RG10, vol. 3181, reel C-11332, file 452, 124-1a. Report Indian Affairs, 4 November 1916.

[116] LAC, RG10, vol. 3181, reel C-11335, file 452, 124-1a. Report Indian Affairs, 4 November 1916; Scott to Ernest Green, 14 November 1916.

Table 6.1: *Known Indian enlistments, November 1916*

Province	Enlistments	Indian male population Ages 16 to 65 (1915)	%
Ontario	862	6,185	13.9
Quebec	101	2,535	4.0
Manitoba	89	2,567	3.5
Saskatchewan	57	1,968	2.9
Prince Edward Island	24	78	30.8
British Columbia	17	6,665	0.26
Nova Scotia	14	558	2.5
New Brunswick	12	428	2.8
Alberta	9	1,529	0.59
Yukon Territory	2	428	0.47
Northwest Territory		1,121	
Total	*1,187*	*24,062*	*4.9*

outside of Ontario believing, like Scott and Graham, that the remainder of the Indian population had been overlooked.[117] Government policy had shifted from unofficially preventing Indians from enlistment in 1914; to official inclusion and sanctioning individual efforts for recruitment in late 1915 and into 1916; to becoming directly involved in promoting the recruitment effort by late 1916.

Unlike Canada, neighbouring Newfoundland engaged in the direct recruitment of its diminutive indigenous population prior to the British request of October 1915. In the spring of 1915, the Newfoundland Patriotic Association initiated recruitment in smaller outports on the island and also in Labrador and included Eskimos in this effort. In January 1915, Governor Davidson complained that, 'Although St. John's has contributed a large portion of young men for the front ... the Outports are still slow to join. Torbay [20 km north of St John's] – a settlement of Dorset [County] men, fine sailors and inured to hardship – has sent no one. Their reason is that they make good money in the summer "pogie" fishing off the New England coast.'[118]

On 1 April 1915, the St John's depot received a telegraph which was relayed to Davidson: 'Mr. Swaffield, Cartwright, Labrador, wishes to know if any recruit Volunteers are needed in St. John's or England [for]

---

[117] LAC, RG24-c-1-a, vol. 1221, file HQ-593-1-7. Memorandums Graham to Campbell, 30 November, 4 December 1916; Cooke to Militia Council and Scott, 15 December 1916.

[118] PANL, MG136, Sir Walter Davidson Papers, file 2.03.001. Diary Entry 11 January 1915.

active service for another Newfoundland Contingent. He says he can get at least fifteen to St. John's.' Davidson's response illustrates the isolation of Labrador communities and, more importantly, the non-existence of recruiting in Labrador itself: 'I propose sending the following reply ... I know so little of life conditions in Labrador that I am uncertain whether they can spare their young men:- "We would welcome recruits from Labrador for another draft of Volunteers for the front. But do not denude coast of labour or leave families without adequate support."' Localized recruitment, including that of indigenous men, was initiated in Labrador shortly after these communications.[119]

Secondary sources, however, misplace the timeframe of this recruitment and of the deployment of at least fourteen indigenous men in 1915, citing that they sailed with F Company. F Company, which was raised in the spring of 1915, was a collection of 242 men from remote regions of the Dominion, including Labrador. According to Davidson, 'A good many are from the northern outports ... not perhaps so smart in their drill as some of the earlier companies, as they have not been brought up in Cadet Corps.'[120] F Company sailed from St John's on 20 June 1915. However, of the known indigenous recruits from Labrador harnessed in the spring/summer of 1915, nine enlisted on 24 July, and one other on 11 August 1915 – after the sailing of F Company. Nominal roles of F Company contain no names of any of the twenty-one known indigenes who served during the war.[121]

One such volunteer to enlist on 24 July 1915 was John Shiwak, an Eskimo hunter and trapper from Rigolet, Labrador. John joined the Legion of Frontiersmen in 1911, based at the Grenfell Mission, where he worked as a handyman for Dr A. W. Wakefield, CO of the Legion of Frontiersmen. According to the Newfoundland Patriotic Association in August 1914, 'his [Wakefield's] Labrador trappers are riflemen but undrilled'.[122] When news of war reached Rigolet in 1914, Shiwak wrote (he had taught himself to read and write) to his friend, novelist and journalist Amy Lacey, whom he had met on a coastal steamer in 1911, explaining that he wanted to be a 'Soljer'. Lacey recorded that he, 'dismissed it as one of his ambitions unattainable owing to his race'. In

[119] PANL, GN2/14, boxes 1–23, file 151. Major Montgomerie and Governor Davidson, 1 April 1915.
[120] G. W. L. Nicholson, *The Fighting Newfoundlander: A History of the Royal Newfoundland Regiment* (London: Thomas Nelson Printers, 1964), pp. 209–11.
[121] PANL, GN2/14, boxes 1–23, file 143. List of Recruits and Next of Kin, 1915–17, Nominal Role F Company; GN19, B-2-3. Service Records Royal Newfoundland Regiment.
[122] PANL, MG136, Sir Walter Davidson Papers, file 2.02.007. Diary Entry 13 August 1914.

July 1915, John enticed two other local Eskimos and one non-Eskimo to enlist in St John's, where they were posted to C Company. Shiwak, who excelled in marksmanship due to his traditional background of 'swatching seals', became a sniper upon reaching France on 24 July 1916 – three weeks after the regiment's devastating losses at Beaumont-Hamel on 1 July. In his unpublished memoirs, Private Howard Morry remembered, 'Johnny Shirvack [sic], a sniper and a good one. He was shy and lonely but I got to be quite friendly with him by talking of seal and duck hunting etc. We'd talk for hours and he'd often say, "Will it ever be over?" He was a great shot and had lots of notches on his rifle stock. He said sniping was like swatching seals.' (See Figure 6.5.)[123]

On 19 September 1915, the 1,076 members of the Newfoundland Regiment landed at Suvla Bay, Gallipoli. During its stay at Gallipoli, the Battalion suffered 45 dead and 80 wounded, excluding 392 who were evacuated for sickness, exposure and frostbite.[124] At the close of 1915, the total enlistment for the Newfoundland Regiment was 2,775, with 1,985 deployed overseas. An additional 1,287 were serving, or attested, in the Royal Navy and it was estimated that 450 to 500 were serving in Canadian or British units. The Newfoundland Patriotic Association noted that, in order to sustain the Battalion in the face of casualties, greater recruiting would have to be initiated in communities outside the direct radius of St John's, including Labrador. Harcourt also urged Davidson that '50% reinforcements be in training at any given time'.[125] The next wave of Eskimo enlistment from Labrador, however, did not occur until the spring of 1917. The year of 1916 saw only one indigenous islander enlist – Andrew Shaw of Little Hearts Ease/Trinity Bay.[126]

While the October imperial desires immediately influenced the positions of Indians, Eskimos and Maori within their respective Dominion formations, the transfer towards inclusion was not as abrupt in the more exclusionist Dominions of Australia and South Africa. Throughout 1915, offers to raise mounted Aboriginal units were submitted to

---

[123] Amy Lacey, 'John Shiwak: An Eskimo Patriot', *Them Days – Stories of Early Labrador* 17/1 (1991); John C. Kennedy, 'John Shiwak', in *Dictionary of Canadian Biography* (University of Toronto Press, 2000); Dean Bruckshaw, 'John Shiwak: An Inuit Frontiersman', *Legion of Frontiersmen: Countess Mountbatten's Own*. www.frontiersmanhistorian.info/canada7. 'Swatching seals' is the process of shooting or clubbing seals as they briefly expose their heads in ice holes to breathe.

[124] PANL, MG632, Patriotic Association of Newfoundland, 1914–19, file 1. Minutes 4 February 1916.

[125] PANL, MG632, Patriotic Association of Newfoundland, 1914–19, file 1. Harcourt to Davidson, 19 November 1914; GN2/14, boxes 1–23, file 193. Newfoundland Colonial Secretary John R. Bennett to Davidson, 4 February 1916.

[126] PANL, GN19, B-2-3, reel 170. Service Records Andrew Shaw.

Figure 6.5 Legion of Frontiersman, John Shiwak, 1911.

military authorities from citizens and government officials. In June 1915, Archibald Meston, as he had done in 1899 during the Boer War, proposed the formation of a mounted unit of Queensland Aborigines. The offer was flatly rejected by the military authorities.[127]

[127] Pratt, 'Queensland's Aborigines in the First AIF', 21.

In 1915, Australia conducted a census of national resources and manpower, as a basis and cover for Prime Minister William Hughes' conscription agenda. Although Aborigines were excluded from military service, men of military age only were included in the survey; a notable departure, given that Aborigines were not included in national censuses.[128] A memorandum by John William Bleakley, Chief Protector for Queensland, required his subordinates to:

> Please compile for war census purposes the following information regarding Aborigines and half-castes in your districts … List of civilised male Aborigines between 18–45 years showing name-town-occupation-wages. List all Aborigines and half-castes with money to credit in bank or other property showing name-sex-adult or child-amount to credit and estimated value of other property known.[129]

By February 1916, enquiries were being submitted by the Chief Protectors of various States as to whether indigenes could be accepted into AIF units. The reply from the Minister of Defence, George Pearce, stated: 'with reference to applications for the enlistment of Aborigines, full-blood, or half-caste, please note that it is not considered advisable that such should be enlisted in the Australian Imperial Forces' (see Figure 6.6).[130]

Nevertheless, Aborigines managed to gain admittance into the AIF, including Douglas Grant of Lithgow, NSW, and the three Blackman brothers from Gayndah, Queensland.

Charles, the youngest, enlisted in Brisbane on 18 August 1915 into the 6th Reinforcements/25th Battalion at the age of nineteen years. Charles is one of the earliest-known Aboriginal recruits to be attested into the AIF. On 27 February 1916, in Cairo, he was taken on strength by the 9th Battalion, which had been the first unit raised in Queensland, and together with the 10th, 11th and 12th battalions formed the 3rd Brigade, 1st Division. On 3 April 1916, the 9th Battalion disembarked at Marseilles, France, bound for the Western Front.[131] The Battalion's first major action in France came during actions at Pozieres (23 July– 7 August 1916), during the Battle of the Somme. Australian casualties totalled 23,000 between 23 July and 5 September 1916. Private

---

[128] Australian Bureau of Statistics, *The Private Wealth of Australia and its Growth as Ascertained by Various Methods, together with a Report of the War Census of 1915* (Melbourne: McCarron, Bird, 1918).

[129] Pratt, 'Queensland's Aborigines in the First AIF' (April/June 1990), 16.

[130] Ibid, 16.

[131] NAA, B2455/1 – 3088591: First World War Service Records of Charles Tednee Blackman; 3088621: First World War Service Records of Alfred John Blackman; 3088646: First World War Service Records of Thomas Blackman.

A QUESTION OF COLOR

"Hullou, Jacky, not enlisted yet?"

"Yes Boss! Tried to join Light Horse, but plurry sergeant turn me down. Him say:
'You too plurry dark for Light Horse'--he, he!"

From The Bulletin, 31 August 1916

Figure 6.6 'A Question of Color: Too Dark for the Light Horse'. (*The Bulletin*, 31 August 1916.)

Blackman recalled this period in a letter of 13 January 1917 to his former employer, J. H. Salter of Biggenden: 'I had 10 month with the Battalion. I have been very lucky cording to what I have been through. Poziers was terrible but Ill return.'[132] While Charles was fighting in France, his older brothers enlisted: Thomas on 11 December 1916, followed roughly a month later by Alfred on 6 January 1917 – both into the 7th Reinforcements/41st Battalion. Following training, privates

---

[132] AWM, PR01679 – Letters, Papers and Postcards from Charles Blackman to Mr J. H. Salter, Biggenden, Queensland. Letter dated 13 January 1917.

Thomas and Alfred Blackman joined the 41st Battalion (11th Brigade, 3rd Division) near Messines, Belgium, on 18 July 1917.

All three brothers participated in the Battle of Passchendaele (Third Ypres) between 31 July and 10 November 1917. Private Alfred John Blackman was wounded in the head and neck by shell fragments on 4 October 1917 while advancing on Passchendaele Ridge. He died of these wounds on 8 October at the 7th Canadian General Hospital in Etaples, France. He is buried at the Etaples Military Cemetery along with 10,773 other Commonwealth soldiers, including 463 Australians.[133] Charles and Thomas participated in the brilliant Canadian and Australian spearhead operation during the Battle of Amiens beginning 8 August 1918. Thomas Blackman received a gun shot wound to his right foot on the 8th and Charles was gassed on the 11th. For Thomas, the war was over. After time in hospital, he was invalided home to Australia. Charles rejoined his battalion on 31 August and survived the war.[134]

Aborigines volunteered for various reasons; one being that service might give them full citizenship rights. Others, like 16-year-olds Mike Flick and Harry Manson from Collarenebri, NSW, enlisted for adventure and to escape mandatory pastoral work.[135] Lastly, the average wage for an Aboriginal male in 1914 was seven shillings and sixpence per week as compared with a private's pay in the AIF of six shillings a day.[136]

The overall number of Aborigines who enlisted in 1915 and 1916, however, was still relatively low. Changes allowing for Aboriginal inclusion into the AIF did not occur until March 1917, as a result of, and in combination with, the rejection of conscription during the first plebiscite of 28 October 1916, and the need to sustain I and II Anzac Corps after their transfer to the Western Front in March to April 1916. Australian forces suffered over 50,000 casualties between July 1916 and June 1917, 27,000 of these during the Somme offensive alone.[137] While recruits had been forthcoming during 1915 and 1916, with yearly totals of 165,912 and 124,355 respectively, by 1917 volunteers were scarce, as evidenced by the 1917 total of only 45,101.[138]

[133] NAA, B2455/1 – 3088591: First World War Service Records of Charles Tednee Blackman; 3088621: First World War Service Records of Alfred John Blackman; 3088646: First World War Service Records of Thomas Blackman.
[134] NAA, B2455/1 – 3088591: First World War Service Records of Charles Tednee Blackman; 3088646: First World War Service Records of Thomas Blackman.
[135] Huggonson, 'Dark Diggers of the AIF', 354.
[136] Huggonson, 'Villers-Bretonneux: A Strange Name for an Aboriginal Burial Ground', 287.
[137] NAA, A11803, 1918/89/137. Voting in Conscription Referendum; AWM38, 3DRL66673/866. C. E. W. Bean Collection, War Service Papers.
[138] Grey, A Military History of Australia, p. 87.

The use of native South Africans outside of the Union's African campaigns was hastened by demands from the imperial government in late 1915 and 1916. Following the successful campaign in GSWA, the first Union soldiers left Africa, the 1st South African Infantry Brigade arriving in Britain in October 1915. This same month, the imperial government specifically addressed the issue of using black and coloured labour in non-African theatres, with the memorandum of 18 October. The memorandum also influenced the formation of South African coloured and Indian units for East Africa.

In September 1915, the imperial government had reached an agreement with the Union on the formation of a Cape coloured infantry battalion (Cape Corps), under the authority and pay of the imperial government and officered by white South Africans. Dr Abdul Abdurahman, president of the African Political Organization from 1905 to 1940, was appointed chair of a recruiting committee: 'Today the Empire needs us. What nobler duty is there than to respond to the call of your King and Country?'[139] Recruiting commenced in Cape Town in October and the target of a thousand men was met by early December. Command of the unit was given to Lieutenant-Colonel George Abbot Morris.

The Battalion (32 European officers and 1,022 coloureds) left Cape Town on 9 February 1916 headed for Mombasa, to reinforce the 2nd South African Infantry Brigade. On 11 February, Smuts assumed command of the imperial forces in East Africa, which included soldiers from South Africa, Britain, India and Rhodesia. The 7th South African Infantry Battalion was composed almost exclusively of Australians and New Zealanders resident in South Africa. Also active during the campaign were Belgian and Portuguese soldiers and colonial troops representing the colonies of the Belgian Congo and Portuguese East and West Africa. By early February, imperial forces exceeded 27,000, excluding African carriers and non-combatants, who would raise the ration strength to approximately 75,000; however, figures for all forces of the East African campaign are subject to dispute.[140] The 'Cape Boys' were initiated into the severe battle conditions of East Africa on 7 March, near the foothills of Kilimanjaro. Immediately, disease, hunger and exhaustion, which became trademarks of the campaign, plagued the Battalion and by the end of April more than half of its men were casualties, hospitalized or sick in rear areas of operations. The corps only reached full strength again in December 1916.

---

[139] Simons, *Class and Colour in South Africa*, p. 179.
[140] Strachan, *The First World War in Africa*, pp. 122–35; Paice, *Tip & Run*, pp. 170–80.

The high death rate among South African blacks, coloureds and whites in East Africa prompted Botha to suspend all recruiting for the campaign in April 1917, despite objections from military authorities. Botha had been informed that local labourers were available, and a general shift towards the 'Africanization' of the campaign occurred. In a private, and therefore presumably sincerely felt, letter, Botha revealed that, 'Nothing has grieved me more, because apart from the dictates of humanity, if there is one thing I have insisted upon during this war it is that the treatment and well being of our Natives who have responded to the call for labourers should be properly provided for in every possible way.' A second reason for cancelling recruitment for East Africa was that Botha was eager to secure more blacks for the SANLC, to which he assigned the highest priority.[141]

In addition to the Cape Corps, two volunteer South African East Indian (Stretcher) Bearer Companies also served in East Africa from 1916 until the end of the campaign (and the war) in 1918. Precedence had been set for these units during the Boer War and also during the Bambatha rebellion. Gandhi had served as assistant superintendent of the unit during the Boer War until it was disbanded in February 1900, when the British abandoned operations to relieve the siege at Ladysmith. The Indian Bearer Company was again formed during the Bambatha rebellion and Gandhi served as its RSM. The use of Indians in any military function was met with hostility from the South African public and newspapers such as the *East Rand Express*:

If Indians are used against the Germans they will return to India disabused of the respect they should bear for the white race. The empire must uphold the principle that a coloured man must not raise his hand against a white man if there is to be any law or order in either India, Africa, or any part of the Empire where the white man rules over a large concourse of coloured people. In South Africa it will mean that Natives will secure pictures of whites chased by coloured men, and who knows what harm such pictures may do?[142]

Although the imperial government had contemplated raising black South African units for European service since October 1915, any proposition forwarded by the War Council was futile without the consent of a wary Union government. During discussions in the Imperial War Council in June 1916, it was proposed to use South African labour forces in Britain itself. The Colonial Office objected to this, arguing that the force would be better utilized closer to the front in France and that the responsibility of segregating the unit would be a burden to the

---

[141] Grundlingh, *Fighting Their Own War*, pp. 89–90.
[142] Plaatje, *Native Life in South Africa*, pp. 282–3.

War Office and might not meet Union standards. Secondly, and more importantly, British trade unions were obstinately opposed to a situation whereby their members could be displaced by foreign workers.[143] Therefore, the imperial proposal relayed to Botha in June was that black labour would be utilized in France. There was a serious labour shortage in Allied forces, which had been heightened by the effects of the Somme offensive. It was thought that black South Africans could add to the labour pool, as well as freeing European and white colonial labourers for combat. In August 1916, the British Commander-in-Chief, Sir Douglas Haig, estimated that the labour shortage exceeded 60,000 men.[144]

Upon receipt of the proposal, Botha met with representatives of his government and his ministry. The conclusion reached was that, 'War necessities are paramount, but this experiment, if given effect to, will require careful supervision and selected instruments. From the point of view of the Union, the sociology of the experiment is the important one.' Discussions also included measures of segregation and control within France and the fact that, 'it would be practicable to proclaim Martial Law in their Camps and Docks'. Furthermore, politicians were concerned about the possible interaction of natives with alcohol, other labourers, and French civilians and women, including prostitutes, whereby the 'Native would think white women cheap'. Exposing black South Africans to the more socially tolerant environment of France, with fewer colour barriers, was an experiment that could 'destroy white hierarchy and virtue at home in South Africa'.[145] The pressure of this 'black peril' on white imaginations caused one pundit to ask, in a letter to the editor of the *Natal Mercury*, 'What do all the half castes bear witness to – the black or white peril?'[146]

Member of Parliament J. G. Keyter argued that, 'when the kaffir returned, he will pretend to be a major or a colonel and the white man his underling, he will have ideas above his station, he will work for no white man and incite his people to agitate for equal rights'. Another opposition member was adamant in his anticipation that, 'Upon their return from Europe, the kaffirs will demand the vote.' Leaders of the SANNC also linked service to emancipation and citizenship: 'If at the conclusion of the war we were able to point to a record of military service, the Constitution would inevitably have to be altered in order that

[143] Grundlingh, *Fighting Their Own War*, pp. 41–2.
[144] See: Ian Malcolm Brown, *British Logistics on the Western Front: 1914–1919* (Toronto: Praeger, 1998).
[145] NASA, SAB, GNLB, 254/369/16. Report Ministry of Native Affairs, 3 June 1916.
[146] Grundlingh, *Fighting Their Own War*, p. 52.

brave soldiers of the Empire might be put in possession of the fullest rights and privileges of citizenship and all that pertain to *Subjects and Soldiers* of the British Empire.' The argument advanced by whites, that any dispatch of natives to Europe was politically perilous, was perceived by the SANNC and black newspapers as 'the best proof that this contingent is a good thing for the natives'.[147]

There are three primary reasons why Botha and his advisors agreed to dispatch a contingent of native labourers to France. The first, according to Botha himself, was that, 'The entire arrangements for the recruiting, officering, equipment, pay and dispatch of this contingent are in the hands of Native Affairs Department, unlike the Native labour corps used in Africa itself which were under control of the Department of Defence. All members of the Union Defence Forces and of the staff of the Union Defence Department must ... give every possible assistance.' By these measures, Botha ensured that he had direct command and control of the unit through his position as Minister of Native Affairs, chiefly via the efforts of Native Affairs secretary Edward Dower and chief clerk Godfrey A. Godley.[148] Given this fact, Botha agreed to the 'experiment', without referring the matter to the House of Assembly, where opposition was bound to occur, stipulating, however, that Britain shoulder the complete cost of the contingent. Authorities reflected on the notion that, 'the scheme provided an ideal opportunity for testing – in what would, it was hoped, be carefully controlled conditions – the practicability and effects of implementation of certain segregatory devices of social control; the lessons and results of this experiment could possibly be utilized in South Africa itself'. Secondly, Botha was protecting South African interests. He was concerned that the imperial government could circumvent the Union by recruiting blacks from its surrounding protectorates of Bechuanaland, Basutoland and Swaziland. In fact, the War Office had already raised this possibility. Botha recognized that British officers, instead of the more racially attuned South Africans, in command of local natives could undermine South African influence in the region. The association of natives, 'side by side with British soldiers who have not been accustomed to deal with them, is regarded as dangerous from the South African point of view'.[149] Lastly, a refusal to comply would, by extension, damage South African claims to the coveted GSWA during peace negotiations.

---

[147] Ibid, pp. 45–52.
[148] NASA, SAB, GNLB, 254/369/16. Botha to all Ministries, 7 September 1916; Memorandum SANLC Recruiting, October 1916.
[149] Grundlingh, *Fighting Their Own War*, pp. 42–3.

Prior to any public announcement, Native Affairs sought the opinion of medical advisors as to the dangers of disease and the effects of the climate in France on natives. After an initially negative report warning of increased malady, a specialist on disease amongst South African native populations, Dr F. Arnold, expressed no objections or significant medical anxieties as to any heightened instances of disease amongst the labour force once deployed to France. The negative conclusions of the original medical committee were, as told to Botha, 'influenced not so much on the purely medical side as from ... opposition to the venture on political and other grounds'.[150]

Colonel S. M. Pritchard was again selected to organize the recruiting for, and to command, the South African Native Labour Contingent (SANLC). He established the main recruiting depot at Rosebank showgrounds in Cape Town.[151] Given his prior experience in recruiting native labour, Pritchard immediately organized a meeting with delegates of the SANNC, as he thought it imperative to gain the support of the black elite. At a meeting in Johannesburg, he invited their comments and concerns, as he had done in 1914 and 1915, but stressed that conditions of service were non-negotiable. The SANNC, unconcerned by Pritchard's motives in wanting to gain congress support as an aid in recruitment, fully endorsed the formation of the SANLC as 'a stepping stone to still closer cooperation between the Government and the Natives'.[152]

With administrative and political understanding consolidated, on 8 September 1916 Botha publicly announced the formation of the SANLC:

I desire to express my appreciation for the good work which the Natives throughout South Africa have performed by furnishing labour for the forces in South Africa, South West Africa, and in East Africa ... You have often expressed your great desire to be allowed to assist overseas, and at the request of His Majesty the King's government, it has been arranged that a contingent of 10 000 labourers should proceed to Europe for service. The contingent will be a military unit under military discipline, employed on dock labour at French ports and not in the fighting line and will be housed in closed compounds.[153]

Botha alluded to the stipulations set by the Union regarding the use of black South Africans in France. The first was that they were non-combatant, rear-echelon labourers. The second, and most prominent

---

[150] Ibid, p. 46.
[151] NASA, SAB, GNLB, 254/369/16. Botha to all Ministries, 7 September 1916; Memorandum SANLC Recruiting, October 1916.
[152] Grundlingh, *Fighting Their Own War*, pp. 57–8.
[153] Gleeson, *The Unknown Force*, p. 25.

in all Union correspondence, was that the SANLC be housed in segregated, closed compounds (similar to those of the Kimberley mines),
preferably away from French towns and villages and the camps of other
labour units. It was also quite evident that, through the medium of this
appeal, Botha was attempting to minimize negative public and media
outcry.

The force was to be composed of 10,000 natives from across the
Union, as well as Basutoland and Swaziland, with the following
quotas: Cape 4,000, Transvaal 4,000, Natal 1,000, Basutoland 500
and Swaziland 500. The plan was for 5 battalions of 2,000 men each,
including Europeans, with one European sergeant to 60 natives. In
total, each battalion had 60 Europeans in administrative and command positions. It was stressed that, 'as for European Pers[ons] only
applications from those unavailable for Active Service [combat] will
receive consideration'. Each battalion was also furnished with one
native chaplain, two native hospital orderlies and eight native inter-
preters. The terms of service for blacks was a one year contract, with
possible reengagement, at a private's pay rate of £3 per month, with
higher rates for more senior ranks and positions. Two-thirds of all pay
was deferred until discharge. All ranks were appointed by battalion
commanders at Rosebank. Upon attestation, the recruit was given the
opportunity to arrange for family allotments from monthly pay but
was not required to do so. Compensation for disablement or death was
set at £30 to £50.[154]

The first recruits arrived at Rosebank on 20 September. Prior to
attestation, men were run through a 'carry test, viz:– carry one hundred pounds (100 lbs) one hundred yards (100 yards)'. Upon successful
completion, the medical examiner was to determine that the recruit
was, 'Sound in limb and body, free from disease or deformities, able to
masticate without artificial aid and able to see without glasses.' Medical
officers were given the discretion to 'express an opinion as to whether
a recruit is coloured or not … rejecting a man on account of colour
must however ultimately rest with the Officer who is responsible for
attestation'. The SANLC was to be made up solely of blacks with coloured men assigned to other specifically designated 'coloured units'.[155]
There was no minimum height or weight requirement, nor was any
consideration afforded to the ability to read, write or speak English

---

[154] NASA, SAB, NTS, 17/363/9108. Circular D.7/16, Overseas Native Labour
Contingent, 18 September 1916; SAB, GNLB, 25/369/16. Memorandum SANLC
Recruiting, October 1916.

[155] NASA, KAB, 1BIZ, vol. 6-2. Department of Defence to all Magistrates, 3 March
1916.

or Afrikaans.[156] While recruiting was under way in South Africa, 1st Anzac was instructed that:

One Company (500 men) of the South African Native Labour Corps will be available for work in your area about November 20th. These men will be accommodated in closed compounds, which must be ready for their occupation ... Lieutenant-Colonel Pritchard, Dir. of Nat. Labour in SA coming to help in set up and assist in arrangements ... That compounds, unless they are situated within town, are sufficiently protected by unclimbable [sic] barbed wire fence or wall, in which all openings are guarded.

The engineers of 1st Anzac were given extensively detailed blueprints for the construction of the compounds.[157]

While the closed compounds were being raised in France, recruiting continued for the SANLC throughout South Africa, and neighbouring protectorates. Botha and Pritchard urged elders, headsmen and the SANNC to help facilitate and expedite recruiting efforts. However, the SANNC, although warm to the formation of the SANLC, was not prepared to render assistance for full-scale recruiting. In return for its cooperation, the SANNC demanded that the intended closed compound system in France be abolished and that a greater number of blacks be appointed to NCO ranks. Although the government flatly rejected both requests, the SANNC decided that, 'It would be folly not to comply, for surely if we do not, then our future ... and general welfare cannot be assured.' Plaatje also reasoned that by aiding in recruitment, the SANLC would provide the men needed to bring the war to an accelerated conclusion and thus make it possible for the SANNC to attend to its grievances, the promoting of which had been postponed in August 1914.[158]

Both the SANNC and the Maori committee were in precarious positions, as bridge organizations between their people and white authorities, and wore two masks. By supporting the war effort, they demonstrated allegiance to white society and government in the hope of gaining social and political equality. They could not, however, be seen by their own people as being adjuncts to a repressive white society. Both organizations distanced themselves from active recruitment in order to maintain a phlegmatic posture. Unlike the SANNC, the members of which were self-appointed, the members of the Maori committee were elected MPs and had to answer to, and be re-elected by, their Maori constituents.

[156] NASA, SAB, NTS, 17/363/9108. Circular D.7/16, Overseas Native Labour Contingent, 18 September 1916.
[157] AWM25, 163/9. 4th Army HQ to I ANZAC, September to December 1916.
[158] Grundlingh, *Fighting Their Own War*, pp. 60–1.

Having secured the cooperation of the SANNC, both Botha and Governor-General Buxton toured South Africa to boost recruitment for the Contingent. However, the influence of the local magistrates and chiefs was the crucial factor in securing recruits. In black areas where the chief was supportive, men enlisted in great numbers, but were reluctant to do so if the local chief or elders were against service. In addition, English churches and religious benefactors to the native populations were asked directly by Botha to stimulate recruiting. They readily offered their assistance in advertising for the SANLC, with the ancillary purpose of promoting their religious agenda.[159] After a visit to the SANLC camp at Rosebank, the Anglican Bishop of Zululand was resolute that, 'a large number of the men belonging to the battalion who were heathens to-day, would come back Christians'.[160] Lastly, black newspapers and publications across South Africa encouraged enlistment: 'Even we Bantu ought to play our part in this war … Without you, your white comrades cannot do anything, because they cannot fight and provide labour at the same time. So you must go and do the labour while your white fellows are doing the fighting.'[161] F. Z. S. Peregrino, an ostentatious Captonian and editor of the *South African Spectator*, published a pamphlet entitled *His Majesty's Black Labourers: A Treatise on the Camp Life of the S.A.N.L.C.*, exhorting enlistment by dramatically glamorizing the benefits of service (see Figure 6.7).[162]

Despite the patriotic appeals and pressing recruitment drive, enlistment did not meet expectations. By January 1917, the initial 10,000 labourers had been recruited; however, during this same month the imperial government urgently asked the Union to furnish a total of 40,000 labourers for the SANLC. The Union response was simply that, although they 'cannot at this stage guarantee a supply of 40,000 they will gladly do everything in their power to meet the request of the Army Council'.[163] During 1917, recruitment efforts and methods were accelerated and broadened.

The October 1915 British memorandums influenced the formation of other colonial indigenous units and also the military inclusion of non-indigenous minority groups within the Dominions. On 26 October 1915, the British West Indies Regiment (BWIR) was established. In

---

[159] NASA, KAB, 1KNT, vol. 22. Botha to Churches of the Union, 11 June 1917.
[160] Grundlingh, *Fighting Their Own War*, p. 62.
[161] Jingoes, *A Chief is a Chief by the People*, p. 72.
[162] NASA, KAB, CMT, 3–930. F.Z.S. Peregrino, 'His Majesty's Black Labourers: A Treatise on the Camp Life of the SANLC (1917)'.
[163] NASA, SAB, GG, vol. 670, 9/93/56–9/93/63. War Office and Buxton, 18 January 1917, 7 February 1917.

Figure 6.7 Recruits of the South African Native Labour Contingent, 1916.

all, twelve indigenous labour battalions were raised, totalling 15,601 men (10,411 from Jamaica), which saw service in East Africa, Palestine, Egypt, Jordan, Italy and France. The BWIR met its initial promise to provide reinforcements of 15 per cent per month and maintained its authorized strength throughout the war.[164] On 30 December 1916, the

---

[164] NA, WO-363-364. Collection British West Indies Regiment and Those Pertaining to the BWIR Destroyed during the Battle of Britain, 1940; Harcourt Papers 445. Report on West Indian Colonies October 1915. Also see: Glenford D. Howe, 'West Indian Blacks and the Struggle for Participation in the First World War', *Journal of Caribbean History* 28/1 (1994), 27–62; Richard Smith, *Jamaican Volunteers in the*

British government secured consent from the Chinese administration to recruit Chinese labourers for the Western Front. The first Chinese 'coolies' arrived in April 1917. The total reached 100,000 by the end of the war and the last were released from service in 1920.[165]

Canadian policies affecting other minorities were also altered during 1916. In 1914, the total black population of Canada was roughly 20,000, the majority living in Nova Scotia and southern Ontario. Throughout 1914 and 1915, official policy forbade the enlistment of black Canadians, although, like Indians, a small number successfully enlisted at the discretion of recruiting officers free of colour prejudice or needing to fill battalion strengths. The 106th Battalion Nova Scotia Rifles is known to have enlisted at least sixteen blacks during late 1915.[166] Most battalion commanders, however, shared the concerns of Lieutenant-Colonel George Fowler, CO of the 104th Battalion, who turned away over twenty black volunteers: 'I have been fortunate to have secured a very fine class of recruits, and I did not think it was fair to these men that they should have to mingle with negroes.'[167] In April 1916, Gwatkin circulated a blunt memorandum to all military district commanders:

The civilized negro is vain and imitative ... in the trenches he is not likely to make a good fighter; and the average white man will not associate with him on terms of equality ... it would be humiliating to the coloured men themselves to serve in a battalion where they are not wanted. In France, in the firing line, there would be no place for a black battalion, CEF. It would be eyed askance; it would crowd out a white battalion; it would be difficult to reinforce.

He concluded that nothing prevented individual battalions from enlisting blacks at their own discretion, and that a segregated labour battalion could be raised to meet their desire to serve in some capacity. On 19 April 1916, Borden agreed to the formation of such a battalion, and authorization that the imperial government would 'be glad to accept such a battalion of Canadian Negroes' was given by the War Office on 11 May. The War Office had previously asked Canada to mobilize

First World War: Race, Masculinity and the Development of National Consciousness (Manchester University Press, 2004).

[165] PANL, MG136, Sir Walter Davidson Papers, file 3.03.006. Diary Entry 4 December 1917; David Payne, 'Forgotten Hands with Picks and Shovels', *Journal of the Western Front Association* (December 2008). Online at: www.westernfrontassociation.com

[166] Dennis and Leslie McLaughlin, *For My Country: Black Canadians on the Field of Honour* (Ottawa: National Defence, 2004), pp. 18–22.

[167] Calvin W. Ruck, *The Black Battalion 1916–1920: Canada's Best Kept Military Secret* (Halifax: Nimbus Publishing, 1987), p. 10.

labour battalions in February 1916, and at roughly the same time it was courting South Africa for expeditionary native labour units.[168]

On 5 July 1916, the No. 2 Construction Battalion, officered by whites,[169] was officially announced and was given authority to recruit blacks from across the country. Objections from military commanders over disease and the troublesome nature of such a unit in winter quarters (although they were Canadians) were immediately voiced. Moreover, recruitment had not been as high as expected, despite the fact that in February 1917 authorization was given to accept blacks from the United States and the Caribbean (171 from these areas eventually served in the Battalion).[170] The Battalion even recruited five Indians from Windsor, Ontario. During training, these Indians, contrary to the stereotype of the 'drunken Indian', were appalled with the drinking and gambling in the unit, and demanded a transfer. When the response was slow, Tuscarora Chief Thunderwater appealed to the Ministry of Militia, claiming 'a natural dislike of association with negroes on the part of Indians'. They were eventually transferred to the 256th Railway Construction Battalion, which had a large Indian component. Thunderwater demanded of Gwatkin, 'that you arrange that Indians and negroes are kept from the same Battalions'. Lieutenant-Colonel Thompson, CO of the 114th Battalion, rejected the offer of black volunteers, claiming that, 'The introduction of a coloured platoon into our Battalion would undoubtedly cause serious friction and discontent.'[171]

On 28 March 1917, the 624 men of the black Battalion left Halifax for Liverpool, well short of the authorized 1,038-man strength. Given its size, it was reconstituted as the No. 2 Construction Company in May 1917 and attached to the Canadian Forestry Corps in the Jura mountains, France. To sidestep policies of confinement and segregation similar to those imposed on the SANLC, the Canadian Ministry of Overseas Military Forces deliberately dispatched the company to this location, which was in the French area of operations, free from such racial policies. When General Headquarters issued instructions to conform to imperial standards, the Canadian Forestry commander, Colonel J. B. White, refused: '[T]he men of this Unit are engaged in exactly

---

[168] Walker, 'Race and Recruitment in World War I', 11.

[169] The only black to be commissioned was the Reverend William A. White, who was bestowed with the honorary rank of Captain, as was customary for military chaplains.

[170] John G. Armstrong, 'The Unwelcome Sacrifice: A Black Unit in the Canadian Expeditionary Force, 1917–19', in *Ethnic Armies: Polyethnic Armed Forces from the Time of the Habsburgs to the Age of the Superpowers*, p. 186.

[171] Walker, 'Race and Recruitment in World War I', 14.

the same work as the white labour with whom they are employed ... no change be made'. The No. 2 Construction Company remained equal to other Canadian Forestry units until its return to Canada on 4 December 1918. In all, over a thousand Canadian blacks served in various battalions during the war, the majority in No. 2.[172]

Asian Canadians were also barred from enlistment until the summer of 1916, when the Ministry of Militia officially authorized their recruitment. Of the roughly two hundred Japanese who saw service, almost all were enrolled in infantry battalions, primarily the 10th, 50th and 52nd Battalions. It is known that fifty-four were killed, while thirteen won the Military Medal (MM) – both overrepresentations, and a testament to their bravery, given the relatively low figure that saw service.[173] While enlistment privileges were extended to certain minorities during late 1915 and 1916, those from enemy countries were treated with harsh restrictions. The 80,000 'unnaturalized enemy aliens' from Germany and Austria-Hungary within Canada were not only refused the right to serve and to vote, but 8,579 were imprisoned under the War Measures Act in 26 'special camps'.[174] Even at this juncture in the war, the need for recruits did not wholly supersede or countermand mercurial, and often unwarranted, racial tensions, heightened by war hysteria.

Similarly, the roughly 3,000 Asians in New Zealand and 44,000 in Australia in 1914 were excluded from the NZEF and the AIF for the duration of the war.[175] However, a handful subverted protocol, or appeared substantially white, and gained entrance into military forces. According to Morag Loh, 'War records give no indication of ethnicity and scanning lists of troops for Chinese-sounding names yields very uncertain results. Some Chinese anglicised their names ... The number of Chinese-Australians ... to serve would have been very small.'[176] The most celebrated was sniper Trooper William (Billy) Sing, born to a Chinese father and a British mother. Sing, nicknamed 'The Assassin', tallied a confirmed 150 (201 unconfirmed) kills during the Gallipoli campaign alone. Three times wounded, gassed and surviving influenza,

---

[172] Armstrong, 'The Unwelcome Sacrifice', 187–8; Walker, 'Race and Recruitment in World War I', 23.
[173] See: Roy Ito, *We Went to War: The Story of the Japanese Canadians who Served in the First and Second World Wars* (Stittsville: Canada's Wings, 1984).
[174] Thompson, *Ethnic Minorities during Two World Wars*, pp. 5–7.
[175] Offer, *The First World War*, p. 169.
[176] See: Morag Loh (ed. Judith Winternitz), *Dinky-Di: The Contributions of Chinese Immigrants and Australians of Chinese Descent to Australia's Defence Forces and War Efforts, 1899–1988* (Canberra: AGPS Press, 1989); Michael Armit, 'The Chinese who Fought for "White Australia" ...', *Migration* (1989), 18–21.

Sing was awarded the DCM and the Belgian Croix de Guerre, before returning to Australia as medically unfit in July 1918.[177]

British and Dominion recruitment policies at the outbreak of war, and into 1915, could not sustain national fighting formations in the face of mounting casualties and expanding expeditionary forces. Pragmatism required the alteration of policies to allow for the inclusion of minorities as both combatants and non-combatants.

---

[177] NAA, B2455/1. Service Records William Edward Sing. He died a pauper at the age of 57.

7   1917–1918: All the King's men

By 1917, the need for manpower to sustain Allied formations became increasingly important as events unfolded on both the Western and Eastern Fronts. By the close of 1917, the Allies faced numerous and immediate strategic and operational problems. Unrestricted German submarine warfare wreaked havoc on trans-Atlantic supply lines. Reinforcements were dwindling; manpower in Allied forces was shrinking and there were increasing numbers of deserters from the French Army. Although the United States entered the war on 6 April 1917, and had the potential to tip the scales in favour of the Allies, it would be months before a significant field force was ready for deployment. Britain, the Dominions and France continued to shoulder the weight of the war. In addition, after the disaster at Caporetto in October to November 1917, the Italians were struggling to maintain a professional field force.[1] Moreover, there was no Allied breakthrough on the Western Front and stalemate and attrition continued.

To compound the Allies' problems, they witnessed the capitulation of their Russian ally and the collapse of the Eastern Front in November 1917. From mid-1917, the Germans began to relocate men and materials to the Western Front in preparation for a massive offensive. By the time the Treaty of Brest-Litovsk was signed on 3 March 1918, forty-four German divisions had already been relocated. Between November 1917 and 21 March 1918, when the *Kaiserschlacht* offensive began, the Central Powers had increased their fighting strength on the Western Front by 30 per cent. By comparison, Allied strength fell by 25 per cent over the same period, the result of the devastating losses sustained during the Passchendaele offensive and the dearth of immediate replacements.[2]

---

[1] Also known as the 12th Battle of the Isonzo, at Caporetto the Italians suffered: 10,000 killed, 30,000 wounded, 293,000 taken prisoner and 400,000 deserters at only a fraction of casualties to the Austro-Hungarian and German divisions.

[2] The net gain of the *Westheer* between November 1917 and March 1918 has been the subject of much debate. See: John Hussey, 'Debate: The Movement of German Divisions to the Western Front, Winter 1917–1918', *War in History* 4/2 (1997), 213–20;

By the beginning of 1917, four Dominions had relaxed enlistment protocols for indigenes. Only Australia still refused its indigenous population entrance into its military forces. The insatiable need for manpower, and the realization of conscription in New Zealand, Canada and Newfoundland, which contrasted with the failure of a second conscription referendum in Australia in December 1917, led to further changes to the approaches to military service for indigenes in all Dominions, including Australia, during 1917 and 1918.

In September 1916, the Canadian National Service Board was created to take a census of Canada's population and resources. The registration of all men and women over the age of 16 occurred in the winter of 1916–17, with the stated objective being to 'gather information in the cause of increased production from an agricultural point of view; to ascertain where labour for essential industries may be found; and to prepare a system of rationing food should it become necessary'. A special section was added, confirming that Indian registration was mandatory, warning that, 'The result of failure to register will be so serious that very much hardship and suffering may occur on your Reserve.'[3] Correspondingly, in February 1917 Duncan Campbell Scott issued all Indian agents with a standard 'Return of Indian Enlistment Form', on which agents were instructed to update original enlistment registers and to provide monthly recruitment returns.[4]

Confusion among Indians was immediate. Many viewed the registration as a means to conscription; others viewed it as conscription itself. Chief Meeshe Keepinais, Swan Lake Manitoba Reserve, wrote to Scott asking that, if 'the Government is going to take the young men all over this country and send them away to the war, we want to know at once if that includes the young Indians of these Reserves'. The Port Simpson, Nisga'a and Kitkatla bands in BC sent a petition to Borden and Scott, adamant that conscription did not apply to them.[5] John Gadieux, from Port Arthur, Ontario, wrote to his agent: 'Go to hell. Me to sign my name on that card, sign your own name and leave me alone. If you think that everyone is a fool like yourself you need not think that I am one.' Many other men, such as Bloods Peter Black Rabbit, George

Tim Travers, 'Debate: Reply to John Hussey: The Movement of German Divisions to the Western Front, Winter 1917–1918', *War in History* 5/3 (1998), 367–70; Giordan Fong, 'Debate: The Movement of German Divisions to the Western Front, Winter 1917–1918', *War in History* 7/2 (2000), 225–35.

[3] LAC, RG10, vol. 6770, reel C-8514, file 452-26-1. Notes on Registration.

[4] LAC, RG10, vol. 6767, reel C-8512, file 452-17. Memorandum: Scott to all Indian Agents, 22 February 1917.

[5] LAC, RG10, vol. 6768, reel C-8511, file 452-20. Petition September 1917.

Long Time Squirrel and John Pace, refused to sign their cards, while others in remote locations were simply ignorant of the registration. Indian Affairs released a statement to its agents in February 1917, stating that, 'the Indians are under obligation ... understand that these cards do not mean enlistment in the overseas battalions, but a census of the industrial strength of the Dominion'. It is unclear if any legal action was taken against Indians who refused to register. Gadieux's letter was passed to the National Service Board, 'since the officers of this Department [Indian Affairs] are not responsible for the enforcement of this Act'.[6]

The worry that the registration was the foundation for conscription was not unfounded, as the Canadian Corps was suffering sustained casualties. From April 1916 to April 1917, the Canadians suffered 75,065 casualties; a further 43,837 were accrued during the remainder of 1917.[7] In January 1917, the total strength of the CEF was 303,149, far below Borden's pledge of half a million. Monthly volunteer rates had plummeted from 28,185 in January 1916 to roughly 5,000 a month for August to December 1916. Total recruitment for the year 1917 was an unpromising 63,611, compared with 176,919 for 1916.[8] Nevertheless, by May 1918, the potent Canadian Corps totalled 123,000 men, a strength increased to as many as 148,000 when augmented by British artillery and support units – attached when the Corps was used as a spearhead formation during the last hundred days.[9] Canadian casualties during the last hundred days totalled 48,632 (excluding 6,511 sick) – roughly 20% of the total (241,000) Canadian casualties. This figure represents 12.8% of all casualties (379,000) sustained by the entire BEF between 8 August and 11 November, despite the fact that the Canadian Corps was roughly 6.7% of its overall ration-strength.[10]

In May 1917, when casualty rates were more than twice that of recruitment, Borden announced his intention to introduce military conscription as 'the battle for Canadian liberty and autonomy is being fought today on the plains of France and Belgium'.[11] It was a fateful decision that further divided English and French-Canadians.

[6] LAC, RG10, vol. 6766, reel C-8511, file 452-12. Gadieux to W. R. Brown (Indian Agent Port Arthur), January 1917; Brown to Scott, 16 January 1917; Scott to Secretary National Service Board, 22 January 1917; McLean to Chiefs Manitoulin Island, 1 February 1917; Dempsey, *Warriors of the King*, pp. 36–7.

[7] Rawling, *Surviving Trench Warfare*, pp. 238–40.

[8] Nicholson, *Canadian Expeditionary Force*, Appendix C.

[9] Rawling, *Surviving Trench Warfare*, pp. 241–2.

[10] See: Shane B. Schreiber, *Shock Army of the British Empire: The Canadian Corps in the Last 100 Days of the Great War* (St Catherine's: Vanwell Publishing, 2004).

[11] Walker, 'Race and Recruitment in World War I', 18.

On 11 June 1917, Borden introduced the Military Service Bill with the objectives of securing more men to promote Canadian interests and autonomy, while legally demanding Québecois participation. Immediately, Scott was flooded with correspondence from both chiefs and agents asking what the regulations were pertaining to Indians. Scott replied that the bill was not yet law; however, he did presume that, if made law, it would apply to all British subjects in Canada, including Indians. Many chiefs and band councils reminded Scott of treaties that prevented Indians from being compelled to go to war in service of Canada.[12]

On 29 August, the Military Service Act legally sanctioned conscription. The decree applied to all male British subjects in Canada, including Indians, Asians and blacks, between the ages of 20 and 45, with men being placed in six classes based on age, marital and dependant status. Those specifically mentioned for exemption were conscientious objectors, the clergy and certain professionals. All others were forced to register in order to apply for individual exemptions. Of the total 142,588 Canadian men registered under the Military Service Act, only 24,132 joined active Canadian battalions.[13]

Petitions flowed to Ottawa, and to the King, from Indian (and Japanese) councils demanding that, because they did not have rights of citizenship, they should not be forced to perform the duties of a fully enfranchised Canadian. Many Indian communities reminded the government of its obligations under the treaties of the 1870s, and the promises of negotiator Alexander Morris, which excluded Indians from conscription. Widely circulated newspapers also ran articles stating the same case on behalf of the Indian population. Within these objections lie the faint articulations of the war aims of Canadian and other Dominion minority groups; if the burdens of the war were to be shared by them, it must result in the extension of equality and citizenship.

On 1 October 1917, Scott informed the Ministry of Militia and the Deputy Minister of Justice, E. L. Newcombe, that his department would support the conscription of Indians. The Ministry of Militia endorsed Scott's decision: 'Indians are British subjects and come under the terms of the Military Service Act, just as any other British subjects.'[14] All male Indians of military age were expected to register

---

[12] LAC, RG10, vol. 6768, reels C-8512, C-8513, files 452-20-1,2,3. Correspondence Scott Concerning Military Service Bill and the Military Service Act.
[13] Walker, 'Race and Recruitment in World War I', 18.
[14] LAC, RG10, vol. 6768, reels C-8512, C-8513, files 452-20-1,2,3. Scott to Newcombe, 1 October 1917.

Figure 7.1 Onondaga Private Tom Longboat of the Six Nations
Reserve buying a 'trench paper', June 1917.

by 10 November 1917. There was no mention of Canada's Arctic
Eskimos – a logical realization of the impossibility of enforcing the Act,
given their remoteness and relatively miniscule population of roughly
3,500. Nevertheless, driven by the necessities of the war, Canada's policy towards Indian military service had shifted to the opposite end of
the spectrum from that of 1914. From originally trying to dissuade
Indians from participation, through the gradual shift between 1915
and 1917 of active recruitment, Ottawa was now demanding, under
law, their participation (see Figure 7.1).

In addition to the protest correspondence directed at Ottawa and
London, many Indians refused to register, while others in remote areas
did not know of the regulation. Others, including entire reserves, as
with the earlier National Service Board registration, refused to comply
out of defiance, some going so far as to conceal their young men. On
the Sarcee Reserve in Alberta, the agent, disgusted with the regulations
of his government, registered all eligible men only to exempt them, citing a fictitious outbreak of tuberculosis in the paperwork submitted

to his superiors in Ottawa. On numerous smaller reserves throughout Canada, all eligible men had already volunteered.[15]

On 16 November, to avoid problems associated with taking legal action against those who failed to register, the deadline for Indians was extended to 1 February 1918. There were, however, individual cases of charges laid against Indians for failing to register. Clefus DeCoine of Lake Wabasca, Alberta, 250 miles north of Edmonton, was charged with breach of the Military Service Act. At the trial, DeCoine needed a Cree interpreter and, obvious to all, had no concept of the Act. The charges were quickly dismissed.[16] Before the closing date of 1 February arrived, Ottawa passed legislation exempting Indians (and Japanese) from the terms of the Military Service Act. On 17 January 1918, an Order-in-Council (PC111) stated:

Whereas petitions and memorials have been received from and on behalf of Indians pointing out that in view of their not having any vote, they should, although natural born British subjects, not be compelled to perform militia service, and that in the negotiations of certain treaties, expressions were used indicating that Indians should not be so compelled, an instance of this recently brought forward being the expression of the Lieutenant Governor in negotiating the North West Angle Treaty as it appears in the despatch of the 14th of October, 1873, quoted in Morris, Treaties of Canada with the Indians, pp. 50 and 69.

18a. Any Indian agent may make application for the exemption of any Indian attached to the Reserve over which such agent has jurisdiction and it shall not be necessary for the Registrar to assign to a local tribunal any application made or transmitted by an Indian agent on behalf of an Indian, but the Registrar shall forthwith issue to such Indian and transmit to the Indian agent for delivery to him a certificate of exemption from combatant military service.[17]

The order also contained provisions whereby any Indian who had enlisted, or been drafted since the Military Service Act was passed, could apply for guaranteed discharge. A stipulation was that these men could only make a submission for discharge on their own behalf through their agent, not through a relative, band council or chief. Another clause of PC111 was that, although all Indians were exempt from military service, all Canadian men and women over the age of 16, including Indians, were still compelled to register under the Military Service Act by 22 June 1918.[18] An unpublicized glitch within PC111, which could have caused

[15] Dempsey, *Warriors of the King*, p. 39.
[16] Ibid, p. 41.
[17] LAC, RG10, vol. 6768, reels C-8512, C-8513, files 452-20-1,2,3. Governor-General in Council: Military Service Act Regulations, 17 January 1918. East Indians were granted exemption three weeks later. Blacks were not exempted, as they enjoyed the franchise.
[18] LAC, RG10, vol. 6768, reels C-8512, C-8513, files 452-20-1,2,3. Department of Militia and Defence: Status of Indians Under the M.S.A., 22 February 1918.

great embarrassment to the government of Canada, was that regulation 18a, and also clause 14a, both stated that, 'Indians were exempt from combat duties'. This implied that Indians could volunteer and serve in home defence units, at reasonable pay rates, without ever leaving Canada. It also meant that those overseas could request transfer back to Canada and serve out the remainder of the war in the home defence force. If this special treatment had been afforded only to Indians, it would have been met with fierce opposition from French-Canadians, who strongly opposed conscription. Rioting nevertheless plagued Montreal during the two days following the passing of conscription, and on the Easter weekend of 1918, Quebec City was engulfed in anti-conscription violence that led to the death of four civilians. Auspiciously, for Scott and the government of Canada, few Indian soldiers discovered these loopholes. There was, however, one exception.

On 31 August 1918, Harry Stonechild, a Peepeekisis who was still serving after being wounded and gassed in France, wrote the following letter to his Saskatchewan Superintendent, W. M. Graham, who forwarded it to Scott: 'I beg your assistance to kindly inform me as to whether these instructions apply to me that were issued by Ottawa at the last Federal Elections. Concerning to Indians who have been drafted into the ranks. May be released from the Army if application is made by themselves or relations. As the Indians do not enjoy their Franchise they have the privilege of now leaving the army if desiring to do so.'[19] Although Stonechild volunteered in August 1915, and was not drafted, he wanted clarification of his rights as an Indian soldier under current law. Scott told Graham that each case should be judged on its own merit, but stated that it would be a dangerous precedent to recommend a return to civilian life for those already in uniform as it might cause undue resentment among other segments of the population: 'It has been thought that a recommendation for the return of one Indian might cause dissatisfaction in the event of a large number of applicants being made ... I may add that there is no truth that enlisted Indians are to be allowed to return to civil life on account of not having the privilege of franchise.'[20]

Stonechild referred to amendments made to the Voters Act by a fretful Borden before the bitter General Federal Election of 17 December 1917. To ensure victory for conscription, Borden introduced two laws

[19] Alistair Sweeny, *Government Policy and Saskatchewan Indian Veterans: A Brief History of the Canadian Government's Treatment of Indian Veterans of the Two World Wars* (Saskatoon: Tyler, Wright & Daniel, 1979), pp. 6–8.

[20] Ibid, p. 9.

to slant the voting in favour of his newly formed Union Party (which included selected opposition members in cabinet). The first, the Wartime Elections Act (20 September 1917), disenfranchised conscientious objectors and Canadian citizens who were born in Central Power countries and immigrated after 1902. The law also gave female relatives of servicemen the vote. Thus, the 1917 election was the first federal election in which some women were allowed to vote, although this alteration did not apply to Indian women. Secondly, the Military Voters Act (27 November 1917) provided a special provision for the enfranchisement, for the upcoming election only, of all soldiers, including Indians. In addition, a special clause for Indian veterans (of the Great War only) stipulated that a governmental representative would be dispatched to reserves in order for them to vote.[21] The Indian Act specified that enfranchisement meant the loss of 'Indian status'; however, the Military Voters Act superseded these articles.[22] In reality, albeit without their knowledge, Indian servicemen had already obtained the right to vote before these alterations. On 4 May 1916, in parliamentary debate, the Minister of Justice, Charles Doherty, quoted a passage from the active Military Service Act: 'Canadian soldiers on Active Military Service during the present war [have the right] to exercise their electoral franchise ... makes no exception of Indians'.[23]

In contrast to Indians, Maori were initially excluded from New Zealand's Military Service Act, yet, at the insistence of Pomare, they were ultimately included. In January 1917, with more Maori reinforcements, the Pioneer Battalion was reorganized into three full Maori companies, including officers, and one *Pakeha* company. The winter of 1917 was a relatively quiet period for the Battalion. During the Battle of Messines (7–14 June 1917) the Battalion was charged with trench digging, light tram-rail construction and wiring parties. The Maori suffered 155 casualties, including 17 killed, before being removed from the line on the 29th.[24] Maori casualty rates were never withheld at any point in the war and were published as supplements in the *Maori Gazette*, despite the fact that in certain locations this honesty hindered recruiting.[25] Notwithstanding, enough Maori reinforcements arrived to create an all-Maori unit. The *Pakeha* company was transferred to an infantry

---

[21] LAC, RG9III, vol. 5081. Dominion of Canada, Military Voter's Act, 1917: Directions of Guidance for Voters.
[22] Dempsey, *Aboriginal Soldiers and the First World War*, pp. 2–3.
[23] Ibid, p. 3.
[24] Cowan, *The Maoris in the Great War*, p. 115.
[25] ANZ, AD1, box 758, record 9/296. Casualty *Kahiti* (Supplements) of the *Maori Gazette*, 25 May 1916.

battalion. On 1 September, the New Zealand (Maori) Pioneer Battalion was officially formed. Inaccurately, secondary sources conclude that the main reason the authorities had the confidence to create a Maori battalion, and maintain its ranks in the face of casualties and disease, was because conscription had been extended to Maori on 26 June 1917.[26] Although Maori recruitment slowed during 1916, from the beginning of 1917 onwards numbers were not a problem and the Maori Pioneer Battalion never fell below its established strength – at the end of 1917 it was 928-strong. Conscription of Maori was not the reason for the formation of the Battalion, nor did conscription actually produce significant reinforcements. Conscription was designed to force service on certain Maori tribes that had not opted to do so voluntarily, most notably in Pomare's district among the Waikato and Taranaki tribes of King Country. In a sense, it was a tool of assimilation, if not punishment, for those Maori who had not supported New Zealand's war effort.

In general, recruitment in New Zealand had stalled throughout 1915; yet, the NZEF, which had maintained an infantry brigade, was enlarged into a division in January 1916. With its deployment to the Western Front in April 1916, and the subsequent bloodletting at the Somme, traditional recruitment was not meeting the demands of the division. A War Census under the National Registration Act, conducted in October to November 1915, revealed that over 60 per cent of eligible men had not yet enlisted.[27] This mandatory registration did not include Maori.

The New Zealand Military Services Bill was introduced on 10 June 1916, followed by the Military Service Act on 1 August, and, like the 1915 registration, did not pertain to Maori. Allen quickly made this exemption known to Maori leaders and communities, while outlining the legal action that would allow for compulsion: 'Natives in the meaning of the Native Land Act 1909 are exempted from registration under the Military Service Act. Section 50, however, provides that the Governor may by proclamation extend the provisions of the Act so as to provide for compulsory calling up of natives for military service within the Expeditionary Force.'[28] The Military Service Act did not apply to other minorities, including Asians and men of German heritage. These small minority populations were barred from enlistment, and excluded from conscription, for the entire war.[29]

---

[26] ANZ, AD1, box 1367, record 66/11. Memorandum: Extension of Military Service Act 1916 to Natives, 26 June 1917.
[27] See: Paul Baker, *King and Country Call: New Zealanders, Conscription and the Great War* (Auckland: University Press, 1988).
[28] ANZ, AD1, box 960, record 29/108. Memorandum: Allen, 9 September 1916.
[29] Baker, *King and Country Call*, pp. 222–3.

Maori recruitment, like that of *Pakeha*, had slowed throughout 1916. Tribes of the Waikato, Taranaki, Maniapoto, Tuhoe and the Ureweras, where special Maori recruiting officers had been active since June 1916, were still resisting recruitment. Pomare expressed the view to the Department of Defence that, 'There is only one way, I am afraid, of getting at the Waikatos, that is by having Section 50 of the Military Service Act, 1916, brought into operation, and I hope you will soon have a proclamation drafted in this connection.' Ngata also concluded that the initial promises of Maori men were just 'wind and words'.[30] Maori companies had only been sustained through the early months of 1916 by the enlistment of Pacific Islanders, who were no longer on active service and not wanted. Furthermore, Pomare's attempt to transfer all Maori serving in other units to Maori companies, in the summer of 1916, did not succeed. After canvassing all New Zealand units, only eight of the forty Maori identified opted for transfer, and Godley and Allen were unwilling to compel the remainder to do so.[31]

During the parliamentary debates concerning the Military Service Act, Pomare, with lukewarm support from the Maori committee, was urging the Department of Defence to pass Section 50 to bind Maori legally to mandatory service. Pomare believed that no distinction should be made between Maori and *Pakeha*: 'It treats every man alike, no matter what his creed, no matter what his wealth, no matter what his colour may be ... I say it should apply to all alike, and for that reason I believe in conscription.'[32] Ngata did not envisage different applications of the Act either, at least not publicly. He did, however, outwardly reflect on his belief that neither Maori nor *Pakeha* would 'voluntarily' cooperate with conscription. Tau Henare, MP for the Northern Maori, in a speech he refused to deliver in English, told Parliament that the reluctance of the Waikato and Taranaki to volunteer was due to residual animosity from the New Zealand Wars and the subsequent confiscation of land. He further instructed that, should conscription apply to men of these tribal communities, 'those blocks of confiscated lands which are not already settled by Europeans should be returned for the use and occupation of the returned native soldiers of those districts'.[33]

Within the debate regarding conscription, the most dominant theme was the refusal of men from King Country to enlist. In the end, this

---

[30] ANZ, AD1, box 960, record 29/108. Pomare to General Sir Alfred Robin, 1 February 1917.

[31] ANZ, AD1, box 734, record 9/32/1. HQ NZ Division to Allen, 5 August 1917; Pomare to Allen, 7 August 1917; Godley to Allen, 13 August 1917.

[32] Cody, *Man of Two Worlds*, p. 119.

[33] O'Connor, 'The Recruitment of Maori Soldiers', 61–2.

refusal led directly to the unofficial imposition of conscription on them alone. As of 6 August 1917, shortly after conscription was applied to Maori on 26 June, Allen sent a memorandum to all MPs to be distributed to their Maori communities:

The compulsion of the Military Service Act need not be feared by the Tribes of New Zealand who voluntarily sent their sons in the services of King and Empire, and if it has become necessary to introduce compulsion so far as the Maori people as concerned it is because one Tribe, at any rate, has not done its duty ... no injustice will be meted out to the loyal and patriotic Maoris who have shown their loyalty in this time of national trial.

Although officially conscription applied to 'some or all North Island Maoris', it was clear that unofficially it was intended to apply to the 'Waikato-Maniapoto Land District' only.[34]

The task of completing a register for the Waikato Maori was an almost impossible feat. Many Maori births were not registered and contemporary government registers were unreliable in almost all categories. Furthermore, according to the Inspector of Recruiting Services, most young men 'no longer visit towns, but have taken back to the country, forests or settlements'. Others that responded asked if the call-up could be delayed until after the autumn shearing and harvest season. These problems led to a delay in gathering the first Maori draft, which did not occur until February 1918. Over 50 per cent of the first ballot failed to appear for their medical boards. Those who could be tracked were imprisoned.[35] When war ended, 552 Maoris had been registered in four ballots, with 254 found ineligible or medically unfit. Of the remaining 298, 11 were serving prison sentences, 139 were unaccounted for, with over 100 arrest warrants unexecuted. Only seventy-four were training at Narrow Neck, with a further seventy-four in the administration process for either duty or imprisonment.[36] No conscripted Maori ever served overseas and, in May 1919, objectors were released from prison and the fifty-seven outstanding warrants annulled.[37]

Despite the fact that no Maori conscripts joined the Maori Pioneer Battalion in France, it was still able to maintain its full strength of over 900 until the end of the war (no more than fifty of these, including officers, were ever *Pakeha*). During the Passchendaele offensive, the

---

[34] ANZ, AD1, box 1367, record 66/11. Memorandum: Allen, 6 August 1917.
[35] ANZ, AD1, box 1367, record 66/11. Inspector of Recruiting Services to Allen, 30 April 1918, 29 May 1918.
[36] King, *Te Puea*, p. 96; Baker, *King and Country Call*, p. 220.
[37] ANZ, AD1, box 1367, record 66/11. Pomare to Allen (with Reply), 20 August 1919; Baker, *King and Country Call*, p. 201.

Figure 7.2 Prime Minister William F. Massey and Sir Joseph G. Ward inspecting the Maori Pioneer Battalion at Bois-de-Warnimont, France, June 1918.

Battalion suffered sixty-one casualties, including fifteen dead. During the German offensives in the spring of 1918, the Battalion suffered forty-seven additional casualties. In the final Allied offensives, the Battalion suffered 207 more casualties for the months of August to October (see Figure 7.2).

At the opening of 1917, Australia had yet officially to endorse the enlistment of Aborigines, although a small number had evaded protocol. Facing a shortage of volunteers, despite a vigorous recruiting campaign, regulations were relaxed concerning the enlistment of 'half-castes'. No alterations, however, were made to the Defence Act, to safeguard Aboriginal exclusion from the ADF after the war when their services would no longer be needed. By July 1916, Australia had five divisions active on the Western Front, which formed the Australian Corps on 1 November 1917. From July 1916 to June 1917, Australian casualties totalled more than 55,000, with another 38,000 suffered during the Passchendaele offensive. On the other hand, recruitment for the expanding AIF totalled 80,854 from December 1915 to April 1916, but thereafter enlistment rates went into continuous decline, numbering only 45,101 for the year of 1917.[38] Furthermore, two attempts at a democratic conscription process failed. By 1917, Australia needed more soldiers to maintain AIF formations.

In March 1917, a military memorandum was sent to all recruiting depots stating that, 'Half-castes may be enlisted in the AIF provided that the examining medical authorities are satisfied that one of the parents is of European descent.'[39] In addition, height requirements had progressively been lowered from 165 cm at the outbreak of war to 155 cm by 1917. By 11 May 1917, all Chief Protectors of Aborigines for each state had announced Military Order 200(2):

Advice has been received from the recruiting committee that half-castes will now be accepted for service in the Australian Expeditionary Forces provided that they satisfy the medical authorities that one parent was of European origin. As the enlistment of full-blood Aborigines is also being advocated, will you [local protectors] as soon as possible ascertain and advise the probable number of full-bloods and half-castes, separately, under 45 years who would be prepared to enlist within the next three months.[40]

Manpower requirements, fuelled by modern war with its ever increasing casualties, necessitated that elements of racial prejudice in 'White Australia' be discarded. In addition to Aborigines, Morag Loh asserts that, 'Chinese-Australians may have been accepted into the army, particularly later in the war, despite the regulations, because of the falling off in recruitment and China's declaration of war on Germany in March 1917.'[41]

In May 1917, active recruiting was initiated in Aboriginal communities. In Lake Tyers, Victoria, enlisted men formed a gum leaf band, which was successfully used in recruiting campaigns throughout Victoria State.[42] Another Aboriginal volunteer from Barambah settlement, dressed in a military uniform, participated in recruiting drives bearing a sign, 'By Cripes! I'll Fight for White Australia.'[43] Eighteen men from Barambah were recruited, but ten were released for being 'full-bloods'. Nevertheless, there was a significant increase in Aboriginal enlistment after May 1917.[44] According to Rod Pratt, known Aboriginal enlistment

---

[38] Robson, *The First A.I.F.*, pp. 77, 137, 165–6.

[39] Pratt, 'Queensland's Aborigines in the First AIF', 17.

[40] Huggonson, 'Dark Diggers of the AIF', 353.

[41] Armit, 'The Chinese who Fought for "White Australia"...', 20.

[42] Alick Jackomos and Derek Fowell, *Forgotten Heroes: Aborigines at War from the Somme to Vietnam* (Melbourne: Victoria Press, 1993), p. 14.

[43] Pratt, 'Queensland's Aborigines in the First AIF', 19.

[44] AWM, CN R940.4030994 A938. List of Australian Indigenous Servicemen who Served in World War One (Work in Progress), January 2007; AWM27, 533/1. Returns

totals for Queensland were: ten for 1915, twenty-one for 1916, rising to fifty for 1917, with thirty-two of these enlisting between July and December.[45] According to Bleakley, 'Large numbers immediately volunteered, all claiming to come within that category [half-caste]. The recruiting officers scratched their heads, as one of them said, "some of these are the blackest half-castes I've ever seen". It seemed a shame to disappoint them, but most, if not all, wormed themselves in at other centres and got into uniform eventually.'[46] Many claimed to be part Indian. Others, including Richard Martin, who falsely listed his place of birth as Dunedin, New Zealand, claimed to be Maori. Albert Tripcony explained his dark complexion by telling recruiters that he came from Italy. Australia was willing to accept Maori into the AIF, given their performance at Gallipoli and in France, under the pretence of Maori martial and racial hierarchy.[47]

Although Aboriginal recruits were judged on their physical appearance, they were also given credit for their ability to read and write, which was evidence of both an education and assimilation. One possibility for the inclusion of educated 'full-bloods' was an unofficial amendment to the May 1917 policy insinuating that those who had been closely associated with whites, or who had been raised by white families, could enter service.[48]

Newfoundland initiated a second campaign to recruit the indigenous population of Labrador during 1917. Since Gallipoli, the Newfoundland Regiment had sustained devastating casualties. In less than 30 minutes on 1 July 1916, at Beaumont Hamel, the regiment suffered 733 casualties of 801 men engaged. After taking part in minor engagements (including 239 casualties at Gueudecourt in October 1916) the Battalion suffered 486 casualties (including three Eskimos) at Monchy-le-Preux between 12 and 15 April 1917, during the denouement to the Arras offensive. Battalion casualties during the Passchendaele offensive totalled 200. Following the Battle of Cambrai (November to December 1917), during which the regiment suffered almost 350 casualties, total strength stood at only 250 men. Although these actions resulted in the regiment gaining the title 'Royal' in December 1917, recruitment and maintaining battalion strength were

Showing Particulars of Men of Aboriginal Percentage who Enlisted and Served Abroad with the A.I.F.
[45] Pratt, 'Queensland Aborigines in the First AIF', 18.
[46] J. W. Bleakley, *The Aborigines of Australia: Their History – Their Habits – Their Assimilation* (Brisbane: Jacaranda Press, 1961), p. 170.
[47] Lindsay Watson, 'Barambah or Cherbourg: It's All the Same', *Kurbingui Star* (No Date), 10.
[48] Watson, 'Better Than a One-Eyed Man', 5.

serious problems and conscription had been openly discussed in government since January 1917. In contrast to these casualty rates, total enlistment for the year 1916 was only 1,089.[49]

During the final two years of the war, the political and military organizations of Newfoundland witnessed wholesale change. In July 1917, an official Ministry of Militia was created, headed by John R. Bennett. In September, Governor Davidson became Governor of New South Wales and was replaced by Sir Charles Alexander Harris. In December, Prime Minister Morris resigned in favour of William F. Lloyd. While these changes occurred, recruitment stagnated; St John's had been drained of most eligible men, while the outports still lagged behind. Conscription became a realistic measure and was supported by the primarily Protestant government officials and population of St John's, but was opposed in the smaller Catholic outports. From August to October 1917, only 344 recruits were accepted as medically fit. Canada had passed the Military Service Act in August 1917, and in September, Bennett met with Borden and his Canadian counterpart, Sir Albert Edward Kemp, to discuss the Act and its broader implementation.[50]

Prior to Bennett's visit to Ottawa, and Newfoundland's debate over conscription, recruitment of indigenous men from Labrador was again questioned. Elite, white members of Labrador communities were still uncertain as to the recruitment regulations pertaining to Eskimos. On 10 July 1917, W. R. Grieve, chair of the Newfoundland Recruiting Committee, received a cable from Dr Harry L. Paddon, stationed at the Grenfell Association in Indian Harbour, Labrador. Paddon's letter confirms the confusion, neglect and mistrust of governance in Labrador, including during the war years, while also representing the general political and social realities of all indigenes of the Dominions:

I want to enlist your interest in the question of Labrador recruiting ... as a limited number of natural snipers are available, but rather hard to get. Seven men from Hamilton Inlet have ... determination to volunteer at the end of this summer's fishery. At the time the war broke out ... they [Eskimos] were underrepresented, unemployed, largely uneducated, in fact underdeveloped in every way. Moreover, the population is so scattered that ... words meant little to such people [but] many of them see that it is their war, & they have an interest in ending it. Lectures & lantern slides & amateur recruiting may have had a little effect. The lack of any resident administrative, worthy of the name, on this Coast; & the constant chaos, neglect & injustice necessarily resulting

---

[49] PANL, MG632, Patriotic Association of Newfoundland 1914–19 – file 1. Casualties.
[50] PANL, GN2/14, box 14, file 200. Maj. Montgomerie, GOC HQ St John's to Colonial Secretary Arthur Mews, 7 September 1917; Borden from Governor Harris, 8 October 1917.

from the unintelligent efforts of summer trippers [recruiters], maintain a constant deep resentment, & certainly add greatly to the difficulty in recruiting. 'We owe nothing because we get nothing.' 'We couldn't be worse off if the Germans took the country.' These are, honestly wide spread sentiments. It is hard to point out ... that the argument that sacrifice now is the best way to win recognition in the future also fails to take hold, where, in 110 years there has been neither representation, Commissioner, Justice, Employment or more than a bare smattering of Education. These facts must be faced, Sir, to understand the situation. These regrettable truths leave the Country apathetic, when one would long to see her bearing a greater share of the War's evils & earning a greater share of its blessings. I am honestly trying to combat this. But a little encouragement from Newfoundland might do far more than personal effort ... Politicians in the past at any rate, have not thought this Dependency worth bothering about: &, while we have but little to offer, I do trust that you will give kindly consideration to the facts & reasons I have laid before you.

Paddon also questioned the policy of war-time allowances to dependants and enlistment regulations, asking: 'Is a man worth sending so long as he is sane & physically fit?'[51]

The letter was passed to both Bennett and Governor Davidson, with Grieve stating 'that this is much too large a matter for me to take up'. This answer mirrored that of Duncan Campbell Scott regarding the Canadian registration of 1916–17 – in the event of uncertainty, or facing a question of jurisdiction, it was convenient and politically safe to forward responsibility. Bennett offered Grieve advice, which avoided larger political issues and pertained to recruitment alone: 'The standard has been relaxed since March 1915 by the reduction of height to five feet [from 5'3"] and by the reduction of weight to one hundred and twelve pounds [from 120 lbs], for eighteen years of age [from nineteen] ... Unless a man is almost an idiot it would be hard to turn him down.' The need for manpower is evident in Bennett's response, but realistic special consideration was also afforded to all men in Labrador, including indigenes, given their remote locations and adverse living conditions: 'Early in the war His Excellency the Governor laid down the rule that we would not receive recruits of married men living in Labrador or others having women and children depending on them.' Bennett was referring, not to official policy, but rather to Davidson's earlier reply of April 1915 to Mr Swaffield's offer of fifteen men from Cartwright, Labrador.[52] Three Eskimos in Paddon's charge enlisted following this correspondence.[53]

[51] PANL, GN2/14, box 13, file 146. Paddon to W. R. Grieve, 10 July 1917.
[52] PANL, GN2/14, box 13, file 146. W. R. Grieve to Paddon, 26 July 1917; file 165. John R. Bennett to Colonial Secretary R. A. Squires, 21 August 1917.
[53] PANL, GN19, B-2-3, reels 235, 238. Service Records John Blake, Frederick Freida, Thomas Flowers.

Although conscription had been looming in Newfoundland since early 1917, voluntary recruitment efforts were maintained with limited success until the spring of 1918. On 9 April 1918, Governor Harris received a telegram from the War Office outlining the urgency for reinforcements for the Battalion, which was 170 men short of its authorized strength: '[A]t least 300 men will be required from Newfoundland as early as possible in order to bring the Battalion up to strength, and an additional sixty men per month will be required to maintain it in the field. His Majesty's Government trust that your Government will be able to supply these men.' The alternative was to break up the regiment and form two Newfoundland companies within a Canadian battalion. With conscription looming, a last intense campaign to stimulate recruiting was undertaken. Although 725 recruits were secured in April, the best monthly total since February 1915, officials realized it would not be enough.[54]

On 27 April, the War Office issued Harris another cable: 'Battalion short of men. Training Depot England has no men to send forward. Absolutely essential men for Regiment be provided without delay and referring of Conscription Act to people would result in loss of valuable time.'[55] The Military Service Act was introduced on 11 May 1918, patterned almost identically on that of Canada. By war's end, only 3,629 men had been registered, of which only 1,573 were found to be medically fit. Although these men proceeded to Britain for training in September 1918, hostilities ended before any were posted to the Battalion. No conscript ever served at the front.[56] Conscription was never applied to indigenous Newfoundlanders. In response to questions regarding conscription in Labrador, the Ministry of Militia simply stated that, 'This department has not issued any instructions and has not been authorized to deal with this matter.'[57] This is yet another example illustrating a Dominion's lack of clear policy or forethought regarding indigenous service.

In South Africa, recruiting for the SANLC had achieved the initial goal of 10,000 by January 1917, but numbers were far too low to meet the increased request by imperial authorities for 40,000. Conscription, in the official and legal sense, as sanctioned in other Dominions, was not an option for the Union government. The implementation of a binding military service act for blacks could have sparked open

---

[54] Nicholson, *The Fighting Newfoundlander*, pp. 438–9.
[55] PANL, GN2/14, box 11, file 113. War Office to Governor Harris, 27 April 1918.
[56] Nicholson, *The Fighting Newfoundlander*, p. 439.
[57] PANL, GN2/14, box 11, file 103. GOC HQ Major Montgomerie to Governor Harris and Recruiting Committee, May 1918.

rebellion. Alternative methods to secure recruits for the SANLC were implemented during 1917, with marginal success. There were multiple reasons for the lack of volunteers but, as Grundlingh accurately points out, 'all are traceable to one underlying theme: basic mistrust of the white man'.[58] Many chiefs and individuals felt there was no good reason to serve a country or an empire for which they held no affinity, or were hostile towards, given the recent 1913 Natives Land Act. Although the SANLC was technically an imperial unit, most natives did not make this distinction and still viewed it as an arm of the repressive Union government. This was expressed unanimously by the chiefs of Western Pondoland: 'Why should there be a difference between the men at the Docks and those in the fighting line? To-day the Union Government should do away with the colour bar before we go overseas. General Botha said we should be one. In many ways we are not one.'[59]

In addition, many feared the unknown, including the voyage: 'At a meeting the spokesman said that none were going; that they were frightened of crossing the sea.' Stimela Jason Jingoes commented, upon his return from France in 1918, of the 'superstition that no black person could cross the sea and return again ... Few believed that we really were soldiers.'[60] This point was especially true after the sinking of the transport ship SS *Mendi* on 21 February 1917, during which 619 members of the SANLC lost their lives (including twelve whites).[61] After the *Mendi* disaster many magistrates shared the expressed view of the Chief Magistrate at Lusikisiki: 'The news of the loss of a ship with 600 natives ... may have the effect of extinguishing any little hope there may have been of getting any [recruits] out.'[62] Showing some commitment to honesty, the *Mendi* casualty lists were made public on the orders of Botha, and printed in black newspapers much to the detriment of future recruiting, as exemplified by the Matatiele magistrate: 'I do not know who is responsible for these [casualty lists] appearing in the papers but the natives here certainly associate going to France with dying by and through these lists.'[63]

---

[58] Grundlingh, *Fighting Their Own War*, p. 72.
[59] NASA, KAB, CMT, 3/925. Meeting of Magistrate Pondoland/Umtata with Chief Mangala and Chiefs of Western Pondoland, 10 November 1916; Correspondence to Magistrate Umtata from Chiefs Mangala, Nongqansa, Jiyajiya, 23 October to 10 November 1916.
[60] Jingoes, *A Chief is a Chief by the People*, p. 91.
[61] NA, WO-107/37. After Action Report: Work of Labour Force during the War, November 1919.
[62] NASA, KAB, CMT, 3/925. Magistrate Lusikisiki to Native Affairs, 12 March 1917.
[63] NASA, KAB, CMT, 3/930. Magistrate Matatiele to Native Affairs, 24 August 1917; Memorandum from Botha regarding *Mendi*, 23 March 1917.

Other blacks resented the fact that they were labourers. According to H. M. Tyali, SANLC veteran and returned recruiter: '[M]en of no weapon, men of no training to any sort of weapon to go through the big waves and dangers of Germans ... we should be trained in the art of carrying arms that we may do our bit ... and we do not wish to be treated like women.'[64] Furthermore, men working in the mines or on farms had a steady income without the risk of going to war, despite the higher SANLC salary (an average rate of 10/- per month), in addition to free food and a uniform afforded by service. Although enlisting in March 1917, Jingoes weighed this option: 'Why should I go? I'm getting a good salary here. Mr. Sack's is a fine employer. I'm having an admirable time right here. Over there, people are dying!'[65] In addition, many men were threatened by their employers, or by the white farmers whose land they leased, that, if they joined, their families would suffer the consequences while they were away. Many black farmers also viewed recruiting as a governmental scheme to entice men away in order to seize land in their absence. They were right. In 1917, the government initiated (although did not pass) the Native Administration Bill, which outlined further segregation policies and the creation of 'reserves', in accordance with the 1913 Land Act.[66]

More importantly, the Chamber of Mines, the railway administration and other employers with a large black labour force refused to cooperate with recruitment. Fearing a shortage of labour, and higher costs if a large segment of their workforce was diverted to Europe, these organizations were unresponsive to the call for recruits. Botha expressed his belief that, 'Europeans in close touch with the Natives have perhaps not realized the importance of the labour aspect, and may not therefore have been as enthusiastic in making recruiting a success as they would otherwise be.' Given this lack of cooperation, it is not surprising that men with mining experience did not constitute a large percentage of the SANLC. As of May 1917 only 38% of the roughly 14,000 recruits had worked in a mining industry in the past three years, with 53% not at all.[67] Blacks who recruited for the mines were given a per capita grant and often exaggerated the dangers of overseas service, enhancing the already common belief among blacks that those who went to France were nearly all dead. The policy of non-cooperation illustrated by the Chamber of Mines was at odds with its policy during the campaign in GSWA. A surplus of labour then had allowed them to extend to

---

[64] NASA, KAB, 1LSK, vol. 13. H. M. Tyali to Chief Magistrate Transkei, 28 May 1917.
[65] Jingoes, *A Chief is a Chief by the People*, p. 73.
[66] Willan, 'The South African Native Labour Contingent', 69.
[67] NASA, SAB, GNLB, vol. 254/369/16. SANLC Headquarters Log, 10 April 1917.

the Union significant numbers of labourers for three-month contracts. However, the Chamber of Mines refused to supply labour for the East African campaign.[68]

Lastly, and arguably the greatest factor in the failure to secure recruits, was the 'press-ganging' and intimidation used by recruiting agents, despite Pritchard's assurance to the SANNC that, 'no pressure or other influence would be exercised in order to induce Natives ... *The system would be voluntary*.'[69] After the poor initial response, the most popular recruiting tactic was the intimidation of men and chiefs to supply quotas. Threats of being deposed, and the suspension of subsidies, were used to induce them to cooperate. To avoid being pressed into service, many men simply vanished into the bush to stay clear of recruiting agents. Chiefs reported that, 'only old men come to the meetings and the young and able-bodied keep away'. Other schemes were devised to combat the lack of recruits, including inflated promises by some recruiters of exemption from poll tax and pass laws, as well as of free land and heads of cattle upon return. These fictitious exemptions were never Union policy and were never granted, although the idea of offering cattle incentives was discussed.[70]

The possibility of releasing an estimated '4,000 Native prisoners who would immediately be available' for service was contemplated in October 1917 but never carried out, although a certain number of outstanding criminals from Witwatersrand did find a safe haven in the contingent.[71] Another method to stimulate recruitment was the publication of positively couched letters from members of the SANLC in black newspapers.[72] The Department of Native Affairs also instructed the adjutant of the SANLC to 'send newspaper articles from European Papers dealing with SANLC to SA for translation and distribution to aid recruitment'.[73] In reality, many members of the SANLC had written to their local magistrates, or directly to Botha or Governor-General Buxton, expressing their desire for representatives of the Union to convey to their people that they were being well treated and that 'there is no need for them to be afraid to come over here'.[74]

---

[68] Grundlingh, *Fighting Their Own War*, pp. 59–60.
[69] Ibid, p. 59.
[70] NASA, SAB, NTS, vol. 9108/18/363–28/363. Correspondence Regarding Exemptions/ Recruitment, 1917–19.
[71] NASA, SAB, GG, vol. 674/9/93/136. Report on Native Prisoners for Service, 4 October 1917; Grundlingh, 'The Impact of the First World War on South African Blacks' (The ASA Conference, Washington D.C., November 1982), 3.
[72] NASA, KAB, 1TBU, vol. 25. Native Affairs to all Magistrates, 16 July 1917.
[73] NASA, KAB, CMT, 3/930. Circular No. 19 Native Labour Contingent, 14 July 1917.
[74] NASA, KAB, 1KNT, vol. 22. Native Interviews and Letters with/to Governor-General Buxton.

Sol. Plaatje shared the views of other SANNC members and educated blacks, that 'by going to France our people should realize that they are going to a university of experience ... six months in France would teach them more than ten years in Kimberley [mines]; it was just like a great educational institution without having to pay fees'.[75] Grundlingh asserts that, 'For the educated African elite, who enrolled in numbers disproportionate to the size of their class in the total black population [25 per cent of the total SANLC], the idea to prove their loyalty to the "civilising" Imperial power in an hour of need, as well as the notion that service abroad was an educative experience, were important considerations.'[76] In April 1917, policy was initiated to use returned members of the SANLC for recruiting purposes. H. M. Tyali, a returned SANLC recruiter, recognized, in his letter sent directly to Botha in May 1917, the need for further recruits to promote black equality:

I also believe that the whole Empire had had some doubts that a race like the Natives of South Africa who were disarmed and kept like little children would gladly accept the call from the King ... Let the Government today think of a Native, let the Empire know that the Native of South Africa should be given a situation of better rights ... to-day Government should be asked to push the Native to a higher stage ... the necessity of the Native to be enlisted in the same rights with the white men to-day is seen ... it is the white race who rebelled during this War but all eyes were looking on Natives to rebel against the Government ... all your endeavours should be as they are to uplift Native races both in politics and social.[77]

Nevertheless, the average black South African, ignorant of political motives, and simply trying to survive, did not see service in the same light. Enlistment rates into the SANLC, whether secured by fair means or foul, did not meet expectations. In April 1917, the Commissioner of Swaziland wrote to Buxton: 'It is regrettable that little interest in the War, or desire to serve, is manifest among them [Natives] ... In any case it seems unlikely that sufficient number will be forthcoming to warrant formation of separate Swazi Companies.'[78] This statement was repeated in a letter from the Commissioner of Bechuanaland to Buxton that same month: 'All of opinion that few recruits will be obtained. Natives are away on lands ... it appears useless to attempt to raise further separate Bechuanaland Protectorate Companies.'[79] Recruitment

---

[75] Willan, 'The South African Native Labour Contingent', 66–7.
[76] Grundlingh, 'The Impact of the First World War on South African Blacks', 3–4.
[77] NASA, KAB, 1LSK, vol. 13. H. M. Tyali to Magistrate Transkei and Botha, 28 May 1917.
[78] NA, DO-119/922. Commissioner Swaziland to Buxton, 20 April 1917.
[79] NA, DO-119/923. Commissioner Bechuanaland to Buxton, 17 April 1917.

among the Zulu was only 300 by March 1917, despite intensive efforts by the magistrates of Natal: 'Meetings with Zulu Chiefs and headsmen and people ... there were some 12,000 [present], of which number some 9,000 were of the ages ranging from 18 years to 50 ... they refused absolutely to go anywhere or do anything connected to the war. They had seen enough and suffered enough during the Boer War.' The Union had not done itself any favours by selecting as a recruiting official Sir George Leuchars, who led the ruthless suppression of the Bambatha rebellion.[80] The numbers of recruits secured for the SANLC from the individual provinces and protectorates by June 1917 (and January 1918) reflected the uneven spread of volunteering (see Table 7.1). The presentation by the Union of gift rifles to chiefs who aided recruiting serves as an excellent indicator of the enthusiasm of local native leaders.

The Transvaal produced roughly 55 per cent of the total numbers for the SANLC. This disproportionate representation was the result of two factors. The first was that a severe drought afflicted the Transvaal in the spring of 1917, when recruitment efforts were at their peak. Secondly, according to Buxton, 'The native there no doubt are somewhat more under control of their Chiefs, and the Chiefs there are more under control of the Government than elsewhere ... the legitimate pressure by Officials has produced a greater result than it has produced elsewhere.' Whether the pressure was legitimate or not, recruiting efforts, coinciding with drought and famine, produced a higher rate of enlistment in the Transvaal, especially in the north, where the drought was most severe.[81]

In addition to requests for labour, the imperial government asked the Union for native combatants for use on the Western Front. On 28 March 1917, Buxton received a cable from the War Office, 'desirous of replacing white personnel in certain Artillery Units in France by [18,300] Native personnel enlisted in South Africa or Indian ... for the duration of the war'. Buxton answered the Colonial Secretary, Walter Hume Long, without consulting Botha or Smuts. Buxton's detailed response alluded to all racial, social, political and military realities current in South Africa:

Natives could not be relied upon for service in the fighting lines ... Any endeavour to recruit for Combatant service would immediately prejudice recruiting for the South African Native Labour Contingent and would undoubtedly prevent Government from securing anything approaching numbers of labourers already asked for as a matter of urgency by the Army Council. Those who

[80] NASA, KAB, CMT, 3/930. Report of Magistrates, Natal, 9 July 1917.
[81] Grundlingh, *Fighting Their Own War*, pp. 76–8.

Table 7.1: *SANLC native enlistment rates, June 1917 and January 1918*[1]

Province or protectorate	Native population (1911 Census)	Enlistments June 1917	% population	Enlistments January 1918	% population	Gifts of rifles
Transvaal	1,219,845	9,924	0.81	13,578	1.11	26
Cape Colony	1,007,468	1,764	0.18	6,959	0.58	13
Transkei	186,706	1,487	0.80	Included in Cape Colony	Included in Cape Colony	Included in Cape Colony
Natal	962,490	629	0.07	1,487	0.15	4
Orange Free State	352,985	569	0.16	787	0.22	1
Bechuanaland	84,636	449	0.53	575	0.68	3
Basutoland	403,111	252	0.06	1,457	0.36	4
Swaziland	100,000	55	0.06	55	0.06	0
Totals	*4,317,241*	*15,129*	*0.35*	*24,561 ~total*	*0.57*	*51*

[1] NASA, KAB, 1PDE, vol. 15, file 362/14. SANLC Enlistments, 2 June 1917; SAB, NTS, Vol. 9107/11/363. Territorial Classifications of SANLC, 12 January 1918; SAB, GG, Vol. 670/9/93/56–9/93/63. Gifts of Rifles to Headsmen and Chiefs, December 1917; 1911 Census in *Colonial Office Lists 1918*, pp. 318–56.

oppose Native labourers being sent ... by asserting that they will sooner or later be employed in the fighting line ... would be regarded as confirmed. The men would not come under control of officers accustomed to deal with Natives; it would not be possible to keep them in closed compounds; and apart from other objections the effect of their association side by side with British soldiers ... is regarded as dangerous from the South African point of view ... control maintenance of strict discipline, and special arrangements for housing can easily be swept away under the pressure of military exigencies and thus leave the Natives unprotected from risks and ill effects of free social and other contact which are unmistakably feared by a large section of the Europeans of South Africa. Politically the proposal would cause embarrassment in view of the antagonistic attitude of a section of people of this country to the employment of Natives overseas for Any form of War service.

The issue was given no further consideration and was not broached again by the War Office.[82]

There were alterations, however, to the deployment of Cape coloureds. The Cape Corps (Battalion) had been active in a combat role in East Africa since February 1916, and was rotated back to Durban in December 1917. A second battalion of Cape coloureds was raised in June 1917 and was transferred from Portuguese East Africa to German East Africa in late 1917. After seeing limited combat action, the battalion was released from duty in July 1918, and half were demobilized by December 1918. The second half, however, was amalgamated into the 1st Battalion, which was deployed to Egypt in April 1918. In July, the unit, as part of General Edmund Allenby's Egyptian Expeditionary Force, occupied lines northwest of Jerusalem. The unit fought under Allenby's command for the remainder of the war, arriving back in South Africa in August 1919. In fact, from March to May 1919, the unit participated in quelling the Egyptian revolution, which spurred Egypt's independence from Britain in 1922. Nearly 7,000 coloureds served in the two Cape battalions between 1915 and 1919, with 450 killed or dead from disease.[83]

Although the Cape coloured battalions were officially imperial units, not part of the UDF, the precedent for using coloureds in segregated combat units with European officers had been set by the British during South Africa's colonial period. During the First World War, the units were not deployed to a European theatre, nor were they ever intended, or wanted, for such a purpose. In the tradition of the Cape Corps, they were used first in Africa and then in the secondary theatre of Palestine.

[82] NASA, SAB, GG, vol. 673/9/93/112–9/93/135. War Office to Buxton, 28 March 1917, and Reply, 3 April 1917.
[83] Gleeson, *The Unknown Force*, pp. 68–94.

Therefore, the deployment did not upset the historical status quo and received little political or social commentary within South Africa itself. Moreover, the Cape coloured units were financed by the imperial government – a stipulation made by South Africa for all coloured and native units.

Coloured men did, however, serve in Europe in a non-combatant role as labourers and drivers. The Cape Corps Labour Battalion (CCLB) was established in June 1916 'on behalf of the Imperial Government for overseas service'. By May 1917, the unit, consisting of roughly two thousand men, was tasked to the British Army Service Corps, working at the French ports of Boulogne, Dunkirk and Le Havre. The Battalion was one of the last units to leave France (and only after Botha's insistence), returning to South Africa in July 1919.[84] Another coloured unit, the Cape Auxiliary Horse Transport (CAHT), was authorized in March 1917 as an imperial unit. Coloured units similar to the CAHT had been used in the GSWA and GEA campaigns, and 60 per cent of the 3,500 to see service in the CAHT had participated in one or the other, with a small number having served in both. The CAHT was primarily located at the same ports as the CCLB. Enlistment for both units was for the duration of the war plus six months, as was standard for both French and British colonial labour units by the time of their formation.[85]

The mixing of coloureds with blacks did not occur in any units raised in South Africa, a distinction left over from British colonial rule, and from the enhanced rights and racial profiling given to coloureds in the Cape Province. Coloured units were not billeted in closed compounds. Botha stressed the importance, 'of not having Cape Coloureds working anywhere near SANLC [so] as to keep compound system in order and natives under control'.[86] In addition, both the CAHT and the CCLB were raised at a time when recruitment for the SANLC had stagnated and these coloured units offered a convenient way to secure more labour. The distinction between coloureds and blacks was emphasized in a memorandum from the Department of Defence to all recruiting depots for both the CAHT and the CCLB:

Numbers of aboriginal natives [blacks] are sent forward from various centres for the above units [CAHT and CCLB] and then have to be returned to their homes resulting in unnecessary expense. It is difficult to lay down any hard and fast rules by which the community of 'coloured men' may be defined ... The

[84] NASA, KAB, 1PDE, vol. 15/362/14. Cape Coloured Labour Corps.
[85] NASA, KAB, 1PDE, vol. 15/362/14. Cape Auxiliary Horse Transport Memorandum, 6 March 1917; Gleeson, *The Unknown Force*, p. 55.
[86] NA, WO-107/37. After Action Report: Work of Labour Force during War, November 1919.

object is to exclude aboriginal natives ... it should be noted that Bastards crossed with Hottentots and Europeans, good men of Griqua descent and dark skinned men from Slaves [Indians and Asians] and coloured women may be accepted; and where doubt exists manner of living as well as appearance must be considered.[87]

This is another example of the stress placed on the differences between 'half-castes' and 'full-bloods' in South African (and Australian) policies and societies. This distinction was not as pronounced in the societies and policies of New Zealand, Newfoundland and Canada.

The first Battalion of the SANLC arrived at Le Havre on 20 November 1916, followed by the second on 10 December. Although instructions initially recommended the need to, 'keep the men of the same tribe, e.g., Zulus, Basutos, etc., in the same unit ... in the same station and to avoid mixing on the work', similar to the system in the mines, this policy was not enforced in France for three reasons. The first was that there was a variance in the numbers of men from each tribe, and homogenous companies of certain tribes were unsustainable due to lack of numbers.[88] Secondly, a unified Directorate of Labour was created in the British General Headquarters in December 1916 to coordinate an effective administration of the undersized labour pool. As a consequence, the degree of control exercised by the white officers and administrators of the SANLC was reduced. The imperial directorate immediately disbanded the battalion structure of the SANLC in favour of smaller, more mobile companies, which were spread over various labour stations. This action was an immediate affront to the policies of the Union, exercised by Pritchard in France, in regards to the stringent controls imposed on the SANLC. After all, the experiment of the SANLC was intended to be a test for the implementation, under strictly controlled conditions, of devices of social control, the lessons of which could be utilized in South Africa itself.[89] Lastly, it was argued that the mixing of tribes would lessen the possibility of organized violence, rebellion or strikes amongst members of the same ethnic or tribal groupings.[90] It was reported that, 'Although in South Africa it had been regarded as important to keep the different races [tribes] separate while at work, in France it became recognised that mixing them up was equally if not more successful. No cases of conflict owing to racial

---

[87] NASA, KAB, 1PDE, vol. 15/362/14. Department of Defence to all Recruiting Depots, 16 May 1918.

[88] NA, WO-107/37. After Action Report: Work of Labour Force during the War, November 1919.

[89] Willan, 'The South African Native Labour Contingent', 71–3.

[90] Grundlingh, *Fighting Their Own War*, p. 124.

jealousy ever occurred here and it was in some cases beneficial to mix them together because they were easier to handle and friendly competition in the work resulted.'[91]

Nevertheless, in December, Pritchard met with the Directorate of Labour to ensure that South African demands were not disregarded. As things stood, the first two battalions of the SANLC, divided into smaller sub-units, were scattered, not only in the French channel ports, but also in forward supply areas close to the front. The first directive was that the term 'Kaffir' be substituted with 'SA Native as the Basutos, Zulus, and Swazis find it as a term of opprobrium'.[92] Secondly, although it was the intention to employ the contingent exclusively on dock work at the French ports, it was proposed and accepted to 'extend the usefulness of the Contingent by increasing the scope of employment to include roadmaking, quarrying and work incidental to forestry, all of which work it is perhaps needless to add will be away from any danger zone ... the difficulties of segregation which would arise in towns would be reduced if the Natives were engaged on such work'.[93] Furthermore, Pritchard added that, 'the South African natives were unsuitable for work in any dangerous area, and their contracts prohibited this ... Owing to the presence South of the River Somme of Chinese labour recruited by the French, whose administration was in the opinion of some British experts far too lax, it was decided ... the retention of the S.A.N.L.C. in Army Areas was of short duration.'[94]

While moving the SANLC away from the front and north of the River Somme also had its drawbacks, namely it would be closer to urban areas, this was regarded as the lesser of two evils, and the SANLC was relocated to main camps at Le Havre, Rouen, Dieppe and Abancourt. SANLC headquarters was based in Rouen, and the records office at Dieppe. Segregated hospitals in Dieppe and Boulogne were also formed with native orderlies. The SANLC could not be moved, however, until special compounds were erected; therefore, relocation, although occurring in stages, was not completed until April 1917.[95] The movements were hastened after 19 January 1917 due to the death from shellfire of a SANLC labourer. This was not reported as a combat casualty, at the insistence of Pritchard: 'Should the report get about that casualties

[91] NA, WO-107/37. After Action Report: Work of Labour Force during the War, November 1919.
[92] NASA, SAB, GNLB, vol. 254/369/16. HQ Log SANLC, December 1916.
[93] NASA, KAB, 1PDE, vol. 15/362/14. Circular Instructions SANLC, December 1916.
[94] NA, WO-107/37. After Action Report: Work of Labour Force during the War, November 1919.
[95] NASA, SAB, GNLB, vol. 254/369/16. HQ Log SANLC, December 1916.

amongst natives ... are caused by Shell-fire the result will be disastrous from a recruiting point of view.' Haig assured Botha in April that, 'the policy of employing this labour outside shelled areas will be followed as far as the exigencies of the service admit'.[96]

In March 1917, Pritchard issued all white officers and administrators with an *Appendix to Notes for Officers of Labour Companies (South African Native Labour)*. Members of the SANLC were not allowed to leave camp unless escorted by white personnel. They were not allowed in local shops, pubs, businesses or private dwellings without white escort, nor were they allowed to be in possession of alcohol or 'dagga' (marijuana) within the camps (they had brought 'dagga' with them from South Africa). Unauthorized personnel and locals were not allowed within the camps, and interaction with locals, especially women, and other labour units was to be minimized, 'to avoid familiarity between Europeans and Natives'. Lastly, with the Cape Coloured Labour Battalion stationed at Rouen, it was 'imperative' to relocate the Cape boys as they, 'were treated as soldiers, the former [SANLC] were segregated; it would have been impossible to enforce the rules by which the South African natives were restricted to compounds if they had seen the Cape Boys alongside them allowed practically unlimited freedom'. It was also stressed that all natives 'were under the Army Act and military discipline'.[97] However, prior to the removal of SANLC units from forward areas in April 1917, these regulations would have been impossible to maintain (see Figure 7.3).

Free time was also strictly controlled. The twelve black chaplains who accompanied the contingent taught classes ranging from English language instruction to geography, maths and music. A philanthropic Committee for the Welfare of Africans in Europe was formed under the Earl of Selbourne and was responsible for the donation of a multitude of equipment: books and newspapers, teaching supplies, sporting equipment, musical instruments, gramophones and records, winter clothing, games and bibles. Total donations exceeded £5,000 by August 1917. The Aborigines Protection Society, while procuring commodities for the contingent, supported the compound system as a necessary measure for the security and welfare of the men. Under the supervision of whites, sporting matches and other amusements took place, and, in some cases, were mandatory. For propaganda purposes,

---

[96] NASA, SAB, NTS, vol. 9106/1/363–7/363. Memorandum Acting Director of Native Labour, 26 February 1917; Haig to War Office and South Africa GHQ, 13 April 1917.

[97] NA, WO-107/37. After Action Report: Work of Labour Force during the War, November 1919.

Figure 7.3 'Smiling and Warm: Members of the SANLC Enjoy
Some Down-time', February 1917.

to portray the SANLC as happy and well-maintained, concerts of
singing and dancing were performed for locals, troops and military
officials.[98]

While Haig and other British politicians offered the services of
British NCOs and officers to aid in the maintenance and supervision of
the SANLC, Botha and Buxton refused to admit any British soldiers
into the SANLC, stating that they had no experience in dealing with
natives. In reality, a small number of the white members of the SANLC
transferred to South African fighting units. They were replaced, first
by men from the British Army medically unfit for combat, and later by
men sent from South Africa, who met the requirements of whites in the
SANLC: '[A] combined knowledge of the Native, Military procedure,
and labour [not fit for fighting units]'.[99]

---

[98] NASA, KAB, CMT, 3/930. Pamphlet: British Africans in Europe and the Work of
the Welfare Committee; Sloley, 'The African Native Labour Contingent and the
Welfare Committee'.

[99] NASA, SAB, GG, vol. 670/9/93/56–9/93/63. Botha to Buxton, 16 February 1917;
Haig to War Office, 2 June 1917.

Originally, the highest rank for blacks was that of sergeant. Rank structure, however, was immediately altered in France, with lance-corporal the highest rank for blacks and corporal the lowest for whites – an arrangement which ensured that blacks could never outrank their white overseers.[100] Furthermore, uniforms, described 'as the most atrocious, vile-smelling cotton velveteen; brown, shoddy and sloppy looking', confirmed the reality that the members of the SANLC were not equal to other soldiers and labourers of the British empire, nor to the white members of the contingent dressed in the usual khaki UDF uniforms. The shoddy brown uniform, void of insignia or markings aside from rank, and large floppy 'outback' style headdress were designed to degrade and visibly differentiate natives, who placed a symbolic attachment on a uniform as recognition of their equal status as men in service of king and empire. An educated member of the SANLC wrote home to his local newspaper, 'The suit of brown corduroy certainly lowered the status of the Native labourers in the eyes of the other troops.'[101] The Union had thus accomplished its goal.

Other equipment and clothing was issued in response to health concerns during the harsh winter of 1916–17. Since the boots issued originally did not properly fit and caused medical problems, new wider and shorter 'Russian ankle-boots' were procured in June 1917, and hospital admittance due to foot problems became almost non-existent.[102] Diet and food were adequate and deliberately mirrored the ratios and types consumed by natives in South Africa. While there were complaints about food, particularly the 'mealie-meal', these were not out of the ordinary for men in military service. In addition, although the winter was colder than usual, winter clothing and socks provided by the welfare committee augmented issued uniforms. Lastly, sanitary conditions in the camps and the two segregated hospitals were well maintained and, in reality, were superior to the norm for natives in South Africa.[103] In general, health problems were much lower than anticipated.

Frostbite did occur and eleven men lost limbs as a result; however, frostbite was not unusually high within the SANLC. Pritchard stressed to Botha and the War Office that, 'In no case were men sent to work who had suffered from frostbite or allied conditions unless they were

---

[100] NASA, KAB, 1TBU, vol. 25. Circular D. 12/17, May 1917.
[101] Grundlingh, *Fighting Their Own War*, p. 101.
[102] NASA, SAB, NTS, vol. 9106/1/363–7/363. Report: Director of Labour Corps GHQ, 15 November 1917; NA, DO-119/924. Overseas Native Labour Medical Report, 23 April 1917.
[103] NASA, SAB, GG, vol. 670/9/93/56. Medical Reports SANLC and Weekly Ration Table.

fit, and I do not remember any complaint being made to this effect.' The few cases of venereal disease discovered had been contracted in the Union prior to deployment. The most common illnesses were pulmonary disorders, primarily tuberculosis, which accounted for 65 per cent of hospital admissions. Pritchard summarized the general health and welfare of the SANLC in November 1917:

> It is generally admitted that the average physical condition … fell below what may be described as the South Africa 'Mine Standard', while the weather conditions during the winter and spring were of abnormal severity … I am of the opinion that the remarkably low sick and mortality rates recorded during the past year, afford a complete repudiation of any suggestion of neglect or lack of solicitude on the part of those responsible for the well being of the Native personnel.

The two hospitals (800 beds) were never more than half occupied and contingency plans to provide an additional 1,000 beds never had to be implemented.[104] SANLC HQ in France recorded that many of the men hospitalized with various diseases could have been eliminated in South Africa and urged officers at Rosebank to 'ensure more stringent medical examinations' were carried out (see Figure 7.4).[105]

Although there were minor problems with health, the SANLC provided valuable service and was recognized for its contribution. Prejudice accounted for some officers reporting that blacks worked more slowly and less efficiently than white labourers; however, this was not the general attitude. Herbert Sloley of the Aborigines Protection Society recorded that he 'had the advantage of hearing the opinions of officers of the Royal Engineers, Army Service Corps, Commissariat, Transport and Ordnance Departments, and the general estimate of the African native as a labourer appears to have been that, man for man, he is equal to any other class of labourer employed behind our lines'.[106] Praising the SANLC served two functions. The first was simply that, in all probability, members of the SANLC performed on par with other labourers. Secondly, there was a desire for the 'experiment' to be seen as a success, and extolling the work of the natives gave support to the decision to employ them in France. Praise of the SANLC was a political tool used to silence pessimists and ease political retribution from opposition leaders who opposed the 'experiment'.

---

[104] NASA, SAB, NTS, vol. 9106/1/363–7/363. Report: Director of Labour Corps GHQ, 15 November 1917; SAB, GG, vol. 670/9/93/56. Medical Reports SANLC.

[105] NASA, SAB, NTS, vol. 9107/17/363. SANLC Medical Report HQ, 21 December 1917.

[106] Sloley, 'The African Native Labour Contingent and the Welfare Committee', 205.

Figure 7.4 Two members of the SANLC 'greasing' their feet,
February 1917.

In February 1917, Pritchard wrote to Edward Dower, Secretary of
Native Affairs: 'I am assured of the benefits that may be anticipated to
accrue to all in South Africa by the presence here and active association
of its Native peoples with this vast War, the teachings of which will
open the eyes of and inspire the Natives in a manner that many years
of even the most enlightened & progressive Native Administration
could never bring about.'[107] Also, in February 1917, the Department
of Native Affairs issued a memorandum to all magistrates: 'Not only is
the work performed by the natives of a high standard but their behaviour is most satisfactory whilst the percentage of sickness is small ...
[S]pare no efforts in your endeavours to secure recruits as the need is
most urgent.'[108] In January 1917, the War Office had pressed for the
unrealistic increase of the recruitment target, from an already unten-
able goal of 40,000, to 50,000.[109]

---

[107] NASA, SAB, GG, 673/9/93/112–9/93/135. Pritchard to Dower, 15 February 1917.
[108] NASA, KAB, 1PDE, vol. 15/362/14. Memorandum of 19 February 1917.
[109] Willan, 'The South African Native Labour Contingent', 81.

The deployment of the SANLC did not last until the end of the war. One reason for its early departure from France could have been avoided during the creation of the unit in 1916. Unlike all other South African soldiers and labourers, including coloureds, original SANLC contacts were for a total of twelve months. It was rationally deduced in November 1917 that, 'existing Labour only available for 9 months after deduction journey time ... hence proposition for 12 months from landing in France'. By this time 3,432 members of the SANLC had already returned to the Union, having served out their twelve-month contracts. This short duration of service was an administrative and financial burden, and undermined the effectiveness of the actual labour force in France. Furthermore, recruiters, facing an existing lack of enthusiasm for the contingent, reported to Native Affairs that, 'Proposal of enlisting Natives for the duration of the war plus an additional 6 months [as was customary] ... would practically terminate recruiting for the Contingent in South Africa.' Confusion over policy was evident on 3 December when Native Affairs issued an instruction to recruiters to change service to the norm of 'duration of war plus six months thereafter'. However, a second memorandum was sent concerning 'Shortage of Shipping and of repatriation of Natives'. It was instructed: 'You are therefore requested to take immediate steps to stop recruiting ... All persons, both European and Native, engaged in recruiting, should be immediately withdrawn from this duty.'[110]

On 15 December, Botha, after consultation with the senior members of Native Affairs, sent a circular to all magistrates and administrators of the SANLC: 'Army Council concur that in view of difficulties of maintaining compound system ... all recruiting should be stopped ... Although both Chinese and Egyptians are compounded the restrictions are not nearly so rigorously carried out as regards the former [SANLC], while the latter are of negligible quantity.' All contracts were ordered to be cancelled, and men paid accordingly, before being sent home. On 4 January 1918, Botha issued the official statement, for widest distribution, of the termination of the SANLC:

For reasons of a purely military nature His Majesty the King through his Army Council has intimated to the Union Government that recruiting for the South African Native Labour Contingent should cease forwith [sic], and that no further companies of native labourers should be dispatched overseas. In Conveying this decision to you the Right Honourable the Prime Minister General Botha

---

[110] NASA, SAB, NTS, vol. 9107/16/363. Memorandums of 3 November 1917, 3 December 1917; SAB, GG, vol. 670/9/93/56–9/93/63. List: Natives Repatriated as of 21 November 1917; Recruitment Memorandum, 3 November 1917.

wishes to emphasize how much he and the Government appreciate the loyal and splendid manner in which Chiefs, Headsmen and people throughout the Union responded to his original call for recruits for the Corps and for the way reinforcements have since come forward ... In conclusion, General Botha confidently trusts that by their work and behaviour in this country the men who have already returned, or who will return in due course from France will set such an example which cannot but result in the inculcation of discipline and sustained industry amongst the natives throughout the Union.[111]

At this time the strength of the SANLC in France was 11,349. In total, 25,048 native men were recruited, of whom 20,205 served in France. The last contingent of forty-two men arrived in France on 5 January 1918, after which time the SANLC was rotated, piecemeal, back to South Africa. By March the SANLC total in France had been reduced to 8,046. Aside from a small number of men in hospitals, or retained for administrative duties, all men of the SANLC were returned to the Union by September.[112] Haig delivered his thanks to the last contingents of the SANLC: 'My warm appreciation of the good work done by them for the British Army during their stay in France. They have rendered loyal and excellent service wherever they have been employed and I send them my heartiest thanks and all good wishes for a prosperous journey home.'[113] Throughout 1917 the SANLC had constituted roughly 20 per cent to 25 per cent of the total British labour force.[114]

The SANLC was recalled as a result of political, social and racial realities. Reports had filtered through South Africa of the impossibility of maintaining the compound system to the standard set by Union politicians and expected by white civilians. Although rumours exaggerated the freedom, and the contamination, of the natives by their association with French civilians, French women and the soldiers of other nationalities, segregation, although attempted, was not as complete as had been promised. Returned SANLC officers told Nationalist Party opposition leaders that, 'the compound system had entirely failed in its objectives'. With the opening of a new session of Parliament in January, Botha, who had failed to answer questions relating to the SANLC convincingly

[111] NASA, SAB, NTS, vol. 9107/16/363. Memorandum to all Chiefs, Headsmen and People, 4 January 1918.
[112] NASA, SAB, NTS, vol. 9107/11/363. Strengths of the SANLC; NA, WO-107/37. After Action Report: Work of Labour Force during the War, November 1919. Secondary sources all list that 20,887 natives served in France. This is incorrect. This was the number of men who left South Africa. The reduced number of 20,205 accounts for the losses on the *Mendi*, deaths at sea and those left on stops due to sickness before reaching France.
[113] NASA, SAB, GNLB, vol. 254/369/16. Memorandum Haig, 26 September 1918.
[114] Grundlingh, *Fighting Their Own War*, p. 96.

during the prior session, was not prepared to face the imminent criticism from the opposition. The experiment, therefore, had to be abandoned to satisfy the political and racial status quo of the Union, and to safeguard Botha's hold on power.

Elite and educated blacks were aware of the realities behind the Union's decision, as expressed by the SANNC: '[T]his dramatic cancelling of a pact already signed and entered into will give rise to feelings of suspicion that the reasons for this cancellation are more of a political than a military nature, for, curiously enough, it synchronises with the re-assembling of Parliament.'[115] Manpower requirements, to satisfy imperial needs and demands, did not wholly override South African political will or social and racial anxieties. General Smuts delivered a speech, on 22 May 1917 at the Savoy Hotel in London, outlining his perceptions of natives, the war and the future of South Africa:

There are many people in South Africa … who do not feel certain that our white experiment will be a permanent success, or that we shall ever succeed in making a white man's land of Southern Africa; but at any rate, we mean to press on with the experiment … With us there are certain axioms now in regard to the relations of white and black; and the principal one is 'no intermixture of blood between the two colours' … We were not aware of the great military value of the natives until this war. This war has been an eye-opener in many new directions … I hope that one of the results of this war will be some arrangement or convention among the nations interested in Central Africa by which the military training of natives in that area will be prevented, as we have prevented it in South Africa. It can well be foreseen that armies may yet be trained there, which under proper leading might prove a danger to civilization itself … We shall always have a difficult question not only in Central but in Southern Africa. Unlike other British Dominions, our future as a white civilization is not assured for the reasons which I have given.[116]

Although the experiment alluded to in Smuts' address was ongoing, and arguably lasted until 1994, the experimental trial of native labourers in France ended in September 1918 (see Figure 7.5).

With the SANLC repatriated by September 1918, South Africa avoided two significant problems which occurred after the armistice of 11 November. First was the issue of indigenous soldiers and labourers stationed in Germany during its occupation by the Allies. Second was the difficult process of mass repatriation during the winter months of 1918 and 1919. The sheer number of Dominion (and other foreign) soldiers in Europe created a logistical burden on administrative and transport mechanisms. Repatriation was a laborious and lengthy process,

[115] Willan, 'The South African Native Labour Contingent', 81.
[116] Smuts, *Jan Christian Smuts*, pp. 194–5.

Figure 7.5 General Jan C. Smuts inspecting a unit of the SANLC in
France, 1918.

which required men to linger in haphazard staging camps in Britain
and France, ultimately leading to a lapse in discipline. After years of
war and military regulation, these men – not occupied by any significant work, wanting to return home and exposed to large quantities of
alcohol – vented their frustrations in often riotous behaviour.

Australia, on Hughes' dogged insistence, flatly rejected to have any
elements of the AIF contribute to the occupation force. The Royal
Newfoundland Regiment was also excluded from the occupation
force. The Battalion was relieved on 26 October following the Battle
of Ooteghem-Inghem Ridge. Depleted, and lacking available reinforcements, it was returned to England for repatriation. Elements of
the Canadian Expeditionary Force did take part in the occupation of
Germany. Given that Indians were scattered across various Canadian
formations, no differentiation was afforded them in regards to occupying German towns. The Black No. 2 Construction Company, however,
was deliberately returned to Canada on 4 December 1918.

At the armistice, the Maori Battalion was supporting the New Zealand
Division on the River Sambre, two miles shy of the Belgian border.

On 28 November the Battalion began marching, reaching Stembert (roughly twelve miles from the German border) on 19 December with a view to entraining at Cologne. On the 20th, however, the divisional commander, Sir Andrew Russell, instructed the Battalion to proceed to Dunkirk for demobilization. Russell visited the Battalion on the 24th and 'got them together and made a small speech of farewell – they all looked and were very happy'. By all accounts the soldiers were aware of, and resented, this racial discrimination, but were content to be returning to New Zealand. The decision to exclude the Maori Battalion from New Zealand's occupation force was an imperial one.[117] The Maori Pioneer Battalion left England for New Zealand on 28 February 1919. During the voyage, before arriving at Auckland on 6 April, they were instructed in 'general education, agriculture, motor mechanics and book-keeping'. The Battalion was one of only two New Zealand units to return to the Dominion as a formed body (the Tunnelling Company was the other).[118]

After the armistice, pre-war British codes of conduct, regarding the participation of indigenous men in Europe, were reinstated. The British authorities, who were more sympathetic to the Germans than the retributive French, deemed it inappropriate to have a European country occupied by indigenous soldiers. Unlike the British, the French used colonial African and Asian units during the occupation, in the face of Anglo-American objections. In fact, between 1919 and 1921, the number of French colonial soldiers in Germany varied between 25,000 and 45,000, to the indignation and stern objections of the German authorities and civilian population. The 'Black Horror on the Rhine' was seen by Germans as an affront to European and white racial supremacy. British officer and author, Robert Graves, recalled that, 'the presence of semi-civilized coloured troops in Europe was, from the German point of view, we knew, one of the chief Allied atrocities. We sympathized.'[119] In 1928, when Hitler was expounding his philosophies of *Mein Kampf* and preaching against 'the de-Germanization, Negrification, and Judaization of our people', there were still 1,000 to 2,000 French colonial soldiers stationed in the *Reich*.[120]

The concern regarding positioning Dominion indigenes in Germany officially affected only the Maori Battalion. The problems related to

[117] Christopher Pugsley, *On the Fringe of Hell: New Zealanders and Military Discipline in the First World War* (Auckland: Hodder & Stoughton, 1991), p. 289.
[118] Gould, 'Maori and the First World War', 299.
[119] Smith, *Jamaican Volunteers in the First World War*, p. 62.
[120] See: Keith L. Nelson, 'The "Black Horror on the Rhine": Race as a Factor in Post-World War I Diplomacy', *Journal of Modern History* 42/4 (1970), 606–27.

the repatriation of vast national forces, however, were a concern for all Dominions and, by association, Britain itself. Discipline among the labourers of the SANLC, connected to the compound system and twelve-month contracts, was one reason for its premature return to South Africa. On 23 July 1917, at Dieppe, a riot broke out in the SANLC camp after a labourer was arrested for insubordination. His platoon stormed the gates of the guard house in an attempt to free him. The guards opened fire, killing four blacks and wounding thirteen others, including two whites.[121] A second episode occurred on 15 November 1917, during the repatriation of a contingent, shortly before official discussion over the complete removal of the SANLC from France. Eight men, Basutos from northern Transvaal, on board the *H.M.T. Miltiades*, refused to obey the military police, who were Zulu, stating that their twelve-month contracts had expired. A small riot broke out during which one man was killed and another wounded. Eight men were convicted in Cape Town and given twelve years' imprisonment. This incident was not made public. In the interest of race relations in the Union, and to prevent further violence within the SANLC, Botha overrode military authority to have the men released in May 1918. Aside from these major incidents, there are mentions of 'minor strikes' by small sub-units in France. Six individual cases of drunkenness and insubordination are also recorded, all occurring in 1918.[122] Although flogging had been banned in the British (and Dominion) Army in 1881 (for white troops), this was a common punishment for black troops in GSWA and GEA and, to a lesser extent, for the SANLC in France.[123]

While awaiting repatriation, Maori also displayed a lack of discipline, both in France and England, uncharacteristic of their record of good behaviour throughout the war. In late 1917, newspapers in New Zealand published unsubstantiated articles about the lewd and drunken behaviour of Maori soldiers. In reality, only seven charges were laid at Narrow Neck Camp against Maori, all for drunkenness or obscene language. Peacock added that, 'they are very well behaved'.[124] It was after the armistice, prior to embarkation for New Zealand, that major disciplinary lapses occurred. On New Year's Eve in Rouen, an officer

---

[121] NASA, SAB, NTS, vol. 9107/12/363. Report: Riot at No. 7 Camp Dieppe, 23 July 1917.

[122] NASA, SAB, GG, vol. 675/9/93/175. Report: Mutiny of the *Miltiades*, 15–23 November 1917.

[123] Grundlingh, *Fighting Their Own War*, p. 91.

[124] ANZ, AD1, box 873, record 24/246. Newspaper Articles 'Beer and Crayfish', *Auckland Observer, N.Z. Observer*, 6, 7 October 1917; Peacock to NZMF HQ, 7 November 1917.

was shot and killed by a Maori soldier, with another badly beaten. Two other Maori soldiers were convicted of rape. When in Dunkirk, picquets were placed throughout the streets of the town, 'Anticipating that the Maoris might get mixed up in rows with Americans, French and British soldiers'. Also, two cases had been reported 'of Maoris, while on leave, discharging firearms [German trophy revolvers] one case in France and one in London'.[125] In February, at Larkhill on Salisbury Plain, the most serious incident occurred: 'A party of Maoris about 20 or 30 strong have just broken into our canteen, stolen a 36 gallon cask of Ale, and are now rolling it towards the Amesbury Road ... Some of them have pistols and are covering their retirement.' A prolonged fight ensued, during which two British soldiers were wounded. New Zealand HQ was told by the War Office to ensure that, 'the necessary steps may be taken to prevent recurrences of this disgraceful hooliganism and ill discipline'.[126]

Disciplinary problems of this nature were by no means exclusive to the Maori, and there is no evidence to suggest that they behaved any worse than *Pakeha* soldiers or those of other nationalities. On the night of 10 December 1918, in retaliation for the murder of a New Zealand soldier by a local Arab, members of the New Zealand Mounted Brigade (accompanied by a small number of Australians and British) ransacked and razed the village of Surafend in Lebanon. After herding out women, children and the elderly, the troops entered the village, burning huts and assaulting the occupants, killing between twenty to thirty-five men, leaving many others severely wounded.[127] By comparison, on that same night in Le Havre, France, mutineers from the Royal Artillery torched several depots.[128] Between November 1918 and March 1919 there were thirteen separate disorders involving Canadian troops in Britain. The largest, the Kinmel Park (Wales) riot of 4–5 March, which encompassed 15,000 Canadian rioters dissatisfied with housing conditions, lack of food and delays in pay and repatriation, resulted in five men killed and twenty-five seriously wounded.[129]

Throughout the war, British civilians and authorities, including Haig, viewed Dominion soldiers as undisciplined and prone to sexual deviancy. The latter is certainly supported by the higher rates of venereal

---

[125] ANZ, AD10, box 1, record 2/25. Ennis to NZEF HQ London, 6 January 1919; Report Administration NZEF, UK, 7 February 1919.

[126] Pugsley, *On the Fringe of Hell*, p. 290.

[127] Ibid, pp. 287–8.

[128] See: Douglas Gill and Gloden Dallas, *The Unknown Army: Mutinies in the British Army in World War One* (New York: Schocken Books, 1985).

[129] Nicholson, *Canadian Expeditionary Force*, p. 532.

diseases among Dominion soldiers (most notably the Australians and Canadians), compared with other nationalities.[130] The unrest and violence during repatriation no doubt added to the negative reputation of the British colonials. On the other hand, British soldiers were granted leave in Britain throughout the war and were repatriated more quickly, while men from the Dominions had no such luxuries; many had been away from home for more than three or four years.

[130] See: W. G. Macpherson, *History of the Great War Based on Official Documents: Medical Services. Diseases of the War* (London: HMSO, 1923), vol. II; W. G. Macpherson et al. (eds.), *The British Official Medical History of the Great War* (London: HMSO, 1922), vols. I, II; Philippa Levine, *Prostitution, Race, and Politics: Policing Venereal Disease in the British Empire* (New York: Routledge, 2003).

8   Indigenous soldiers

Indigenous peoples participated in all aspects of the war both on and off the battlefields. While racial estimations influenced the standing of indigenes as soldiers, their military participation correspondingly influenced racial perceptions. The exposure of indigenous soldiers to the wider world and their association with soldiers and civilians from other nations altered their perceptions of themselves, their home nations and white countrymen. Racial and martial perceptions of indigenous soldiers were formed, modified or confirmed during the war by all nationalities. Indigenes also formed their own observations and estimations of themselves within the profession of arms, their home Dominions and the broader empire.

Racial perceptions influenced the creation of units, the military trade of certain all-indigenous formations, and the roles and ranks of indigenes. Cynthia Enloe describes this occurrence as a combination of 'political reliability' weighed against 'martial race' aptitude, whereby each identifiable group was assigned a military occupation (or unit) in keeping with maintaining domestic state security. In summary, a group that possessed martial propensities, and was politically reliable (assimilated), such as the Maori, was trusted to perform a military function, usually reserved for whites, within a homogenous unit under their own officers. Those deemed high on the martial scale but lower on the reliability/assimilation scale, were relegated to combat support occupations, in homogenous units, strictly controlled and segregated by white officers and NCOs, such as the SANLC. Thus, homogenous units occurred at both ends of the spectrum, the difference being the race of those ranks entrusted with command and control, and whether the formation's function was combatant or auxiliary. The possibility existed of groups that were highly martial but politically unreliable being excluded wholesale, if they had recently rebelled. This was the perception of many South Africans in relation to the use of blacks in any military capacity, especially the Zulu who had rebelled in 1906.

Table 8.1: *Dominion indigenes: political and military reliability against roles and units*

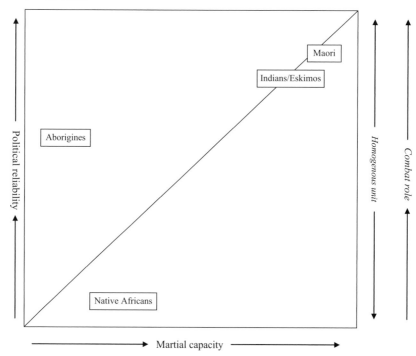

Those identifiable groups that fell in the middle of the scale were integrated, for the purposes of assimilation, and to enhance their reliability, in all manners of military occupation, as happened to Indians, Eskimos and Aborigines. The latter, although thought to be void of martial qualities, were relatively reliable, and therefore were scattered in both role and unit (see Table 8.1).

German perceptions of indigenous peoples were well established before the war. Prior to 1914, Germany, aside from its own experiences and observations of its colonial subjects, had shown a fascination for indigenous peoples, and they were well represented in popular culture. Carl Hagenbeck, founder of the modern zoo, displayed foreign animals and indigenes during European tours and in *Volkerschau* at his popular Tierpark (outside Hamburg), which opened in 1874. Between the opening of his park and 1913, he displayed and toured with Samoans, Laplanders and various African peoples. In 1886, a group of Eskimos from Hopedale, Labrador, and over sixty Indians from Bella Coola, BC, were part of his exhibition. Hagenbeck influenced Geoffroy de Saint-Hilaire's creation of the 'human zoo' exhibition in Paris, operating between 1877 and 1912, attracting roughly one million visitors per year. The Parisian World Fairs of 1878 and 1889 presented exhibitions of indigenous peoples from across the globe. Buffalo Bill Cody's Wild West Show, featuring prominent headliners such as Annie Oakley, Métis Gabriel Dumont and Sioux Chief Sitting Bull, toured Europe, including Germany, between 1887 and 1889.[1] Cody's show also included Australian Aborigines, two of whom served in the 34th Battalion (AIF) during the war.[2] Thomas A. Britten points out that, 'the German people held a long-standing affinity for Native Americans, one that stretched back to the nineteenth century'. He also attaches importance to 'Wild West Shows', and to letters and stories sent home to Europe by German immigrants to North America.[3]

The foremost influence on German perceptions of North American Indians, and their martial proclivities, was that of the German novelist Karl May (1842–1912), described in *Der Spiegel* as having a reputation 'greater than that of any other author between Johann Wolfgang von Goethe and Thomas Mann'. His works were translated into 20 languages, sold 30 million copies and were read by an estimated 300 million individuals. His four-novel series, *Winnetou* (1893–1910), about an Apache chief, describes the Apaches as noble warriors and honourable people, but also includes lengthy passages describing such practices as torture and scalping. The series was received with great acclaim, in both Germany and Austria, along with other books discussing Indian history and culture. Between 1912 and 1963, German cinema produced twenty-three films based on May's novels.[4] *Indian Boyhood* (1902) by Dr Charles Eastman, a Sioux, was translated into German in 1912 (fourth edition 1914).[5] In 1920, German veteran Ernst Jünger published his autobiographical account of the war, *In Stahlgewittern* (The Storm of Steel), and made reference to May's works: 'Memories of my

---

[1] See: Carl Hagenbeck, *Beasts and Men: Being Carl Hagenbeck's Experiences for Half a Century Among Wild Animals* (London: Longmans, Green and Co., 1912); Nigel Rothfels, *Savages and Beasts: The Birth of the Modern Zoo* (Baltimore: Johns Hopkins University Press, 2002). Many of these Bella Coola Indians returned to their communities having been converted to Catholicism while in Europe, creating divisions which still persist in their communities to this day.
[2] Huggonson, 'Aboriginal Diggers of the 9th Brigade, First AIF', 217.
[3] Britten, *American Indians in World War I*, p. 107.
[4] Kenneth William Townsend, *World War II and the American Indian* (Albuquerque: University of New Mexico Press, 2000), pp. 33–5.
[5] Britten, *American Indians in World War I*, pp. 107–8.

192 Indigenous Peoples and the First World War

third grade class and Karl May came back to me, as I was crawling on my stomach through the dew-covered and thorny grass, careful not to make the least noise, for, fifty metres in front of us, was the entrance to the English trench that detached itself like a dark line in the shadow.'[6]

During the First World War, select German propaganda was aimed at reassuring soldiers that they were not facing the warriors depicted in May's novels. An article in *Rheinische Zeitung* stated that there were no Indians fighting on the Western Front as they were dying out because they were 'thoroughly degenerated from drink'.[7] In contrast, another German propaganda source suggested that the British Army was in numerical decline, and all replacements from the colonies were indigenes. New Zealanders were all Maori, while North American soldiers belonged to the 'Choctaws, Blackfeet, or Ojibwa'.[8] Another German propaganda poster and postcard, entitled 'England's Only Available Army', depicted British soldiers as a rag-tag collection of cartoonish, *assegai*-wielding Africans.[9] Aware of the deployment of the SANLC, the Germans, according to prisoners and downed airmen, targeted its camps during air raids, and in late 1917 dropped leaflets on the SANLC camp at Dieppe: 'But in this war, I hate Black people the most. I do not know what they want in this European war. Where I find them, I will smash them.' In light of this, a member of the SANLC told the *Cape Times* that, 'Our assegais are no good now; they could not reach an aeroplane.'[10]

Testimonies from prisoners of war, from both sides, also offer an insight of German perceptions of indigenous soldiers during the war. A German taken prisoner during the Battle of Vimy Ridge told Private Andrew McCrindle that his superiors warned him, 'Not to be taken prisoner, as the Canadians are all Red Indians who would scalp them'.[11] There is no factual evidence supporting the scalping of enemies by Indians during the war. An officer captured by the US 32nd Division during the Battle of Soissons (18–22 July 1918) asked his captors what percentage of the division was Indian. An American officer captured prior to the Battle of Mihiel (12–15 September 1918) was surprised

---

[6] Ernst Jünger, *The Storm of Steel* (London: Chatto & Windus, 1929), p. 5.
[7] Britten, *American Indians in World War I*, p. 108.
[8] Dempsey, *Warriors of the King*, p. 63.
[9] Robb, *British Culture and the First World War*, p. 13.
[10] Jingoes, *A Chief is a Chief by the People*, pp. 88–9; Grundlingh, *Fighting Their Own War*, p. 127.
[11] Ted Barris, *Victory at Vimy: Canada Comes of Age, April 9–12, 1917* (Toronto: Thomas Allen, 2007), p. 185.

to be asked by interrogators how many 'Indians there were opposing the Boches [Germans] in that sector'.[12] A captured German document confirmed that during the St Mihiel campaign additional snipers were detailed to 'kill Indians' as they were 'greatly superior' to other troops. A confiscated letter from a soldier of the Sixth Jaeger Regiment stated that, 'The Indians of the Sioux tribe were identified in one of the last attacks. After the war Karl May can write another book about his experiences with the Redskins.'[13]

Accounts from Dominion indigenes taken prisoner also offer an insight into German perceptions. Six Nations Mohawk, William Foster Lickers, who enlisted in September 1914, was captured during the 2nd Battle of Ypres. He was tortured and beaten by his prison guards to see if 'Indians could feel pain', and was left paralysed for the remainder of his life.[14] Aboriginal Driver Frank Balser, serving in Egypt with the 5th Light Horse, was taken prisoner by Indian Cavalry who, not knowing Australians could be 'coloured', thought he was an Arab spy.[15]

Full-blood Aborigine, Douglas Grant, serves as the most emblematic case study. When Grant was roughly twelve months old, he was rescued from death by Scotsman Robert Grant, after his parents were killed during a punitive raid on their camp. He was raised by the Grant family in Lithgow, NSW, where he received an education and trained as a draughtsman, while acquiring his adoptive father's Scottish accent. Grant enlisted in 1915, but was released for being a 'full-blood'. Six months later, with the aid of his influential father, Grant successfully joined the 13th Battalion. He was taken prisoner on 11 April 1917 at Reincourt, France, during the Battle of Bullecourt. Grant was placed in the 'coloured section' of the prisoner camp along with Indian *sepoys* and black troops. Initially, his captors thought he was a Gurkha, but during his medical examination, Grant approached Dr Hermann Klaatsch and reminded him that they had met in 1905 at the Australian Museum, where Grant's father was employed as the senior taxidermist. Subsequently, Grant was moved to a white camp, closer to Berlin, so he could be scientifically studied. German scientists and anthropologists took great interest in Grant, taking photographs and measurements. The famed sculptor, Rudolf Marcuse, modelled his bust in ebony.

[12] Dianne Camurat, 'The American Indian in the Great War: Real and Imagined', unpublished MA thesis, Institut Charles V of the University of Paris VII (1993), Section 1.2.3.
[13] Britten, *American Indians in World War I*, p. 109.
[14] Lackenbauer and McGowan, 'Competing Loyalties in a Complex Community', 100.
[15] Watson, 'Better Than a One-Eyed Man', 13.

Dr Leonard Adam, a German scientist, recalled his relationship with Grant during the war:

I first met the man in 1918 in a south Berlin suburb, while I was working with the Royal Prussian Photographic Commission. Our objective was to collect material on languages, songs and dialects among Allied prisoners, and of course we regarded Grant as something of a prize. In fact, he was not very useful for any study of the Australian aboriginal; he had been removed from the tribe, and he regarded the natives with almost as much curiosity as we did. Like his fellow prisoners, though, we quickly learned that he was a man of superior intellect. He was a gentleman, and very honest, and he was appointed by the prisoners themselves to be in charge of the receipt of all the Red Cross parcels which made their drab life tolerable. He was not particularly interested in sport, and he spent most of his spare time either discussing literature or reading. His favourite author, I remember, was [Thomas] Carlyle.[16]

Grant enclosed one of these pictures in a letter home to his parents: 'I am well & as comfortable as circumstances will permit. I am working everyday, which helps to pass the time away. I often weary for home ... The Australian Red Cross sends me three packets of groceries a fortnight ... I had my photograph taken the other day & I am sending you a copy, by which you will see I am looking well ... You really cannot understand what happiness the receipt of letters does afford me.' (See Figure 8.1.)[17] These feelings were not shared by Andrew Shaw, a Newfoundland Indian, taken prisoner, after being wounded, on 12 April 1918: 'I have received no Red Cross packages and *I am suffering terribly* from my hip wound.' Shaw was repatriated to London, during a wounded prisoner exchange, on 11 September 1918.[18]

The Allies, and individual indigenes, played upon German perceptions and stereotypes. *Stars and Stripes*, the official publication of the AEF, published four articles detailing the heroics of the 'American Indian against the Prussian Guard'.[19] *The Indian School Journal* also circulated a commentary exaggerating Indian bellicosity: 'A Sioux soldier was so full of fight that during the last two weeks of action he could not be kept in his dugout long enough to have his wound stripes sewn on his sleeves.'[20] In response to the alleged German anxiety over fighting Indian soldiers, certain American regiments suggested the idea of using Indians, wearing traditional dress and appurtenances, to conduct night

---

[16] Harry Gordon, *The Embarrassing Australian: The Story of an Aboriginal Warrior* (London: Angus & Robertson, 1963), pp. 26–8.
[17] Mrs Margaret Beadman (AWM), Private Collection.
[18] PANL, GN19, B-20-3, reel 170. Service Records Andrew Shaw.
[19] Camurat, 'The American Indian in the Great War', Section 1.1.
[20] Britten, *American Indians in World War I*, pp. 100–1.

Figure 8.1 Private Douglas Grant with Australian, Private Harry Avery, and an unidentified British soldier.

raids.[21] After the war, Duncan Campbell Scott romantically portrayed the impression Germans had of Canadian Indians:

If singled out by the foe for particular mention, it may be claimed for the Indians, who were depicted by the Germans in warpaint and with feathers, with scalping knives and tomahawks, ready to carry out … their treacherous and cruel practices. No doubt, the Germans had a wholesome fear of the Canadian methods of fighting, of the efficiency of our sharp-shooters, and the sudden, desperate nature of our trench raids … as for the Indian himself, there

[21] Ibid, p. 109.

is no doubt that he excelled in the kind of offensive that had been practiced by his ancestors and was native to him.[22]

In reality, many Indians either played on the stereotypes conferred upon them, or did indeed practise their traditional customs. Many wore moccasins, especially snipers and scouts, as they were quieter than boots. Others, like George Strangling Wolf, adhered to the ancient beliefs of the warrior ethos as witnessed by Mike Mountain Horse:

Another custom ... in the life of a warrior on the eve of battle was to cut away a small portion of his body as an offering ... In those dark days of 1917 ... George Strangling Wolf, while praying, took a needle out of his 'housewife' (a soldier's name for a sewing kit) and inserted it into the skin near his knee. He then took an army knife and sliced off that portion of the flesh which he was holding out taut with the needle. Pointing in the direction of the sun, and still holding the small portion of bloody flesh in his hand, George offered prayer.[23]

There are countless recorded instances of Indian soldiers bellowing war chants and 'whoops'. Standing-Rock Sioux, Charlie Rogers, of the 18th American Infantry Regiment, 'who was the match for 20 Huns, leaped over the parapet swinging his old rifle over his head. He let out a yell he had been saving for years, and it was a genuine war-whoop.'[24] Mountain Horse relayed a similar anecdote: 'I released my pent up feelings in the rendering of my own particular war song ... though some of my companions assured me that my war whoops had stopped the war for at least a few seconds, I have never been able to ascertain exactly what was Jerry's reaction to my outburst.'[25] He also mentions that he used Indian war medicines and ceremonies when preparing for battle. Mountain Horse even went so far as to paint Blackfoot Confederacy victory symbols on the captured guns of an entire German battery during the Battle of Amiens, an indication that he felt he was fighting for the nations of both Canada and the Blood (see Figure 8.2).[26]

In the South African tradition, blacks were used as labour, both in Africa and Europe, under command of white South Africans. Although coloureds served as combatants in the secondary theatres of the Middle East and Africa itself, this was not a departure from the colonial experience, and their deployment to Europe was in the function of labourers and transporters. In keeping with past practice, black and coloured South African units were respectively homogenous, save for white

[22] Dempsey, *Warriors of the King*, p. 63.
[23] Mountain Horse, *My People, the Bloods*, pp. 74–5.
[24] Britten, *American Indians in World War I*, p. 101.
[25] Mountain Horse, *My People, the Bloods*, p. 30.
[26] Dempsey, *Warriors of the King*, pp. 48, 58.

Figure 8.2 Blood Indian recruits of the 191st Battalion, CEF, Macleod, Alberta, 1916.

officers and senior NCOs. Rank was dependent on race. The highest rank for a black in the SANLC was lance-corporal; the lowest for a white was corporal, one rank higher. Coloureds deployed to European theatres were represented in all ranks except those of officers, while coloured units serving outside of Europe did contain some coloured officers. Black and coloured 'soldiers' were also paid less than their white South African counterparts and were identified by wearing relatively unmilitary uniforms, signifying their inferior position as labourers and non-citizens of the Union.

The Maori, from the outset of the war, were maintained as a homogenous unit, or sub-unit, save for the brief break-up of Maori companies after Gallipoli. The homogenous Maori Battalion, however, was mustered as a secondary, albeit front-line, pioneer battalion for service in Europe. The majority of the officers were Maori, save for the CO and the adjutant. Maori had rights equal to those of *Pakeha* under the Constitution; they were politically represented in Parliament and were, in general, politically reliable as an indigenous entity. They were collectively viewed as the pinnacle of global indigenes and had a reputation as fierce warriors. The role and ranks of Maori during the war, including equality with *Pakeha* in pay and uniform, reflect these contemporary realities, not to mention their immediate, distinctive inclusion in the NZDF at the outbreak of war and the power conferred on the Maori committee.

Aboriginal Australians were represented in a wide variety of functions within the AIF, although 58 per cent served in infantry battalions and 26 per cent in mounted units. The abnormally high mounted representation can be attributed to the fact that most were familiar with horses due to their mandatory agricultural occupations. Of the confirmed pre-war occupations of Aboriginal soldiers, 71.5 per cent had vocations which required familiarity with horses.[27] In addition, most Aborigines met the rigid requirements for mounted units that, 'Men to be good shots ... good riders and bushmen, accustomed to finding their way about in a strange country.'[28] Elyne Mitchell, daughter of General Sir Henry George Chauvel, commander of the Anzac Mounted Division Light Horse and Desert Mounted Corps, recalled in her work, *Light Horse: The Story of Australia's Mounted Troops*:

The 11th [Light Horse] received a batch of reinforcements among whom were thirty Aboriginals, who proved to be very good soldiers. Because of their superb sight and hearing, they were excellent on outpost duty, though one troop sergeant who had four Aborigines on a listing post one night, said that they heard so many suspicious sounds inaudible to anyone else, that he was compelled to 'stand to' all night.[29]

During the Battle of Beersheba (31 October 1917), in southern Palestine, the 11th Light Horse contained at least twenty-nine Aborigines.[30] Aborigines were well represented in the Remount Units, the horsebreakers for Australian mounted units.[31] Indigenous Australians also served in the following formations in both Europe and the Middle East: engineer, medical, machine gun, signal, mortar, veterinary, railway, camel, training and tunnelling.[32]

Although most were privates, Aboriginal soldiers were represented in both commissioned and non-commissioned ranks and were paid at standard AIF rates. Harry Hawkins of Queensland reached the rank of

[27] AWM27, 533/1. Returns Showing Particulars of Men of Aboriginal Percentage who Enlisted and Served Abroad with the A.I.F.; Watson, 'Aboriginal and Torres Strait Islander Soldiers of the First World War'.
[28] Ross, *The Myth of the Digger*, p. 32.
[29] Elyne Mitchell, *Light Horse: The Story of Australia's Mounted Troops* (Melbourne: Macmillan Press, 1978), p. 86.
[30] Mrs Margaret Beadman (AWM), Private Collection.
[31] Huggonson, 'Aboriginal Roughriders of World War 1', 70; Huggonson, 'Aboriginal Diggers of the 9th Brigade, First AIF', 217.
[32] Watson, 'Aboriginal and Torres Strait Islander Soldiers of the First World War', 7–18.

warrant officer 1, while George Kennedy attained the rank of warrant officer 2. There is also overwhelming evidence to suggest that Reginald Saunders, an officer during the Second World War and Korea, was not the first man of Aboriginal descent to receive a commission. Although the names will be withheld out of customary respect for Aboriginal tradition and kin, a soldier of Aboriginal descent from NSW served with the 6th Light Horse as a lieutenant, while another from Western Australia was a lieutenant with the 51st Battalion.[33]

Given the limited membership of Aborigines in Australian military formations in the past, and their late inclusion in the AIF, no thought was given to creating an all-Aboriginal unit. Aboriginal inclusion was dependent upon the need for manpower and was intended to meet shortages during the war. The extension of inclusion into the ADF was not projected to carry over into peacetime. A homogenous Aboriginal unit would have been a tacit recognition of their value as soldiers, a step which was racially and socially incompatible with contemporary Australian culture and political discourse. As such, it would have also undermined Australian efforts to promote assimilation. This point also applied to Canadian Indians.

The roles and representation of Indians and Eskimos in the CEF and the Royal Newfoundland Regiment reflected the duality of the racial and martial perceptions of the 'noble savage'. Many recruiters and battalion commanders believed that, given the history and military prowess of Indians, they had innate abilities in tracking, scouting and shooting, while possessing a certain degree of 'bloodlust'. Many also believed that Indians had keener eyesight, especially night vision, and better hearing, and could navigate by instinct. In reality, many Indians filled the roles of snipers and scouts, excelling in both functions given their civilian experience as hunters and trappers. All thirty-five Ojibwa recruited from Fort William, in northern Ontario, became snipers.[34]

Corporal Francis Pegahmagabow claimed 378 unofficial kills, which also ranked him the premier sniper in the entire Allied forces. In March 1917, while recovering from shellshock in England, Pegahmagabow wrote directly to Scott, asking him to intercede to allow him to return to his 1st Battalion:

I cannot return to my duty in France, they won't let me go ... Alex Logan [his agent at Parry Sound] will tell I have been a good boy at home and I am glad

---

[33] AWM, CN R940.4030994 A938. List of Australian Indigenous Servicemen who Served in World War One (Work in Progress), January 2007; AWM27, 533/1. Returns Showing Particulars of Men of Aboriginal Percentage who Enlisted and Served Abroad with the A.I.F.

[34] Dempsey, *Aboriginal Soldiers and the First World War*, p. 4.

to say that I feel just as lively as I was when I first enlisted 7th August 1914. There is no reason why they should keep or delay me back here. It isn't because I got wounded on Sept. 24th last, my wound does not bother me at all … For my part I would sooner fight my human enemy while I am trying to fight my spiritual enemy [post traumatic stress disorder] as well. Give them a tap to let me go back to my hunting Fritz in France. The reality of soldiering is nothing to me, although I had twenty months under shell fire in France, which I found is not half as bad as it is back here in England. Any soldier will contradict my idea between peace and war, chuck him in the clink for me, he is a-pologetic. [I was] awarded a medal [Military Medal] last June. I want another one while I have a chance.[35]

Although Pegahmagabow won the Military Medal three times (one of only thirty-eight Canadians to accomplish this feat), his unofficial tally of 378 kills is disputed and is symptomatic of Duncan Campbell Scott's poetic licence for propaganda purposes. In late 1919, Scott declared that Corporal Francis Pegahmagabow 'bears the extraordinary record of having killed 378 of the enemy'. In reality, during the presentation of his Military Medal and two bars by the Prince of Wales (future King Edward VIII) in Toronto in August 1919, Pegahmagabow boasted to reporters that he had tallied 378 kills during the war. Eager to show Indian contributions to the war effort, Scott, using newspaper articles and Pegahmagabow's statements, made this number 'official' in his department's year end report for 1919. This figure has since become fact in Canadian history, although it has never been corroborated by evidence or by accounts in either the official records of Pegahmagabow's 1st Battalion or by observers. Unlike most snipers, who worked in pairs, he operated alone.[36] Nevertheless, Pegahmagabow's war record and decorations are evidence of his skill and bravery as a sniper.

Another notable Indian sniper was Lance-Corporal Henry 'Ducky' Norwest of the 50th Battalion, a Métis of Cree ancestry from Edmonton, Alberta. Norwest tallied 115 kills. The former rancher, trapper and rodeo performer earned the MM with bar, making him one of 830 Canadians to be awarded this double honour. Norwest was killed on 18 August 1918 during the Battle of Amiens. That same day his CO issued a tribute: 'I doubt if anyone in the Canadian Corps or in the whole British Army had a finer record than he … His Indian blood possibly helped him in his work, possibly inherited his patience and cunning from his hunting forbears … his example an inspiration'. According

[35] LAC, RG10, vol. 3181, reel C-11335, file 452, 124-1a. Letter Pegahmagabow to Scott, 8 March 1917. Many doctors believed it impossible for Indians to suffer shellshock because of their upbringing and innate stoicism.

[36] Adrian Hayes, *Pegahmagabow: Legendary Warrior, Forgotten Hero* (Sault Ste. Marie: Fox Meadow Creations, 2003), pp. 35–43.

to the memoirs of the 50th Battalion, 'Our famous sniper … Henry Norwest carried out his terrible duty superbly because he believed his special skill gave him no choice but to fulfil his indispensable mission.' On his grave marker, his friends inscribed: 'It must have been a damned good sniper that got Norwest.'[37] According to a German prisoner of war, his reputation and fame were known to them, and they feared him.[38]

The records of other Indians also give credence to their exceptional skill as marksmen. Ojibwa Lance-Corporal Johnson Paudash (21st Battalion), Hiawatha band, Keene, Ontario, amassed eighty-eight kills and won the MM. A trio of Indian snipers from the 8th Battalion recorded impressive numbers. Lance-Corporal John Ballendine, a Cree from Battleford, Saskatchewan, finished the war with fifty-eight. Private Philip McDonald, a Mohawk from Akwesasne, was credited with forty, before being killed on 3 January 1916. Lastly, Private Patrick Riel, grandson to Louis Riel, accumulated thirty-eight notches. He was killed eleven days after McDonald.[39] Other notable snipers were Ojibwa brothers Pete and Sampson Comego, Ojibwa Private Roderick Cameron, and George Stonefish, a Delaware from Moraviantown, Ontario. Sampson Comego was killed on 10 November 1915, but in his short period of service tallied twenty-eight kills.[40]

Royal Newfoundland Regiment sniper Lance-Corporal John Shiwak was killed by shellfire on 20 November 1917 during the Battle of Cambrai. Shiwak's company commander, Captain R. H. Tait, called him a 'great favourite with all ranks, an excellent scout and observer, and a thoroughly good and reliable fellow in every way'. Another officer dubbed him, 'the best sniper in the British Army'.[41] Another notable Eskimo who served in the regiment was Frederick Freida of Hopedale, Labrador. In 1951, Freida joined the newly created Canadian Rangers, a formation of Indians and Eskimos tasked to patrol the remote Canadian Arctic, while engaging in traditional hunting and trapping.[42]

While excelling as snipers and scouts, Canadian Indians were employed in every branch of the combat arms and auxiliary formations except for the Royal Tank Corps. Albert Cochrane and Edward Lavallee, both from Saskatchewan, joined the Royal Naval Canadian

[37] LAC, RG9III-D-3, vol. 4941, reel T10748, file 441. War Diaries 50th Canadian Infantry Battalion.
[38] Dempsey, *Warriors of the King*, pp. 52–3.
[39] LAC, RG9III-D-3, vol. 4918, reel T10710–10711, file 369. War Diaries 8th Canadian Infantry Battalion.
[40] Scott, *Report of the Deputy Superintendent General*, pp. 15, 27.
[41] Kennedy, 'John Shiwak', 1.
[42] Gaffen, *Forgotten Soldiers*, p. 29.

Volunteer Reserve, and Kenneth McDonald of the Yukon joined the Royal Navy.[43] Three members of the defunct 114th Battalion, Lieutenants James David Moses, Oliver Milton Martin (both Mohawks from Six Nations) and John Randolph Stacey, a Mohawk from Kahnawake, Quebec, all served as pilots in the Royal Air Force (RAF). Stacey was killed on 8 April 1918, and Moses on 1 August 1918.[44] Martin went on to serve in the Second World War, attaining the rank of brigadier-general, the highest position ever attained in the Canadian Forces by an Indian.[45] American General John Pershing's French interpreter was Mohawk William Newell, a graduate of Syracuse University.[46]

At least seventeen Indians were commissioned officers in the CEF during the First World War (sixty-four American Indians were commissioned in the AEF). Seventy per cent had prior military service in the Canadian Militia (one was a permanent Militia officer prior to the war) and all came from professions which required an education, including law, teaching, engineering and skilled trades. Simply stated, Indians were commissioned according to their level of assimilation. This is not to say, however, that these Indians viewed themselves as assimilated, nor did it mean that they had rejected their Indian culture.

Indians also served in other campaigns apart from the Western Front. David Bernardan, a Salish Bella Coola from BC, was one of thirty-eight Canadians of the First Overseas Canadian Pioneer Detail, which operated barges on the Tigris and Euphrates rivers in Mesopotamia from 1916 onwards.[47] Privates William Thompson and John Munninguay, of the Peguis Reserve, Manitoba, served on the Western Front with the 203rd Battalion. Afterwards, they served in the 5,300-strong Canadian Siberian Expeditionary Force, at Vladivostock, from October 1918 to May 1919.[48] Two other Peguis Indians were attached to the Serbian Army and served on the Balkan Front from 1916 to 1918.[49]

While certain commanders possessed a romanticized view of the martial qualities of the Indian and tasked them accordingly, others perceived the Indian negatively. Many were placed in auxiliary units in non-combat roles, stereotyped as ill-educated and best suited for manual labour. Indians were well represented in the six battalions of the

[43] Dempsey, *Warriors of the King*, p. 61.
[44] Scott, *Report of the Deputy Superintendent General*, pp. 16–17.
[45] Gaffen, *Forgotten Soldiers*, p. 24.
[46] Barsh, 'American Indians in the Great War', 279.
[47] Scott, *Report of the Deputy Superintendent General*, p. 20.
[48] Dempsey, *Warriors of the King*, pp. 65–6.
[49] Scott, *Report of the Deputy Superintendent General*, p. 19.

Figure 8.3 An Indian soldier of the CEF Forestry Corps, *c.* 1917–18.

Canadian Forestry Corps (see Figure 8.3) and in the 256th Railway Construction Battalion (or 10th Battalion Canadian Railway Troops).

An all-Indian battalion never materialized during the First World War for numerous reasons. The first was the availability of reinforcements without conscription. Given the high casualty rates, and the relatively low Indian male population of military age (roughly 11,500), it was considered unlikely that enough replacements could be mustered to support a battalion once engaged in combat. Had the Maori Battalion been designated an infantry, rather than a pioneer, unit, it is doubtful that it would have been able to maintain its strength, given the lack of volunteers, and the failure to enforce conscription on Maori.

Secondly, there was concern within the Departments of Indian Affairs and the Militia that, if formed piecemeal from various Indian nations, there could be, as Gwatkin remarked, a worry as to 'whether coming from different tribes, they would fight among themselves'. In addition, many Indians did not speak English; therefore, exercising proper command and control would have been difficult given the multiplicity of Indian languages that would make up any all-Indian unit. Scott recognized this problem during the initial Indian recruiting campaign of early 1916:

[T]he usual routine of drill must be undergone by every soldier to fit himself to take his place in the ranks; and lack of knowledge of English is a very great disadvantage in receiving instruction. Under the circumstances I am of the opinion that it would be well to confine the efforts in recruiting to reserves ... where most of the Indians have been in closer touch with white people and have a knowledge of the English language.[50]

Many government officials and senior military personnel also regarded the CEF as a tool of assimilation. It must be remembered that the Ministry of Militia did not endorse the concept of homogenous French-Canadian battalions either, thus alienating a great number of French-Canadian men who would otherwise have enlisted. Had an all-Indian unit been formed, the French would have objected, or demanded the same conditions, adding to an already volatile ethnic situation.

Thirdly, the well-documented susceptibility of Indians to tuberculosis troubled the senior staff of the Canadian Red Cross: '[W]hen they went into lower altitudes, and became subjected to poisonous gases, this tendency would also immediately break out into tuberculosis and instead of the Indians being an assistance in numbers they would be a burden on the medical and Red Cross service.' Finally, W. M. Graham, Inspector General of Indian Agencies for southern Saskatchewan, argued that, 'If they went into the front as a unit, and if by chance they went into action and suffered tremendous casualties, there would always be a feeling among their friends at home that their sons had been placed in a more dangerous position than the whites. Of course this would not be the case ... the old Indian is quite primitive and does not understand things as we do.'[51] In retrospect, Graham's insight, albeit

[50] LAC, RG10, vol. 6766, reel C-8511, file 452-13. Letter Scott to W. B. Brown (Indian Agent Port Arthur, Ontario), 21 March 1916.
[51] LAC, RG10, vol. 6766, reel C-8511, file 452-13. W. J. Dilworth (Indian Agent Blood Agency, Alberta) to Scott, 17 January 1916; Dempsey, *Warriors of the King*, p. 24. In 1940, the Canadian Tuberculosis Association reported that for every hundred Canadian soldiers to be killed in the Great War, six died of tuberculosis. The United States' policy towards their Indian soldiers was very similar to that of Canada. They

containing elements of prejudice, was quite remarkable. Many colonial and Dominion units were perceived by their home governments (who exercised little discretion over their soldiers, especially prior to 1917) as being used as 'cannon fodder' by the British high command.

The 114th and 107th battalions were the closest any units came to being Indian. The 114th was broken up in November 1916, to reinforce other units, including the 107th. Shortly after arriving in England, on 1 February 1917, the 107th, containing over five hundred Indians, was officially converted to a pioneer battalion. There is no evidence to suggest that this decision was influenced by the Maori unit of the same designation. By this time, all newly formed Canadian battalions were being broken up as reinforcements. There was, however, a need for auxiliary units in the Canadian Corps. Lieutenant-Colonel Campbell pleaded with authorities to have his battalion re-mustered as a pioneer battalion, referring to his Indian soldiers' 'ability to adapt themselves without complaint to awkward circumstances and bad weather, which rendered their efficiency as a pioneer battalion far above the average'.[52] On 28 May 1918, after over one year of service, the 107th was disbanded and its members scattered across the 1st Canadian Engineer Brigade.[53]

What was similar across all Dominions was that those entrusted with command and control were hand-picked for their experience and familiarity with the culture and, in certain cases, language of the indigenes under their command. The officers for the Maori Contingent, including the CO and adjutant, were all selected by the Maori committee, followed by approval from the Ministry of Defence. Carkeek recalled that in order to uphold tribal *mana* and to assure both Maori and English proficiency, 'Care had to be exercised in selecting the non-commissioned and commissioned officers of the contingent. However, this was soon accomplished as special classes were formed for the purpose and only the best were selected.'[54]

The Canadian Ministry of Militia (aided by Indian Affairs) chose commanders for the 114th and 107th who were comfortable, and familiar, with the culture of their soldiers. Lieutenant-Colonel Glen Campbell was loaned by Indian Affairs from his position as Chief Inspector, to raise and lead the 107th Battalion. Campbell was deeply

---

maintained a policy of integration. However, they did have units that were made up primarily of Indians, such as the 142nd, 158th and 358th Infantry Regiments.
[52] Scott, *Report of the Deputy Superintendent General*, p. 15.
[53] LAC, RG150, 1992–93/166, 1434. Service Records Glen Campbell; LAC, RG9III-D-3, vol. 5010, reel T10859, file 725. War Diaries, 107th Pioneer Battalion.
[54] Carkeek, *Home Little Maori Home*, p. 10.

involved with Indian communities through his ranching and trapping and could speak Cree and Ojibwa. He also married Harriet, a Saulteaux (Ojibwa) and daughter of Chief Keeseekoowenin.[55] The CO of the 114th Battalion, Lieutenant-Colonel Andrew T. Thompson, was born in Cayuga astride the Six Nations Reserve. Thompson joined the 37th Haldimand Rifles, as a captain, in 1892, and proceeded to serve as the regiment's CO for eight years, before becoming the local Member of Parliament.[56] Thompson was also an Honorary Chief of the Six Nations.[57] Lieutenant-Colonel James K. Cornwall, CO of the 8th Battalion Canadian Railway Troops, which contained more than fifty Indians, had lived among the Indians of Alberta and Manitoba, hunting and trapping, before becoming the Peace River Member of Provincial Parliament (MPP) in the Alberta Legislature. He was fluent in Cree, Chipewyan and Dogrib. Not only did he interpret, he also taught his Indian soldiers to speak some English, as did Campbell.[58]

For the SANLC, Grundlingh asserts that, 'The background typical of the white staff who had been appointed after such careful scrutiny is well illustrated by the career of the commanding officer of the contingent, Col. S. M. Pritchard.' He emigrated from England in 1894 and joined the Basutoland Mounted Police. After serving as the private secretary to the Commissioner of Basutoland, Pritchard was appointed the Chief Inspector of Native Labour in the colony. In 1903 he was promoted to be assistant director of the South African Native Labour Bureau and became head director in 1914, shortly before the war. He was tasked with raising native labour for the GSWA campaign, before commanding the SANLC.[59] Likewise, all administrators, officers and senior NCOs under his command were hand-picked for their experience and familiarity with 'the mentality and customs [of blacks and] combined knowledge of the Native, Military Procedure and Labour'. Botha even took it upon himself to make the final appointments, indicative of his anxiety over the deployment of blacks to Europe, the need to maintain the compound system and the associated political repercussions. By September 1917, 146 members of the Native Labour

---

[55] LAC, RG10, vol. 4063, reel C-10204, file 402890. Correspondence Regarding the Appointment of Glen Campbell as Chief Inspector of Agencies, Reserves and Inspectorates in Manitoba, Saskatchewan, Alberta and the Northwest Territories. Also Subsequent Work While on Loan to Department of Militia & Defence and Death as Lieutenant-Colonel in France.
[56] LAC, RG150, 1992–93/166, 9622. Service Records Andrew Thompson.
[57] Scott, *Report of the Deputy Superintendent General*, p. 7.
[58] Dempsey, *Warriors of the King*, pp. 25–7.
[59] Grundlingh, *Fighting Their Own War*, pp. 102–3.

Bureau, in addition to former mine compound managers, were in Europe, employed with the SANLC.[60]

Indigenous inclusion in white, British-society-based militaries was problematic. Traditional leadership in many indigenous communities and warrior societies rested with the people themselves. Leaders and war chiefs were appointed, followed out of respect, and could be replaced at the discretion of the people. Military dress and deportment were foreign to many who joined from remote areas or had little previous contact with whites. Acclimatization to army discipline also proved difficult. Traditionally there were not the same sharp distinctions between a war chief and warriors compared with the disparity between commissioned officers and the ranks. For example, Indian Private John Ratt was disciplined for failing to salute an officer. During his hearing he remarked that at home, 'when we meet a man there we speak to him one time. No speak anymore to same man all day. Down here me salute everytime [sic] me pass man?'[61] It is difficult to discern objectively the degree of adjustment, or hardships, faced by indigenes in Dominion forces, as the majority of information is highly anecdotal.

Mountain Horse remarked that, 'I can readily appreciate the easy adjustment of the white man to the strict disciplinary measures of the army, but to apply the same rules and regulations to young undisciplined natives was quite another matter.' He recalled George Strangling Wolf turning out on parade 'wearing elk teeth earrings, with an elk teeth necklace to match, and a gaudy red handkerchief around his neck. The crown of his hat was cut away to let in the air, and he was noisily chewing gum, much to the discomfort of the man next to him in line.' Mountain Horse also mentions that Private Bumble Bee Crow Chief, a Blood who spoke no English, was struck from the battalion strength after he refused to cut his long braids. When leaving camp, Bumble Bee scolded his fellow Blood Indians: 'Don't be foolish like these white soldiers. I hear they call the war off everyday for mealtime. You boys want to keep on shooting even if you see them sitting down to eat.'[62] For the Plains Indians, long hair was symbolic of superiority. The records also indicate that many Indians adorned their tents with traditional artefacts, some even wearing traditional headdress. The Blackfoot and Blood went so far as to create a word in their languages for Germans, loosely translated as 'pointed helmets'.[63]

---

[60] NA, WO-107/37. After Action Report: Work of Labour Force during the War, November 1919; NASA, KAB, NTS, vol. 9107/8/363. SANLC Civil Servants.

[61] Britten, *American Indians in World War I*, p. 113.

[62] Mountain Horse, *My People, the Bloods*, pp. 141–2.

[63] Gaffen, *Forgotten Soldiers*, p. 22.

Two other prominent factors facing indigenous servicemen were introductions to western culture and to the English language. Many indigenous soldiers came from remote communities, which adhered to their cultural norms and traditions and had limited interaction with whites. For example, William Semia, an Ojibwa from northern Ontario, spoke no English when he enlisted in the 52nd Battalion. A fellow Ojibwa taught him rudimentary English during recruit training in Port Arthur, where he saw, for the first time, a modern city and, to his disbelief, grocery stores.[64] John Campbell, an Eskimo from the Yukon Territory, made a three-thousand mile journey by trail, canoe and river-steamer to enlist at Vancouver.[65] John Waymistigoos from the Duck Lake Reserve spoke no English; yet, he was accepted into the Forestry Depot as he showed proficiency with carpentry tools. Duncan Campbell Scott received reports from across Canada throughout 1916 of 'Indians who could not speak a word of English want[ing] to join up, but the fact that they could not understand English was an obstacle that prevented their enlistment'.[66] Carkeek recounts that some of his Maori comrades had never seen a big city and were thrilled to visit Auckland:

[T]he men took the opportunity of going into Auckland where they entered into the various amusements of the city with great gusto and glee ... walk shyly and bashfully into the city ... half admiring the shiny brass buttons on the ill-fitting tunic and practically disgusted with the almost bell-bottomed trousers [before the issue of proper NZEF uniforms]. Every now and then each would give an occasional glance into the shop windows to see how he looked in general ... Fully seventy-five percent of these men never had any military training before. They were the essence of the raw recruit, but willing to learn the modern arts of war.

In Colombo, Egypt, France and Britain, Carkeek records the excitement of the men when visiting the sights of the towns and cities while on leave.[67]

For South African blacks the shock of the journey and deployment to France was arguably more pronounced than for other indigenes, given the high level of prejudice in South Africa. When docking in Sierra Leone, members of the SANLC were amazed to see 'the people of that territory were pure black negroes of very high educational attainments equal to that of the best European'.[68] Jingoes mentions that, in Liverpool, 'the girls of that place arrived with teapots, cups, and

[64] LAC, RG10, vol. 6771, file 452-29. Service Records.
[65] LAC, RG10, vol. 3180, file 452-124-1A. Service Records.
[66] Dempsey, *Warriors of the King*, pp. 26-7.
[67] Carkeek, *Home Little Maori Home*, pp. 9-16.
[68] Willan, 'The South African Native Labour Contingent', 78.

biscuits to serve us with tea. They were so friendly, and we warmed
to their concern … Although white women had served us with tea in
Cape Town, we knew they were only doing it because we were going to
war. These girls were different … How could there be a country where
black men were treated the same as white men?' He goes on to state
that he 'landed at Calais … to be met by French people, men, women,
and girls. All were laughing and shaking our hands.' Jingoes met a
British labourer, William Johnstone, on the docks of Dieppe and the
two became good friends: 'We hit it off at once and spent our breaks
drinking tea and taking about our two countries, until at last we were
close friends. After the war we corresponded for many years.'[69]

In fact, in late 1917, Pritchard arranged a strictly controlled propaganda tour of England and Scotland for four black chaplains of the
SANLC, accompanied by white officers, to impress upon them 'the
greatness of Britain'. An accompanying officer reported afterwards that,
'Colonel Pritchard as O. C., and South Africa as a country, will have no
reason to be anything but satisfied with the result of the tour … I believe
that the scheme has produced nothing but good … for the future.'[70]

The compound system, however, was not as segregated as planned.
When marching to and from the camps and work areas, members of the
SANLC were greeted by French women. Many noted their addresses
and, through letters delivered by children, formed relationships with
these women. While most were caught, others appear to have been successful in sneaking out of camp for rendezvous with French women,
including prostitutes. An intercepted letter reads:

Dear Lady – I am so pleased that I can't even tell anybody, and I am much
anxious if this note could be received by you. Then I am kindly asking you, if
possible you will be so kind to do me a favour and call round our camp tonight
at 8:30. I am in the first hut by the second gate as you go down … If you too
late, do cleverly come, approach the door and give a small knock. I will hear
you. And I will then explain to you about my notion concerning you. I beg to
remain with best greetings of love to you.

After this incident, directives were given to SANLC commanders,
and the local population, instructing them that, 'It is absolutely essential that the Kaffir should regard white women as unapproachable …
[P]eople who suffer from this levity on the part of white women … are
the wives and daughters of our settlers in the black man's country, who
live in deadly peril of rape and murder.'[71]

[69] Jingoes, *A Chief is a Chief by the People*, pp. 80–93.
[70] Willan, 'The South African Native Labour Contingent', 82.
[71] Grundlingh, *Fighting Their Own War*, p. 112.

Following the war, the chief censor in South Africa, J. M. Weaver, intercepted and destroyed ten letters from French women to returned members of the SANLC. Weaver argued that these letters 'will give the natives the wrong impression as to their relative position with regard to Europeans'.[72] By comparison, Lance-Corporal Harold Frazer, an Aborigine from Goodooga, New South Wales, married an English woman (Rose) while recovering from wounds and gas poisoning in England. After the war, they settled in New South Wales, where Harold became an expert opal cutter.[73] Aborigine Private Gordon Naley married Cecilia Karsh from Fulham, London. They left England together and settled at his home in Barmera, South Australia.[74] Canadian Private Joseph DeLaronde, an Ojibwa from Lake Nipigon, Ontario, married the English nurse who tended his wounds while convalescing. The couple returned to his reserve after the war. Two other Indian soldiers are known to have married British war brides.[75]

By all accounts, indigenes enjoyed the culture and people of Britain and France, despite the fact that British and French society held ignorant, if not romantic, perceptions of indigenes. British propaganda promoted the war as a joint imperial effort and lauded the national war efforts of its colonies and Dominions. According to George Robb, 'Visual depictions of the imperial "family of nations" appeared frequently on war posters and commercial advertisements, though the images typically privileged British people by placing them front and centre, flanked by people from the white dominions, with Indians and Africans in the background.' (See Figure 8.4.) Dominion loyalty was illustrated through propaganda films such as: *Sons of the Empire*; *Canadians on the Western Front*; *New Zealand Troops in France*; *A Chinese Labour Contingent*; and *A South African Native Labour Contingent*.[76] A Canadian national newspaper exclaimed in May 1916 that the imperial war effort 'reminds one of the human colour-box in the war as a whole, for the world armies include all shades of flesh, from the whitest of white faces to the blackest ebony, with all the variegated shades in between'.[77]

Canadian Frank Ferguson recalled in his diary the story of a young boy asking him and his mates who they were. After responding that they were Canadians, the young boy exclaimed, 'Strike me pink, Cannydians, and you're white!' Ferguson added that, 'I suppose he

---

[72] Grundlingh, 'The Impact of the First World War on South African Blacks', 4.
[73] Huggonson, 'Aboriginal Diggers of the 9th Brigade, First AIF', 216.
[74] Huggonson, 'Aboriginal POW's of World War One', 11–12.
[75] Scott, 'The Canadian Indians and the Great World War', 328.
[76] Robb, *British Culture and the First World War*, pp. 14–15.
[77] LAC, RG10, vol. 3180, C-11335, 45-124-1a. Unknown Newspaper, 6 May 1916.

Figure 8.4 Members of the Maori Pioneer Battalion having formal afternoon tea, with King George V looking on from the back-left wall, *c*. 1917.

shared the popular idea that all Canadians were redskins.' Another Canadian, H. J. Elliot, wrote to his parents, amused that the people in Britain 'have great ideas about Canada. They imagined we were all wild savages or cowboys that lived in tents, and forests were everywhere, and no farm land.' Willard Melvin echoed this British perception in a letter to his father: 'A Canadian up here is something of a curio, you can hear people on the street saying, "There's a Canadian", like I was a strange animal of some kind!'[78] In an incident relating to the SANLC reported to Governor-General Buxton, 'A white officer, when a batch of natives landed at Portsmouth on their way to France, took some of them into a shop. The shopman said: "These are Zulus, I suppose." The officer, somewhat hypercritically, said, "No, Am-a-Zulu" (Amazulu being plural for Zulu). "Oh! Really, are you?"' Aborigine Douglas Grant recalled a humorous encounter with a young girl while visiting his father's former

[78] Tim Cook, *Shock Troops: Canadians Fighting the Great War Vol. 2, 1917–1918* (Toronto: Penguin Group, 2008), pp. 47–8.

village in the Orkneys. As he chatted to a shopkeeper in his Scottish brogue, a young girl shrieked, 'Mither, come quick. Here's a poor wee Scottie come back from Australia, and he's been burned black!'[79]

From anecdotal evidence, letters and diaries, Dominion indigenes enjoyed European culture, and contact with the relatively unprejudiced local populations. Aboriginal Private, Roland Carter, mentioned in a letter while convalescing in England that, 'I am getting good treatment here. Last Friday I went in the town to see the moving pictures. All the Native[s] went … I am having a good time here.'[80] SANLC labourer E. H. Lesuthu wrote to his magistrate exclaiming that, 'We have seen most wonderful things of the civilized Nations … France is a most beautiful looking country mostly in summer when everything looks green … We enjoy ourselves.'[81] Aborigine, Lance-Corporal Charles Blackman (see Figure 8.5), wrote numerous letters home to his pre-war employer in Biggenden, Queensland, describing his leave and his life as a soldier:

1 July 1917: I suppose you will be glad to hear that I have been on leave to England for ten days. I had a glorious time there, one can't help having a good time because the people in England think the world of yer and they take yer all over the place and show you everything you wish to see and look after you well.

15 October 1917: It is nice to get a few letters now and then as I always been a lonely soldier till I went on leave in England … There are quite a few Biggenden lads in the ninth Battalion with me but it matter who we meet so long as a few of us can get together we can always be found laughes or with the *big fresh smile up* and dont worry so long as we get back home someday.

29 October 1917: I expect you know what we feel like over here or you have a good idear its terrible painful and serious but yet it can't make us lad down harted All my cobber [mates] are in Blighty having a spell with slite wound they are coming back geragly. after the war we are going to have a look all over England Scotland + Ireland so we will see some sites yet … so far we haven't see any better places than Australia. France is beautiful but it rains to mutch why you never see the sun here one thing is the clouds here never need to thunder the guns do all the thundering + the splashes they make is just like lightening they make more noise than those thunderstorms you have in Australia. I would rather be in a thunderstorm than a Battle … from your sincerely friends lonely soldier

23 November 1917: The last time up in the line I killed five german I did it because they held up thir hand till we got about ten yards off them and then the dirty bruits threw bombs at us so that's why I killed them. If they hadent thrown bombs at us we would have taken them Presnors and they would have been alright. This totles ten for me since I been in France that all good hall for

---

[79] Clark, 'Aborigines in the First AIF', 24.
[80] Kartinyeri, *Ngarrindjeri Anzacs*, pp. 20–1.
[81] NASA, KAB, CMT, 3–930. E. H. Lesuthu to Magistrate, 22 June 1917.

Figure 8.5 Lance-Corporal Charles T. Blackman, 1917 and 1918.

one man isn't it I have done my bit I think the next time up Ill get some more and Ill kill all I can. this is not half of what I could tell you about the Battle in France. What a soldier don't know it not worth known we seen some sites of all kind ... I have see quite enough of it before.

6 July 1918: I wish I was returning to Australia today I think this war is a nuisense it keeping us away to long ... I havent seen any place like Aussie yet in this

Figure 8.5 (*cont.*)

world … everyday you can hear dozens of fellows saying I wish I was in Aussie now. The reply is you've got a lot of mates Digger.[82]

---

[82] AWM, PRO1679. Charles Blackman: Letters, Photographs. Blighty is slang for England, derived from the Hindustani word *vilayati*, meaning foreigner.

Within Blackman's letters lie several subtle, yet important, themes of not only the service of indigenes, but of all soldiers. He alludes to the loneliness and homesickness of soldiers, the camaraderie felt by men in arms, within both national formations and smaller sub-units, and, for indigenes, their acceptance by other soldiers, regardless of race. A benefit of war service was the interaction of whites and indigenes, something not common within their home nations. Letters home from indigenes only represent those who could read and write, and say nothing about those who could not. The latter group may have felt a greater alienation as they were less accustomed to white culture, and estrangement from their traditional communities and customs augmented an already strange and traumatizing war.

This issue, however, was more pronounced for Indians and Eskimos than for their Dominion counterparts. Maori and native South Africans were grouped in homogenous units, and, for the most part, shared a common language, customs and civilian experience. They experienced the war alongside fellow indigenes. Aborigines who were accepted into the AIF were primarily, although not without exception, half-castes who spoke English and were relatively assimilated. Indians and Eskimos, many of whom spoke no, or very little, English and came from remote communities, were scattered across all formations of the CEF. W. M. Graham, Inspector General of Indian Agencies for southern Saskatchewan, received three letters from Indians expressing their loneliness: "'Most of my Indian pals are either Blighty or killed. Two of us Indian boys are left, four of them have paid the price … I tell you letters are very interesting, especially when your chums are away from you." *Elijah Dickson*; "It makes us boys long to get back … And how proud we feel of the reserve we are doing our duty for." *John Walker*; "I am quite interested in the news of our reserve. Many is the time I wish I was back in my native country." *Abel Watech*.' Mountain Horse wrote home while in hospital: 'I am rather lonely … I have not talked Blackfoot for over six months.'[83]

While the inability of Indians to speak English was problematic, there was one exception. The American 'Code-Talker' programme of Second World War fame had roots in the First World War. In October 1918, E Company, of the 142nd (US) Infantry Regiment which contained 208 Indians, called on two of its eighty-nine Choctaw soldiers to transmit messages in their Indian language. Regimental commander, Colonel A. W. Bloor, believed, 'it was hardly possible that Fritz would be able to translate their dialects and the plan to have these Indians translate

[83] Dempsey, *Warriors of the King*, pp. 60–1.

telephone messages was adopted'. A training school was opened for Indian transmitters. During the last two months of the war, various units of the 36th and 41st Divisions employed Indians as telephone operators. It is not known if this practice was adopted by the Canadian Expeditionary Force, although there is evidence to suggest that Cree men might have been used in this function. During the Second World War, both the American and Canadian forces created official code-talker programmes.[84]

At Armentières, on the night of 10–11 July 1916, eighty-five Maori soldiers conducted trench raids. According to battalion orders, 'No rifles and bayonets will be taken. Officers and sappers will carry revolvers. Other ranks will be armed with *meres* ... Only Maori will be spoken by all parties after leaving the starting point.'[85] It is interesting that traditional Maori weapons (*meres*) were preferred and used (although homemade clubs and batons were quite common for raiding parties of all nationalities), and that it was a conscious command decision to speak only in the Maori tongue. The Maori language would be utilized again as a means of safeguarding communications in the Second World War with the 28th (Maori) Battalion and during operations in the 1960s in Borneo.

For indigenous soldiers, visits by the King and other dignitaries and politicians provided affirmation of their worth as members of the imperial war effort. In 1917, the SANLC was visited by the King of Belgium, followed by French parliamentarians, including Blaise Diagne. According to Jingoes, 'When they arrived, there was a black man among them, and we assumed that he was simply there to accompany his white masters. We were all staggered when these men were introduced, for the pitch-black man held a high position in the Government.' Diagne was the commissioner of recruitment for Senegal and a deputy in the French Assembly. Jingoes also remembered that, 'we were told that there was no colour bar at all in France, and that a person was elected to office because of his education and ability; the man in question had degrees behind his name ... It was our first experience of living in a society without a colour bar.'[86]

On 10 July 1917, the SANLC was inspected by King George V, accompanied by Queen Mary, the Prince of Wales and Haig. During his address, the King remarked that, 'The loyalty of my native subjects

---

[84] See: William C. Meadows, 'North American Indian Code Talkers: Current Developments and Research', in *Aboriginal Peoples and Military Participation: Canadian & International Perspectives*, pp. 161–213.

[85] Battalion Orders No. 1, 8 July 1916, in Cowan, *The Maoris in the Great War*, pp. 85–7.

[86] Jingoes, *A Chief is a Chief by the People*, p. 87.

in South Africa is fully shown by the helpful part you are taking in this world-wide war ... You are also part of my great armies fighting for the liberty and freedom of my subjects of all races and creeds throughout the empire.'[87] M. L. Posholi mused that, 'We saw him, George V, our king, with our own eyes ... To us it is a dream, something to wonder at.'[88] On orders from the Department of Native Affairs, the King's speech was translated and printed 'in Kafir and sesuto [sic] languages', for distribution in South Africa.[89] Similarly, Blood Private George Strangling Wolf was elated to have seen 'the Great White King' while in England.[90] Lieutenant Frederick Loft, a Mohawk, represented the Iroquois Confederacy as a Pine Tree Chief, in an audience with the King on 21 February 1918. The confederacy, in a demonstration of autonomy, had unilaterally declared war on Germany in April 1917 as an ally of both the United States and the British empire.[91]

While the necessities of war led to the inclusion of Dominion indigenes, their presence in Allied forces was the subject of debate. Although Allied forces and propaganda praised the contribution of the imperial family, racial considerations and prejudice influenced the position and standing of indigenous soldiers and all aspects of their participation. The level of equality varied across Dominions and was based on pragmatic considerations and the desire to maintain the overall balance between indigenous and white populations within all Dominions. The Germans also deplored Britain's and France's employment of indigenes as combatants on the Western Front and in the occupation forces following the war. The exposure of indigenous soldiers to those from other nations and to countries relatively void of significant racial prejudice influenced their perceptions of whites, their home Dominions and themselves. Their inclusion influenced the perceptions of white soldiers, politicians and governments with regard to indigenes as peoples and soldiers.

[87] NASA, KAB, CMT, 3–930. Speech King George V, 10 July 1917.
[88] Grundlingh, 'The Impact of the First World War on South African Blacks', 6.
[89] NASA, KAB, CMT, 3–930. Memorandum from Native Affairs, 23 July 1917.
[90] Dempsey, *Warriors of the King*, p. 58.
[91] Donald B. Smith, 'Fred Loft', in Frederick E. Hoxie (ed.), *Encyclopedia of North American Indians* (New York: Houghton Mifflin Harcourt, 1996), p. 345. This distinction is not a hereditary title like those of other Iroquois Sachems (Chiefs). The title and position in the Great Council of Chiefs were given because of extraordinary abilities and actions. Pine Tree Chiefs could not (unlike hereditary Chiefs) be dehorned (deposed) by Clan Mothers, although the council and the people could be told to 'be deaf to his voice and advice'.

9   The home front

The enthusiasm for the war effort among indigenes was evident within indigenous communities on the home fronts and was shared by women as well as men. Indigenous women served as nurses and were active in patriotic organizations. Indigenous peoples donated money to war funds and contributed to the agricultural and industrial output of the Dominions. Edith Montour, of the Six Nations Reserve, served as a nurse with the US Medical Corps. By 1917, she was stationed in Vittel, France, treating wounded soldiers: 'Sometimes we would walk right over to where there had been fighting. It was an awful sight ... whole towns blow[n] up'.[1] Fourteen American Indian women served as nurses.[2] An unknown number of Maori nurses were also present in New Zealand field hospitals. Allen wrote to Pomare on 3 September 1915 that, 'I have already authorized the Commandant to secure a certain number of Maori nurses for the front.' However, he stipulated that, 'I do not deem it prudent to let them go except under the charge of an experienced pakeha matron or nurse.'[3] While no black South African nurses accompanied the SANLC to Europe, they were present in black veteran hospitals in the Union itself. In April 1916, the Ministry of Native Affairs made this recommendation: 'Since Native nurses are required for work solely amongst Natives, which there is no prospect of White nurses ever undertaking and which it is undesirable White nurses should undertake, the establishment of a Junior Certificate for Natives would not appear in any way to endanger the prestige of the nursing profession generally or to discourage Natives from aspiring to the European nursing standard.'[4]

The greatest contribution made by indigenous women was on the home front through patriotic organizations. Maori women were active

---

[1] Summerby, *Native Soldiers, Foreign Battlefields*, pp. 17–19.
[2] Barsh, 'American Indians in the Great War', 280.
[3] ANZ, AD1, box 758, record 9/296. Allen to Pomare, 3 September 1915.
[4] NASA, SAB, GNLB, vol. 254/369/16. Report of Native Sub-Committee and King Edward VII Order of Nurses, 19 April 1916.

in national war organizations, as well as Maori-specific associations, such as 'Lady Liverpool's and Mrs. Pomare's Maori Soldiers' Fund'. In 1917, Maori leaders, doubting the government's sincerity in proposing equality in repatriation programmes, set up the Maori Patriotic Committee to raise private funds among Maori. The money was used for the welfare of Maori veterans. The possibility of buying land for veterans was considered but never initiated.[5]

Aboriginal women in Queensland and Northern Territory auctioned hand-made crafts for the Patriotic Fund and also participated in Red Cross fund-raising displays. Melbourne saw a large Aboriginal population growth during the war years, as many women took up occupations in essential war industries, which had been previously reserved for whites.[6] According to Bleakley, 'the aborigines' most valuable contribution to the war effort was the labour they were able to provide for the rural industries, in relief of the men who were away on military service … [E]mployers were readily offering increased rates of pay to obtain men.'[7] Aborigines followed news of the war, as witnessed by Jimmie Barker, 13 years of age when war broke out: 'We knew little about what was happening overseas, but everyone was talking about it. Suddenly it made a difference to us. People bought newspapers and there was more knowledge of world events. Even school children became aware of other places and of the importance of such occurrences as the sinking of the *Emden* and the fighting at Gallipoli.'[8]

Black South African women were asked by the Red Cross and the Governor-General's Fund to donate 'curios for selling from Natives'. In some cases, these women were paid small sums for their crafts. A native kraal was erected outside the SANLC Rosebank depot in Cape Town in September 1918, 'in connection with entertainment which is being arranged by the SANLC for the purpose of raising funds … in aid of the "Red Cross" funds and to sell native assegais, knobkerries, sticks, shields, bangles, skins, gourds, or any Native curios'.[9] By 1916, natives had donated 'according to their small means, to several war funds … the Basutos had given £2700 to the National Relief Fund … while the Zulus, Tembus and Pondos were still collecting'.[10]

---

[5] Hill, *State Authority, Indigenous Autonomy*, pp. 105, 109.
[6] Jackomos and Fowell, *Forgotten Heroes*, p. 14; Pratt, 'Queensland's Aborigines in the First AIF', 19.
[7] Bleakley, *The Aborigines of Australia*, p. 171.
[8] Jimmie Barker (as told to Janet Mathews), *The Two Worlds of Jimmie Barker: The Life of an Australian Aboriginal 1900–1972* (Marrickville: Southwood Press, 1977), p. 87.
[9] NASA, KAB, 1PDE, vol. 16. CO SANLC Depot Cape Town to Department of Native Affairs, 4 September 1918.
[10] Plaatje, *Native Life in South Africa*, p. 312.

In Newfoundland, the Women's Patriotic Association, founded in August 1914 by Lady Margaret Davidson, had grown to include 15,000 volunteers at 218 branches by 1918. According to Dr Paddon, at the International Grenfell Association in Indian Harbour, Labrador: 'My wife runs a girls' club which has raised $160.00, from the few able to contribute, by needlework & a basket social ... My wife has written Lady Davidson to ask for a little word of encouragement to the Labrador girls from her.'[11] By the end of the war, Newfoundland had raised over $1 million for war funds.[12]

Canadian Indian women formed Patriotic and Red Cross societies on their own reserves. They made bandages, knitted various items of clothing and raised funds by selling traditional crafts. The Canadian Red Cross Society stated that the articles made by Indian women were the finest quality of knitting and sewing they received. The Six Nations Women's Patriotic League, formed in October 1914, produced the greatest yield of needlework of any reserve. In addition, Indian women and men worked in munitions factories.[13]

Canadian Indian donations to Patriotic Funds were used as a propaganda tool to increase monetary offerings by all Canadians. In November 1916, the Honorary Secretary of the Patriotic Fund, Sir Herbert Ames, received a letter from an Onion Lake, Saskatchewan Cree, Moo-che-we-in-es, with his contribution of $1.50. Ames wrote to Scott: 'We are now looking for every human story we can get to help our campaign for the Canadian Patriotic Fund ... Can you get the story, or could you get him to write a letter, as to why he made the subscription? We can use this to our advantage in the press.' Moo-che-we-in-es was persuaded to write a note using Cree syllabics, which was translated into English:

You asked me to tell you a story about how it came into my mind to pay a little towards 'War Money'. I heard there was a big war going on over there and I feel like I want to help you in some way and the best I can do is to send a little money for I can't go myself as I am nearly blind. This is to show you I like to help you. I am an Indian. I heard that other Indians were going to give 25 cents each out of their treaty money. I give $1.50 out of the money from the Government for beef I sell the Agency. I am about 50 years old and my wife and two sons are living with me and my son's wife and her child. That is the way I make up that $1.50 – 25 cents for six. I shake hands to you, Moo-che-we-in-es.

The letter was passed on to Ames, who quickly wrote Scott, 'That letter ... is one of the best things I have seen ... If you have anything

[11] PANL, GN2/14, box 13, file 146. Dr H. L. Paddon to W. R. Grieve, 10 July 1917.
[12] Newfoundland-Labrador Heritage, 'Managing the War Effort: The Home Front'. www.heritage.nf.ca
[13] Dempsey, *Aboriginal Soldiers and the First World War*, pp. 4–6.

Figure 9.1 Moo-che-we-in-es Canadian Patriotic Fund poster, *c.* 1917.

more as good as this, send it on. We could always utilize advanta-geously any human story.'[14] Moo-che-we-in-es' letter was made into a Patriotic Fund poster that was used across Canada, including reserves (see Figure 9.1).

[14] LAC, RG10, vol. 6762, file 452-2. Ames to Scott, November 1916; Moo-che-we-in-es to Scott, 4 December 1916; Ames to Scott, 15 December 1916.

Table 9.1: *Indian patriotic donations (Cdn $)*[1]

Province	Patriotic Fund	Red Cross	Local Patriotic and Red Cross funds	Other war funds and Belgian Relief Fund	Total
Saskatchewan	4,961.00	326.55	11,945.75	24.60	17,257.90
Ontario	6,927.55	697.00	2,759.15		10,383.70
Alberta	3,143.65	230.10	4,775.65	507.50	8,656.90
BC	447.11	359.25	4,241.00		5,047.36
Manitoba	811.60	1,029.50	1,178.50		3,019.60
Quebec	50.00	25.00	100.00	5.00	180.00
Total	*16,340.91*	*2,667.40*	*25,000.05*	*537.10*	*44,545.46*

[1] LAC, RG10, vol. 6762, file 452-3. Native Contributions to War Funds; Scott, *Report of the Deputy Superintendent General*, pp. 20–5.

By the end of the war, Indians had donated almost $45,000 to war funds, or 43 cents per Indian (see Table 9.1). A further $8,750.00 was not accepted, as particular bands were not in a financial position to make the donations requested out of their monthly funds.

Mountain Horse proudly stated that, 'From the outset of this colossal struggle the Red Man demonstrated his loyalty to the British Crown in a very convincing manner. Patriotic and other war funds were generously subscribed to, and various lines of war work participated in at home.'[15] American Indians purchased $25 million worth of Liberty Bonds during the war.[16] Indians also purchased Victory Bonds, although few were in a financial position to do so. The Ministry of Indian Affairs refused requests by reserves to invest their band funds from Ottawa in Victory Bonds, given that the accumulation of interest would be the same, since all Indian funds belonged to the government.[17]

Despite the substantial donations to the Canadian Patriotic Fund, which was designed to aid families of soldiers in hardship, Indian families could not draw on its resources: 'The dependants of these Indian soldiers are wards of the Government, and draw living rations from the Government and have no rents to pay, hence since they are a charge on the Government of Canada, and as the Government of Canada is responsible for their maintenance, and for these reasons we cannot recommend that they participate in the distribution of the Patriotic

[15] Mountain Horse, *My People, the Bloods*, p. 139.
[16] Britten, *American Indians in World War I*, p. 133.
[17] LAC, RG10, vol. 6770, file 452-23. Victory Bond Contributions.

Figure 9.2 'Canadian Patriotic Indian Chiefs', *c*. 1915–16.

Funds.' Only after the executive of the Patriotic Fund was made aware of Indian contributions was the policy changed in April 1917, so that 'families of Indians who have listed be treated in the same manner as those of other nationalities' (see Figure 9.2).[18]

Despite the contributions of indigenous peoples on and off the battle-field, Dominion governments continued the long-standing practice of appropriating indigenous land. In 1917, Arthur Meighen, Canadian Minister of the Interior and Indian Affairs, launched the Greater Production Effort programme to increase agricultural production on Indian reserves: 'We will still leave him enough to trap on, but even if we did not, thirty bushels of wheat to the acre is a lot better than a few squirrels caught by the Indian.'[19] Section 90, sub-sections 2 and 3 of the Indian Act were altered, under the argument that many reserves were

[18] LAC, RG10, vol. 6762, file 452-2. Correspondence: Indian Affairs and Patriotic Fund, 1917.
[19] S. D. Grant, 'Indian Affairs Under Duncan Campbell Scott: The Plains Cree of Saskatchewan 1913–1931', *Journal of Canadian Studies* 18/3 (1983), 30.

too vast to be completely utilized by the Indians. It was amended so that these lands, if not sold to the government, would be expropriated and leased to whites for agricultural pursuits. In total, 313,398 acres of reserve land were subject to these actions.[20] According to Meighen, it was necessary to remove power from 'what one may call reactionary or recalcitrant Indian bands to check their own progress by refusing consent to the utilization of their funds or vacant land for their own advantage'.[21]

Sub-section 2 of the revision gave the federal government power, 'to deal with the council of a band who through some delusion or misapprehension acts in a manner contrary to the best interests of the band, and refuses to sanction expenditures which the Governor in Council may consider necessary for the welfare and progress of the band'. The need for expenditures to increase agricultural productivity was specifically mentioned, and the Indian Act was further amended to make use of 'idle' band funds for investment in the Greater Production Effort. The government could dictate the use of reserve land and band funds, with or without the consent of band councils. Sub-section 3 referred particularly to 'large areas of land on Indian reserves [in western Canada] capable of pasturing cattle or producing wheat, and it is desired that all obstacles to the utilization of these lands should, in as far as possible be removed'.[22] On 23 April 1918, Meighen issued a statement in the House of Commons concerning his productivity campaign: 'We need not waste any time in sympathy for the Indian, for I am pretty sure his interests will be looked after ... The Indian is a ward of the Government still. The presumption of the law is that he has not the capacity to decide what is for his ultimate benefit in the same degree as his guardian, the Government of Canada.'[23] Sarah Carter believes that the inspiration for Meighen's programme 'may have come from the American example, launched in 1917, when the Bureau of Indian Affairs mobilized behind a plan to see that every tillable acre on Indian reservations be intensely cultivated'.[24]

The Blood Indians of Alberta serve as a case study for the modifications made to the Indian Act for the Greater Production Effort.

[20] E. Brian Titley, *A Narrow Vision: Duncan Campbell Scott and the Administration of Indian Affairs in Canada* (Vancouver: University of British Columbia Press, 1986), pp. 40–1.
[21] Sarah Carter, '"An Infamous Proposal": Prairie Indian Reserve Land and Soldier Settlement after World War I', *Manitoba History* 37 (1999), 13.
[22] Dempsey, 'The Indians and World War One', 5–6.
[23] Titley, *A Narrow Vision*, p. 41.
[24] Carter, '"An Infamous Proposal": Prairie Indian Reserve Land and Soldier Settlement after World War I', 12.

A 1916 government proposal to sell 90,000 acres had been refused by the Bloods. The head chief filed charges of bribery, fraud and intimidation against the federal government through the Ministry of Indian Affairs. Although no legal action was ever taken, the government halted its attempt to seize the land. On 15 February 1918, the government invoked the new amendments and large tracts of land (90,000 acres) were forcibly leased to white farmers; the Indians living on that land were dispossessed. Although the years 1916 and 1917 saw the Blood Reserves produce the highest yields of grains and cattle of any in Canada, in 1918 they were deprived of their lands to increase their own production. Meighen claimed that the campaign to increase productivity on reserves had been a great success, with the 1918 crop the best in history; however, statistics indicate otherwise. In the fiscal year 1916 production reached 388,731 bushels of wheat. By 1918, the year Meighen cited as showing an increase, only 255,884 bushels were harvested. Production on the Blood Reserve fell from 65,000 bushels in 1917 to 5,000 bushels in 1919. This scheme, however, remained in effect until 1922.[25]

Indian lands were also used directly by the Canadian military. In April 1917, Camp Mohawk was opened by the Imperial Munitions Board (IMB) on the Tyendinaga Mohawk Reserve, Ontario, as a training facility for the Royal Flying Corps. After 'considerable discussion and explanation' the elected (Indian Act) band council agreed to lease the land providing that the IMB would compensate for all damages to infrastructure and livestock, and that local Indians be given preference for internal jobs. The training school accommodated roughly 900 to 1,000 airmen at any given time throughout 1918. The camp was closed at the end of the war, but was again utilized, with Mohawk consent, during the Second World War. Although there were minor disagreements and tensions among Tyendinaga residents, the council and the IMB, the situation surrounding Camp Mohawk was generally cooperative and indicative of J. R. Miller's observation that Indians were proactive and adopted strategies 'to counter attempts to control their lives and eradicate their traditions'. A similar situation occurred on the Sarcee Reserve in Alberta in 1915, where land was leased for a military facility.[26]

Land was also a source of contention in New Zealand. The expropriation of Maori land under the 1909 Native Land Act, followed by the 1913 Native Land Amendment Act, created animosity among Maori

[25] Dempsey, 'The Indians and World War One', 5–7.
[26] Lackenbauer, *Battle Grounds*, pp. 39–82, 264.

who refused to sell land or were forced to relinquish title. The issues of land, and the refusal of Kingite tribes to enlist, came to a head on 2 April 1916 in the Urewera Mountains. Three police parties, totalling sixty-seven men, descended on Prophet Rua Kenana's community of Maungapohatu. In a half-hour battle two Maori were killed (Rua's son and uncle) and an unknown number wounded, while four police were also wounded. Six Maori, including Rua, were arrested. Between 1909 and 1920, Maori had relinquished title, by fair means or foul, to an additional 2.3 million acres. An official calculation in 1920 stated that Maori retained less than a million acres, 'that may be considered suitable for settlement'.[27]

In South Africa, the enforcement of the 1913 Natives Land Act and cattle dipping regulations had the potential to ignite violence, a situation which worried the Union government and white citizens. Although magistrates reported that black military recruits and local populations had, 'generally speaking behaved themselves quite well' during the war, there was one instance of armed rebellion in South Africa.[28] On 12 November 1914, groups of armed Hlubi in the Matatiele district of the Transkei destroyed dipping tanks and razed a number of white-owned stores. Chief Magistrate W. T. Brownlee summoned every available member of the Citizen Force to quell the uprising. Hlubi resistance melted away by the 19th, when confronted with superior firepower and a greater number of troops than anticipated. After-action reports indicated that the Hlubi perceived there to be a lack of police and militia in the area, due to enlistment, and seized the opportunity to rebel against white authority.[29]

While Canada did not witness an Indian rebellion during the war years, American Indians did revolt against the US draft. In June 1917, efforts to register Navajos and Utes were suspended in Colorado, after tribes threatened to attack the town of Ignacio. In June 1918, over two hundred Creeks in Oklahoma, angry over the draft regulations, killed three farmers and exchanged shots with US militiamen.[30]

In Singapore, on 15 February 1915, 950 Indian *sepoys* mutinied against their British superiors and British rule, killing 47 British soldiers and civilians. Soldiers of the West Indies Regiment rioted in Taranto,

[27] Hill, *State Authority, Indigenous Autonomy*, pp. 92, 101, 110.
[28] NASA, SAB, NTS, vol. 9108/18/363–28/363. Reports on South African Railways and Harbours/Memorandums Behaviour of Natives, 1916–18.
[29] Grundlingh, 'The Impact of the First World War on South African Blacks', 15.
[30] Barsh, 'American Indians in the Great War', 281.

Italy, in December 1918, over second-class treatment and work duties.[31] The 1917 Barue rebellion in Mozambique, and the earlier 1915 uprising in Nyasaland led by John Chilembwe, were precipitated by the conscription of Africans. The root of both rebellions, however, was the subjugation of African people by colonial powers. Similar disturbances occurred in Nigeria and in French West Africa, provoked by the militant *Senusiyyah* Islamic brotherhood.[32] As Robert Holland points out, 'Overall, however, the war was the occasion of such troubles, not their cause.' In March 1919, when addressing the British African Society, Sir Harry Johnston, the veteran Victorian proconsul, remarked that these occurrences marked 'the beginning of revolt against the white man's supremacy in Africa'.[33]

Racial violence continued after the war. In India, growing protest against British rule led to the Amritsar massacre of April 1919, during which British-led Indian soldiers fired into crowds, killing 400 civilians. This became the setting for Gandhi's first collective campaign against British rule. In Jamaica, Trinidad and British Honduras, returning indigenous soldiers and sailors attacked whites and looted homes and businesses chanting anti-white slogans. By 1919, there were 20,000 blacks in Britain (a majority working on the docks), many former merchant marines or war labourers. With the onset of post-war unemployment, resentment towards black workers heightened. During the summer of 1919, there were riots across Britain – in Barry, Cardiff, Liverpool, Glasgow, Newport, South Shields and London. White mobs, including soldiers from the Dominions awaiting repatriation (mostly Australians and South Africans), attacked labour recruitment centres, black boarding houses, homes and shops. According to the *Liverpool Courier*, 'One of the chief reasons of popular anger behind the present disturbances lies in the fact that the average negro is nearer the animal than is the average white man, and that there are women in Liverpool who have no self-respect.'[34]

Dominion governments continued to expropriate indigenous land and used the war itself as the justification for doing so. The issue of land led to minor revolts in South Africa and New Zealand; however,

---

[31] Robb, *British Culture and the First World War*, pp. 22–3.
[32] Melvin E. Page, 'Introduction: Black Men in a White Man's War' in Melvin E. Page (ed.), *Africa and the First World War* (London: Macmillan, 1987), p. 7.
[33] Robert Holland, 'The British Empire and the Great War, 1914–1918' in Judith M. Brown and Wm. Roger Louis (eds.), *The Oxford History of the British Empire, Vol. IV: The Twentieth Century* (Oxford University Press, 1999), p. 121.
[34] Robb, *British Culture and the First World War*, pp. 29–31.

larger rebellions against European colonial rule occurred throughout Africa and in other regions of empire. The consequences of the expropriation of indigenous land and the failure to grant indigenous soldiers (and their families) equal rights, despite active war participation, was a harbinger of things to come. At the end of the war, indigenous veterans entered a period of peace with prejudice.

10   Peace with prejudice

For all nations, the sacrifice of the First World War was measured in blood and the staggering tally of the butcher's bill. This was no different for the indigenous peoples of the Dominions. Although the Union of South Africa had serious concerns over the health of its indigenes in a foreign environment, as did all Dominions, deaths within the SANLC during its active period were low, given that 607 men died in the 1917 *Mendi* sinking alone. In total, 1,107 men of the 25,048 who enlisted in the SANLC died (see Table 10.1).

Of the 1,463 whites enrolled in the SANLC, 20 died (1.4%), as compared with 4.4% of natives. However, when only those who died overseas are considered, the numbers are more comparable: 0.6% of whites and 1.2% of natives. In 1926, the Department of Native Affairs finalized the total number of native deaths at 1,167, the additional 60 having died in South Africa after repatriation due to disease apparently caused by war service (more probably from influenza). In July 1918, medical authorities stated that 6–7 per cent of the natives of the SANLC had tuberculosis.[1]

Approximately 102,000 blacks and coloureds were mobilized during the war and almost 95,000 served in active theatres; however, numerous men served in more than one campaign. While numbers vary, the most accurate estimates conclude that between 80,000 and 85,000 individual indigenous South Africans served. The official history states that 5,635 blacks and coloureds died, although the actual number was probably higher. The overall number of men wounded, or hospitalized with disease, was not tabulated.[2]

Indigenous Australian soldiers came from all geographical areas of the country, including one Torres Strait Islander. The sixty-five known

---

[1] NASA, SAB, NTS, vol. 9106/1/363–7/363. Medical and Casualty Report SANLC, 29 July 1918.
[2] NASA, SAB, NTS, vol. 9107/9/363. G. A. Godley to Smuts, 15 January 1919; NA, WO-107/37. After Action Report: Work of Labour Force during the War, November 1919.

Table 10.1: *SANLC native casualties*[1]

Cause of death	Number of deaths	Place of death	Number of deaths
Tuberculosis	256	S.A. before embarkation	11
Other pulmonary diseases	108	At sea proceeding	619
Other diseases	99	Overseas	312
Accidents	631	At sea returning	47
Combat-related	1	S.A. after repatriation	118
Total	*1,107*	*Total*	*1,107*

[1] NASA, SAB, NTS, vol. 9107/11/363. Report SANLC Strengths and Casualties, 30 September 1919.

Tasmanians came from both Tasmania and the Flinders Islands.[3] The bulk of Aboriginal soldiers came from states with a high percentage of half-castes or a more assimilated society, such as Victoria. The Western Australia Recruiting Committee never deviated from pre-war policy forbidding Aboriginal enlistment, which explains the relatively small number of recruits given its high Aboriginal population (see Table 10.2).[4]

Of these known Aboriginal soldiers, 83 were killed, 125 wounded and 17 became prisoners of war. Including the POWs, the casualty rate was 39% as compared with 65% across the entire AIF.[5] This can be attributed to the fact that Aboriginal enlistment regulations were relaxed in May 1917, after the Australian bloodletting during 1916 and early 1917. Also, roughly 26 per cent of Aborigines served in mounted units which incurred lower casualty rates than their infantry counterparts.

In total, 2,668 Maori served overseas during the Great War, suffering 1,070 casualties (336 dead {132 of disease}, 734 wounded), amounting to a 40% casualty rate, compared with 59% for *Pakeha* who saw active service. This discrepancy can be attributed to the late arrival of the Maori to Gallipoli and their subsequent role as pioneers. In

[3] AWM, CN R940.4030994 A938. List of Australian Indigenous Servicemen who Served in World War One (Work in Progress), January 2007; AWM27, 533/1. Returns Showing Particulars of Men of Aboriginal Percentage who Enlisted and Served Abroad with the A.I.F. This author also wishes to acknowledge Andrea Gerrard for providing reliable and revisionist statistics for those soldiers from Tasmania.
[4] Huggonson, 'The Dark Diggers of the AIF', 353.
[5] AWM41, 914. Figures for the Australian Aborigines who Served in the War of 1914–18 in A.I.F. and were killed, wounded, not wounded; Andrews, *The Anzac Illusion*, p. 216; Mrs Margaret Beadman (AWM), Private Collection.

Table 10.2: *Known state enlistments and Aboriginal populations*[1]

State	Full-blood	Half-caste	Total population (1926)	Known enlistments	% half-caste	% of total
NSW	1,031	6,035	7,066	209	3.5	3.0
Victoria	55	459	514	56	12.2	10.9
Queensland	13,604	4,047	17,651	182	4.5	1.0
S. Australia	2,531	1,452	3,983	41	2.8	1.0
W. Australia	22,222	2,420	24,642	15	0.62	0.06
N. Territory	19,853	689	20,542	6	0.87	0.03
Tasmania	0	Unknown	Unknown	65		
Torres Strait Islands	Unknown	Unknown	Unknown	1		
Unknown				5		
Totals	*59,296*	*15,102*	*74,398*	*580*	*3.6*	*0.73*

[1] Yarwood and Knowling, *Race Relations in Australia*, p. 250. The composition of Aboriginal population is an estimate based on figures from 1926, as Aborigines were never included in any federal or state censuses. However, most scholarship gives the Aboriginal population during the war as between 70,000 and 80,000; therefore, the 1926 figure of 74,398 is a reasonable estimate. Torres Strait Islands is not a state, rather a distinct geographical area. Although one is known to have enlisted, there are possibly ten others who are as of yet unconfirmed. I wish to acknowledge the contributions of Andrea Gerrard at the University of Tasmania for providing the statistics for the Aborigines of Tasmania.

addition, 631 Pacific Islanders served overseas, although only 458 were attached, for various (often short) periods of time, to the Maori unit.[6] Although the Maori contribution should not be neglected, total Maori enlistments/conscripts (2,816) represented only 5.3% of the total Maori population, compared with 11.7% for the remainder of New Zealand.[7]

The casualty rates among the indigenous peoples of Canada and Newfoundland cannot be precisely calculated, since race was generally not recorded on military records. However, of the twenty-one known Eskimos and Indians to serve in the Royal Newfoundland Regiment, two were killed, five were wounded and one was taken prisoner – a 38 per cent casualty rate, matching that of the total Newfoundland forces.[8]

[6] ANZ, AD78, box 18, record 27/161: Maori Battalion: Casualties, Decorations and Awards; AD78, box 8, record 23/35: Casualties, Honours, Enlistments, Maoris, Rarotongans and Niue Islanders.
[7] ANZ, AD1, box 734, record 9/32/1. War File, 4 March 1919; Godley to Allen, 4 March 1919; Baker, *King and Country Call*, p. 221.
[8] PANL, GN19, B-2-3. Service Records.

It is estimated that 4,000 Canadian Indians served in the CEF, suffering 1,200 casualties, a 30% rate. For example, 292 men from the Six Nations Reserve served overseas (roughly 6.5% of the total reserve population, compared with 5.4% for Canada). Of this total, thirty-five were killed, fifty-five were wounded and one was taken prisoner, representing an overall casualty rate of 31%. The lesser Indian casualty rate, compared with the larger CEF, can be attributed to the high proportion of Indians who served in support units, such as forestry, labour and pioneer battalions. The figure of 4,000 represents 35% of Indian males of military age, roughly equal to that of white Canadians and comparable with the Australian white percentage of 38.7%.[9] This was a substantial commitment, given that most Indian enlistment occurred after December 1915. It was testimony to the historical and contemporary allegiance of Indians to the British Crown, directly or via Canada itself (see Figure 10.1).

When making any statistical comparisons and conclusions among indigenes, it is important to note the policies, including conscription, and dates of indigenous inclusion into Dominion forces. For example, of the total Aboriginal population only 0.73% served. However, the AIF only officially accepted half-castes and they were the majority who served. When service is equated to the total half-caste population, the percentage rises to 3.6%. Other factors to consider are their roles as soldiers, their theatres of deployment and the overall casualty rates of the Dominion force in which they served. All factors must be weighed in association to formulate an accurate representation of the burden of service for individual Dominion indigenes or to draw accurate comparisons (see Table 10.3).

In addition to war casualties, the 1918–19 'Spanish Influenza' pandemic devastated indigenous populations significantly more than their white counterparts. The drastically lower socio-economic standing of indigenous peoples, their lack of access to health care, and their well-documented susceptibility to Old World diseases, most notably tuberculosis, were all factors in the higher proportion of sickness and deaths due to the influenza virus. Although global death figures are estimates, recent research concludes that roughly 50 million people died worldwide, compared with a total 10 million war service deaths or 16 million war-related deaths, including civilian fatalities.

---

[9] LAC, RG10, vol. 6762–6808. List of Native Canadians Killed or Wounded; Scott, *Report of the Deputy Superintendent General*. It has been accurately counted that roughly three hundred Indians died during the war. Based on Canadian casualty rates, the total Indian casualties would be roughly 1,200.

Figure 10.1 Stoney Indians at Armistice Day celebration,
High River, Alberta, 1918.

Australia suffered a mortality rate of 2.3 per 1,000 compared with 4.3
in the United Kingdom, 5.5 in New Zealand (for non-Maori) and 6.4 in
Canada. However, mortality was higher amongst non-Europeans, with
some Aboriginal communities, such as Barambah and Taroom, being
almost wiped out.[10] In Queensland, Bleakley realized that Aborigines
were going 'down like corn before the reaper'. Stringent measures
were introduced to limit Aborigines' exposure to whites and infected
Aboriginal groups, and to prevent them from 'going bush', with some
degree of success.[11] It is not known how many Aborigines succumbed to
influenza but it is estimated that the percentage was much higher than
for non-Aboriginal Australians. Total Australian deaths are estimated
at 12,000. Following the war, the Aboriginal population continued

[10] Humphrey McQueen, 'The "Spanish" Influenza Pandemic in Australia, 1912–1919'
in Jill Roe (ed.), *Social Policy in Australia: Some Perspectives, 1901–1975* (Melbourne:
Cassell Australia, 1976), p. 141.
[11] Bleakley, *The Aborigines of Australia*, pp. 173–4; Huggonson, 'Aborigines and the
Aftermath of the Great War', 4.

Table 10.3: *Dominion First World War statistics*[1]

Category	Canada	Australia	New Zealand	South Africa	Newfoundland	Totals	UK
Non-indigenous population, 1914	7,879,000	4,917,949	1,099,449	1,383,510	251,726	15,531,634	46,089,249
Mobilized	629,000	417,000	129,000	182,000	12,500	1,369,500	6,147,000
% total population	8.0	8.5	11.7	13.2	5.0	8.8	13.3
Served in theatre	422,405	331,781	98,950	160,000	9,700	1,022,836	5,000,000
% total population	5.4	6.7	9.0	11.7	3.9	6.6	10.8
% mobilized	67.2	79.6	76.7	87.9	77.6	74.7	81.3
Casualties (including dead)	241,000	216,000	59,000	21,000	3,800	540,800	2,556,014
% mobilized	38.3	51.8	45.7	11.5	30.4	39.5	41.6
% in theatre	57.1	65.1	59.6	13.1	39.2	52.9	51.1
Indigenous population, 1914	*103,774*	*80,000 est.*	*52,997*	*5,081,490*	*1,700 est.*	*5,319,961*	
Mobilized			*2,816*	*102,110*			
% total population			*5.3*	*2.0*			
Served in theatre	*4,000 est.*	*580*	*2,668*	*94,843*	*21*	*102,077*	
% total population	*3.9*	*0.73*	*5.0*	*1.9*	*1.2*	*1.9*	
% mobilized			*94.7*	*92.9*			
Casualties (including dead)	*1,200 est.*	*225*	*1,070*	*5,635 dead*	*8*	*8,138*	
% mobilized	*30.0*	*41.3*	*38.0*	*5.5*			
% in theatre			*40.1*	*5.9*	*38.1*	*8.0*	

[1] Indigenous data is listed in italics. A record of sources would be too lengthy to list. Numbers from archival, primary and secondary sources, censuses and official histories were scrutinized and compared. Numbers listed above are either exact or based on a compilation of all sources available and listed as the most reasonable (up to date) statistics. Statistics are only provided where they can be accurately determined. This author recognizes the discrepancies that exist in the statistical analysis of Great War figures. Nevertheless, the statistics provided are reasonably accurate and are suitable to demonstrate the comparative qualities of the Dominions and the United Kingdom. One could also look at UK enlistments in racial terms. For example, out of 140,000 Irish volunteers, 65,000 were Catholic, even though Catholics outnumbered Protestants three to one. South African statistics skew Dominion totals (usually decreasing). For example, excluding South Africa, the Dominion in theatre casualty percentages would be 37.4% for indigenes and 60.2% for non-indigenes. Academic arguments relating to casualty rates are common in war historiography, especially when dealing with the Dominions, both compared with each other and when tallied against those of the UK. For example, theories include the idea that Dominion forces suffered greater casualty rates than those of the UK because they were used as cannon fodder by British high command; or that Canada suffered a lower percentage of casualties than Australia or New Zealand due to Currie's abilities and the combat prowess of Canadian soldiers (despite General Monash's acknowledged brilliance and the record of Anzac soldiers). See the works of Gary Sheffield, John Terraine and Robin Neillands for an analysis of these arguments. Most academic works, however, do promote and laud the fighting qualities of the Dominion forces and the Scottish Highland battalions.

its decline until the Second World War, when populations began to increase, climbing to 87,000 by 1947.[12]

In New Zealand, roughly 9,000 people succumbed to influenza, including an estimated 2,300 Maori. The *Pakeha* death rate was 5.5 per 1,000, while the Maori death rate was 42.3 per 1,000; an estimated 4 per cent of the Maori population died in the last two months of 1918 alone.[13] Buck, acting as Health Officer for Maori, wrote that influenza 'must figure as the severest setback the race has received since the fighting days of Hongi Hika. Influenza in three months caused more casualties to the Maoris than the campaigns in Gallipoli, France and Belgium.'[14] In the New Zealand protectorate of Western Samoa, 7,500 islanders succumbed to influenza, representing a shattering 25 per cent of the island's population. American Samoa stayed free of the disease due to a strictly enforced quarantine. In addition, in 1918, Maori susceptibility to tuberculosis remained five times higher than for non-Maori, and infant mortality was still three times higher for Maori than other New Zealanders.[15] However, the Maori population continued to rise slowly, reaching roughly 90,000 on the eve of the Second World War.

Influenza affected one in six Canadians, resulting in more than 50,000 deaths nationwide, including an estimated 3,500 Indians (3 per cent of the total Indian population). The Indian/Eskimo death rate was six times higher than the rest of Canada, while tuberculosis rates were twenty times higher for indigenes than whites.[16] An article for *Emerging Infectious Diseases* outlines that, 'In various communities of Canada ... mortality rates were estimated to be 3–70x higher for indigenous than for non-indigenous populations.'[17] Following the war, the Indian population began a slow recovery and by 1939 had increased to 118,406.[18]

[12] See: L. R. Smith, *The Aboriginal Population of Australia* (Canberra: ANU Press, 1980).
[13] Geoffrey W. Rice, *Black November: The 1918 Influenza Pandemic in New Zealand* (Christchurch: Canterbury University Press, 2005), 17, pp. 159–61; Belich, *Paradise Reforged*, pp. 113, 193.
[14] Condliffe, *Te Rangi Hiroa*, p. 142.
[15] Howard Phillips and David Killingray, 'Introduction' in Howard Phillips and David Killingray (eds.), *The Spanish Influenza Pandemic of 1918–1919: New Perspectives* (London: Routledge, 2003), p. 10.
[16] Lisa Sattenspiel and Dawn Herring, 'Structural Epidemic Models and the Spread of Influenza in the Central Canadian Sub-Arctic', *Human Biology* (1998), 3; 'Death in Winter: Spanish Flu in the Canadian Subarctic', in *The Spanish Influenza Pandemic of 1918–1919: New Perspectives*, pp. 173–90.
[17] John F. Brundage and G. Dennis Shanks, 'Deaths from Bacterial Pneumonia during 1918–19 Influenza Pandemic', *Emerging Infectious Diseases* 14/8 (2008), 1193–9.
[18] Dominion Bureau of Statistics, *The Canada Year Book 1940* (Ottawa: King's Printer, 1941), p. 1062.

The statistics were similar for the indigenous populations of Newfoundland. An estimated 2,050 people died on the island of Newfoundland. The death rate in Labrador, however, reached 10% of the total population and 30% of the Eskimo population. The Eskimo villages of Hebron and Okak were literally erased. At Hebron, 68 of the 100 residents died. At Okak, 204 residents from a total of 263 succumbed to the disease by December 1918, and by January every male from Okak was dead. At Sillutalik, the flu killed forty of forty-five residents, while thirteen of eighteen people died at Orlik.[19]

In South Africa, the official death toll, reported as 140,000, underestimated black and coloured mortality. It was stated that 127,745 'Blacks, Coloureds and Indians' died, while white deaths totalled 11,726. Using these statistics, indigenous death rates were more than double those of whites.[20] Over 30 per cent of the black Kimberley miners died. However, revised figures estimate that total indigenous deaths were closer to 275,000. It is thought that the arrival of flu in South Africa, or more accurately the second wave, coincided with the return on 13 and 18 September 1918 of two troopships to Cape Town, carrying 1,274 and 1,769 men respectively of the SANLC.[21]

In addition to sharing in the suffering and casualties of war, indigenous soldiers also shared in the accolades. All Dominion indigenous soldiers were awarded the standard Imperial War and Victory Medals, save for black South Africans. While South African coloureds and blacks from British Protectorates received the two decorations (although whites received the medals in silver and non-whites in bronze), blacks from South Africa did not. Complaints were lodged by black veterans as late as 1971; however, a final decision to withhold the medals from blacks was taken in 1925. Ironically, in December 1918, unaware that the black members of the SANLC would not receive the imperial honours, Pritchard forwarded the names of ninety-two blacks, 'submitted with the recommendation that appropriate recognition of their services may be granted them'. As a result, six blacks were awarded the Meritorious Service Medal (MSM), their names being published in the *London Gazette* on 3 June 1919. Coloured South Africans of the Cape Corps were also awarded sixteen Distinguished Conduct Medals (DCM), eight Military Medals (MM) and thirty-four Mention in Dispatches (MID).[22]

---

[19] Jenny Higgins, 'The 1918 Spanish Flu in Newfoundland and Labrador', Newfoundland and Labrador Heritage, 2007.
[20] Brundage and Shanks, 'Deaths from Bacterial Pneumonia during 1918–19 Influenza Pandemic', 1193–9.
[21] Phillips and Killingray, 'Introduction', 9.
[22] Clothier, *Black Valour*, pp. 165–6; Gleeson, *The Unknown Force*, pp. 45–6, 94.

Three Aboriginal Australians were awarded the DCM, nine the MM, three the MID and one the Military Cross (MC). Lindsay Watson attributes the lack of Aboriginal medal winners, not to racism, but to the fact that roughly 26 per cent served in theatres outside the Western Front, where units generally received 50 per cent fewer decorations than those engaged in the main European theatre. The late entry of Aborigines into the AIF also influenced medal totals.[23] The Maori Contingent/Battalion (including *Pakeha*) received: three Distinguished Service Orders (DSO) – Buck being the single Maori, nine MC, four DCM, thirty-nine MM, nine MSM, forty-two MID and thirteen foreign decorations, including the French and Belgian Croix de Guerre, the Italian Bronze Medal and the Serbian Order of the White Eagle.[24]

While the number of Canadian Indians awarded honours is not officially known, Veterans Affairs states that 'at least 50 medals were awarded to aboriginal people in Canada for bravery and heroism'.[25] Lieutenant Alexander Smith (Six Nations) won the MC and Pegahmagabow was awarded the MM three times, making him one of only thirty-eight Canadians to accomplish this feat during the war. Enlisting with his brother in April 1916, Private Francis Misinishkotewe, an Ojibwa from Manitoulin Island, Ontario, was awarded the Cross of the Order of St George (Fourth Class), the highest Imperial Russian military decoration.[26] Of the known twenty-one indigenous Newfoundlanders, none were awarded decorations.

Canadian Indian Private Daniel Pelletier remarked after the war that, 'The army treated us all right ... there was no discrimination "over there" and we were treated good.'[27] This relative equality, however, was not manifest in governmental veteran policies, as Indians reverted back to being wards of the state under the paternalistic Indian Act. After the war, the government of Canada introduced financial and farm land grant programmes for veterans. The first and largest of these initiatives was the Soldier Settlement Act (SSA) of 1919 (an amendment to the 1917 Act).

The SSA provided veterans the opportunity to obtain Dominion lands at no cost, or to purchase farms and equipment at low interest

---

[23] Coulthard-Clark, 'Aborigine Medal Winners', 244–8; Watson, 'Aboriginal and Torres Strait Islander Soldiers of the First World War', 4; Mrs Margaret Beadman (AWM), Private Collection.

[24] ANZ, AD78, box 18, record 27/161: Maori Battalion: Casualties, Decorations and Awards; AD78, box 8, record 23/35: Casualties, Honours, Enlistments, Maoris, Rarotongans and Niue Islanders.

[25] Veterans Affairs Canada at: www.vac-acc.gc.ca

[26] Gaffen, *Forgotten Soldiers*, pp. 111–12.

[27] Dempsey, *Warriors of the King*, p. 51.

rates. The Act specified, however, that the Ministry of Indian Affairs was charged with the administration of all benefits, allowances and pensions for Indians, 'thus avoiding the confusion which would inevitably arise if their affairs were administered partly by the Department of Indian Affairs and partly by the Soldier Settlement Board'. Although the amendments gave Duncan Campbell Scott 'all powers of the Soldier Settlement Board except those of expropriation', applications by Indian veterans were subject to the approval of their individual Indian agents, 'who have personal knowledge of the capabilities and needs of Indian returned soldiers'.[28] For example, Pegahmagabow's application for a farm land grant was not endorsed by his agent, Alexander Logan, who cited that Pegahmagabow 'was disabled and suffered from dementia', and that the site chosen 'was most out of the way place for a successful farmer'. Although Pegahmagabow wrote directly to Indian Affairs, and to the Soldiers Aid Commission, he received no land, loans or grants under the SSA.[29]

As with other governmental policies, the SSA conflicted directly with a 1906 amendment to the Indian Act which stated: 'No Indian or non-treaty Indian resident in the provinces of Manitoba, Saskatchewan, Alberta or the Territories shall be held capable of having acquired or acquiring a homestead or pre-emption right under any Act respecting Dominion lands ... in the said provinces and territories.'[30] This discrepancy was illuminated when many veterans applied under the SSA to take up farming on their respective reserves. Reserve land could be used personally by any Indian but could not be owned by any Indian, as it remained the property of the Crown. Nevertheless, it was 'proposed to settle the Indian soldiers as far as possible on reserves belonging to the bands of which they are members ... without the consent of the council of the band'.[31] Thus, the small number of Indians who received reserve lands were given a 'Certificate of Possession' of little legal value. Indians were also wary of applying for land grants off reserve, as their fears that they would lose their Indian status, and the rights and governmental obligations associated with it, were substantiated.[32]

While it is known that ten Indians in Ontario and Quebec and six from the Prairie Provinces received land grants off reserve without losing status, most applicants were denied this right. Only one in ten Indian veterans who applied received loans or land grants on reserve.

[28] LAC, RG10, vol. 11154, reel C-V-8, file 34. Soldier Settlement Act, 1919.
[29] Hayes, *Pegahmagabow*, pp. 44–6.
[30] LAC, RG10, vol. 4048, file 357. Indian Act.
[31] Scott, *Report of the Deputy Superintendent General*, pp. 28–9.
[32] Dempsey, 'The Indians and World War One', 8.

Table 10.4: *Indian land sold or confiscated under the Soldier Settlement Act*[1]

Province	Acres	Paid ($)	Per acre ($)
Saskatchewan	69,803	831,148	11.91
Alberta	15,887	169,462	10.67
British Columbia	154	12,280	79.74
Totals	*85,844*	*1,012,890*	*11.80*

[1] Gaffen, *Forgotten Soldiers*, p. 135.

By 1920, only 160 had received loans. According to Scott, 'the needs of an Indian farmer would not perhaps be as extensive as the needs of a white farmer'. He maintained that loans should be kept as 'low as possible in order not to burden the settler with too large a repayment'.[33] Many were denied land as band councils simply ignored the ministry and refused the allocation of land to veterans, as personal ownership of land was not customary among most Indian nations; land remained communal, as people belonged to the earth, not the other way around. Many other veterans simply did not apply as they feared overriding the band councils and the alienation of their communities that would ensue.

The government also used the SAA to expropriate reserve land. As immigrants of the influx from eastern Europe at the turn of the century had been granted most of the fertile Crown land in the prairies, more suitable farm land had to be found to meet the needs of the SSA. A 23 April 1919 Order-in-Council (P.C. 929) granted the Ministry of Indian Affairs (under the Regulations of the Soldier Settlement Act, 1919) authority to expropriate reserve land 'not under cultivation or otherwise properly used' without the consent of the Indians or their councils. Under this law, almost 86,000 acres of reserve lands were confiscated and given to white veterans (see Table 10.4).[34]

Indians of Vancouver Island protested to the ministry that parcelling their lands to white veterans 'would be unfair to those of our race who are sleeping in France and Flanders. This is what the Kaiser would have done to us all, whites and Indians, if he had won the war.'[35] When

[33] Carter, '"An Infamous Proposal"', 16.
[34] R. Scott Sheffield, *A Search for Equity: A Study of the Treatment Afforded to First Nations Veterans and Dependants of the Second World War and the Korean Conflict* (Ottawa: Department of Indian Affairs, April 2001), p. 6; Gaffen, *Forgotten Soldiers*, p. 135.
[35] Carter, '"An Infamous Proposal"', 16.

an elderly Sioux man was asked in conversation with his agent what should be done with the Kaiser, he replied that he should be 'confined to a reservation, given an allotment, and forced to farm'. He added that the agent should tell the Kaiser that, 'Now you lazy bad man, you farm and make your living by farming, rain or no rain; and if you do not make your own living don't come to the Agency whining when you have no food in your stomach, and no money, but stay here on your farm and grow fat till you starve.'[36]

After petitioning the government, knowing that the land would be taken without compensation, most bands settled for token monetary sums. However, even the $1.01 million that was awarded to the Indians for the 85,844 acres was not given directly to the bands; rather, it was held in trust by the Ministry, who promised to disperse the money to the various reserves when it saw fit. The 18,223.4 acre Ochapowace Cree Reserve in Saskatchewan was confiscated for $164,160, under protest from the band and the nearby white community. The Cree were forced to relocate to the Sioux Reserve at Dundurn. The money was withheld by the Ministry, to be used and divided at a later date, and neither the Cree nor the Sioux (traditional enemies) were consulted about their forced co-habitation.[37]

In conjunction with the Order-in-Council, an unofficial arrangement was made between the SSA and the Ministry of Indian Affairs to minimize the amount of land given to Indian veterans on the reserves, as reserve land could only be appropriated if it was not in 'proper use'.[38] The obvious outcome was that unused reserve land was taken by the SSA, leaving little for Indian veterans, as it was known by the Ministry that they were wary of applying for off-reserve land grants. These arrangements reduced the amount of reserve land for Indians, both veterans and non-veterans, while procuring more fertile farm land for non-Indian veterans under the SSA; hence, Indian applications for land, loans and grants subsequently diminished. According to the 1927 Sixth Report of the Soldier Settlement Board of Canada, only 224 land grants or loans had been issued to Indian veterans, 'most in the Province of Ontario [184 of 224] … The Indians mostly had their locations on the reserves.'[39]

Indian veterans also did not receive equal consideration for pensions, disability or War Veterans' Allowance. Although many did receive

[36] Britten, *American Indians in World War I*, pp. 185–6.
[37] Dempsey, *Warriors of the King*, p. 77.
[38] 'Canadian Indians and World War One', 71.
[39] Gaffen, *Forgotten Soldiers*, p. 36.

small compensations, on a random, individual case basis, others were denied on account of being 'Indian'. No common policy existed within the Departments of Indian Affairs, the Militia or Veterans Affairs relating to pensions and monetary allocations. Under the War Veterans Allowance Act, only enfranchised Indians living off reserve were entitled to the same benefits as non-Indian veterans: 'Returned Indian soldiers are subject to the provisions of the Indian Act and are in the same position as they were before enlisting.' Therefore, the allowances of $40/month for a single and $70/month for a married veteran accorded by the Act were not available to non-enfranchised Indian veterans – the vast majority. The same discriminatory policy extended to the Last Post Fund, established in 1909 to prevent veterans of Her Majesty's forces from being buried in a pauper's grave without recognition. These courses of action were seen as further governmental assimilation attempts by trying to force Indians to vacate reserves in order to gain their financial dues. The discriminatory policies of the War Veterans' Allowance Act and the Last Post Fund were not altered for the benefit of Indian veterans until 1936.[40] Furthermore, any pension or disability relief to Indian veterans residing on reserve was administered by local agents. A resentful Corporal Pegahmagabow had to ask his agent John Daly to release his veteran funds in allotments, despite the fact that he was short of money and supporting a wife and six children: 'He get [sic] it tied up in the bank so I could only get it with his approval. Then when I call for it, he expect me to get down on my knees for it and get sore before he would write me out a cheque.'[41]

Under these policies very few Indians enjoyed the franchise. A 1918 amendment, 122 A (1), to the Indian Act stated that: 'An Indian who holds no land in a reserve, does not reside on a reserve, and does not follow the Indian mode of life ... and satisfies the Superintendent General that he is self-supporting and fit to be enfranchised, and surrenders all claims whatsoever to any interest in the lands of the band to which he belongs ... the Governor-General may order that such an Indian be enfranchised.'[42] Any application for enfranchisement also had to be accompanied by an endorsement from a clergyman, priest, notary public or justice of the peace and an Indian agent that the applicant was, 'of good moral character, temperate in habits and of sufficient intelligence ... and report of the earning capacity of the individual Indian'.

---

[40] LAC, RG10, vol. 6771, file 452-37-40. Correspondence: Indian Affairs, Last Post Fund, Canadian Legion and Department of Pensions and National Health, 1932–36.

[41] Hayes, *Pegahmagabow*, pp. 61–3.

[42] Scott, *Report of the Deputy Superintendent General*, p. 31.

To become enfranchised the applicant needed to be willing to renounce his Indian culture and heritage and become assimilated. By 1921, only 227 Indians, all from Ontario (212 from the Six Nations Reserve), had been enfranchised under the new legislation. The department also forwarded the idea of the enfranchisement 'of individual Indians or a band of Indians without the necessity of obtaining their consent ... where it was found upon investigation that the continuance of wardship was no longer in the interests of the public'.[43]

Some whites acknowledged the valuable participation of Indians during the war, and advocated their equality. Ronald Haycock asserts that:

They [Canadians] began to explore the Indian in closer detail, to see the miniscule evils of the white man's own creation and to develop an attitude that wanted a humane improvement in the administration of Indians and the conception of him. The focus became clearer again with the holocaust of war. The Indian was made to appear as if he responded with equal alacrity as did other Canadians – indeed more so. In the reader's mind he was again performing a definite role. As in the days when his forebears by their military value were playing active parts and thereby forcing attention, so he did in this war. It is likely, however, that Canadians were ready to look willingly this time, for the literature indicates the stage was set. War brought it into place faster ... Social interest, awareness of the 'whole' Indian, a desire for reform and active government sympathy were replacing paternalism, Social-Darwinism and noble savage concepts of the beginning of the century ... The Indian became once more a power. He came to be of importance as he was during his part in the fur trade or as a military force ... During the Great War he had offered his service to the nation. Now he offered his condition at a time when Canadians wanted to better it – now he offered his culture at a time Canadians wanted to tolerate and preserve it as a worthy contribution to the national life.[44]

For example, in 1921, W. Everard Edmonds, secretary of the Historical Society of Alberta, wrote an article, 'Canada's Red Army', for the widely distributed *Canadian Magazine of Politics, Science, Art and Literature*, which was also printed by several newspapers:

[I]ndications are not wanting that a race that has slept for centuries is now awakening to life ... This is one of the results of the War. The Indian feels that he has done a man's work, and he will never again be content to stand aside, uttering no word in matters that directly concern him. The spirit of unrest has taken hold of him and is expressing itself in various forms of race consciousness ... That our Indians deserve full citizenship can be doubted by no one who recalls the splendid part they played in the greatest struggle of all time ... more than 4,000 enlisted for active service with the Canadian Expeditionary Force, while there were probably many cases of Indian enlistment that were

[43] Ibid, p. 31.
[44] Haycock, *The Image of the Indian*, pp. 90–1.

not reported ... If then, the Indian desires the full privileges of Canadian citizenship, shall we not grant him what he asks? We have long regarded him as a child, but it was no child's part he played in the War.[45]

Haycock, however, rightly asserts that only in the 1960s, during a time of sweeping social awareness and political and racial consciousness, did journalists again discuss the cause of the Indian. Enfranchisement was finally granted to Indians in 1960. Although the war may have briefly given awareness to whites, and perhaps government, it did not bring equality or cultural recognition. As Indian sacrifice and participation in the war faded from memory, little attention was given to their social, political or cultural position within Canada, despite the fact that indirectly, the war spawned the creation of a Canadian pan-Indian organization.

Indian veterans were instrumental in the creation of the first nationwide Indian political organization – the League of Indians of Canada. Six Nations Mohawk, Frederick Loft, a lieutenant in the Canadian Forestry Corps during the war, drew up the principles of the organization in 1919:

Not in vain did our young men die in a strange land; not in vain are our Indian bones mingled with the soil of a foreign land for the first time since the world began; not in vain did the Indian father and mothers see their sons march away to face what to them were unknown dangers. The unseen tears of Indian mothers in many isolated reserves have watered the seeds from which may spring those desires and efforts and aspirations which will enable us to reach the stage when we will take our place side by side with the white people, doing our share of productive work and gladly shouldering the responsibility of citizens in this, our country.[46]

The constitution of the League of Indians also included passages concerning denouncement of the residential school system, equality in post-war veteran programmes, and the creation of an accommodating Canadian–British–Indian political forum. Clearly, Loft and other Indian veteran members, including Pegahmagabow, associated Indian participation in the war with the principles of self-determination and equality as citizens of Canada: 'The principal aim of the League ... is equality for the Indian as a citizen – equality, that is, in the two-fold meaning of privilege and responsibility; and to achieve this objective, our first emphasis must be upon improved educational and health care programs.'[47] They also believed that a unified Indian stance, through a

---

[45] W. Everard Edmonds, 'Canada's Red Army', *Canadian Magazine of Politics, Science, Art and Literature* 54/5 (1921), 340–2.

[46] Ibid, 342.

[47] Grant, 'Indian Affairs Under Duncan Campbell Scott', 34.

political organization, could challenge the government and the Indian Act. According to Loft, 'We must be heard as a nation.'[48]

Indian Affairs immediately tried to undermine Loft's authority by proposing to force enfranchisement upon him, thereby removing his Indian status, and to eliminate 'troublemakers and educated Indians from the ranks as a whole'.[49] Viewing the League as a threat, the Ministry also amended the Indian Act, whereby bands were prohibited from donating funds to Indian political organizations. Nevertheless, the League of Indians of Canada held its inaugural meeting in Sault Ste. Marie, Ontario, in September 1919. Annual meetings were held in other provinces over the next four years. In 1927, to nullify further the ability of Indians to form structured resistance, the Indian Act was amended, making it illegal for status Indians to organize politically, or to retain legal council in forwarding claims against the government.

By the early 1930s the League had splintered into smaller Indian political organizations such as the League of Indians of Western Canada, the Indian Association of Alberta and the Union of Saskatchewan Indians.[50] Although the founding League of Indians of Canada had few tangible accomplishments, it was a precedent for future national Indian assemblies and it served Indian Affairs with notice that Indians had the education, motivation and aptitude to challenge governmental policies. Edmonds noted in 1921 that, 'mighty movements are stirring and one knows not what the next hour may bring forth ... Tribes far removed from each other, unknown to each other and hitherto uninterested in each other, are now corresponding and exchanging opinions ... The formation of a National Indian League is one way in which the Red Man has expressed his new found manhood.'[51] In fact, in 1924, a group of Iroquois, led by Cayuga Chief Deskaheh, travelled to Geneva and presented a petition to the League of Nations on 4 November, unsuccessfully pressing the claim of Iroquois Confederacy sovereignty under Article 17 of the League's covenant. Deskaheh had previously petitioned the King and the Colonial Office during a trip to London in 1921 and travelled throughout Europe from 1923 to 1925, soliciting the support of European nations.[52]

---

[48] Peter Kulchyski, 'A Considerable Unrest: F. O. Loft and the League of Indians', *Native Studies Review* 4/1–2 (1988), 101.

[49] Ibid, 106–7.

[50] Hayes, *Pegahmagabow*, pp. 49–51. In 1920, American Indians formed the political organization, American Indians of the World War (AIWW).

[51] Edmonds, 'Canada's Red Army', 340–2.

[52] Townsend, *World War II and the American Indian*, p. 118.

Veterans also impacted on political realities within their individual reserves. Pegahmagabow became Chief of his Parry Island band in 1921, a position he held until 1925 when he became band councillor until 1936. John Moses argues that, 'As with groups of Great War veterans elsewhere across the country who felt a disconnect between the magnitude of their wartime sacrifices overseas and the political, economic and social prospects to which they returned in peacetime, so too did Six Nations veterans of the Great War return to an environment that they found unresponsive to their needs and aspirations.' He asserts that the forced implementation, by Indian Affairs, of an elected band council on the reserve, as opposed to the traditional Longhouse Chiefs, was due to the demands of veterans, and Lieutenant-Colonel Andrew T. Thompson (114th CO): '[N]ewly returned Six Nations veterans of the Great War constituted an elite body at the forefront of this movement for profound political change ... [T]his new system was an appropriate reward for their wartime service.'[53]

In 1923, Thompson was appointed by the federal government to investigate the political organizations of the Six Nations Reserve after a series of confrontations involving rival factions, the Royal Canadian Mounted Police and a Longhouse group led by Deskaheh. Completed in November 1923, Thompson's report suggested the establishment of an elected band council under the Indian Act. In favour of his veteran soldiers, he argued that, 'The separatist party [Deskaheh and supporters], if I may so describe it, is exceptionally strong in the Council of Chiefs, in fact it is completely dominant there. Its members maintain ... that not being British subjects they are not bound by Canadian law, and ... the Indian Act does not apply to the Six Nations Indians.' Without consulting Six Nations representatives, the government deposed the traditional Longhouse Council and, though voter participation was exceedingly small, as it was boycotted by traditional Iroquois, a new council was elected in October 1924.[54] These political divisions between supporters of the elective Indian Act system and those who maintain the Longhouse are central to the political fissures which currently exist on many Iroquois/Mohawk reserves.

---

[53] John Moses, 'The Return of the Native: Six Nations Veterans and Political Change at the Grand River Reserve, 1917–1924' in *Aboriginal Peoples and the Canadian Military: Historical Perspectives*, pp. 117–28.

[54] Andrew T. Thompson, *Report by Col. Andrew T. Thompson Commissioned to Investigate and Enquire into the Affairs of the Six Nations Indians, 1923* (Ottawa: King's Printer, 1924), pp. 12–13; Ronald Niezen, 'Recognizing Indigenism: Canadian Unity and the International Movement of Indigenous Peoples', *Comparative Studies in Society and History* 42/1 (2000), 123–4.

Scott remarked in 1919 that, 'The Indians deserve well of Canada, and the end of the war should mark the beginning of a new era for them.'[55] Instead of ushering in a new era for Indians, the Ministry of Indian Affairs continued to dominate all aspects of reserve life and little change materialized during the interwar decades. The Great Depression compounded the deteriorating socio-economic condition of Indian communities. Indians remained wards of the Crown, under the paternalistic jurisdiction of Indian Affairs. The residential school system was not abolished until the 1960s, despite governmental knowledge of the sexual and physical abuse and rampant disease within the schools. The first institutions were running by the 1840s and the last vestige of the programme ceased in 1996 with the closing of White Calf College in Saskatchewan. In 1919, 322 schools were operational nationwide (the majority in the western provinces), accommodating 11,952 Indian children.[56] Between 1894 and 1908 mortality rates in western Canadian schools ranged from 35% to 60% over a five-year period (five years after entry 35% to 60% of children had died), according to a 1909 report by Indian Affairs medical superintendent, Dr Peter Bryce. These statistics were made public in 1922, after Bryce, no longer attached to Indian Affairs, published his findings. Similarly, another report of 1922 concluded that 50 per cent of children in western schools had tuberculosis.[57] In 2005, a $1.9 billion compensation package was announced by the federal government and on 11 June 2008, Prime Minister Stephen Harper issued a formal apology to residential school victims and families on behalf of the government and people of Canada. That same month, modelled on the 2005 South African example, a nation-wide, $60 million government-sponsored, residential school Truth and Reconciliation Commission was established. The first 'National Event' discussion and open-floor was held in Winnipeg in June 2010.[58]

In 1917, the Minister of the Interior and Indian Affairs, Arthur Meighen, who succeeded Borden as prime minister in 1920, summarized the relationship between Indians and Canada during the Great War: 'It is an inspiring fact that these descendants of the aboriginal inhabitants of a continent so recently appropriated by our own ancestors should voluntarily sacrifice their lives on European battlefields, side by side with men of our own race, for the preservation of the ideals

[55] Scott, 'The Canadian Indians and the Great War', 19.
[56] Scott, *Report of the Deputy Superintendent General*, p. 32.
[57] See: John S. Milloy, *A National Crime: The Canadian Government and the Residential School System 1879–1986* (Winnipeg: University of Manitoba Press, 1999).
[58] The website for the commission is www.trc.ca

of our civilization, and their staunch devotion forms an eloquent tribute to the beneficent character of British rule over a native people.'[59] Such a statement contrasts with the negligible impact Indian participation in the war had on the broader social and political realities of Indians within Canada.

Aboriginal Australians also found that racial prejudice was less pronounced within the AIF among soldiers. According to the daughter of an Australian veteran, 'After the war, for many years, [Douglas] Grant visited my father Mark on Anzac Day from Lithgow. The two had become good friends in the POW Camp.'[60] A machine gunner in the 3rd Division vocalized his displeasure at having to eat with an 'Abo'. He was met with threats of 'a bloody smack on the snout' as proof of soldiers' equality. Years later, the Aboriginal soldier recalled that, 'The next day he came looking for me, and we sat down to eat together. He turned out to be my best mate … and we stayed good friends after the war.'[61]

Following the war, however, Aboriginal soldiers returned to Australia to find that war service had not changed racial intolerance or legal rights. Post-war programmes for Aborigines were almost indistinguishable from those of Canada in both form and function. The Department of Repatriation for NSW approached the Ministry of Defence asking 'if an aboriginal who has served with the A.I.F. is, after discharge, still under the restrictions imposed by this [Aborigines] Act'. The Ministry bluntly stated that, 'The fact of an aboriginal having served with the A.I.F. does not remove him from the care or supervision exercisable by the Board appointed for the protection of Aborigines under the Aborigines Act, 1909, neither does it relieve that Board of its duties towards the Aboriginal.'[62] This 'supervision' included the financial control for legislating Aboriginal wages, but also their private finances. Charles Blackman applied for repatriation aid in June 1921. He was denied all benefits of repatriation programmes, on account of being an Aborigine and that, 'he did not make application within the stipulated period of twelve months after discharge'.[63] Pegahmagabow's postwar experience would have been identical had he been an Australian Aborigine instead of a Canadian Indian.

Similar to Indians giving up status under the Indian Act to gain citizenship, half-caste Aborigines could apply for exemption certificates,

[59] Dempsey, 'The Indians and World War One', 2.
[60] Letter, Private Collection.
[61] Gordon, *The Embarrassing Australian*, pp. 36–7.
[62] NAA, A2487 1919/3202. Memorandum from Ministry of Defence, Melbourne to Department of Repatriation, NSW, 12 April 1919.
[63] NAA, A2487/1 217220 – Repatriation of Corporal Charles Blackman, 1921.

judged by a tribunal. Decisions were based on their level of assimilation, education and worth. By accepting a certificate, an Aborigine was no longer recognized as such under individual Australian state laws, was enfranchised, and could live and work outside of his Aboriginal reserve or community. For example, Section 33 of Queensland's 1897 Aboriginals Protection and Restriction of the Sale of Opium Act read: 'It shall be lawful for the Minister to issue to any half-caste, who, in his opinion, ought not to be subject to the provisions of this Act, a certificate, in writing under his hand, and that such half-caste is exempt from the provisions of this Act and the Regulations.' In short, it was a means of assimilation, although very few who applied were ever granted certificates. For example, prior to 1940, of the 14,000 NSW Aborigines eligible to apply, only 1,500 were issued with certificates. In Queensland from 1908 to 1967 only 4,092 certificates were issued. War service did not automatically warrant the issue of an exemption certificate.[64]

Upon repatriation, in all states except Queensland, Aboriginal soldiers were given the lump sum of their withheld pay. In Queensland, Bleakley maintained control of all Aboriginal accounts and condemned military authorities for distributing their entire reserve pay to be wasted on 'vice and drink'. Bleakley's arrangement has been referred to as 'stolen wages'.[65] Esme Fisher, wife of Aborigine veteran, Frank Fisher (11th LHR), complained about the arrangement: 'I am having a bit of trouble with my husband's military pay, I used to draw at the Murgon Post Office, and Mr. Bleakley has taken it to Brisbane without my consent, and I don't see why I can't draw my husband's pay here.'[66] All Aboriginal finances were kept in trust by the local protector and no Aborigine had direct control or access to his finances.

In addition, returning Australian soldiers were granted a war gratuity based on duration of service, only withheld in the event of dishonourable discharge. Aboriginal veterans, although entitled to the same money, were subjected to an oral examination by their local protector, who in turn answered to the Aboriginal Protection Board, regarding each individual's ability to 'handle money ... would he be intelligent enough to be allowed care of his own bond? Is he in employment, if not why?'[67] While some veterans did receive this allotment, it was based on an arbitrary system, and the granting of this entitlement was by no

---

[64] Judi Wickes, '"Never Really Heard of It": The Certificate of Exemption and Lost Identity', *The Australian National University Electronic Collection* (2008) at: www.epress.anu.edu.au

[65] Bleakley, *The Aborigines of Australia*, p. 170.

[66] Pratt, 'Queensland's Aborigines in the First AIF', 37.

[67] Ibid, 37.

means universal for Aboriginal veterans – most were rejected. Some veterans possessing exemption certificates were denied the allotment.[68]

Australia instituted the Soldier Settlement Scheme, whereby returned servicemen would be allotted parcels of free land for farming or development. The programme, initiated in South Australia in 1915, was made universal across all states by 1917. Under these state programmes the federal Parliamentary War Committee advised that Crown land be used where at all possible.[69] Given that Aborigines lived on Crown land, a number of Aboriginal reserves were seized, or reduced in size, and the populations relocated in order to parcel out the land to white veterans. At Warangesda, NSW, 1,410 acres of Aboriginal land was expropriated in 1926 under the Returned Soldier Settlement Act.[70] Only one Aboriginal veteran is known to have been allocated land under the Soldier Settlement Scheme. WO2 George Kennedy of the 6th Light Horse was granted 17,000 acres at Yelty, NSW. Kennedy's final resting place was recently rediscovered in a cemetery in Condobolin as simply a numbered peg. Aboriginal veterans or their families did not receive military burial services or funeral compensation as did non-Aboriginal veterans.[71]

What many Aboriginal veterans found humiliating was the denial of entrance into any establishment serving alcohol. While in service they fought, died and drank alongside their white comrades; yet, they could not share a drink with their mates in Australia. As Private Herbert Milera remembered, 'While I was in military uniform, I was granted all the privileges one could think of, even going into an hotel and having a glass of beer. Now it is all over … I am practically No-Body.'[72] Interviewed in 1950, George Dutton, an Aborigine from Queensland who was rejected for enlistment in 1914, was still bitter about the inequality during the First World War: 'These darkies have got no right to go fighting for whites that stole their country. Now they won't let 'em into the hotel. They've got to gulp down plonk [alcohol] in the lavatory.'[73]

The manifestation of these frustrations was the formation of political activist groups. In 1923, Frederick Maynard founded the Aborigines' Progress Association or Aboriginal Progressive Association (APA) in

---

[68] Huggonson, 'Aborigines and the Aftermath of the Great War', 3.
[69] NAA, A2487 1919/11073. The Discharged Soldiers' Settlement Act 1917, Queensland.
[70] Huggonson, 'Aborigines and the Aftermath of the Great War', 7; AWM, Private Collections.
[71] NAA, A2487 1919/3202. Position of the Australian Aboriginal Soldier; Inglis, *Sacred Places*, pp. 457–8.
[72] Hall, *The Black Diggers*, p. 79.
[73] Pratt, 'Queensland's Aborigines in the First AIF', 38.

Sydney. In consultation with veterans, this organization publicly campaigned for equal rights and called for the cessation of the 'educational' removal of Aboriginal children. Continuously hounded by police, the organization operated formally for only three years.[74] William Cooper, father of Private Daniel Cooper (killed in action on 20 September 1917), founded the Australian Aborigines League (AAL) in Melbourne in 1933. His organization incorporated smaller activist groups, formed bonds with sympathetic trade unions and petitioned the Australian governments and King George V for equal rights. In 1939 at the outbreak of the Second World War, Cooper wrote to the federal Minister of the Interior:

I am the father of a soldier who gave his life for his King on the Battlefield and thousands of coloured men enlisted in the A.I.F. They will doubtless do so again though on their return last time, that is those who survived, were pushed back to the bush to resume the status of aboriginals ... the aboriginal now has no status, no rights, no land and ... nothing to fight for but the privilege of defending the land which was taken from him by the white race without compensation or even kindness. We submit that to put us in the trenches, until we have something to fight for, is not right ... the enlistment of natives should be preceded by the removal of all disabilities ... Can we not have a 'Balfour Declaration' for natives of a national home in Australia. It will cost nothing to give the native born in the land the same rights, not merely of the persons of European blood, but of Maoris and ... Asiatic peoples.[75]

On 26 January 1938, the 150th anniversary of the first British settlement in Australia, Cooper implemented the concept of a 'National Day of Mourning'. The publicity of the event secured the leadership of the AAL a meeting with the Prime Minister and the Minister of the Interior. In February, members of the AAL were successful in submitting evidence to a Parliamentary Select Committee of Inquiry on Aboriginal affairs.[76]

Perhaps the greatest tragedy of the First World War era concerning Aborigines was what is now referred to as the 'Stolen Generations'. Although the systematic removal of Aboriginal children had occurred as early as 1869, policies were amended and became more stringent at the turn of the century. In 1913, the South Australian Royal Commission on Aborigines reported that, 'the problem is now one of assisting and training that native so that he may become a useful member of the community ... To achieve this object ... it is necessary for more direct Government control ... the principal duties of the board will be

---

[74] Huggonson, 'Aborigines and the Aftermath of the Great War', 7.
[75] Jackomos and Fowell, *Forgotten Heroes*, pp. 9–10.
[76] Huggonson, 'The Dark Diggers of the AIF', 355.

to see that all aboriginal and half-caste children are educated … the
greatest hope for the aboriginal race.'[77] Based on the 1897 Queensland
Act, successive acts and amendments in all states pursued a policy
whereby Aboriginal children were removed, without parental consent,
from their communities and placed in institutionalized 'educational'
care. Although reading, writing and arithmetic were part of the syl-
labus, the priority was placed upon training for domestic service for
girls and farming, carpentry and manual labour for boys.[78] By 1912,
in Western Australia, all children of Aboriginal descent were expelled
from, and subsequently forbidden entry into, state schools. In August
1918, Aboriginal farmer, John Kickett, voiced his disapproval to his
MP: 'I have five of my people in France fighting, since you were here
for your election one has been killed which leaves four as my people
are Fighting for Our King and Country Sir, I think they should have
the liberty of going to any State school.'[79] This national practice was
not abolished until 1969, two years after the franchise was extended
to Aborigines, and awareness was made global by the acclaimed movie
Rabbit-Proof Fence (2002), based on Doris Pilkington-Garimara's book,
Follow the Rabbit-Proof Fence (1996), detailing the experiences of her
mother and two aunts.[80] On 13 February 2008, four months before
Canada, Prime Minister Kevin Rudd issued a formal apology on behalf
of Australia, although no compensation package was proposed.

The participation of Aborigines during the First World War did little
to change the public perception of Aborigines. In 1928, William Murray,
a veteran of Gallipoli, led several punitive expeditions in the Northern
Territory in retaliation for the killing of dingo hunter, Frederick Brooks.
The total number of Aboriginal deaths varies between 31 and 110, the
consensus being roughly 60 deaths, including women and children.
What became known as the Coniston Massacre was deemed by a 1929
Board of Inquiry to be 'justified, and that the natives killed were all
members of the Walmulla [sic] tribe from Western Australia, who were
on a marauding expedition, with the avowed object of wiping out the
white settlers'. This massacre was not an isolated event; two others
occurred in 1924 and 1926.[81]

---

[77] Stone, *Aborigines in White Australia*, p. 148.
[78] Broome, *Aboriginal Australians*, pp. 102–4.
[79] Peter Biskup, *Not Slaves, Not Citizens* (St Lucia: University of Queensland Press, 1973), p. 154.
[80] Doris Pilkington, *Follow the Rabbit-Proof Fence* (Brisbane: University of Queensland Press, 1996).
[81] Australian Institute for Aboriginal and Torres Strait Islander Studies, *Report on the Administration of North Australia for the Year 1929* (March 1930).

In New Zealand, between 1910 and 1930, 3.5 million acres passed out of Maori title, including 681,000 acres during the war itself, leaving only four million acres in Maori possession by 1930.[82] In addition, portions of Maori land were secured for the settlement of repatriated veterans under the Discharged Soldiers' Settlement Act 1915 and the 1917 amendment. Although Maori veterans were entitled to the same benefits as *Pakeha*, only thirty-nine Maori soldiers (or 1.7%) were assisted in acquiring land under this scheme compared to 10% of *Pakeha* veterans. On 28 March 1916, government legislation ensured that, for the purposes of repatriation programmes, benefits and pensions, Maori soldiers were to be treated on identical terms as *Pakeha*. Given this policy of equality, racism does not seem to have been a primary factor in the low number of land grants to Maori; veterans preferred to return to their Maori communities rather than secure land far removed from their traditional tribal locations. Nevertheless, Maori leaders continued to petition the government over land and treaty rights, and in 1926 a Maori delegation travelled to London to petition King George V.[83]

From anecdotal evidence, black South African labourers shared the belief of one SANLC member that, 'when we heave a heavy load, we know that we kill a Hun'.[84] Jingoes recounted that, 'Although at that time politics and Independence were a long way off, we were aware, when we returned, that we were different from other people at home. Our behaviour, as we showed the South Africans, was something more than they expected from a Native, more like what was expected among them of a white man.' Z. F. Zibi remarked that, 'We are not here [in France] as Mfengu, Xhosa and other tribes. We are conscious of the fact that we Blacks are united in staying together ... Therefore we shall never be deceived ... Otherwise it would mean that we are like people who share mat but quarrel – in such cases one never sleeps well.'[85] Nevertheless, the overwhelming attitude of whites, both within the SANLC and in South Africa, was expressed by an SANLC officer in France: 'When you people get to South Africa again, don't start thinking that you are Whites, just because this place has spoiled you. You are black, and you will stay black.'[86]

[82] Dick Scott, *Ask that Mountain: The Story of Parihaka* (Auckland: Heinemann/Southern Cross, 1975), p. 198; Smith, *A Concise History of New Zealand*, p. 147.
[83] Ashley Gould, 'Soldier Settlement in New Zealand after World War I: A Reappraisal' in Judith Smart and Tony Wood (eds.), *An Anzac Muster: War and Society in Australia and New Zealand 1914–1918 and 1939–1945 Selected Papers* (Victoria: Monash University, 1992), pp. 116–24; Gould, 'Maori and the First World War', 299.
[84] Page, 'Introduction: Black Men in a White Man's War', 8.
[85] Grundlingh, *Fighting Their Own War*, p. 124.
[86] Jingoes, *A Chief is a Chief by the People*, pp. 92–3.

South African soldiers received a war gratuity of £4 upon repatriation. The Department of Native Affairs stipulated, with no exceptions, that, 'The gratuity is only issuable [sic] to the European personnel, S.A.N.L.C.' It was added that, 'They [natives] were never entitled to them (gratuity, vocational training, loans, or money for purchase of land) and this department would be lacking in its duty were it to encourage idle hopes which are fore-doomed to disappointment.' Furthermore, natives were required to pay poll and hut taxes even if they had been out of the country for military service. It was arranged, however, that coloureds receive the gratuity, 'as they earned less than they would have in civil employment whereas the SANLC earned equivalent or better than the mines'.[87] In addition, while white and coloured veterans could retain their uniforms, blacks could only do so after their already lower-quality uniforms were 'stripped of all buttons, rank and insignia'. Native Affairs did, however, instruct all districts that blacks and coloureds requiring further medical treatment after discharge, 'directly related to active service ... shall be treated as civilians but are to be given free treatment and in the event of death burial at public expense'.[88]

Buxton declared in December 1918 that, 'the war has proved to you that your loyalty was well placed; and I can assure you that it will not be forgotten'. However, black contributions to the war effort were quickly forgotten and policies of segregation were amplified. The unequal treatment of black veterans led A. K. Xabanisa to conclude tersely that, 'I am just like a stone which after killing a bird, nobody bothers about, not cares to see where it falls.' The SANNC sent a delegation of five men to England in April 1919 to press their claims for equal rights and remind the imperial government of black war service; the SANLC was the only sub-Saharan African unit to see service in Europe.[89] The delegation was a dismal failure. Frustrated and cynical, the SANNC lapsed into a period of stagnation during the 1920s, finding it difficult to adopt new strategies to forward black grievances.

The war did have a drastic impact on the demography of South Africa. The number of black miners remained constant between 1914 and 1919. Black farmers or sharecroppers, however, did not share the benefits of white farmers who witnessed a 'remarkable prosperity due to the war'. South African agricultural exports increased 62 per cent

---

[87] NASA, KAB, 1LSK, vol. 13. Army Order No. 17/1919 – War Gratuity; SAB, NTS, vol. 9108/18/363–28/363. Native Affairs Memorandums 10, 22 May 1918, 29 January 1920, 29 March 1921.

[88] NASA, KAB, 1UTA, 6/1/200. Native Affairs to all Districts, 13 August 1917; KAB, 1TBU, vol. 25. Department of Public Health to Senior Medical Officers, 6 July 1920.

[89] Grundlingh, *Fighting Their Own War*, pp. 129, 134–5.

during the war. The land acts prior to the war had undermined natives to such an extent that they could not share in the benefits of the war boom.[90] Furthermore, blacks who were wealthy with cattle prior to the war were left impoverished by the expropriation of their livestock for war purposes. Following the war, they were supplanted by veterans, who had accrued enough capital to buy cattle even at inflated prices.[91] Through the prestige of cattle, certain veterans assumed leadership, usurping power within their communities, at the expense of former leading men.

Given the 1913 Land Act, and with little opportunity for profit farming, blacks became increasingly urbanized during the inter-war years. Black workers employed in urban industries, excluding mines, rose by 83 per cent from 1915–16 to 1919–20, totalling roughly 114,000 by 1920. By 1936, the total black urban population was 1,150,000, compared with 508,000 in 1914.[92] Movement to urban centres, however, was not an escape from Union policies of racial containment. The 1923 Native Urban Areas Act strictly controlled movement of blacks between rural and urban cantons. Urban status, given only to employed men, was temporary and required a pass. These men lived in segregated communities and municipal authorities had jurisdiction over black urban inclusion. Blacks were only welcome in urban areas when satisfying white needs.[93]

Furthermore, the cost of living in South Africa increased by 15.1 per cent between 1914 and 1918. White wages were adjusted, black wages were not. This factor was the key component in labour unrest or 'strike fever' following the war. While most strikes were violently repressed, the 1920 strike of 71,000 miners on the Witwatersrand forced mine owners to increase black wages by 25 per cent. However, Grundlingh concludes that:

[T]here is no satisfactory evidence that ex-contingent [SANLC] members were in the vanguard of sustained and coherent black resistance to white domination. For example, no indication could be found that former members were involved in the black industrial unrest ... Nor does it appear, on a somewhat different level, that veterans acted as 'modernisers' in rural societies ... Ultimately, then, military service was not a crucial variant in determining political behaviour.[94]

[90] Ibid, p. 156.
[91] Page, 'Introduction: Black Men in a White Man's War', 18.
[92] Walshe, *The Rise of African Nationalism in South Africa*, p. 105.
[93] Union of South Africa, *Natives (Urban Areas) Act, Act No. 21, 1923* (Pretoria: Government Printer, 1923); Paul Maylam, 'The Rise and Decline of Urban Apartheid in South Africa', *African Affairs* 89/354 (1990), 57–84.
[94] Grundlingh, *Fighting Their Own War*, pp. 132, 152, 169.

Following the war, indigenous military service reverted back to pre-war Dominion defence policy, since no official alterations were made to these acts during the war years. The service of indigenous men was no longer a pragmatic requirement. Aborigines were once again excluded wholesale. Blacks and coloureds had served their primary function as labourers during the war and their services were no longer required. In New Zealand, some of the 'right types' of Maori were admitted into the NZDF; however, it was believed that an inundation of roughly nine thousand Maori of military age would be disadvantageous in mixed units. Thus, Maori inclusion was the same as it had been prior to the war – one of limited inclusion for those deemed to be assimilated.[95] The situation for Canadian Indians was identical.

[95] Haami, 'Maori in the Armed Forces', 302.

Conclusion

The pragmatic realization of the need for manpower, allied with the October 1915 requests of the imperial government, provided for the military inclusion of Dominion indigenes during the First World War. Had the war been short and limited in its requirements for men and materials, indigenes would have remained subjugated spectators. The First World War, however, was a global conflict and encompassed the terrain and populations of peoples that belonged, willingly or otherwise, to established European empires; thus, these indigenous peoples were solicited to participate. Many eagerly embraced the opportunity to serve as equals within Dominion forces, while demonstrating their loyalty to the empire and their home nations.

Nevertheless, racial considerations, including probable outcomes, were foremost in all decisions pertaining to the use of indigenous men in a military capacity. The military inclusion of indigenes was never intended to outlast the war, as defence acts were not formally altered, but rather, were ignored to meet military exigencies, chiefly the need for manpower. All facets of their military service were carefully weighed and applied, so as not to upset the existing racial, social and political realities of Dominion societies, while at the same time satisfying strategic war objectives – greater autonomy, sub-imperialism of the Antipodes and South Africa, and access to enhanced economic markets for all Dominions. In a war of attrition, providing manpower for national expeditionary forces, to supplement the senior British Expeditionary Force, was the most conspicuous avenue to achieve these ambitions.

The inclusion of indigenes in Dominion formations was a continuation of past, official or unofficial, policies and practices. Historical tradition dictated that indigenes were used only when, and where, they were required. Their use during the First World War was not an exception to this principle; however, never before had they been called upon in such magnitude. Yet, the evolution of indigenous inclusion was gradual and paralleled increasing Dominion contributions and the amplification of the war in its entirety. In 1914, the majority of indigenous leaders and peoples greeted the war with enthusiasm and immediately offered their services, and donations, to King and country. Indigenous elites and political organizations viewed war service as a tool to gain equality and respect within the broader spheres of imperial and Dominion politics and society. By 1915, Dominion politicians and military officials viewed indigenous service as a pragmatic necessity to meet national strategic intentions, while also using participation to further domestic indigenous policy. For the Dominions with European demographic superiority, the war was an instrument of assimilation, while for South Africa, where Europeans were outnumbered by blacks by a 4:1 ratio, war was used to experiment with policies of pre-apartheid segregation.

Aware of indigenous grievances and demands, in 1914, Dominion governments actively resisted and blocked indigenous attempts for inclusion in the war effort when viable. With Dominion manpower sufficient at this point in the war to meet demands and commitments, indigenous participation was not needed and, therefore, was generally not accepted. In South Africa, although a select few blacks and coloureds may have been used as armed scouts during the Boer Rebellion, the majority of blacks were used as labourers during both the rebellion and in GSWA. This was in keeping with South African tradition and current defence policy, and blacks were always intended to be employed for military labour within the confines of Africa. Maori, technically equal to *Pakeha*, were placated and allowed partial inclusion as non-combatants for garrison duty in Egypt. By imperial design, Maori were excluded from the New Zealand force raised for the Boer War, so in 1914, Massey hesitated (although did request) to permit Maori combatant privileges. A select number of Canadian Indians circumvented the non-official and confusing policy of exclusion to enlist in the CEF; however, most were denied enlistment. Australian Aborigines were excluded wholesale from the AIF. Lastly, the Indian and Eskimo populations of Newfoundland-Labrador were too small and remote to be given any attention in a military capacity, as Newfoundland was the least prepared for war of any Dominion.

According to James Walker, at the onset of war the participation of indigenes was guided, 'by a set of presumptions about their abilities which dictated the role they were to play [or not play] and which limited the rewards they were to derive'.[1] As the war progressed, however, and Dominion forces expanded and accrued the horrific casualty rates of trench warfare on the Western Front and Gallipoli, official and

---

[1] Walker, 'Race and Recruitment in World War I', 3.

unofficial Dominion exclusionist policies regarding indigenous service were ignored (although not legally changed). Pragmatism dictated the inclusion of minorities as both combatants and non-combatants. The roles of Dominion indigenes within these expanding forces differed, and were predicated upon immediate needs and contemporary racial policies and anxieties.

The years of 1915 and, more explicitly, 1916, saw a relaxation in restrictive policies, coupled to the imperial requests of October 1915, and, in some cases, active governmental recruitment of indigenous men for combatant and non-combatant units. In June 1915, Maori were re-mustered into a homogenous combat, pioneer battalion and were deployed to Gallipoli and, subsequently, to the Western Front. In December 1915, Indians were officially sanctioned to enlist in all units of the CEF. In late 1916, the 107th and 114th battalions arrived in England with 50 per cent Indian representation. In September 1916, the Union initiated recruitment for the SANLC, bound for France. Newfoundland-Labrador undertook specific recruitment drives in the Outports and Labrador in the summer of 1915, which included Indians and Eskimos. The primary target, however, remained the non-indigenous male population. While a small number of Aborigines, predominately half-caste, evaded exclusionist protocol to enlist in the AIF, their numbers remained small. Australia maintained an official 'white only' policy. In all instances, however, the service of indigenous men and their military application was dependent upon internal state security and conventional racial norms, within the parameters of fuelling Dominion enlistment, which in all cases began to decline throughout 1916.

On 5 January 1916, Britain introduced the first of a series of Military Service Acts, which initiated conscription. New Zealand followed suit, passing the Military Services Bill on 10 June 1916. Initially, it imposed conscription only on *Pakeha*, but came to include Maori, at the insistence of Pomare, in June 1917, as was legally permitted. Conscription in Australia was rejected by referendum in October 1916 by a margin of 2 per cent. A second plebiscite, held on 20 December 1917, was rejected by a greater margin. Nevertheless, under the Constitution, conscription would not have applied to Aborigines. Canada introduced compulsory service with the controversial Military Service Act of August 1917, to the indignation of most French-Canadians. Its application to Indians was confused and capricious. While initially included, treaty rights eventually allowed for Indian omission. Lastly, Newfoundland passed its own Military Service Act on 11 May 1918, and made no specific reference to its diminutive indigenous populations.

During 1917 and 1918, the inclusion of indigenes was broadened and included active recruitment. Half-caste Aborigines were officially admitted, and specifically recruited, into the AIF. The SANLC and coloured units were used as labour on the Western Front, and coloured combatants served in Africa and the Middle East. The Maori Battalion maintained full strength while active in France and Belgium. Canadian Indians were specifically recruited for forestry companies, as well as infantry reinforcements. Newfoundland initiated a second recruitment campaign in Labrador and the Outports in 1917. These shifts in policy were directly related to the manpower needs of expanding Allied forces. Racial concerns, however, still permeated all aspects of indigenous participation. The SANLC 'experiment' was terminated for racial and political reasons before the end of hostilities. Britain excluded indigenes, including the Maori Battalion, from occupation forces in Germany, and pre-war exclusionist policies were reinstated at the armistice. Nevertheless, indigenes shared equally in the burdens of war.

They voluntarily aided the empire in its time of need, despite prejudicial governmental actions and policies, and many sought equality as recompense. As mentioned, Arthur Marwick asserts that, 'in modern war there is a greater participation on the part of larger underprivileged groups in society, who tend correspondingly to benefit, or at least develop a new self-consciousness ... a strengthened market position and hence higher material standards for such groups; it also engenders a new sense of status, usually leading to a dropping of former sectional or class barriers'.[2] The elevated participation of Dominion indigenes during the First World War was a potential catalyst to achieve these benefits and to accelerate their attainment of equal rights. This did not happen. In the case of Dominion indigenes and First World War participation, Marwick's argument can be dismissed. The Dominions, however, did accrue the benefits of significant war contributions, although the filtering of reward did not descend the rungs of hierarchy to their indigenous peoples.

One-fifth of President Woodrow Wilson's Fourteen Points alluded, in some manner, to the interests of indigenous populations. Yet, as Margaret MacMillan points out, 'no one had actually bothered to consult the Africans or Pacific Islanders'. During the 1919 Paris peace talks, and discussions surrounding League of Nations 'protectorate' mandates, Australia's Hughes, New Zealand's Massey, both Botha and

---

[2] See: Arthur Marwick, *War and Social Change in the Twentieth Century: A Comparative Study of Britain, France, Germany, Russia and the United States* (London: Palgrave Macmillan, 1974).

Smuts of South Africa, and France's Clemenceau were all hostile to these ideals and to Wilson's overtures. For Clemenceau, the colonies were a symbol of power, 'and held what France badly needed: manpower ... If France received mandates under the League, would there be niggling restrictions on the recruitment of native soldiers for overseas duty?' For France, it was preposterous to commit resources to its proposed mandates, if it could not recruit volunteers to defend it if needed. Lloyd George reluctantly agreed: 'If this clause meant that he [Clemenceau] had a right of raising troops for a general war, he was satisfied ... So long as M. Clemenceau did not train big nigger armies for the purposes of aggression, that was all the clause was intended to guard against.'[3]

As for the former German colonies in Africa and the Pacific, Smuts remarked that their inhabitants were 'barbarians to whom it would be impracticable to apply any ideas of political self-determination in the European sense'.[4] For Australia, New Zealand and South Africa, all harbouring sub-imperialist interests, their war contributions were leveraged to demand the annexation of neighbouring German colonial possessions. South Africa sought the absorption of GSWA. Smuts argued that white South Africans understood the natives and 'had established a white civilization in a savage continent and had become a great cultural agency all over South Africa'. New Zealand courted Samoa, while Australia coveted New Guinea and the Bismarck Archipelago; a strategic design to limit Japanese southern expansion. For these Dominions, the war was fought to preserve the integrity of the 'white Dominions'.[5]

Clemenceau invited 'the cannibals', as he teasingly referred to Australia and New Zealand, to present their case. After heated debate, Wilson harshly asked Hughes (whom he loathed): 'Am I to understand that if the whole civilised world asks Australia (and NZ) to agree to a mandate in respect of the islands [New Guinea, the Bismarck Archipelago and Samoa], Australia is prepared still to defy the appeal of the whole civilised world?', to which Hughes antagonistically replied, 'That's about the size of it, President Wilson.' The French welcomed the rancour evident among Britain and her Dominions. A member of the Australian delegation remarked: 'Of course he [Hughes] is being used as a Catspaw [sic] by the French who want the Cameroons, Togo

---

[3] MacMillan, *Paris 1919*, pp. 99–104.
[4] Ibid, p. 99.
[5] A significant reason for Allied intervention in Siberia, via Vladivostock, was to prevent Japanese expansion in the 'Pacific Rim'. The others were primarily economic. Halting the spread of Bolshevism, as evidenced by the inaction of allied forces in Siberia, was not the priority, as was promulgated.

Land & Syria.' Borden, the senior Dominion statesman, always cogni-
zant of British–American tension – while trying to enhance Canadian
wellbeing in the 'North Atlantic triangle' – urged Hughes and Massey
to be reasonable.[6]

In the end, the Dominions were mollified with compensation.
Australia and New Zealand got their islands and to South Africa went
the much coveted GSWA. After all, the imperial government had asked
these Dominions to invade these German colonies in September 1914.
The stance of Dominion leaders at the peace talks exemplified their
refusal to grant self-determination and equality to colonial possessions
and peoples, let alone to their domestic indigenes.

Following the war, paternalistic and authoritative Dominion indigenous policies prevailed, and recognition for their unprecedented military
contributions were fast, if not conveniently, forgotten. War service did
not alter the socio-economic or political realities of indigenous peoples
in the Dominions. Military participation, and home front contributions, did not hasten the attainment of equal rights or enfranchisement
(for those other than Maori). During the war, and through repatriation or soldier settlement acts, Dominion governments continued the
long-standing practice of expropriating indigenous land. In certain
cases, the war itself was used as the reason for the confiscation of land.
Indigenous veterans were denied access to most repatriation and veteran programmes. Instead, they returned to their pre-war position of
wards of the state, under various paternalistic governmental laws, which
promoted assimilation in Australia, New Zealand, Newfoundland and
Canada and enhanced segregation in South Africa.

Historians claim that a heightened sense of esteem, attained by indigenes through Great War participation, translated into political action
for equality. While a new found self-worth was realized by individual indigenous veterans, or specific communities, it did not permeate
the broader spheres of Dominion society, to any significant degree.
Although in some cases indigenous veterans were instrumental in
organizing indigenous political organizations, these bodies did little to
change governmental policy or to accelerate the attainment of equal
rights. The social standing of indigenous peoples within the dominant
British-based Dominion societies remained one of exclusion and subjugation. While the Dominions benefited from the use of indigenes, in

---

[6] MacMillan, *Paris 1919*, pp. 99–106. After the Second World War, the UN took over
the mandates. As European empires crumbled, it gave independence to the territories
it had inherited, save for one exception. South Africa refused to give up Southwest
Africa. Only in 1990 did Namibia gain independence, following a lengthy internal
guerilla war (1966–90) often labelled the Namibian War of Independence.

sheer manpower or cheaper labour for example, indigenes accrued little benefit from service, aside from military pay or the fulfilment of individual motivations for enlistment.

Although the elevated participation of indigenes during the First World War had the potential to promote equality, this was never the objective of any Dominion government. Howard Zinn argues that, 'Liberation [from oppression] from the top would only go so far as the interests of the dominant groups permitted. If carried further by the momentum of war, the rhetoric of a crusade, it could be pulled back to a safer position … those who made the war would organize its consequences.'[7] Thus, indigenous grievances were overshadowed by those of other minority European groups in the Dominions. The war created social and political divides between British and French in Canada, between English and Irish in Australia and between British and Afrikaner in South Africa. Given that the war ushered in a new sense of patriotic national identity among the British segments, placating these acrimonious relationships was paramount in the consolidation of the settler-state and to the prosperity and cohesive security of the 'white Dominions'. Jonathan Vance's Canadian paradigm is also representative of the racial atmosphere and post-war realities in all Dominions:

Native Canadians and non-Natives who were sympathetic to their cause, pointed to the war as the ultimate proof of their dedication to Canada and their right to equal treatment in the new nation. At the same time, English Canadians confidently expected the war to be the basis for a final reconciliation with French Canada. The war's legacy would provide the impetus for both groups to become, not Native Canadians or French Canadians, but Canadians pure and simple … The myth's weakness lay, not in the fact that it had too little grounding in the realities of wartime, but in the fact that its rhetoric was too often contradicted by the realities of peacetime. The memory of the war might have been able to work its magic among immigrants, Natives, and French Canadians if it had been accompanied by some substantive steps towards the society it envisioned. As it was, the myth promised far more than it was ever able to deliver.[8]

The war forever transformed the empire, both legally and culturally. The culmination of the considerable contributions made by the Dominions during the Great War occurred with the ratification of the Statute of Westminster in 1931. This legal arrangement granted the Dominions absolute autonomy over all aspects of domestic and foreign policy, including war. The Dominions had officially shrugged off the yoke of British

[7] Howard Zinn, *A People's History of the United States, 1492–Present* (New York: HarperCollins, reprint, 2005), pp. 171–2.
[8] Vance, *Death So Noble*, pp. 245, 258.

rule and had the opportunity to advance indigenous-specific courses of action different from those promulgated by Whitehall and British politicians, who had long ceased cohabitation with the indigenous peoples of their former empire.

The indigenous peoples of the Dominions, through the bonding of a common war trial, were willing to enter into Dominion societies as equals. The Dominions rejected this offer, and refused to acknowledge the shared experience of the First World War and, more importantly, the benefits which could have been derived from it. The First World War was, for the Dominions, the transformative, even pivotal, event in the twentieth century, and the sacrifices of indigenous soldiers and communities shaped the eras that followed. These experiences challenged notions of indigenous identity, as well as their constitutional/political status and their appropriate place in national orders, the influences of which are still evident today.

The more recent pan-indigenous politicization, revival and focus on this matter demonstrate not only its continuing relevance, but also the lasting legacy of the failure of British settler societies to address enduring indigenous injustices. An understanding of the participation of indigenous peoples during the First World War places their contributions in a broader, trans-national context, coupled to the sacrifices common to all citizens and soldiers. It also underscores elements of the war experience which were unique to them. Comparison, by removing blinding national barriers and affiliations, must foster a broader cultural awareness for both indigenous and non-indigenous peoples, while promoting an agenda of mutual understanding and respect. The First World War, by way of a collective mobilization, could have been this mechanism. Unfortunately, it was not, and this issue remains unresolved.

On 13 September 2007, the United Nations General Assembly adopted the Declaration on the Rights of Indigenous Peoples. While it is not legally binding, the UN stated that it does 'represent the dynamic development of international legal norms' and is 'an important standard for the treatment of indigenous peoples that will undoubtedly be a significant tool towards eliminating human rights violations against the planet's 370 million indigenous people and assisting them in combating discrimination and marginalisation'.[9] The declaration was referred to, and passed by, the General Assembly with 143 countries voting in favour, 11 abstaining and 4 voting against. These four countries were: Canada, Australia, New Zealand and the United

---

[9] United Nations Permanent Forum on Indigenous Issues at: www.un.org

Table 11.1: *Indigenous service in the world wars*

	Population 1914	Enlistments 1914–18	Percentage	Population 1939	Enlistments 1939–45	Percentage
Canada	103,774	4,000	3.9	118,406	4,250	3.6
Australia	80,000	580	0.73	82,000	6,000	7.3
New Zealand	52,997	2,816	5.3	90,000	16,000	17.8
South Africa	5,081,490	102,110	2.0	7,990,000	117,000	1.5

States. Australia and New Zealand have since changed their votes in favour, in 2009 and 2010 respectively. In March 2010, the Governor-General of Canada, Michaelle Jean, announced in her Speech From the Throne that the government will take 'steps to endorse this aspirational document in a manner fully consistent with Canada's Constitution and laws'. The United States has made no overtures of support.[10]

While international indigenous political rights remain in abeyance, their value as soldiers continued after the First World War. The unprecedented mobilization of indigenous men, between 1914 and 1918, set the precedent for their inclusion in future Dominion expeditionary forces. During the Second World War, indigenous men were again asked to participate. Although social and racial conditions within the Dominions varied, pragmatism, and the need for manpower, once again forced the admittance of indigenes into military formations. Many of the themes and policies regarding indigenous service in the Great War were repeated during the Second World War (see Table 11.1).

In October 1939, the New Zealand Department of Defence formed the 28th (Maori) Battalion. A committee of five Maori MPs, chaired by Paraire Paikea, was responsible for the coordination of the Maori war effort, reminiscent of that of the First World War. In July 1940, an aging Ngata wrote to Buck:

The Government has accepted a Battalion, which is now in England and will soon be in the thick of it. The response to recruiting is better than in the last war ... The material is good, but in my humble opinion not as tough or as resourceful as that of 25 years ago ... The War of 1914–1918 has brought

---

[10] The abstaining nations were: Azerbaijan, Bangladesh, Bhutan, Burundi, Colombia, Georgia, Kenya, Nigeria, Russian Federation, Samoa and the Ukraine. An additional thirty-four states were absent from the vote.

this one about, because the peacemakers discounted the old motive of ngaki mate [vengeance] … and the international philosophers will have to devise new terminologies for human relationships.[11]

The 28th Battalion sailed, 681 strong, in May 1940 and received its baptism of fire in Greece in March 1941. In 1943, a second Maori Battalion was raised for home defence in response to the Japanese threat and was used to reinforce the 28th Battalion active in North Africa. In March 1943, Second-Lieutenant Moana-Nui-a-Kiwa Ngarimu was posthumously awarded the Victoria Cross for actions at Tebaga Gap, Tunisia. The 28th Battalion served in Italy for the remainder of the war. During the Second World War, 16,000 Maori voluntarily enlisted (conscription was not applied to Maori) from a total population of approximately 90,000. Of the 3,600 who saw combat with the 28th Battalion, 680 were killed and another 1,712 wounded. Lieutenant-General Sir Bernard Freyberg, commander of the 2nd NZEF, commented that no infantry battalion 'had a more distinguished record, or saw more fighting, or, alas, had such heavy casualties as the Maori Battalion'.[12]

After the war, a significant shift in demographics altered the composition of the NZDF. Maori numbered roughly 115,000 in 1950, and were increasingly urban. In 1950, the CGS, Major-General K. L. Stewart, ended the practice of forming distinct Maori units. Hence, no large-scale distinct Maori units, save for a gun crew within the 16th Field Regiment and a transport platoon within the 10th Transport Company raised in 1952, were formed either for the Korean War or in the territorial force. Maori soldiers, however, were increasing their proportion in the NZDF. Maori composed 15% of New Zealand soldiers who served in the Korean War. Likewise, of the 709 men of the New Zealand Battalion sent to Malaya in January 1958, 22.9% were Maori.[13] In 1978, Major-General B. M. Poananga became CGS, the first Maori to hold this position. The current Chief of Defence Force, Lieutenant-General Jeremiah Mateparae, is the second Maori to be appointed commander of New Zealand forces. Presently, roughly 30% of the NZDF

---

[11] M. P. K. Sorrenson (ed.), *Na To Hoa Aroha From Your Dear Friend: The Correspondence between Sir Apirana Ngata and Sir Peter Buck 1925–1950* (Auckland University Press, 1988), vols. 1–3, p. 247.

[12] Monty Soutar, 'Maori War Effort Overseas in the Second World War' in *The Oxford Companion to New Zealand Military History*, pp. 309–11.

[13] Ian McGibbon, *New Zealand and the Korean War Vol. II: Combat Operations* (Oxford University Press, 1996), pp. 197, 366, 467. In 1954, the army alleged that 1,600 of the 4,000 men who saw service in Korea (40 per cent) were of Maori descent, although this has since been historically and academically refuted. The true percentage of Maori soldiers during the Korean War falls somewhere between 15 and 19 per cent.

are Maori, a rate nearly double their representation in the general population, although this figure is much less in the officer corps.[14] In 2007, the Maori population of 632,900 accounted for 15% of the 4.25 million New Zealanders.[15]

At the outbreak of the Second World War, Australian Aborigines could enlist. In May 1940, however, the Military Board issued a memorandum stating that the enlistment of persons of non-European origin or descent was 'neither necessary nor desirable'. Those already in service were not discharged. After the 1942 Japanese bombing of Darwin and the need for more soldiers, the ADF unofficially relaxed its policy of Aboriginal exclusion, stimulating a wave of enlistment. Aboriginal political organizations petitioned the government to form an 'Aboriginal unit'. Although this did not transpire, by war's end over 6,000 men of Aboriginal descent, from a total population of 82,000, had served in home defence, labour and expeditionary units.[16]

In 1949, Aboriginal veterans were enfranchised, yet wholesale enfranchisement of Aborigines only occurred in 1967. The ADF officially repealed its discriminatory policy excluding Aborigines from service in 1951. Aboriginal soldiers thus served in Korea, Vietnam and Borneo. In 1987, the first Aborigine graduated from Australia's Royal Military College.[17] Grazia Scoppio concludes that Aborigines 'are under-represented in the ADF, where they constitute less than 0.5 percent of the Regular Force. However, the proportion of indigenous members is higher in the Army Reserve. The interviewees speculated this to be the case because the Reserves tend to have more of a presence in indigenous communities.' The Deputy Director of Recruiting for the ADF stated that strategies are in place to promote 'Indigenous achievement and culture within the wider ADF'.[18] The 2006 census reported an Aboriginal population of 517,000, representing 2.6 per cent of the total population.[19]

During the Second World War, 4,250 indigenous Canadians served out of a total indigenous population of roughly 120,000.[20] As a

---

[14] Haami, 'Maori in the Armed Forces', 302–3.
[15] Statistics New Zealand, 2007 Census. www.stats.govt.nz
[16] NAA, A1608 D45/2/3. War 1939. Enlistment of Aborigines in AIF; Hall, *The Black Diggers*, pp. 35–45.
[17] Huggonson, 'The Dark Diggers of the AIF', 356; Huggonson, 'Too Dark for the Light Horse'.
[18] Grazia Scoppio, 'Diversity Best Practices in Military Organizations in Canada, Australia, the United Kingdom, and the United States', *Canadian Military Journal* 9/3 (2009), 24.
[19] Australian Bureau of Statistics, 2006 Census. www.abs.gov.au
[20] Sheffield, 'Indifference, Difference and Assimilation', 71.

percentage, fewer Indians served during the Second World War than the First World War. Nevertheless, Indians served with distinction. Ojibwa Sergeant Tommy Prince, a member of the joint Canadian/American 1st Special Service Force ('The Devil's Brigade'), was awarded the MM and was one of only fifty-nine Canadians to win the American Silver Star. Prince went on to serve in the Korean War. However, like his glorified American Indian counterpart, Ira Hayes (immortalized by the Iwo Jima flag-raising photo and by singer Johnny Cash), Prince died an alcoholic and in squalor.[21] Hayes was one of over 25,000 American Indians to serve in the Second World War out of a total population of 287,970 (or 8.7 per cent).[22] US Forces were officially desegregated (with reference to Negroes) in 1951, although it took a decade to visibly appear in the general rank and file. American Indians are well represented in modern US Forces. The 4.3 million American Indians equates to 1.5% of the total US population. Comparatively, Indians represent 1.8% of the entire US Forces. Currently, over 1,300 indigenous Canadians are serving in the Canadian Forces, representing 2% of the total Canadian Forces and 1.7% of the Regular Force.[23] The 2006 census recorded an indigenous population of 1.2 million (or 3.7% of the total Canadian population), with 47% under the age of 25 years. Roughly five thousand indigenous Canadians of this total reside in Newfoundland-Labrador.[24]

Following the Great War, the socio-economic and political conditions for natives in South Africa deteriorated to a greater extent than for indigenes in other Dominions. The drastic segregationist policies of South Africa were reflected in the UDF. During the Second World War, roughly 117,000 blacks and coloureds served in supportive capacities similar to the First World War. In 1947, the Cape (Coloured) Corps became a permanent force battalion. It was disbanded in 1949, and was

[21] See: P. Whitney Lackenbauer, 'A Hell of a Warrior: Remembering the Life of Sergeant Thomas George Prince' in Bernd Horn (ed.), *Intrepid Warriors: Perspectives on Canadian Military Leadership* (St Catherine's: Vanwell, 2007), pp. 95–138. Ira Hayes was photographed raising the flag at Iwo Jima. He died at age 32 of alcoholism and exposure in a remote desert in Arizona. He was the subject of the 1961 movie, 'The Outsider', and the inspiration for Johnny Cash's 1964 title, 'The Ballad of Ira Hayes'. Hayes was recently portrayed in Clint Eastwood's 2006 'Flags of Our Fathers'. Prince was portrayed in the 1968 movie, 'The Devil's Brigade'. Prince died in 1977 at the age of 62 in a Salvation Army Hostel in Winnipeg, Manitoba.
[22] Gaffen, *Forgotten Soldiers*, 76.
[23] Lieutenant-General Andrew B. Leslie, Foreword to *Aboriginal Peoples and Military Participation: Canadian & International Perspectives*; Scoppio, 'Diversity Best Practices in Military Organizations in Canada, Australia, the United Kingdom, and the United States', 26.
[24] Statistics Canada, 2006 Census. www.statcan.gc.ca

reinstated as a permanent force unit in 1963. Throughout its existence, however, no coloureds were permitted as officers and the unit was never used in a combat role. Blacks, on the other hand, were barred from military service.

In 1970, coloured and Indian units were formed, under their own officers, but under no circumstances did these officers command white troops. Blacks were also permitted to join segregated service and support units. Recruitment, training and all military postings were segregated: 'in the 1960s and early 1970s, the SADF [South African Defence Force] was as racist as any institution of Verwoerdian apartheid'. In 1977, coloureds were permitted to train as combat soldiers, under their own officers. In 1979, with the need to expand the SADF, the government contemplated the inclusion of 'representatives of other population groups'. In 1982, Minister of Internal Affairs Frederik de Klerk (who ultimately, with Nelson Mandela, ended apartheid) stated bluntly that, 'You can't ask a man to fight for his country if he can't vote.' At this point, only 11% of the SADF was non-white. Limited advances were made by coloureds and blacks in the SADF throughout the 1980s and early 1990s, as apartheid policies began to disintegrate. By 1990 there were ten black officers in the SADF, and in 1991, the first blacks were admitted into the military academy. By 1993, 40% of the SADF was black, 14% coloured and Indian, and 46% white.[25] The SADF, like all other institutions, underwent drastic alterations following the first post-apartheid national elections in 1994, as full integration was implemented in the newly created South African National Defence Force. The population of South Africa, as of 2007, was roughly 47 million, composed of 79.5% black, 9% white, 9% coloured and 2.5% Asian and Indian.[26]

Similar to the European populations of the Dominions, indigenous reserves and communities erected war memorials honouring their dead immediately after the First World War and memorials are scattered across indigenous communities in all former Dominions. In addition, indigenous soldiers were not excluded from national honour rolls or Dominion/Imperial European monuments, such as the Menin Gate in Ypres or the Canadian Vimy Memorial in France. Explicit governmental recognition, however, was slower, and finally bestowed in the last two decades of the twentieth century, within a general atmosphere of reconciliation among western societies and international organizations such as the United Nations.

---

[25] Greg Mills and Geoffrey Wood, 'Ethnicity, Integration and the South African Armed Forces', *South African Defence Review* 12 (1993).

[26] Statistics South Africa. www.statssa.gov.za

Indigenous peoples now have collective national memorials, similar to those at Vimy, Gallipoli, Delville Wood and Beaumont Hamel. In 1993, as part of the United Nations 'Year of Indigenous People', an anonymous, non-Aboriginal, citizen erected a simple Aboriginal war memorial on a rock at the base of Mount Ainslie behind the Australian War Memorial (museum) in Canberra. On 21 June 2001, on the Canadian National Aboriginal Day, the government unveiled the National Aboriginal Veterans Monument in Confederation Park in Ottawa. Members of the SANLC who died in France are buried around a memorial stone in the British Arques-la-Bataille cemetery in France. Although the South African National Memorial at Delville Wood was unveiled in 1926, only in 1986 was a bronze plaque added commemorating the sinking of the *Mendi* and the sacrifices of the SANLC. The names of the *Mendi* dead are also listed on seventeen panels at the Hollybrook Memorial in Southampton, honouring those who have no grave but the sea. In 1995, Queen Elizabeth II unveiled a memorial in Soweto to the *Mendi* dead, as representation of the sacrifice of native South Africans during the war. Lastly, in 2004, en-route to South Africa from its construction in a German shipyard, the SAS *Mendi* stopped where the SS *Mendi* sank to lay wreaths of remembrance. A sister ship, SAS *Isaac Dyoba*, was named in honour of the Reverend Isaac Dyoba who calmed the men on the *Mendi* in 1917.[27] The New Zealand National War Memorial, inscribed in English and Maori, was dedicated on Anzac Day 1932. It represents all New Zealanders, including Maori, who have died in war. In 1926, the government of New Zealand unveiled a Niuean (Pacific Islander) Roll of Honour and Memorial, complete with a captured German field gun, in Alofi. In 1993, the sole surviving Maori Battalion King's Colour, thought to have been lost, was dedicated to the New Zealand Army under the 1919 orders of King George V.[28]

Schools, military bases, statues and other landmarks in the former Dominions honour select indigenous soldiers by bearing their names. For example, in 2006, the headquarters for the 3rd Canadian Ranger Patrol Group was renamed after Corporal Francis Pegahmagabow. A school in Lethbridge, Alberta, bears the name (Sergeant) Mike Mountain Horse Elementary School. Sergeant Tommy Prince has the following honours in his name: a statue, a school, a street, a Canadian Forces base and a separate drill hall, two educational scholarships for indigenous Canadians and a Cadet Corps. Captain Reginald Saunders,

---

[27] NASA, SAB, GNLB, vol. 254-369-16. South African Native Labour Contingent During the Great War; G. Swinney, 'The Sinking of the SS Mendi, 21 February 1917', *Military History Journal* 10/1 (1995).

[28] ANZ, IT1, box IT122/3 – Part 1. Roll of Honour Niue, 10 September 1926.

son of a First World War veteran and thought to be the first commissioned Aborigine, has a Canberra street bearing his name. An educational scholarship is offered in New Zealand honouring Second-Lieutenant Moana-Nui-a-Kiwa Ngarimu, VC.

Raymond Aron asks in his seminal work *The Century of Total War* (1954) if, after the Great War, governments would 'favour the rise and promotion of the minority which has contributed decisively … to the historic advance?'[29] The war presented just such an opportunity. During the war, however, European minorities in the Dominions violently protested certain governmental actions. The most salient episodes were the 1914–15 Boer Rebellion, the actions of Irish-Australian civilians and soldiers during the 1916 Easter Uprising, and the French-Canadian anti-conscription riots of 1917. Many also refused to enlist in military forces. On the other hand, indigenous political organizations and leaders suspended political lobbying until after the cessation of hostilities. Aside from isolated Maori hostility in the Urewera Mountains in 1916, indigenous peoples did not resort to domestic violence to pursue political agendas. They remained loyal to both King and country, and willingly participated in the war effort.

Indigenous peoples contributed to all aspects of the First World War, demonstrating their eagerness to actively engage in Dominion societies, *and* in their defence, as equals. Many expected that through such purpose and sacrifice, Dominion administrations would reinterpret the place of indigenous peoples in national frameworks, resulting in full inclusion as citizens. The residual effects of this failed opportunity to promote indigenous advancement after the war are evident in the current political and social environments of all former Dominions.

Although the Great War for Civilization ended more than ninety years ago, for the indigenous peoples of Canada, Australia, New Zealand and South Africa, the war for cultural, territorial and socio-economic equality and recognition is still being fought today.

---

[29] Raymond Aron, *The Century of Total War* (Boston: Beacon Press, 1955), p. 319.

Bibliography

MANUSCRIPT, ARCHIVAL AND LIBRARY COLLECTIONS

ALEXANDER TURNBULL LIBRARY, WELLINGTON, NEW ZEALAND

Bulletin No. 3. Journal Kept in New Zealand in 1820 by Ensign Alexander McCrae
P920GOD1949. Letters of General Sir Alexander Godley

ANDREW BONAR LAW PAPERS, HOUSE OF LORDS RECORD OFFICE/
PARLIAMENTARY ARCHIVES, LONDON, UK

Vols. BL/50–BL/64

ARCHIVES NEW ZEALAND (ANZ), WELLINGTON, NEW ZEALAND

AD1 10/230. Nominal and Embarkation Rolls of Maori and Pioneer Battalion
AD1 734 9/32. Maoris: Offering Services in Expeditionary Force
AD1 734 9/32/1. Maori Contingents, N.Z.E.F.
AD1 734 9/32/5. Medical Arrangements Maori Contingent, E.F., 1914
AD1 734 9/32/8. Officers for Maori Contingents, N.Z.E.F.
AD1 734 9/32/11. Maoris Relieving Section of Troops in Samoa
AD1 757 9/276 Parts 1–2. Maori Contingent Active Service Correspondence
AD1 758 9/296. Casualties Maori Contingent
AD1 775 10/254. Training Maori Contingent No. 2 Auckland
AD1 810 13/67. Badge for Maori Contingent, E.F.
AD1 813 13/148. Cook Islanders Joining Maori Contingent
AD1 869 24/146. Niue Islanders from Expeditionary Force: Instructions, Discharge
AD1 873 24/246. Discipline: Maoris on Leave
AD1 960 29/108. Recruiting of Maori General File
AD1 992 31/419/20. Maori Contingent Pay and Allowances
AD1 994 31/426/4. Allotments Cook and Other Islanders
AD1 1007 31/1077. Allowances Children Maori Soldiers, N.Z.E.F.
AD1 1020 32/20/17. Liquor Maori Soldiers: Complaints re Maori Soldiers being Refused Admittance to Certain Hotels and Establishments
AD1 1021 32/23. Canteen for Maori Contingent, Avondale Auckland, 1914
AD1 1062 39/91. Progress Reports: Maori Contingent, E.F.

AD1 1062 39/110. Progress Reports: 3rd Reinforcements and Maori Contingent on Voyage

AD1 1108 43/175. Appointment 2IC Maori Contingent

AD1 1108 43/210. Officers: Maori Contingent

AD1 1132 45/67. Formation of Band: Maori Contingent, E.F.

AD1 1135 46/104. Uniform and Clothing Maori Contingent

AD1 1276 51/276. Establishment of Library for Maori Contingent, E.F.

AD1 1278 51/361. Standing Orders Maori Camp: Capt. H. Peacock

AD1 1290 51/727/18. Regimental History Maori Pioneer Battalion, N.Z.

AD1 1332 59/60. Appointment Chaplain for Maori Contingent No. 2

AD1 1339 59/132. Chaplains Maori Contingent, Prisoners of War

AD1 1367 66/11. Correspondence: Maoris Under the Military Service Act

AD1 1367 66/22. Men of New Zealand Samoan Expeditionary Force Called Up Under the Military Service Act

AD10 1 2/25. Disturbances: Maori Pioneer Troops while Abroad

AD10 20 42/4. Reports: Officers Maori Contingents

AD78 6 22/4. Islanders Returning: Despatch to Homes & Discharges from N.Z.E.F.

AD78 8 23/35. Return: Casualties, Honours, Enlistments, Maoris, Rarotongans and Niue Islanders

AD78 18 27/161. Maori Battalion: Casualties, Decorations and Awards

IT1 IT122/3 Part 1. Niue Islanders: Medals, War Graves, Roll of Honour, Memorial

MA1 376 19/1/473. Maori Battalion Embarkation Rolls, 1914–18

MA52 10h. Maori Contingents and Reinforcements, 1914–18

The Treaty of Waitangi, 1840

WA1 1/3/1 XF363. Ordnance: 3rd, 4th Bn Rifle Bde and 3rd Maori, February 1916, Egypt

WA1 1/4/2 11. Letters from Sir James Carroll to Maori Contingent, 1916

WA97 1. Unit Diaries Maori Contingent and Pioneer Battalion

WA97 2. Routine Orders

WA97 3. Unit Records Maori Contingent and Pioneer Battalion

WA97 3/1. N.Z. Maori Contingent 1914–16, Numerical Roll and Gallipoli

WA97 3/16. Registration Roll for Maori Contingent

WA97 3/17. Nominal Roll N.Z. Maori Contingent, 1915

HON. SIR JAMES ALLEN RG (ALLEN PAPERS)

Allen, J. 1/2 1 2 M1/15 Parts 1–6

Allen, J. 1/2 1 7 D1/6

Allen, J. 1/2 1 9

AUSTRALIAN INSTITUTE OF ABORIGINAL AND TORRES STRAIT ISLANDER STUDIES, CANBERRA, AUSTRALIA

PMS4475. The Aboriginal Anzacs Database

PMS4766. David Huggonson, 'The Dark Diggers of the AIF'. Paper: Work in Progress

AUSTRALIAN WAR MEMORIAL (AWM), CANBERRA, AUSTRALIA

AWM6 217. New Zealand Expeditionary Force – Maori Contingent, July 1915

AWM25 163/9. Correspondence Relating to the Employment of South African Labour Units 'Kaffir Labour' Labour Battalion South African Natives, War Establishment, 1916

AWM26 13/74. Organization of 4th and 6th Divisions and Supervision of Natives, February to March 1916

AWM27 533/1. Returns Showing Particulars of Men of Aboriginal Percentage who Enlisted and Served Abroad with the A.I.F.

AWM38 3DRL 6673/866. C. E. W. Bean Collection: War Service Papers

AWM41 914. Figures for the Australian Aborigines who Served in the War of 1914–18 in A.I.F. and were Killed, Wounded, Not Wounded

AWM43 A2. Official History, 1914–18 War: Biographical and Other Research Files

AWM44 11/1–6, Parts 1–5. Conscription

AWM93 12/5/222. Request for the File Relating to Service with the AIF of Australian Aborigines

AWM265 32/2/62. AWM Acquisitions and Donations to Collection Aborigines Protection Board

PR01679. Letters, Papers and Postcards of LCpl. Charles Tednee Blackman, 9th Bn, A.I.F.

AWM 1DRL/0428. Australian Red Cross Society Bureau Papers, 1914–18/ Prisoners of War

AWM R940.4030994 A938. List of Australian Indigenous Servicemen Who Served in World War I

AUSTRALIAN WAR MEMORIAL PRIVATE COLLECTIONS

Australian Teachers History. Indigenous Australians at War. 2003

Document Concerning 29 Aboriginal Servicemen of the 4th Australian Light Horse Brigade during the Battle of Beersheba, 31 October 1917

Letter from King George V to Private Douglas Grant, 1918

Watson, Lindsay. 'Better Than a One-Eyed Man: An Incomplete History of Queensland's Indigenous Soldiers of the Boer War and World War One'. (Unpublished paper, University of Queensland, 1999)

'Richard Martin, Minjerribah Man' (Unpublished paper)

LEWIS VERNON HARCOURT PAPERS, BODLEIAN LIBRARY, OXFORD, UK

Vols. 443–445. General Correspondence and Papers, 1913–15

Vols. 462–467. Official and Private Correspondence, 1910–16

Vol. 468. General Correspondence, 1910–15

Vols. 471–472. Weekly Secret Notes from Lord Buxton, High Commissioner and Governor General of South Africa, 1914–15

Vols. 473–474. Private Correspondence with Lord Buxton, 1914–15

Vol. 479. Correspondence with Sir Ronald Munro Ferguson, Governor General of Australia, 1914–17

Vol. 490. Correspondence with Lord Liverpool, Governor of New Zealand, 1912–17

Vols. 508–509. Reports on Operations in British Dominions and Colonies and German Territories, 1914–15

Vol. 512. Correspondence, Memoranda and Printed Papers Concerning Foreign and Domestic Wartime Matters, 1914–16

Vols. 552–557. Foreign Office Telegrams, 1914–16

LIBRARY AND ARCHIVES CANADA (LAC), OTTAWA, CANADA

RG9-II-B-9, vol. 33. Sailing Lists 107th Battalion

RG9-II-B-9, vol. 36, file 624. Various Documents relating to the 114th Overseas Battalion

RG9-II-B-10, vols. 21, 38. Nominal Rolls, 107th Overseas Battalion

RG9-II-B-10, vols. 31, 38. Nominal Rolls, 114th Overseas Battalion

RG9-II-B-11, vol. 5. After Orders, 107th Overseas Battalion

RG9-II-B-11, vol. 5. After Orders, 114th Overseas Battalion

RG9-III-D-3, vol. 4918, reel T-10710–10711, file 369. War Diaries 8th Battalion CEF

RG9-III-D-3, vol. 4941, reel T-10748, file 441. War Diaries 50th Battalion CEF

RG9-III-D-3, vol. 4941, reel T-10748, file 442. War Diaries 52nd Battalion CEF

RG9-III-D-3, vol. 4946, reel T-10753–10754, file 460. War Diaries 160th Battalion CEF

RG9-III-D-3, vol. 4990, reel T-10825, file 641. War Diaries 1st Brigade Canadian Engineers

RG9-III-D-3, vol. 5010, reel T-10859, file 725. War Diaries 107th Pioneer Battalion CEF

RG10, Indian Affairs – vol. 2837, reel C-11284, file 171,340. Six Nations Agency – Correspondence Regarding a Resolution of the Six Nations Council Regarding the Formation of a Regiment on the Reserve to be known as the Royal Six Nations Regiment

RG10, Indian Affairs – vol. 2991, reel C-11307, file 215,977. Correspondence Regarding the Desire of Numerous Indian Bands across Canada to go to South Africa Along with a Possible Contingent from the Six Nations, Reports of Rumours Circulating in the North West that Indians Wish to Join the Boer Force in the Transvaal and Donations to the Patriotic Fund by Other Bands and Orders in Council Regarding these Matters

RG10, Indian Affairs, Red Series, vols. 3180–3182. Files Concerning Indian Enlistment and Service

RG10, Indian Affairs, vol. 3195, reel C-11338, file 492,946. Six Nations Agency – Investment by the Band in War Loan Bonds, 1917

RG10, Indian Affairs, vol. 3200, reel C-11338, file 505,265. Correspondence between the Department of Indian Affairs and the War Purchasing Commission

RG10, Indian Affairs, vol. 3230, reel C-11344, file 578,855. Correspondence Regarding the Sales Tax and the War Tax as it Applies to the Indian Affairs Branch, 1922

RG10, Indian Affairs, vol. 3236, reel C-11345, file 600,337. Correspondence Regarding the Use of Indian Workers Particularly to Alleviate the Labour Shortages during the War (Newspaper Clippings)

RG10, vol. 4063, reel C-10204, file 402,890. Correspondence Regarding the Appointment of Glen Campbell as Chief Inspector of Agencies, Reserves and Inspectorates in Manitoba, Saskatchewan, Alberta and the Northwest Territories. Also Subsequent Work while on Loan to Department of Militia & Defence and Death as Lieutenant-Colonel in France

RG10, Indian Affairs, Red Series, vols. 6762–6808. Lists of Native Canadians Killed or Wounded and Settlement, Separation and Pension Claims and Files Concerning Indian Enlistment and Service

RG10, Indian Affairs, vols. 7484–7536. Files Concerning Soldier Settlement

RG10, Indian Affairs, vol. 11154, reel C-V-8, file 34. Soldiers Settlement Act Regulations

RG24-C-1-a, vol. 1543, file 1. Badges, Demobilization, 107th Battalion

RG24-C-1-a, vol. 1562, file 1. Pay and Pay Sheets, 114th Overseas Battalion

RG24-C-1-a, vol. 1568, file 1. Mobilization Accounts, Inspection Reports, 107th Battalion

RG24-C-8, vol. 4380, file 1-MD2-34-7-89. WWI Organization: 114th Overseas Battalion, Haldimand County

RG24-C-8, vol. 4596, file 1. Organization 107th Overseas Battalion

RG24-C-8, vol. 4602, file 1. Military District Records: 107th Battalion

RG150–1, vol. 94, files 1–3. Daily Orders 107th Battalion

RG150–1, vol. 95. Various Documents relating to the 114th Overseas Battalion

RG150–7, vol. 376. Nominal Rolls, Officers, 114th Overseas Battalion

Canada. Dept. of National Defence, Accession 1964-114. Photography

Soldiers of the South African War (1899–1902) Personal Files. Various Canadian Native Soldiers

Soldiers of the First World War (1914–18) Personal Files. Various Canadian Native Soldiers

NATIONAL ARCHIVES (NA), KEW, LONDON, UK

CO 323. Aboriginal Protection Society Correspondence 1914–19 – Peace Terms

CO 418. Colonial Office Australia: Original Correspondence, 1889–1922

CO 532. Colonial Office War: Dominions Original Correspondence

CO 537/359–375. Colonial Office: Action on Outbreak of War, 1912

CO 551. Colonial Office Union of South Africa: Original Correspondence

CO 616. Colonial Office: Dominions War of 1914 to 1918 Original Correspondence

DO 119/922. Swaziland: Overseas Native Labour Contingent, 1917

DO 119/923. Bechuanaland Protectorate: Overseas Native Labour Contingent, 1917

DO 119/924. Overseas Native Labour Contingents Medical Report, 1917

HO 45/10667. Albert Medal: Neighbour Australian Aboriginal Awarded, 1911–13

PRO 30/57/62. Birdwood to Kitchener: Sporadic Fighting and the Maori Contingent, July 1915

WO 32/7938. South Africa/Boer War: Title for Australian Bushmen Rhodesian Defence Force

WO 95/267. 1st Army: 2nd Bn South African Native Labour Contingent, Oct. 1916–Apr. 1917

WO 95/4352. Maori Contingent, July 1915

WO 107/37. Report: Work of the Labour Force during the War, 1919

WO 363/364. Collection British West Indies Regiment

NATIONAL ARCHIVES OF AUSTRALIA (NAA), CANBERRA, AUSTRALIA

A1 1915/6691. Protection of Aborigines, Correspondence, 1901–14

A1 1916/22219. Board for the Protection of Aborigines, 1914–16

A6 1901/232. Aborigines Protection Society London – Conditions of Aborigines in the Australian Colonies, 1900–1

A1608 D45/2/3. War 1939. Enlistment of Aborigines in AIF

A2487 1919/3202. Position of Australian Aboriginal Soldiers

A2487 1919/11073. Information Regarding the Discharged Soldiers' Settlement Act 1917, Queensland

A6443. General Correspondence Files relating to the Australian Contingents in the South African (Boer) War

A11803 1918/89/137. Voting in Conscription Referendum

B2455. First World War Service Records

NATIONAL ARCHIVES OF SOUTH AFRICA (NASA),
CAPE ARCHIVES DEPOT (KAB), CAPE TOWN, SOUTH AFRICA

1/BIZ, vol. 6/2. Overseas Native Labour Contingent Memorandums and Correspondence

CMT, vol. 3/924. Weekly Returns of Recruitment for Overseas Native Labour Contingent

CMT, vol. 3/925. Native Labour Contingent for Overseas Memorandums and Documents

CMT, vol. 3/926. Native Labour Contingent Discontinuance of Recruiting

CMT, vol. 3/929. Native Labour Contingent for Overseas

CMT, vol. 3/930. Native Labour Contingent for Overseas

1/CT, vol. 15/9. Native Prisoners of War Detention Cape Town

1/ELN, vol. 68. Native Labour Act

1/ELN, vol. 71. Overseas Native Labour Contingent Appeals for Recruits/ Messages from General Botha

1/IDW, vol. 26. Native Labour Contingent Contracts

1/KNT, vol. 22. Native Labour Overseas Contingent Correspondence/Native Labour Overseas Contingent Memorandums/Native Labour German East Africa

3/KWT, vol. 4/1/242. Wages of Native Labourers during the War

1/LSK, vol. 13. Native Labour Contingent

1/PDE, vol. 5. Native Labour Recruiting

1/PDE, vol. 8. Native Labour for Service on Railway Line/Complaints by Defence of Native Labour Recruits

1/PDE, vol. 15. South African Native Labour Contingent
1/PDE, vol. 16. Defence – Native Labour Recruits/Governor General's Fund Native Contribution in Curios/SANLC Casualties/Correspondence SANLC
1/PDE, vol. 18. South African Native Labour Contingent Allowances to Dependants
1/TBU, vol. 25. South African Native Labour Contingent
1/UTA, vol. 6/1/200. South African Native Labour Contingent Attestations Native and Cape Coloured Recruits
1/VGB, vol. 17/3. WWI: Recruiting for Cape Coloured Auxiliary Horse Transport

NATIONAL ARCHIVES OF SOUTH AFRICA (NASA), CENTRAL ARCHIVES DEPOT (SAB), PRETORIA, SOUTH AFRICA

GG, vol. 600. War 1914: German South West Africa, Native Labour
GG, vol. 670. War 1914–17: Army Imperial, Native Labour Contingent
GG, vol. 673. War 1914–17: Army Imperial, Native Labour Contingent Private Letters
GG, vol. 674. War 1914–17: Army Imperial, Native Labour Contingent Proposal to Enlist Native Prisoners for Volunteers
GG, vol. 675. War 1914–18: Mutiny among Members of the South African Native Labour Corps
GG, vol. 692. Shipping: Loss of Transport Mendi, South African Native Labour Contingent
GG, vol. 729. Codes/Telegraphs Reporting Casualties in the South African Native Labour Contingent
GNLB, vol. 189. European War: Native Labour in the Union and German South West Africa
GNLB, vol. 224. Native Labour: East Africa
GNLB, vol. 226. Native Labour: Basutoland and the Recruiting of Certain Boys
GNLB, vol. 254. South African Native Labour Contingent: Gifts and Comforts/Appointments Natives/Compensation to Dependants of Natives Lost in the Mendi Disaster/Cessation of Recruiting
MNW, vol. 258. War Crisis: Native Labour Supply for Mines
NTS, vol. 9106. South African Native Labour Corps: Allotments to Dependants
NTS, vol. 9107. South African Native Labour Corps: Recruitment Statistics/ Recruitment of Criminals/Appointment of Commissioned Officers
NTS, vol. 9108. South African Native Labour Corps: Behaviour of Recruits
NTS, vol. 9109. South African Native Labour Corps: Closing Down of Recruiting Depots
PM, vol. 1/1/35. European War: Supply of Native Labour for Railway Construction in German South West Africa
URU, vol. 174. Regulation No. 24 and No. 49 of the Native Labour Regulations
URU, vol. 266. Withdrawal of Regulation No. 24
URU, vol. 293. Regulations under the Native Labour Regulations Act, 1911

PROVINCIAL ARCHIVES OF NEWFOUNDLAND AND
LABRADOR (PANL), ST JOHN'S, NEWFOUNDLAND-LABRADOR

GN2/14, boxes 1–23. World War I: Newfoundland Regiment/Contingent and Royal Naval Reserves; Colonial Secretary's Office/Office of the Governor of Newfoundland: Correspondence, Legislation and Memorandums, 1914–22

File 14: Proposed Enlistment of Miners and Seamen
File 79: Labrador Wireless Stations, 1914–15
File 90: Recruits and Volunteers, 1914–18
File 103: Exemptions from Military Service
File 105: Military Service Board, Conscription and Exemptions
File 107: Military Service Act, Exemptions and War Graves
File 113: Correspondence Regarding Conscription
File 143: List of Recruits and Next of Kin, 1915–17
File 146: Patriotic Association Recruiting Committee
File 151: Recruitment, 1915–17
File 163: Recruitment, 1914–18
File 165: Recruitment, 1914–17
File 193: Correspondence Relating to the Newfoundland Regiment
File 200: Department of Militia, 1917–18
File 300: Recruitment and Volunteers
File 301: Granting of the Title 'Royal' to the Newfoundland Regiment and Other Matters
File 302-13: Correspondence, Recruitment and Mobilization of the Newfoundland Royal Naval Reserves

GN19 B-2-3 reels: 56, 115, 116, 118, 126, 170, 235, 238, 306
Personnel War Records for the Royal Newfoundland Regiment
GN19 B2302 Aa-2-4: Royal Newfoundland Regiment War Diaries, 1914–19
MG105. James Patrick Howley Fonds
MG136 – Governor Sir Walter Davidson Papers, boxes 1–2
BOX 1
File 2.02.007: Diary 8–22 August 1914
File 2.02.008: Diary 1–27 December 1914
File 2.03.001: Diary 1–31 January 1915
File 2.04.001: War Diary 29 July–7 August 1914
BOX 2
File 3.03.006: Visit to France in Support of Newfoundland, December 1917

MG146. Regulations for Fishing off the Coast of Labrador issued by Hugh Palliser, Governor of Newfoundland and the Coast of Labrador, 28 August 1765
MG148. Catholic Cadet Corps (St John's) Fonds, 1905–20
MG225. James A. Simms Fonds
MG228. William Keen Fonds
MG438. G. W. L. Nicholson Fonds

MG592. Great War Veteran's Association Fonds
MG632. Patriotic Association of Newfoundland, Complete Files: 1914–19
File 1: Minutes General Meetings 1914–19
File 13: Recruiting Committee, 1916
File 17: Newfoundland War Contingent Committee
File 20: Correspondence Colonial Office
File 21a–f: Correspondence Prime Minister's Office, 1914–19
File 22a–f: Correspondence Governor's Office, 1914–19
File 28: Rates of Pay Newfoundland and Canadian Forces
File 32: Prisoners of War
File 35: Recruitment, 1914–15
File 37: Nominal Rolls Royal Newfoundland Regiment, 1914–18

QUEEN ELIZABETH II MILITARY MUSEUM, WAIOURU,
NEW ZEALAND

1986.1644. Diary: Egypt and Gallipoli, Private William Dundon
1989.689. Letters: France and Britain – Private A. R. Bailey
1991.2781. Letters: New Zealand, England and Western Front – William
    Malcolm
1994.3310. The Maori Soldier: A Precise
1996.612. Diary: 2nd Lieutenant Edwin Percy Greatbatch
1996.615. Collection: Lieutenant Edwin P. Greatbatch
1999.117. Mana Maori: Questions of Authority on the East during the
    Nineteenth Century
1999.1086. Narrative Gallipoli: Private James Whiteford Swan
1999.3229. Letters of RSM Percival Gunn McIntosh
2005.887. Diary Gallipoli: Sapper Garland Oswald Morgan

SOUTH AFRICAN NATIONAL DEFENCE FORCE
DOCUMENTATION CENTRE, PRETORIA, SOUTH AFRICA

Unsorted Documents Pertaining to the South African Native Labour
    Contingent and Native First World War Service

WALTER HUME LONG PAPERS, BRITISH LIBRARY, LONDON, UK

Vol. 62404. Correspondence with Andrew Bonar Law, 1907–22 and Herbert
    Henry Asquith, 1907–23
Vols. 62421–62424. General Correspondence and Documents, 1916–19
Vol. 62437. Bound Albums – Official Documents and Policy, 1915–18

OTHER SOURCES

Aborigines Protection Society. *Annual Reports, 1907–1909.* (London: P. S. King
    & Son, 1909)
    Colonial Policy in New Zealand. (London: Edward Stanford, 1864)

Middle Island, New Zealand. (London: T. W. Nicholson, 1865)

Native Labour in South Africa – Report 29 April 1903. (London: P. S. King & Son, 1903)

New Zealand Government and the Maori War of 1863–64 with Special Reference to Confiscation of Native Lands. (London: William Tweedie, 1864)

Adams, Peter. *Fatal Necessity: British Intervention in New Zealand 1830–1847.* (Auckland University Press, 1977)

Allen, Chadwick. *Blood Narrative: Indigenous Identity in the American Indian and Maori Literary and Activist Texts.* (Durham: Duke University Press, 2002)

Allen, Robert S. *His Majesty's Indian Allies: British Indian Policy in the Defence of Canada, 1774–1815.* (Toronto: Dundurn Press, 1992)

Anderson, Gary C. *Sitting Bull and the Paradox of Lakota Nationhood.* (New York: Longman, 1996)

Anderson, Ian. *Sitting Bull's Boss: Above the Medicine Line with James Morrow Walsh.* (Surrey: Heritage House, 2000)

Anderson, Ross. *The Forgotten Front: The East African Campaign 1914–1918.* (Gloucestershire: Tempus Publications, 2004)

Andrew, C. M. and A. S. Kanya-Forstner. 'France, Africa, and the First World War', *The Journal of African History* **19**/1, World War I and Africa (1978), 11–23

Andrews, E. M. *The Anzac Illusion: Anglo-Australian Relations during World War I.* (Cambridge University Press, 1993)

Anon. 'Canadian Indians and World War One', *Saskatchewan Indian Federated College Journal* **1**/1 (1984), 65–72

Armit, Michael. 'The Chinese who Fought for "White Australia"...', *Migration* (1989), 18–21.

Armitage, Andrew. *Comparing the Policy of Aboriginal Assimilation: Australia, Canada and New Zealand.* (Vancouver: University of British Columbia Press, 1995)

Armstrong, John G. 'The Unwelcome Sacrifice: A Black Unit in the Canadian Expeditionary Force, 1917–1919', in N. F. Dreisziger (ed.), *Ethnic Armies: Polyethnic Armed Forces from the Time of the Hapsburgs to the Age of the Superpowers.* (Waterloo: Wilfrid Laurier University Press, 1990), 178–197

Aron, Raymond. *The Century of Total War.* (Boston: Beacon Press, 1954)

Australian Bureau of Statistics. *The Private Wealth of Australia and its Growth as Ascertained by Various Methods, together with a Report of the War Census of 1915.* (Melbourne: McCarron, Bird, 1918)

Baker, Donald G. 'Australian and Anglo Racism: Preliminary Explorations', in F. S. Stevens (ed.), *Racism: The Australian Experience: A Study of Race Prejudice in Australia, Volume 3 – Colonialism.* (Sydney: Australia and New Zealand Book Company, 1972)

Baker, Paul. *King and Country Call: New Zealanders, Conscription and the Great War.* (Auckland: University Press, 1988)

Ball, Desmond (ed.), *Aborigines in the Defence of Australia.* (Sydney: Australian National University Press, 1991)

Ballara, Angela. *Te Kingitanga: The People of the Maori King Movement.* (Auckland: University Press, 1998)

Barker, Jimmie (as told to Janet Mathews). *The Two Worlds of Jimmie Barker: The Life of an Australian Aboriginal, 1900–1972.* (Marrickville: Southwood Press/Australian Institute of Aboriginal Studies, Canberra, 1977)

Barris, Ted. *Victory at Vimy: Canada Comes of Age, April 9–12, 1917.* (Toronto: Thomas Allen Publishers, 2007)

Barsh, Russel Lawrence. 'American Indians in the Great War', *Ethnohistory* **38**/3 (1991), 276–303

Bean, C. E. W. *ANZAC to Amiens.* (Canberra: Australian War Memorial, 1946)
The Story of ANZAC. (Queensland: University Press, 1921)

Belgrave, Michael. *Historical Frictions: Maori Claims & Reinvented History.* (Auckland University Press, 2005)

Belich, James. *Making Peoples: A History of the New Zealanders from the Polynesian Settlement to the End of the Nineteenth Century.* (Auckland: Penguin Press, 1996)
'The New Zealand Wars', in Ian McGibbon (ed.), *The Oxford Companion to New Zealand Military History.* (Oxford University Press, 2000), 370–84
The New Zealand Wars: And the Victorian Interpretation of Racial Conflict. (Auckland University Press, 1986)
Paradise Reforged: A History of the New Zealanders from the 1800s to the Year 2000. (Auckland: Allen Lane Penguin Press, 2001)
The Victorian Interpretation of Racial Conflict: The Maori, the British, and the New Zealand Wars. (Montreal: McGill-Queen's University Press, 1989)

Bell, Steven A. 'The 107th "Timber Wolf" Battalion at Hill 70', *Canadian Military History* **5**/1 (1996), 73–8

Benn, Carl. *The Iroquois in the War of 1812.* (University of Toronto Press, 1999)
Mohawks on the Nile: Natives Among the Canadian Voyageurs in Egypt 1884– 1885. (Toronto: Dundurn Group, 2008)

Bernstein, Alison R. *American Indians and World War II.* (Norman: University of Oklahoma Press, 1991)

Berton, Pierre. *Vimy.* (Toronto: Penguin Books, 1986)

Bickford, Anne. 'Aboriginals in New South Wales after 1788', *Magazine of the Royal Australian Historical Society* **4** (1989), 8–12

Biggar, H. P. (ed.), *The Voyages of Jacques Cartier including Cartier's Narratives of 1534.* (Ottawa: King's Printer, 1924)

Biskup, Peter. *Not Slaves, Not Citizens.* (St Lucia: University of Queensland Press, 1973)

Bleakley, J. W. *The Aborigines of Australia: Their History – Their Habits – Their Assimilation.* (Brisbane: Jacaranda Press, 1961)

Bliss, Michael. *Right Honourable Men.* (New York: HarperCollins, 1994)

Boahen, Adu A. *African Perspectives on Colonialism.* (Baltimore: The Johns Hopkins University Press, 1987)

Bohan, Edmund. *To be a Hero: A Biography of Sir George Grey.* (Auckland: HarperCollins, 1998)

Borden, Robert. *Canada in the Commonwealth: From Conflict to Co-operation.* (Oxford: Clarendon Press, 1929)
Special Session of Parliament, August 1914. (Ottawa: King's Printer, 1914)

Boulton, Major Charles. *I Fought Riel: A Military Memoir.* (Toronto: James Lorimer & Company, 1985)

Reminiscences of the North-west Rebellions: With a Record of the Raising of Her Majesty's 100th Regiment in Canada, and a Chapter on Canadian Social and Political Life. (Toronto: Grip Printing and Publishing Co., 1886)

Britten, Thomas A. *American Indians in World War I: At Home and at War*. (Albuquerque: University of New Mexico Press, 1997)

Brook, Jack. 'The Irony of Dharuk Survival', *Magazine of the Royal Australian Historical Society* 4 (1989), 13–14

Broome, Richard. *Aboriginal Australians: Black Reponses to White Dominance 1788–2001*. (Sydney: Allen & Unwin, 2001)

Brown, Ian Malcolm. *British Logistics on the Western Front: 1914–1918*. (Toronto: Preager, 1998)

Brown, Judith. 'War and the Colonial Relationship: Britain, India and the War of 1914–18', in M. R. D. Foot (ed.), *War and Society*. (London: Elek Books, 1973)

Brown, O. E. A. *Settlers of the Plains*. (Gilbert Plains: The Maple Leaf Press, 1953)

Bruckshaw, Dean. 'John Shiwak: An Inuit Frontiersman', *Legion of Frontiersman History, Canada* (2007)

Brundage, John F. and G. Dennis Shanks. 'Deaths from Bacterial Pneumonia during 1918–19 Influenza Pandemic', *Emerging Infectious Diseases* **14**/8 (2008), 1193–9

Buchan, John. *The History of the South African Forces in France*. (London: Thomas Nelson and Sons, 1920)

Bumsted, J. M. 'The West and Louis Riel', in J. M. Bumsted (ed.), *Interpreting Canada's Past: Vol. 2, Post-Confederation*. (Toronto: Oxford University Press, 1993), 64–74

Burns, Patricia. *Fatal Success: A History of the New Zealand Company*. (Auckland: Heinemann Reid, 1989)

Cain, P. J. and A. G. Hopkins. *British Imperialism: Crisis and Deconstruction, 1914–1990*. (Essex: Longman, 1993)

Calamai, Peter. 'Beothuk Mystery', *McMaster University Science Writer* (2005), 1–4

Callwell, C. E. *Small Wars: Their Principles and Practice*. (Reprint. Lincoln: University of Nebraska Press, 1996)

Cameron, D. E. Captain. 'Royal Six Nations Regiment', *The Indian Magazine, Brantford* **3**/4 (1896), 1–4

Cannadine, David. *Ornamentalism: How the British saw their Empire*. (London: Penguin, 2001)

Capon, Alan R. *His Faults Lie Gently: The Incredible Sam Hughes*. (Ontario: Floyd W. Hall, 1969)

Carkeek, Rikihana. *Home Little Maori Home: A Memoir of the Maori Contingent 1914–1916*. (Wellington: Totika Publications, 2003)

Carter, Sarah. '"An Infamous Proposal": Prairie Indian Reserve Land and Soldier Settlement after World War I', *Manitoba History* 37 (1999), 9–21

Cell, Gillian T. *English Enterprise in Newfoundland 1577–1660*. (Toronto: University Press, 1969)

Chadwick, G. A. 'The Anglo-Zulu War of 1879 – Isandlwana and Rorke's Drift', *South African Military History Journal* **4**/4 (1978)

Clark, C. D. 'Aborigines in the First AIF', *Australian Army Journal* **286** (1973), 21–6.

Clendinnen, Inga. *Dancing with Strangers: The True History of the Meeting of the British First Fleet and the Aboriginal Australians, 1788.* (Edinburgh: Canongate Books, 2005)

Clothier, Norman. *Black Valour: The South African Native Labour Contingent, 1916–1918, and the Sinking of the Mendi.* (Pietermaritzburg: University of Natal Press, 1987)

Coates, Ken. *A Global History of Indigenous Peoples: Struggle and Survival.* (Hampshire: Palgrave Macmillan, 2005)

'Learning from Others: Comparative History and the Study of Indigenous–Newcomer Relations', *Native Studies Review* **16**/1 (2005), 3–14

Cody, Joseph F. *28 (Maori) Battalion: Second New Zealand Expeditionary Force.* (Wellington: Historical Publications Board, 1956)

Man of Two Worlds: Sir Maui Pomare. (Wellington: A. H. & A. W. Reed, 1953)

Colonial Office, *The Colonial Office Lists for 1914–1919.* (London: Waterlow & Sons, 1914–19)

Commonwealth of Australia. *Australian Defence Act, 1903.* (Melbourne: Office of Legislative Drafting and Publishing, 1903)

Condliffe, J. B. *Te Rangi Hiroa: The Life of Sir Peter Buck.* (Christchurch: Witcombe & Tombs, 1971)

Connor, John. *The Australian Frontier Wars, 1788–1838.* (Sydney: University of New South Wales Press, 2002)

Cook, Tim. *At the Sharp End: Canadians Fighting the Great War 1914–1916.* (Toronto: Penguin Group Canada, 2007), vol. I

Shock Troops: Canadians Fighting the Great War 1917–1918, Vol. 2. (Toronto: Penguin Group Canada, 2008)

Coombes, Annie E. *Rethinking Settler Colonialism: History and Memory in Australia, Canada, Aotearoa New Zealand and South Africa.* (Manchester University Press, 2006)

Cooper, James Fenimore. *The Last of the Mohicans.* (New York: H. C. Carey & I. Lea, 1826)

Coulthard-Clark, C. D. 'Aborigine Medal Winners', *Sabretache* **18**/4 (1977), 244–8.

Cowan, James. *The Maoris in the Great War.* (Auckland: Whitcombe & Tombs, 1926)

The New Zealand Wars and the Pioneer Period Vols I–II. (Wellington: W. A. G. Skinner Government Printing, 1923)

Crook, Paul. *Darwinism, War and History: The Debate over the Biology of War from the 'Origin of Species' to the First World War.* (Cambridge University Press, 1994)

Darwin, John. 'A Third British Empire? The Dominion Idea in Imperial Politics', in Judith M. Brown and Wm. Roger Louis (eds.), *The Oxford History of the British Empire, Volume IV: The Twentieth Century.* (Oxford University Press, 1999)

Daunton, Martin and Rick Halpern (eds.), *Empire and Others: British Encounters with Indigenous Peoples, 1600–1850.* (Philadelphia: University of Pennsylvania Press, 1999)

Davis, Shelby Cullom. *Reservoirs of Men: A History of the Black Troops of French West Africa*. (Westport: Negro Universities Press, 1970)

Dawson, Robert MacGregor. *The Development of Dominion Status 1900–1936*. (London: Oxford University Press, 1937)

Defence Headquarters, General Staff. *The Union of South Africa and the Great War 1914–1918 – Official History*. (Pretoria: The Government Printing and Stationery Office, 1924)

Deloria Jr., Vine. *Custer Died for Your Sins: An Indian Manifesto*. (Norman: University of Oklahoma Press, 1988)

Dempsey, James. *Aboriginal Soldiers and the First World War*. (Ottawa: Library and Archives Canada, 2006)
    'The Indians and World War One', *Alberta History* **31**/3 (1983), 1–8
    'Persistence of a Warrior Ethic Among the Plains Indians', *Alberta History* **36**/1 (1988), 1–10
    Warriors of the King: Prairie Indians in World War I. (Regina: Canadian Plains Research Center, 1999)

Department of External Affairs. *Documents on Canadian External Relations, Vol. I, 1909–1918*. (Ottawa: Queen's Printer, 1967)

Department of Indian Affairs. *Annual Reports of the Department of Indian Affairs (1913–1919)*. (Ottawa: Department of Indian Affairs, 1913–19)
    Basic Departmental Data, 2003. (Ottawa: Department of Indian Affairs, 2003)
    Indians of Ontario: An Historical Review. (Ottawa: Department of Citizenship and Immigration Indian Affairs Branch, 1962)

Difford, Ivor D. *The Story of the 1st Battalion Cape Corps*. (Cape Town: Hortors, 1920)

Dubow, Saul. *Racial Segregation and the Origins of Apartheid in South Africa, 1919–36*. (London: Macmillan, 1989)

Edmonds, W. Everard. 'Canada's Red Army', *Canadian Magazine of Politics, Science, Art and Literature* **54**/5 (1921), 340–2

Enloe, Cynthia H. *Ethnic Soldiers: State Security in Divided Societies*. (Markham: Penguin Books, 1980)

Evans, Julie, Patricia Grimshaw, David Philips and Shurlee Swain. *Equal Subjects, Unequal Rights: Indigenous Peoples in British Settler Colonies, 1830–1910*. (Manchester University Press, 2003)

Ferguson, Niall. *The Pity of War: Explaining World War I*. (London: Penguin Press, 1998)

Fogarty, Richard S. *Race and War in France: Colonial Subjects in the French Army, 1914–1918*. (Baltimore: The Johns Hopkins University Press, 2008)

Fong, Giordan. 'Debate: The Movement of German Divisions to the Western Front, Winter 1917–1918', *War in History* **7**/2 (2000), 225–35

Foster, Hamar. 'Indigenous Peoples and the Law: The Colonial Legacy in Australia, Canada, New Zealand and the United States', in D. Johnston and D. Ferguson (eds.), *Asia Pacific Legal Developments*. (Vancouver: University of British Columbia Press, 1998), 466–500

Fournier, Suzanne and Ernie Crey. 'Killing the Indian in the Child: Four Centuries of Church-Run Schools', in Roger C. A. Maaka and Chris Andersen (eds.), *The Indigenous Experience: Global Perspectives*. (Toronto: Canadian Scholars' Press, 2006), 141–9

Fowler Jr., William M. *Empires at War: The Seven Years' War and the Struggle for North America, 1754–1763.* (Toronto: Douglas & McIntyre, 2005)

Fox, J. E. J. 'From Pleasantville to Englebeimer', *Veteran Magazine* 7/1 (1928), 69–70

Franco, Jere' Bishop. *Crossing the Pond: The Native American Effort in World War II.* (Denton: University of North Texas Press, 1999)

Fredrickson, George M. 'From Exceptionalism to Variability: Recent Developments in Cross-National Comparative History', *Journal of American History* **82**/2 (1995), 587–604

Freeman, Victoria. 'Attitudes Toward "Miscegenation" in Canada, the United States, New Zealand, and Australia, 1860–1914', *Native Studies Review* **16**/1 (2005), 41–69

Fuller, J. G. *Troop Morale and Popular Culture in the British and Dominion Armies 1914–1918.* (Oxford: Clarendon Press, 1990)

Gaffen, Fred. *Cross-Border Warriors: Canadians in American Forces, Americans in Canadian Forces from the Civil War to the Gulf.* (Toronto: Dundurn Press, 1995)

  Forgotten Soldiers. (Penticton: Theytus Books, 1985)

Gammage, Bill. *The Broken Years: Australian Soldiers in the Great War.* (Victoria: Penguin, 1990)

Gardiner, Wira. *Te Mura O Te Ahi: The Story of the Maori Battalion.* (Auckland: Reed Books, 1992)

Garson, N. G. 'South Africa and World War I', *Journal of Imperial and Commonwealth History* **8**/1 (1979), 69–85

Gates, J. M. 'James Belich and the Maori Pa: Revisionist History Revised', *War & Society* **19**/2 (2001), 47–68

Gibson, Tom. *The Maori Wars: The British Army in New Zealand 1840–1872.* (London: Leo Cooper, 1974)

Gill, Douglas and Gloden Dallas. *The Unknown Army: Mutinies in the British Army in World War One.* (New York: Schocken Books, 1985)

Gillen, Mollie. *The Founders of Australia: A Biographical Dictionary of the First Fleet.* (Sydney: Library of Australian History, 1989)

Gleeson, Ian. *The Unknown Force: Black, Indian and Coloured Soldiers Through Two World Wars.* (Cape Town: Ashanti Publishing, 1994)

Glen, Frank. 'Australian Involvement in the New Zealand Wars', in Ian McGibbon (ed.), *The Oxford Companion to New Zealand Military History.* (Oxford University Press, 2000), 384–5

Goldfrank, Esther Schiff. *Changing Configurations in the Social Organization of the Blackfoot Tribe during the Reserve Period.* (New York: J. J. Augustin, 1945)

Goldie, Terry. *Fear and Temptation: The Image of the Indigene in Canadian, Australian, and New Zealand Literatures.* (Kingston: McGill-Queen's University Press, 1989)

Goldstein, Robert A. *French–Iroquois Diplomatic and Military Relations 1609–1701.* (Paris: Mouton, 1969)

Gordon, Harry. *The Embarrassing Australian: The Story of an Aboriginal Warrior.* (London: Angus & Robertson, 1963)

Gorst, J. E. *The Maori King or, The Story of our Quarrel with the Natives of New Zealand.* (London: Macmillan, 1864)

Gould, Ashley. '"Different Race, Same Queen": Maori and the War', in John Crawford and Ian McGibbon (eds.), *One Flag, One Queen, One Tongue: New Zealand, the British Empire and the South African War 1899–1902.* (Auckland: University Press, 2003), 119–27

'Soldier Settlement in New Zealand after World War I: A Reappraisal', in Judith Smart and Tony Wood (eds.), *An Anzac Muster: War and Society in Australia and New Zealand 1914–1918 and 1939–1945. Selected Papers.* (Victoria: Monash University, 1992)

Government of Canada. *Canadian Soldiers Active Military Services Act, 1916.* (Ottawa: Government Printing Bureau, 1916)

Soldier Settlement Act, 1917, S.C. 1917, C.21. (Ottawa: Government Printing Bureau, 1917)

Soldier Settlement Act, 1919–1923. (Ottawa: Government Printing Bureau, 1919–23)

Graham, Gerald S. *A Concise History of the British Empire.* (London: Thames and Hudson, 1970).

Granatstein, J. L. *Canada's Army: Waging War and Keeping the Peace.* (Toronto University Press, 2002)

Granatstein, J. L. and J. Mackay Hitsman. *Broken Promises: A History of Conscription in Canada.* (Toronto: Oxford University Press, 1977)

Grant, S. D. 'Indian Affairs Under Duncan Campbell Scott: The Plains Cree of Saskatchewan 1913–1931', *Journal of Canadian Studies* **18**/3 (1983), 21–39

Greenway, John. *Bibliography of the Australian Aborigines and the Native Peoples of Torres Strait to 1959.* (Sydney: Angus and Robertson, 1963)

Grey, Jeffrey. *A Military History of Australia.* (Cambridge University Press, 1999)

Grundlingh, Albert. *Fighting Their Own War: South African Blacks and the First World War.* (Johannesburg: Ravan Press, 1987)

'The Impact of the First World War on South African Blacks', ASA Conference, Washington D.C. (November 1982), 1–28

'The Impact of the First World War on South African Blacks', in Melvin E. Page (ed.), *Africa and the First World War.* (London: Macmillan, 1987)

Grundy, Kenneth W. *Soldiers Without Politics: Blacks in the South African Armed Forces.* (Berkeley: University of California Press, 1983)

Gump, James O. *The Dust Rose like Smoke: The Subjugation of the Zulu and the Sioux.* (Lincoln: University of Nebraska Press, 1994)

'A Spirit of Resistance: Sioux, Xhosa, and Maori Responses to Western Dominance, 1840–1920', *Pacific Historical Review* **66**/1 (1997), 21–52

Haami, Bradford. 'Maori in the Armed Forces', in Ian McGibbon (ed.), *The Oxford Companion to New Zealand Military History.* (Oxford University Press, 2000), 301–3

'Maori Traditional Warfare', in Ian McGibbon (ed.), *The Oxford Companion to New Zealand Military History.* (Oxford University Press, 2000), 303–6

Hagenbeck, Carl. *Beasts and Men: Being Carl Hagenbeck's Experiences for Half a Century Among Wild Animals.* (London: Longmans, Green and Co., 1912)

Hall, Robert A. 'Aborigines and Torres Strait Islanders in the Second World War', in Desmond Ball (ed.), *Aborigines in the Defence of Australia.* (Sydney: Australian National University Press), 32–63

The Black Diggers: Aborigines and Torres Strait Islanders in the Second World War. (Sydney: Allen & Unwin, 1989)

Hancock, W. K. and Jean Van Der Poel (eds.), *Selections from the Smuts Papers, Vol. I: June 1886–May 1902*. (Cambridge University Press, 1966)

Hankey, Maurice Lord. *The Supreme Command*. (London: George Allen and Unwin, 1961), vols. I, II

Harrop, A. J. *England and New Zealand: From Tasman to the Taranaki War*. (London: Methuen & Co., 1926)

Hawkins, Mike. *Social Darwinism in European and American Thought, 1860–1945: Nature as Model and Nature as Threat*. (Cambridge University Press, 1997)

Haycock, Ronald G. *The Image of the Indian*. (Waterloo: Lutheran University Press, 1971)

'Recruiting, 1914–1916', in Marc Milner (ed.), *Canadian Military History: Selected Readings*. (Toronto: Irwin, 1998)

Hayes, Adrian. *Pegahmagabow: Legendary Warrior, Forgotten Hero*. (Sault Ste. Marie: Fox Meadow Creations, 2006)

Higgins, Jenny. 'The 1918 Spanish Flu in Newfoundland and Labrador', *Newfoundland and Labrador Heritage* (2007)

Hill, Richard S. *State Authority, Indigenous Autonomy: Crown–Maori Relations in New Zealand/Aotearoa 1900–1950*. (Wellington: Victoria University Press, 2004)

The Story of Policing in New Zealand Volume I: Policing the Colonial Frontier: The Theory and Practice of Coercive Social and Racial Control in New Zealand, 1767–1867. (Wellington: V. R. Ward Government Printer, 1986), parts I, II

Hodges, Geoffrey. 'African Manpower Statistics for the British Forces in East Africa, 1914–1918', *The Journal of African History* **19**/1, World War I and Africa (1978), 101–16

The Carrier Corps: Military Labour in the East African Campaign 1914–1918. (Westport: Greenwood Press, 1986)

Holland, Robert. 'The British Empire and the Great War, 1914–1918', in Judith M. Brown and Wm. Roger Louis (eds.), *The Oxford History of the British Empire, Vol. IV: The Twentieth Century*. (Oxford University Press, 1999)

Holm, Tom. 'Strong Hearts: Native Service in the US Armed Forces', in P. Whitney Lackenbauer et al. (eds.), *Aboriginal Peoples and Military Participation: Canadian and International Perspectives*. (Kingston: Canadian Defence Academy Press, 2007), 127–52

Hopkins, A. G. 'Back to the Future: From National History to Imperial History', *Past and Present* **164** (1999), 198–243

Howe, Glenford D. 'West Indian Blacks and the Struggle for Participation in the First World War', *Journal of Caribbean History* **28**/1 (1994), 27–62

Howe, K. R. *Race Relations, Australia and New Zealand: A Comparative Survey 1770s–1970s*. (Sydney: Methuen Publications, 1977)

Howett, Grant. 'Aboriginal War History', *Arafura Times* **2**/19 (1997), 1–2

Howley, James P. *The Beothuks or Red Indians: The Aboriginal Inhabitants of Newfoundland*. (Cambridge University Press, 1915)

Huggonson, David. 'Aborigines and the Aftermath of the Great War', *Australian Aboriginal Studies* **1** (1993), 2–9

'Aboriginal Diggers of the 9th Brigade, First AIF', *Journal of the Royal Australian Historical Society* **79**/3–4 (1993), 214–23

'Aboriginal POW's of World War One', *Newsletter: The Historical Society of Southern Australia* **105** (1993), 9–12; **106** (1993), 8–11

'Aboriginal Roughriders of World War 1', *Rodeo: Hoofs and Horns* (1990), 70

'Aboriginal Trackers and the Boer War', *Bourke Historical Society: The History of Bourke* **12** (1992), 20

'A Dark Past', *Army Magazine* **13** (1992), 26–7

'The Dark Diggers of the AIF', *The Australian Quarterly* **61**/3 (1989), 352–7

'Too Dark for the Light Horse: An Australian in Germany', *Education* (1987), 24

'Villers-Bretonneux: A Strange Name for an Aboriginal Burial Ground', *Journal of the Royal Historical Society of Queensland* **14**/7 (1991), 285–8

Hull, Isabel V. *Absolute Destruction: Military Culture and the Practices of War in Imperial Germany.* (Ithaca: Cornell University Press, 2005)

Hunt, George T. *The Wars of the Iroquois: A Study in Intertribal Trade Relations.* (Madison: University of Wisconsin Press, 1960)

Hussey, John. 'Debate: The Movement of German Divisions to the Western Front, Winter 1917–1918', *War in History* **4**/2 (1997), 213–20

Huttenback, Robert A. *Racism and Empire: White Settlers and Colored Immigrants in the British Self-Governing Colonies, 1830–1910.* (Ithaca: Cornell University Press, 1976)

Hyam, Ronald. *Britain's Declining Empire: The Road to Decolonisation, 1918–1968.* (Cambridge University Press, 2006)

Idriess, Ion L. *The Desert Column.* (Sydney: Angus & Robertson, 1934)

Inglis, K. S. *Sacred Places: War Memorials in the Australian Landscape.* (Melbourne: Miegunyah Press, 1998)

Ireland, Richard. 'Eligibility of Aboriginals and Torres Strait Islanders for Military Service', *Guide Post* (2005), 9–10

Ito, Roy. *We Went to War: The Story of the Japanese Canadians who Served during the First and Second World Wars.* (Stittsville: Canada's Wings, 1984)

Jackomos, Alick and Derek Fowell. *Forgotten Heroes: Aborigines at War from the Somme to Vietnam.* (Melbourne: Victoria Press, 1993)

Living Aboriginal History of Victoria: Stories in the Oral Tradition. (Cambridge University Press, 1991)

Jackson-Nakano, Ann. *The Pajong and Wallabalooa: A History of the Aboriginal Farming Families at Blakney and Pudman Creeks.* (Canberra: ANU Printing, 2002)

James, Lawrence. *The Rise and Fall of the British Empire.* (London: Little, Brown and Company, 1994)

Jamieson, Melvill Allan. *Medals Awarded to North American Indian Chiefs, 1714–1922 and to Loyal African and Other Chiefs in Various Territories Within the British Empire.* (London: Spink, 1936)

Jauncey, Leslie C. *The Story of Conscription in Australia.* (Melbourne: Macmillan of Australia, 1968)

Jingoes, Stimela Jason. *A Chief is a Chief by the People: The Autobiography of Stimela Jason Jingoes.* Recorded and Compiled by John and Cassandra Perry. (Oxford University Press, 1975)

Johnson, Robert. *British Imperialism*. (New York: Palgrave Macmillan, 2003)

Jünger, Ernst. *The Storm of Steel*. (London: Chatto & Windus, 1929)

Kartinyeri, Doreen. *Ngarrindjeri Anzacs*. (Adelaide: Aboriginal Family History Project, South Australian Museum and Raukkan Council, 1996)

Katzenellenbogen, S. E. 'Southern Africa and the War of 1914–1918', in M. R. D. Foot (ed.), *War and Society*. (London: Elek Books, 1973)

Kawharu, I. H. (ed.), *Waitangi: Maori and Pakeha Perspectives of the Treaty of Waitangi*. (Oxford University Press, 1989)

Kenney, Suzanne. *Mount Tomah: Darug Aboriginal Connections*. (Sydney: BestwayBerk Printing, 2000)

Keshen, Jeff. 'The Great War Soldier as Nation Builder in Canada and Australia', in Briton C. Busch (ed.), *Canada and the Great War: Western Front Association Papers*. (Montreal: McGill-Queen's University Press, 2003)

Kiernan, V. G. *Colonial Empires and Armies, 1815–1960*. (Stroud: Sutton Publishing, 1998)

Killingray, David. 'Repercussions of World War I in the Gold Coast', *The Journal of African History* **19**/1, World War I and Africa (1978), 39–59

Killingray, David and James Matthews. 'Beasts of Burden: British West African Carriers in the First World War', *Canadian Journal of African Studies* **13**/1–2 (1979), 5–23

King, Michael. *Te Puea: A Biography*. (Auckland: Hodder and Stoughton, 1977)

Krebs, Ronald R. *Fighting for Rights: Military Service and the Politics of Citizenship*. (Ithaca: Cornell University Press, 2006)

Krouse, Susan Applegate. *North American Indians in the Great War*. (Lincoln: University of Nebraska Press, 2007)

Kulchyski, Peter. 'A Considerable Unrest: F.O. Loft and the League of Indians', *Native Studies Review* **4**/1–2 (1988), 95–113
  'Primitive Subversions: Totalization and Resistance in Native Canadian Politics', *Cultural Critique* **21** (1992), 171–95

Lacey, Amy. 'John Shiwak: An Eskimo Patriot', *Them Days – Stories of Early Labrador* **17**/1 (1991)

Lackenbauer, P. Whitney. *Battle Grounds: The Canadian Military and Aboriginal Lands*. (Vancouver: University of British Columbia Press, 2007)
  'A Hell of a Warrior: Remembering the Life of Sergeant Thomas George Prince', in Bernd Horn (ed.), *Intrepid Warriors: Perspectives on Canadian Army Leadership*. (St Catherine's: Vanwell Publishing, 2007)

Lackenbauer, P. Whitney and Craig Leslie Mantle (eds.), *Aboriginal Peoples and the Canadian Military: Historical Perspectives*. (Kingston: Canadian Defence Academy Press, 2007)

Lackenbauer, P. Whitney and Katherine McGowan, 'Competing Loyalties in a Complex Community: Enlisting the Six Nations in the Canadian Expeditionary Force, 1914–1917', in P. Whitney Lackenbauer et al. (eds.), *Aboriginal Peoples and the Canadian Military: Historical Perspectives*. (Kingston: Canadian Defence Academy Press, 2007), 89–115

Lackenbauer, P. Whitney and R. Scott Sheffield, 'Moving Beyond "Forgotten": The Historiography on Canadian Native Peoples and the World Wars', in P. Whitney Lackenbauer and Craig Leslie Mantle (eds.), *Aboriginal Peoples and the Canadian Military: Historical Perspectives*. (Kingston: CDA Press, 2007), 209–32

Lackenbauer, P. Whitney, R. Scott Sheffield and Craig Leslie Mantle (eds.), *Aboriginal Peoples and Military Participation: Canadian and International Perspectives*. (Kingston: Canadian Defence Academy Press, 2007)

Lake, Marilyn. *A Divided Society: Tasmania during World War I*. (Melbourne: University Press, 1975)

Lee, David. 'The Métis Militant Rebels of 1885', *Canadian Ethnic Studies* **21**/3 (1989), 13–17

Levine, Philippa. *Prostitution, Race, and Politics: Policing Venereal Disease in the British Empire*. (New York: Routledge, 2003)

Lewis-Maybury, David. 'Indigenous Peoples', in Roger C. A. Maaka and Chris Andersen (eds.), *The Indigenous Experience: Global Perspectives*. (Toronto: Canadian Scholars' Press, 2006), 17–29

Lind, Frank. *The Letters of Mayo Lind*. (St John's: Robinson & Co., 1919)

Lindqvist, Sven. *Terra Nullius: A Journey through No One's Land*. (London: Granta Books, 2007)

Lloyd, T. O. *The British Empire, 1558–1995*. (Oxford University Press, 1996)

Loh, Morag. *Dinky-Di: The Contributions of Chinese Immigrants and Australians of Chinese Descent to Australia's Defence Forces and War Efforts, 1899–1988*. Judith Winternitz (ed.). (Canberra: AGPS Press, 1989)

Louis, Wm. Roger. *Great Britain and Germany's Lost Colonies, 1914–1919*. (Oxford: Clarendon Press, 1967)

Lucas, Charles Sir. *The Empire at War*. (Oxford University Press, 1921), vol. I

Lunn, Joe. 'Kande Kamara Speaks: An Oral History of the West African Experience in France 1914–1918', in Melvin E. Page (ed.), *Africa and the First World War*. (London: Macmillan Press, 1987)
Memoirs of the Maelstrom: A Senegalese Oral History of the First World War. (Oxford: James Curry, 1999)

Maaka, Roger and Augie Fleras. *The Politics of Indigeneity: Challenging the State in Canada and Aotearoa New Zealand*. (Dunedin: University of Otago Press, 2005)

MacEwan, Grant. *Fifty Mighty Men*. (Saskatoon: Western Producer, 1958)
Sitting Bull: The Years in Canada. (Edmonton: Hurtig Publishers, 1973)

MacFarlane, John and John Moses. 'Different Drummers: Aboriginal Culture and the Canadian Armed Forces, 1939–2002', *Canadian Military Journal* **6**/1 (2005), 25–32

MacMillan, Margaret. *Paris 1919*. (New York: Random House, 2003)

Macpherson, W. G. *History of the Great War Based on Official Documents: Medical Services. Diseases of the War*. (London: HMSO, 1923), vol. II

Macpherson, W. G. et al. (eds.), *The British Official Medical History of the Great War*. (London: HMSO, 1922), vols. I, II

Maghraoui, Driss. 'Moroccan Colonial Soldiers: Between Selective Memory and Collective Memory – Beyond Colonialism and Nationalism in North Africa', *Arab Studies Quarterly* **20**/2 (1998), 21–42

Manzione, Joseph. *I Am Looking to the North for My Life: Sitting Bull 1876–1881*. (Salt Lake City: University of Utah Press, 1991)

Marshall, Ingeborg. *A History and Ethnography of the Beothuk*. (Montreal: McGill-Queen's University Press, 1996)

'An Unpublished Map Made by John Cartwright between 1768 and 1773 Showing Beothuck Indian Settlements and Artifacts and Allowing a New Population Estimate', *Ethnohistory* **24**/3 (1977), 223–49.

Marwick, Arthur. *War and Social Change in the Twentieth Century: A Comparative Study of Britain, France, Germany, Russia and the United States*. (London: Palgrave Macmillan, 1974)

Maylam, Paul. 'The Rise and Decline of Urban Apartheid in South Africa', *African Affairs* **89**/354 (1990), 57–84

McGhee, Robert. 'Contact between Native North Americans and the Medieval Norse: A Review of Evidence', *American Antiquity* **49**/1 (1984), 4–26

McGibbon, Ian. *New Zealand and the Korean War*. (Oxford University Press, 1996), vols. I, II

'The Origins of New Zealand's South African War Contribution', in John Crawford and Ian McGibbon (eds.), *One Flag, One Queen, One Tongue: New Zealand, the British Empire and the South African War 1899–1902*. (Auckland University Press, 2003), 1–11

The Path to Gallipoli: Defending New Zealand 1840–1915. (Wellington: GP Books, Department of Internal Affairs, 1991)

McHugh, Paul. *The Maori Magna Carta: New Zealand Law and the Treaty of Waitangi*. (Oxford University Press, 1991)

McIntyre, W. David and W. J. Gardner (eds.), *Speeches and Documents on New Zealand History*. (Oxford: Clarendon Press, 1971)

McKernan, Michael. *Australian Churches at War: Attitudes and Activities of the Major Churches 1914–1918*. (Marrickville: Southwood Press, 1980)

McLachlan, Robert W. *Medals Awarded to Canadian Indians*. (Montreal: Reprinted from *The Gazette* (1886), 1899)

McLaughlin, Dennis. *Fighting for Canada: Chinese and Japanese Canadians in Military Service*. (Ottawa: Department of National Defence, 2003)

McLaughlin, Dennis and Leslie. *For My Country: Black Canadians on the Field of Honour*. (Ottawa: Department of National Defence, 2004)

McLaughlin, Peter. 'The Legacy of Conquest: African Military Manpower in Southern Rhodesia During the First World War', in Melvin E. Page (ed.), *Africa and the First World War*. (London: Macmillan, 1987)

Ragtime Soldiers: The Rhodesian Experience in the First World War. (Bulawayo: Books of Zimbabwe Publishing Co., 1980)

McQueen, Humphrey. 'The "Spanish" Influenza Pandemic in Australia, 1912–1919', in Jill Roe (ed.), *Social Policy in Australia: Some Perspectives, 1901–1975*. (Melbourne: Cassell Australia, 1976)

Meadows, William C. 'North American Indian Code Talkers: Current Developments and Research', in P. Whitney Lackenbauer et al. (eds.), *Aboriginal Peoples and Military Participation: Canadian and International Perspectives*. (Kingston: Canadian Defence Academy Press, 2007), 161–214

Middleton, Richard. *Pontiac's War: Its Causes, Course and Consequence*. (London: Routledge, 2007)

Millar, T. B. *Australia in Peace and War: External Relations 1788–1977*. (London: C. Hurst & Company, 1978)

Miller, J. R. *Lethal Legacy: Current Native Controversies in Canada*. (Toronto: McClelland & Stewart, 2004)

   Skyscrapers Hide the Heavens: A History of Indian–White Relations in Canada. (Toronto: University Press, 2001)

Milloy, John S. *A National Crime: The Canadian Government and the Residential School System 1879–1986*. (Winnipeg: University of Manitoba Press, 1999)

Mills, Greg and Geoffrey Wood. 'Ethnicity, Integration and the South African Armed Forces', *South African Defence Review* **12** (1993)

Ministry of Militia. *Canadian Expeditionary Force Units: Instructions Governing Organization and Administration*. (Ottawa: Government Printing Bureau, 1916)

Mitchell, Elyne. *Light Horse: The Story of Australia's Mounted Troops*. (Melbourne: Macmillan Press, 1978)

Mohlamme, J. S. 'Soldiers without Reward: Africans in South Africa's Wars', *The South African Military History Journal* **10**/1 (1995)

More, Thomas. *Utopia*. (Reprint. Illinois: Harland Davidson, 1949)

Morris, Alexander. *The Treaties of Canada with the Indians of Manitoba and North-West Territories*. (Toronto: Belfords, Clarke, 1880)

Morris, Philip H. *The Canadian Patriotic Fund: A Record of its Activities from 1914–1919*. (Ottawa: The Mortimer Co., 1920)

Morrow Jr., John H. *The Great War: An Imperial History*. (London: Routledge, 2004)

Morton, Desmond. *Silent Battle: Canadian Prisoners of War in Germany 1914–1918*. (Toronto: Lester Publishing, 1992)

Morton, Desmond and J. L. Granatstein. *Marching to Armageddon*. (Toronto: Lester & Orpen Dennys, 1989)

Moses, John. 'Aboriginal Participation in Canadian Military Service: Historic and Contemporary Contexts', *Canadian Army Journal* **3**/3 (2000), 43–7

   'The Return of the Native: Six Nations Veterans and Political Change at the Grand River Reserve, 1917–1924', in P. Whitney Lackenbauer and Craig Leslie Mantle (eds.), *Aboriginal Peoples and the Canadian Military: Historical Perspectives*. (Kingston: Canadian Defence Academy Press, 2007), 117–128

   A Sketch Account of Aboriginal Peoples in the Canadian Military. (Ottawa: Department of National Defence, 2004)

Mountain Horse, Mike. *My People, the Bloods*. (Calgary: Glenbow-Alberta Institute and Blood Tribal Council, 1979)

Nasson, Bill. *Abraham Esau's War: A Black South African War in the Cape, 1899–1902*. (Cambridge University Press, 1991)

   The South African War 1899–1902. (London: Hodder Arnold, 1999)

Neillands, Robin. *The Great War Generals on the Western Front 1914–1918*. (London: Magpie Books, 2004)

Nelson, Keith L. 'The "Black Horror on the Rhine": Race as a Factor in Post-World War I Diplomacy', *Journal of Modern History* **42**/4 (1970), 606–27.

Newman, James L. *The Peopling of Africa: A Geographic Interpretation*. (New Haven: Yale University Press, 1995)

Nicholson, G. W. L. *Canadian Expeditionary Force 1914–1919*. (Ottawa: Queen's Printer, 1962)

The Fighting Newfoundlander: A History of the Royal Newfoundland Regiment. (London: Thomas Nelson Printers, 1964)

Nietzsche, Friedrich. *Beyond Good and Evil.* (New York: Dover Publications, 1997)

Niezen, Ronald. 'Recognizing Indigenism: Canadian Unity and the International Movement of Indigenous Peoples', *Comparative Studies in Society and History* **42**/1 (2000), 119–48

O'Brien, Mike. 'Out of a Clear Sky: The Mobilization of the Newfoundland Regiment, 1914–1915', *Newfoundland and Labrador Studies* **22**/2 (2007), 401–27

O'Connor, P. S. 'The Recruitment of Maori Soldiers, 1914–1918', *Political Science* **19**/2 (1967), 48–83

O'Toole, Fintan. *White Savage: William Johnson and the Invention of America.* (London: Faber and Faber, 2007)

Offer, Avner. *The First World War: An Agrarian Interpretation.* (Oxford: Clarendon Press, 1989)

Office of Census and Statistics. *The Canada Yearbook, 1914–1919, 1939–1940.* (Ottawa: King's Printer, 1915–20, 1940–1)

Omissi, David. *Indian Voices of the Great War: Soldiers' Letters, 1914–1918.* (London: Macmillan, 1999)

The Sepoy and the Raj: The Indian Army, 1860–1940. (London: Macmillan, 1994)

Orange, Claudia. 'An Exercise in Maori Autonomy: The Rise and Demise of the Maori War Effort Organization', in P. Whitney Lackenbauer et al. (eds.), *Aboriginal Peoples and Military Participation: Canadian and International Perspectives.* (Kingston: Canadian Defence Academy Press, 2007), 237–66

The Treaty of Waitangi. (Wellington: Allen & Unwin, 1987)

Page, Melvin E. 'Introduction: Black Men in a White Man's War', in Melvin E. Page (ed.), *Africa and the First World War.* (London: Macmillan, 1987)

'The War of Thangata: Nyasaland and the East African Campaign, 1914–1918', *The Journal of African History* **19**/1, World War I and Africa (1978), 87–100

Paice, Edward. *Tip & Run: The Untold Tragedy of the Great War in Africa.* (London: Weidenfeld & Nicolson, 2007)

Paterson, Hamish. 'First Allied Victory: The South African Campaign in German South-West Africa, 1914–1915', *The South African Military History Journal* **13**/2 (2004)

Patterson, K. David. 'The Influenza Epidemic of 1918–19 in the Gold Coast', *The Journal of African History* **24**/4 (1983), 485–502

Paul, Daniel N. *We Were Not the Savages.* (Halifax: Fernwood Publishing, 2006)

Peled, Alon. *A Question of Loyalty: Military Manpower Policy in Multiethnic States.* (Ithaca: Cornell University Press, 1998)

Perry, F. W. *The Commonwealth Armies: Manpower and Organization in Two World Wars.* (Manchester University Press, 1988)

Pilkington, Doris. *Follow the Rabbit-Proof Fence.* (Brisbane: University of Queensland Press, 1996)

Plaatje, Sol. T. *Native Life in South Africa.* (London: P. S. King and Sons, 1916)

Pointer, Margaret with Kalaisi Folau. *Tagi Tote E Loto Haaku – My Heart is Crying a Little: Niue Island Involvement in the Great War 1914–1918.* (Niue: Oceania Printers, 2000)

Pool, Ian D. *The Maori Population of New Zealand 1769–1971.* (Oxford University Press, 1977)

Pope, Peter E. *The Many Landfalls of John Cabot.* (Toronto University Press, 1997)

Porch, Douglas. *Wars of Empire.* (London: Cassell, 2000)

Pratt, Rod. 'Queensland's Aborigines in the First AIF', *Sabretache* **31** (January/March 1990), 18–22; (April/June 1990), 16–19; (July/September 1990), 26–9; (October/December 1990), 36–8

Preston, Richard A. *Canadian Defence Policy and the Development of the Canadian Nation 1867–1917.* (Ottawa: Canadian Historical Association, 1970)

Pugsley, Christopher. *Gallipoli: The New Zealand Story.* (Auckland: Hodder & Stoughton, 1984)

    'The Maori Battalion in France in the First World War', in John Dunmore (ed.), *The French and the Maori.* (Waikanae, New Zealand: The Heritage Press, 1992)

    'Maori Did Not Invent Trench Warfare', *New Zealand Defence Quarterly* (1998), 33–7

    On the Fringe of Hell: New Zealanders and Military Discipline in the First World War. (Auckland: Hodder & Stoughton, 1991)

    Te Hokowhitu A Tu: The Maori Pioneer Battalion in the First World War. (Auckland: Reed Publishing, 2006)

Rathbone, Richard. 'World War I and Africa: Introduction', *The Journal of African History* **19**/1, World War I and Africa (1978), 1–9

Rawling, Bill. *Surviving Trench Warfare: Technology and the Canadian Corps, 1914–1918.* (University of Toronto Press, 1992)

Ray, Arthur J. 'Constructing and Reconstructing Native History: A Comparative Look at the Impact of Aboriginal and Treaty Rights Claims in North America and Australia', *Native Studies Review* **16**/1 (2005), 15–39

Reitz, Deneys. *Trekking On.* (London: Faber and Faber, 1933)

Renouf, M. A. P. 'Prehistory of Newfoundland Hunter-Gatherers: Extinctions or Adaptations?', *World Archaeology* **30**/3, Arctic Archaeology (1999), 403–20

Returned Sailors and Soldiers Imperial League of Australia (RSSILA). 'Aborigine Diggers: List Grows', *Reveille* (31 October 1931), 15

    'Many Served: A. I. F. Aborigines', *Reveille* (30 November 1931), 22

    'Lever on Britain: Prisoners Suffer', *Reveille* (31 December 1931), 10

    'A. I. F. Aborigines: N. S. W.', *Reveille* (31 January 1932), 20

Rice, Geoffrey W. *Black November: The 1918 Influenza Pandemic in New Zealand.* (Christchurch: Canterbury University Press, 2005)

Rich, Paul B. *State Power and Black Politics in South Africa, 1912–1951.* (London: Macmillan, 1996)

Robb, George. *British Culture and the First World War.* (New York: Palgrave, 2002)

Robson, L. L. *The First A.I.F.: A Study of its Recruitment 1914–1918.* (Melbourne University Press, 1970)

Rolfe, James. *The Armed Forces of New Zealand*. (Sydney: Allan & Unwin, 1999)

Ross, Angus. *New Zealand Aspirations in the Pacific in the Nineteenth Century*. (Oxford University Press, 1964)

Ross, Jane. *The Myth of the Digger: The Australian Soldier in Two World Wars*. (Sydney: Hale & Iremonger, 1985)

Rothfels, Nigel. *Savages and Beasts: The Birth of the Modern Zoo*. (Baltimore: Johns Hopkins University Press, 2002)

Royal Commission on Aboriginal Peoples. *Treaty Making in the Spirit of Co-existence: An Alternative to Extinguishment*. (Ottawa: Canada Communication Group, 1993)

Ruck, Calvin W. *The Black Battalion: 1916–1920: Canada's Best Kept Military Secret*. (Halifax: Nimbus Publishing, 1987)

Russell, Lynette (ed.), *Colonial Frontiers: Indigenous–European Encounters in Settler Societies*. (Manchester University Press, 2006)

Salmond, Anne. *Between Worlds: Early Exchanges between Maori and Europeans 1773–1815*. (Auckland: Penguin Books, 1997)

Sattenspiel, Lisa and Dawn Herring, 'Structural Epidemic Models and the Spread of Influenza in the Central Canadian Sub-Arctic', *Human Biology* **70**/1 (1998), 91–115.

Schreiber, Shane B. *Shock Army of the British Empire: The Canadian Corps in the Last 100 Days of the Great War*. (St Catherine's: Vanwell Publishing, 2004)

Scoppio, Grazia, 'Diversity Best Practices in Military Organizations in Canada, Australia, the United Kingdom and the United States', *Canadian Military Journal* **9**/3 (2009), 17–30

Scott, Dick. *Ask That Mountain: The Story of Parihaka*. (Auckland: Heinemann/ Southern Cross, 1975)

  Years of the Pooh-Bah: A Cook Islands History. (Auckland: Hodder and Stoughton, 1991)

Scott, Duncan Campbell. *The Administration of Indian Affairs in Canada*. (Ottawa: Canadian Institute of International Affairs, 1931)

  'The Canadian Indians and the Great War', in *Canada in the Great War, Vol. III: Guarding the Channel Ports*. (Toronto: United Publishers, 1919), 327–8

  Report of the Deputy Superintendent General of Indian Affairs, Sessional Paper No. 27: The Indians and the Great War. (Ottawa: Department of Indian Affairs, 1919)

Sharp, Andrew. *The Voyages of Abel Janszoon Tasman*. (Oxford: Clarendon Press, 1968)

Sheffield, R. Scott. 'Indifference, Difference and Assimilation: Aboriginal People in Canadian Military Practice, 1900–1945', in P. Whitney Lackenbauer and Craig Leslie Mantle (eds.), *Aboriginal Peoples and the Canadian Military: Historical Perspectives*. (Kingston: Canadian Defence Academy Press, 2007), 57–71

  '"Of Pure European Descent and of the White Race": Recruitment Policy and Aboriginal Canadians, 1939–1945', *Canadian Military History* **5**/1 (1996), 8–15

  The Red Man's on the Warpath: The Image of the 'Indian' and the Second World War. (Vancouver: UBC Press, 2004)

A Search for Equity: A Study of the Treatment Accorded to First Nations Veterans and Dependants of the Second World War and the Korean Conflict. (Ottawa: Department of Indian Affairs and Northern Development, 2001)

Shrimpton, A. W. and Alan E. Mulgan. *Maori & Pakeha: A History of New Zealand.* (Auckland: Whitcombe & Tombs, 1921)

Simons, H. J. and R. E. *Class and Colour in South Africa 1850–1950.* (Harmondsworth: Penguin Books, 1969)

Sloley, Herbert C. 'The African Native Labour Contingent and the Welfare Committee', *Journal of the Royal African Society* 17/67 (1918), 199–211

Smith, Donald B. 'Fred Loft', in Frederick E. Hoxie (ed.), *Encyclopedia of North American Indians.* (New York: Houghton Mifflin Harcourt, 1996), 135

Smith, L. R. *The Aboriginal Population of Australia.* (Canberra: ANU Press, 1980)

Smith, Linda Tuhiwai. 'Colonizing Knowledges', in Roger C. A. Maaka and Chris Andersen (eds.), *The Indigenous Experience: Global Perspectives.* (Toronto: Canadian Scholars' Press, 2006), 91–110

Smith, Philippa Mein. *A Concise History of New Zealand.* (Cambridge University Press, 2005)

Smith, Richard. *Jamaican Volunteers in the First World War: Race, Masculinity and the Development of National Consciousness.* (Manchester University Press, 2004)

Smith, S. Percy. *Hawaiki, the Original Home of the Maori.* (Auckland: Whitcombe and Tombs, 1921)

Smuts, J. C. *Jan Christian Smuts.* (London: Cassell & Company, 1952)

Sorrenson, M. P. K. (ed.), *Na To Hoa Aroha From Your Dear Friend: The Correspondence between Sir Apirana Ngata and Sir Peter Buck 1925–1950.* (Auckland University Press, 1988), vols. 1–3

Soutar, Monty. 'Maori War Effort Overseas in the Second World War', in Ian McGibbon (ed.), *The Oxford Companion to New Zealand Military History.* (Oxford University Press, 2000), 290–311

Speck, Frank G. *Beothuk and Mi'kmaq.* (New York: Museum of American Indian Heye Foundation, 1922)

Stacey, A. J. and Jean Edwards Stacey. *Memoirs of a Blue Puttee: The Newfoundland Regiment in World War One.* (St John's: DRC Publishers, 2002)

Stacey, C. P. *Introduction to the Study of Military History for Canadian Students.* (Ottawa: Directorate of Training Canadian Forces, 1972)

Stanley, G. F. 'The North-West Rebellion', in Marc Milner (ed.), *Canadian Military History: Selected Readings.* (Toronto: Irwin, 1998)

Stapleton, Timothy J. *No Insignificant Part: The Rhodesia Native Regiment and the East Africa Campaign of the First World War.* (Waterloo: Wilfrid Laurier University Press, 2006)

'"They No Longer Care for Their Chiefs": Another Look at the Xhosa Cattle-Killing of 1856–1857', *International Journal of African Historical Studies* 24/2 (1991), 383–92

Stasiulis, Daiva K. and Nira Yuval-Davis. *Unsettling Settler Societies: Articulations of Gender, Race, Ethnicity and Class.* (London: Sage, 1995)

Stevenson, David. *1914–1918: The History of the First World War.* (London: Penguin Books, 2004)

Stevenson, Michael D. 'The Mobilization of Native Canadians During the Second World War', *Journal of the Canadian Historical Association New Series* 7 (1996), 205–26

Stone, Sharman N. (ed.), *Aborigines in White Australia: A Documentary History of the Attitudes Affecting Official Policy and the Australian Aborigine, 1697–1973.* (Victoria: Heinemann, 1974)

Strachan, Hew. *The First World War, Volume I: To Arms.* (Oxford University Press, 2001)

The First World War in Africa. (Oxford University Press, 2004)

Streets, Heather (ed.), *Martial Races and Masculinity in the British Army, 1857–1914.* (Manchester University Press, 2006)

Summerby, Janice. *Native Soldiers, Foreign Battlefields.* (Ottawa: Department of Veterans Affairs, 2005)

Summers, Anne and R. W. Johnson. 'World War I Conscription and Social Change in Guinea', *The Journal of African History* **19**/1, World War I and Africa (1978), 25–38

Sutch, W. B. *The Maori Contribution: Yesterday, Today and Tomorrow.* (Wellington: Department of Industries and Commerce, 1964)

Sutherland, Jonathan and Diane Canwell. *Zulu Kings and their Armies.* (Barnsley: Pen & Sword Books, 2004)

Sweeny, Alistair. *Government Policy and Saskatchewan Indian Veterans: A Brief History of the Canadian Government's Treatment of Indian Veterans of the Two World Wars.* (Saskatoon: Tyler, Wright & Daniel, 1979)

Swinney, G. 'The Sinking of the SS Mendi, 21 February 1917', *Military History Journal* **10**/1 (1995)

Tait, R. H. *Newfoundland: A Summary of the History and Development of Britain's Oldest Colony from 1497 to 1939.* (USA: The Harrington Press, 1939)

The Trail of the Caribou: The Royal Newfoundland Regiment 1914–1918. (Boston: Newfoundland Publishing Co., 1933)

Tate, Michael L. 'From Scout to Doughboy: The National Debate over Integrating American Indians into the Military, 1891–1918', *Western Historical Quarterly* **17**/4 (1986), 417–37.

Tatz, Colin. 'Confronting Australian Genocide', in Roger C. A. Maaka and Chris Andersen (eds.), *The Indigenous Experience: Global Perspectives.* (Toronto: Canadian Scholars' Press, 2006), 125–40

Tench, Watkin. *1788: Comprising a Narrative of the Expedition to Botany Bay and a Complete Account of the Settlement at Port Jackson.* Tim Flannery (ed.). (Melbourne: Text Publishing Company, 1996)

Thompson, Andrew T. *Report by Col. Andrew T. Thompson Commissioned to Investigate and Enquire into the Affairs of the Six Nations Indians, 1923.* (Ottawa: King's Printer, 1924)

Thompson, John Herd. *Ethnic Minorities during Two World Wars.* (Ottawa: Canadian Historical Association, Government of Canada, 1991)

The Harvests of War: The Prairie West 1914–1918. (Toronto: McClelland and Stewart, 1978)

Titley, Brian A. *A Narrow Vision: Duncan Campbell Scott and the Administration of Indian Affairs in Canada.* (Vancouver: University of British Columbia Press, 1986)

Tobias, John L. 'Protection, Civilization, Assimilation', in J. R. Miller (ed.), *Sweet Promises: A Reader on Indian–White Relations in Canada.* (University of Toronto Press, 1991), 127–44

Townsend, Kenneth William. *World War II and the American Indian.* (Albuquerque: University of New Mexico Press, 2000)

Travers, Tim. 'Debate: Reply to John Hussey: The Movement of German Divisions to the Western Front, Winter 1917–1918', *War in History* 5/3 (1998), 367–70

Treager, Edward. *The Aryan Maori.* (Wellington: G. Didsbury Government Printer, 1885)

Tugwell, Maurice and John Thompson. *The Legacy of Oka.* (Toronto: Mackenzie Institute, 1991)

Upton, L. F. S. 'The Extermination of the Beothucks of Newfoundland', *The Canadian Historical Review* 58/2 (1977), 133–53

Vance, Jonathan F. *Death So Noble: Memory, Meaning, and the First World War.* (Vancouver: UBC Press, 1997)

Van der Horst, Sheila T. *Native Labour in South Africa.* (London: Frank Cass, 1971)

Vandervort, Bruce. *Indian Wars of Canada, Mexico and the United States: 1812–1900.* (New York: Routledge, 2006)

  Wars of Imperial Conquest in Africa 1830–1914. (London: Routledge, 1998)

Vayda, A. P. *Maori Warfare.* (New Plymouth: Avery Press, 1960)

Vorbeck-Lettow von, Paul General. *East African Campaigns.* (New York: Robert, Speller & Sons Publishing Inc., 1957)

  My Reminiscences of East Africa. (Nashville: Battery Classics, 1998)

Walker, James W. St. G. 'Race and Recruitment in World War I: Enlistment of Visible Minorities in the Canadian Expeditionary Force', *Canadian Historical Review* 70/1 (1989), 1–26

Walshe, Peter. *The Rise of African Nationalism in South Africa: The African National Congress 1912–1952.* (London: C. Hurst & Company, 1970)

Warwick, Peter. *Black People and the South African War 1899–1902.* (Cambridge University Press, 1983)

West, Ida. *Pride Against Prejudice: Reminiscences of a Tasmanian Aborigine.* (Sydney: Southwood Press, 1984)

White, Bruce. 'The American Army and the Indian', in N. F. Dreisziger (ed.), *Ethnic Armies: Polyethnic Armed Forces from the Time of the Hapsburgs to the Age of the Superpowers.* (Waterloo: Wilfrid Laurier University Press, 1990), 69–88

White, Richard. *The Middle Ground: Indians, Empires, and Republics in the Great Lakes Region, 1650–1815.* (Cambridge University Press, 1991)

Whittall, W. Lieutenant-Commander. *With Botha and Smuts in Africa.* (London: Cassell, 1917)

Willan, B. P. 'The South African Native Labour Contingent, 1916–1918', *Journal of African History* 19/1, World War I and Africa (1978), 61–86

Wilmer, Franke. *The Indigenous Voice in World Politics Since Time Immemorial.* (London: Sage Publications, 1993)

Winegard, Timothy C. 'A Case Study of Indigenous Brothers in Arms during the First World War', *Australian Army Journal* **6**/1 (2009), 191–206

'An Introduction to Charles A. Cooke within the Context of Aboriginal Identity', *Ontario History* **102**/1 (2010), 78–80

Oka: A Convergence of Cultures and the Canadian Forces. (Kingston: Canadian Defence Academy Press, 2008)

Woodward, David R. 'The Imperialist Strategist: Jan Christian Smuts and British Military Policy, 1917–1918', *The South African Military History Journal* **5**/4 (December 1981)

Yarwood, A. T. and M. J. Knowling. *Race Relations in Australia: A History.* (Melbourne: Methuen Australia, 1982)

Zinn, Howard. *A People's History of the United States: 1492–Present.* (New York: HarperCollins, reprint 2005)

MEDIA SOURCES

Brisbane Courier. (15 May 1917), p. 7
(20 June 1917), p. 7
(28 June 1917), p. 8

Brisbane Times. 'Brave Family Spurned by Land they Served'. (28 May 2007)

Hasler, Fay. 'Douglas Grant ... A Man of Exceptional Talent', *Lithgow Mercury.* (5 January 2002)

Regina Leader. 'Indians Are Doing their Bit in the Great War'. (18 November 1916)

The Bulletin. 'Cartoon: A Question of Color'. (31 August 1916)

The New Zealand Observer. 'The Spirit of his Fathers'. (December 1915)

The Queenslander. (9 September 1916), p. 28

The Sydney Mail. 'A Plea for the Australian Aborigines'. (11 July 1917)

Watson, Lindsay. 'Barambah or Cherbourg: It's All the Same', *Kurbingui Star* (no date)

'Special Supplement: Aboriginal and Torres Strait Islander Soldiers of the First World War', *Kurbingui Star*, Zillmere, Queensland. (20 October 2006) (20 pgs)

UNPUBLISHED MATERIALS

Camurat, Diane. 'The American Indian in the Great War: Real and Imagined'. (Unpublished MA thesis for the Institut Charles V of the University of Paris VII, Paris, France, 1993)

McLeod, Donald Wayne. 'The Canadian Indian and World War One: Historical Background and Participation'. (Unpublished MA thesis for the Royal Military College of Canada, Kingston, Ontario, 1979)

ELECTRONIC SOURCES

Hiller, Stanley I. 'For King and Country', Newfoundland and Labrador Heritage Project (2007). www.heritage.nf.ca/greatwar/home

Payne, David. 'Forgotten Hands with Picks and Shovels', Journal of the Western Front Association (December 2008). www.westernfrontassociation.com

Wickes, Judi. 'Never Really Heard of It: The Certificate of Exemption and Lost Identity', The Australian National University Electronic Collection (2008). www.epress.anu.edu.au

Index